Asher Kaufman is Associate Professor of Peace Studies and Director of Doctoral studies at the Joan B. Kroc Institute for International Peace Studies, University of Notre Dame. He previously taught at the Hebrew University, Jerusalem and was a research fellow at the Harry S. Truman Research Institute for the Advancement of Peace. Kaufman is the author of *Contested Frontiers: Cartography, Sovereignty, and Conflict at the Syria, Lebanon, Israel Tri-Border Region* (2014).

To Shimon,

"Yam Shel Ga'agu'a"

REVIVING PHOENICIA

THE SEARCH FOR IDENTITY IN LEBANON

ASHER KAUFMAN

New paperback edition first published in 2014 by I.B.Tauris & Co. Ltd
6 Salem Road, London W2 4BU
175 Fifth Avenue, New York NY 10010
www.ibtauris.com

First published in hardback in 2004 by I.B.Tauris & Co. Ltd

Copyright © Asher Kaufman, 2004, 2014

The right of Asher Kaufman to be identified as the author of this work has been asserted by the author in accordance with the Copyright, Designs and Patents Act 1988.

All rights reserved. Except for brief quotations in a review, this book, or any part thereof, may not be reproduced, stored in or introduced into a retrieval system, or transmitted, in any form or by any means, electronic, mechanical, photocopying, recording or otherwise, without the prior written permission of the publisher.

Every attempt has been made to gain permission for the use of the images in this book. Any omissions will be rectified in future editions.

ISBN: 978 1 78076 779 6
eISBN: 978 0 85773 602 4

A full CIP record for this book is available from the British Library
A full CIP record is available from the Library of Congress

Library of Congress catalog card: available

Table of Contents

Note on Transliteration	vii
Acknowledgements	ix
Preface to the New Paperback Edition	xi

Introduction — 1

Who Were the Phoenicians?	2
National Identities in the Arab Middle East	5
Theorizing Lebanese Nationalism?	8
The French Colonial Idea	13

SECTION I: ORIGINS

Chapter I: First Buds: 1860-1918 — 21

France in the Levant	21
Franco-Maronite Relations	26
The Jesuits in Syria and Lebanon	29
Maronite Clergy and the History of Syria and Lebanon	36
Lay Syro-Lebanese and the Ancient History of Syria	38

Chapter II: Before and After the War — 55

The Syro-Lebanese Community in Egypt	57
Syro-Lebanese in America	70
Between Paris and Beirut: 1913-1919	79
Beirut 1919: Charles Corm and *La Revue Phénicienne*	87

SECTION II: THE MANDATE YEARS

Chapter III: The Mandate Years — 109

The French Mandate and the Lebanese Educational System	110
Université Saint Joseph and Its Graduates	119

Archeology and National Museums 122
1936-1937: A Case Study of Phoenicianism and Its Adversaries 126
Towards Independence 129

Chapter IV: Three Phoenician Currents 141

Charles Corm, the Inspired Maronite Francophone 141
Michel Chiha, the Merchant Republic and the Lebanese Identity 159
Sa'id Aql, Arabophones and Maronite Nationalism 169

Chapter V: The Adversaries 195

Arab-Muslims: Rashid Rida and Shekib Arslan 197
Christian Arab Natinalists:
   Qonstantine Zurayq 200
   Edmond Rabbath 205
   Amin al-Rihani 209
Antun Sa'adeh and the Syrian Social Nationalist Party 215
Muhammad Jamil Bayhum and Sunni Lebanese 220

SECTION III: AFTER INDEPENDENCE AND BEYOND

Chapter VI: Chronicle of a Dream and Disillusionment ... 230

Conclusion: Arabs, Phoenicians and What Lies Between ... 244

Bibliography 251

Index 269

Note on Transliteration

French spelling of names of people and places was used for the most part in order to remain close to their common usages in Lebanon during the Mandate. Otherwise, English transliteration of Arabic follows the rules of the *International Journal of Middle East Studies,* but without diacritical marks.

Acknowledgements

The seeds of this book were planted during my military service as an Israeli soldier in Lebanon. In June 1983 my unit was sent to take over a strategically located villa in the predominantly Christian village of Kfar Falous, a beautiful and picturesque area, 15 km east of Sidon. It was a year after the Israeli invasion into Lebanon and the new political order Ariel Sharon was crafting for Lebanon was already blowing up in his soldiers' faces and in the faces of tens of thousands of Lebanese civilians and militiamen. This operation was targeted against the Christian Phalanges in the region, who, for a reason that was not all clear to me — I was only a peon, straight after basic training — acted too independently. We were told in the briefing that the operation was meant to demonstrate to the Phalanges who was calling the shots. We were not allowed to use our weapons since we operated within a friendly environment and it was no more than a disagreement between allies. Within a few moments after the beginning of the operation we were surrounded by hundreds of these friendly civilians who showed up from all corners and would not let us assume control of the villa. We played cat and mouse with them for the entire day until an agreement was reached between senior Israeli and Phalanges officers. The civilians eventually left and we spent a full week in this villa, the most peaceful week I had spent in Lebanon throughout my entire service. During this week I had the chance to get to know some of these Phalanges. With my then-broken Arabic and their broken English (unfortunately, I did not know a word in French, a language they seemed to have mastered), I learned from some of them that they were not Arabs, that they were Phoenicians. Some told me they hated Muslims and Arabs, others took pride in massacres of Palestinians in which they participated. I was stunned and dismayed. They looked perfectly Arab to me, but what did I know back then? I was barely nineteen years old with very little understanding of Middle East issues, let alone identities. The conversations with them remained imprinted in my mind because it was the only time during my entire service in which I had the chance to actually speak to Lebanese.

Ten years later, I was an MA student at the Department of Islamic and Middle Eastern Studies at the Hebrew University in Jerusalem, looking for a topic for my thesis. By then I had started to be intrigued by the region's multiple layers of identities. The Canaanite movement in Israel fascinated me and I was looking for similar phenomena in Arab society. The Phoenicians from Kfar Falous suddenly resurfaced from the back drawers of my memory. These "Phoenician" Phalanges ended up being the inspiration of my MA, and later PhD theses, and finally this book. I am not sure that if they ever read this book they would like my conclusions but, nevertheless, I suppose that in the very long list of acknowledgements I should begin with them.

The majority of this study is based on my Ph.D. dissertation written at Brandeis University. Words would not be enough to thank my advisor

Avigdor Levy for his assistance and encouragement. I am also indebted to the other members of the committee, Yitzhak Nakash, Kanan Makiya and Sadik al-Azm. I only wish that this remarkable Arab-Israeli cooperation could be manifested in other fields of life as well. The final polish of the study was completed during my post-doctorate at the Harry S. Truman Research Institute for the Advancement of Peace at the Hebrew University in Jerusalem. I am particularly thankful for its director, Amnon Cohen, for his support upon my arrival at the Institute and during the entire duration of my work on this study. The Truman Institute also provided me with financial assistance for the editing of the text for which I am most grateful. I am also very appreciative to the Elie Kedourie Memorial Fund of the British Academy for financing the last necessary stretch of the research. I have infinite gratitude to Lisa Perlman for the editorial work and for her personal touch; and also to Ann Nichols for crossing the t's and dotting the i's. I am also very indebted to Reuven Amitai, who was the head of the Department of Islamic and Middle Eastern Studies when I returned home to Israel. I will always remember and cherish his personal involvement in my professional advancement. Other members of the Hebrew University community deserve my gratitude. Moshe Ma'oz who accompanied my progress since I was his MA student; Elie Podeh who helped with advice about publishing and editing; Miri Hoexter who wisely advised me to change some of the headings; and Yusri Khaizaran who enriched this study through material he freely shared with me from his own research. I am also particularly grateful to Nadim Shehadi, the director of the Centre for Lebanese Studies in Oxford, who was always there when I needed a key to decipher the complex nature of the Lebanese society. The staff of many archives and libraries, "the unknown soldiers" of scholarly works, made this project possible. Among them are the Archives of the French Ministry of Foreign Affairs in Nantes and Paris, the Archives of the Jesuit Order in Vanves, the Zionist Archives in Jerusalem, the National Libraries in France and Israel and the library of the University of Arizona in Tucson, where I sat and wrote the majority of the text, having access to the abundant wealth of American libraries through the free use of the interlibrary loan system. Such research was indeed made possible in part by support from the Institute for Scholarship in the Liberal Arts, College of Arts and Letters, University of Notre Dame. Personal friends were always helpful, some with information and advice, others with moral support. Many thanks to Ginan Rauf, Franck Salameh, Nien-Hê Hsieh, Amy Karpinski, Kay Ellett, Ron Spark, Alan Paris, Kushi Gavrieli, Meira Stern-Glick, the Nichols family — my other home, and the Carlet family.

And finally those who made me who I am. My parents Aviva and Shimon, and my beloved sister and brother Rama and Amir. And finally, my son El'ad who was born a few months before the first edition of the book came out and brought a whole new perspective to my life. Last in order, first in importance, the woman of my life, Cathy, may there be forever spring for you at no less than 28 degrees Celsius.

Preface to the New Paperback Edition*

On 14 February, 2005, exactly one year after the publication of the first edition of this book, Lebanon's former prime minister, Rafiq al-Hariri, was assassinated in central Beirut in a massive explosion that many, including the UN Special Tribunal for Lebanon, attributed to Hizballah's operatives. Al-Hariri is mentioned twice in this book—on the first page and in the concluding chapter—in the context of illustrations of the dissemination of the Phoenician narrative in Lebanon throughout wide sectors of the society that, while fully and unapologetically viewing Lebanon as an Arab state, still endorse specific national traits identified with Phoenicianism: Lebanon as the cradle of Mediterranean civilizations, as a republic of merchants, as a bridge between East and West, and as a business and leisure hub for its Arab neighbors thanks to its relative openness and permissiveness.

The assassination of Rafiq al-Hariri was more than the killing of a political figure by his adversaries. It reflected the struggle between two different approaches to Lebanon as a national and political community. The late Lebanese journalist Gebran Tueni, who shared the same tragic fate as al-Hariri, described this as a struggle between Hong Kong, epitomized by al-Hariri, and Hanoi, epitomized by Hizballah.[1] Nadim Shehadi, another Lebanese intellectual, also used metaphors to describe the two "projects" that have dominated Lebanon since the end of the civil war in 1990. "For the past two decades," Shehadi wrote, "two competing projects have been running in parallel in Lebanon. One aims at building a Riviera, a Monaco of the eastern Mediterranean; the other a Citadel or bunker, at the frontline of confrontation with Israel and the United States."[2] According to Shehadi, the Riviera camp, whose prime architect was al-Hariri, would like to resurrect the pre-civil war cosmopolitan and prosperous Lebanon, in which Beirut functioned as a financial and business centre. Conversely, the Citadel project, led by Hizballah, envisions Lebanon as a strong and militarized state that serves as the spearhead of Arab and Islamic resistance to Israel, or the "usurping entity," and the United States.

In many respects, the Riviera project was modelled after the ideas and vision of Michel Chiha, one of the most important politicians and thinkers who shaped Lebanon's political system during the mandate years (1920-1943) and in their aftermath. Chiha envisioned Lebanon as a "Riviera," where Beirut, the Levantine cosmopolitan city *par excellence*, would operate as an economic, cultural and intellectual hub of the Middle East. As demonstrated in this book, Chiha linked this vision of the country to a particular historical model that emphasized the age-old experience of Lebanon as the historical bedrock of the "Riviera" along the Mediterranean

Sea. Chiha was not a separatist Christian Lebanese, as were some of the supporters of the Phoenician narrative whose stories are recounted in this book. Although he belonged to the Francophone, haute-bourgeoisie circles of Beirut, who at times felt more comfortable in Paris than in any Arab city in the Middle East (other than their own city, Beirut), he was fully cognizant that for Lebanon to survive in the region, it could not turn its back on its Arab neighbors. Consequently, he opposed the establishment of a Jewish state in Palestine and reached out to Sunni politicians, haute-bourgeoisie like himself, in a bid to enable Lebanon to exist as a viable political community. Al-Hariri, a conservative *nouveau riche* Sunni Muslim with an Arab-Islamic education from an impoverished family, hailed from an entirely different socio-economic, religious and educational background, yet he came to embody many (though by no means all) of the ideas about the identity of Lebanon that had first been espoused by Chiha some 50-60 years earlier. Accordingly, the assassins of al-Hariri were attempting to kill not only the politician but also the idea of Lebanon that he personified.

Chiha's version of Lebanon's national identity, some aspects of which were shared by al-Hariri, remained dominant at least until the eruption of the civil war in 1975. This national identity left little to no place for the country's Shi'i community. The Shi'a, the most impoverished, disenfranchised and geographically and socio-economically marginalized community in Lebanon, have developed their own form of Lebanese nationalism, which places them at the centre of the Lebanese "nation" as a subaltern community that emphasizes its Arab and Islamic identities.[3] To achieve this objective, they had to challenge at least two versions of Lebanese nationalism, both of which can be traced to the 1943 National Pact that shaped the country's political system until 1990. The first was developed mainly by Christians (largely, but not only Maronites, as Chiha exemplifies) during the country's first forty years (1920s-1960s). It emphasized the section in the 1943 National Pact that stated that Lebanon "assimilates all that is beneficial and useful in Western civilization."[4] The second was espoused by urban Sunnis such as Riad al-Sulh, one of the drafters of the Pact, and al-Hariri (both from Sidon and, incidentally, both assassinated by Syrian sympathizers), and it emphasized the section in the Pact defining Lebanon as a country with an "Arab face." Although al-Sulh was a member of the "old money" Sunni elite and was educated in French missionary schools whereas al-Hariri only joined this class during the civil war, they shared a vision of Lebanon's Arab identity. Their Arabism was Sunni-centred but they saw Lebanon as a secular polity with close ties to the West and in particular to France.

It was expected that the Shi'a—and by extension their main political parties, Hizballah and Amal—would reject these two interconnected visions of Lebanon's national identity and come up with their own version of Lebanese nationalism. Because of Lebanon's multi-religious composition and the inherent sectarianism that shaped its political life, Lebanese society has always faced the challenge of finding a shared national identity and historical narrative that most if not all of its citizens can endorse. The political ascendancy of Hizballah (and the Shi'i community in general), has only exacerbated this challenge, as the Shi'i organization has rejected the old national narratives, seeking to replace them with its own, and has even linked its version of Lebanese nationalism to an eternal struggle against Israel, thus placing Lebanon, at the very frontline in the conflict against the Jewish state. After Israel withdrew from South Lebanon in 2000, the tension between Hizballah's "Lebanon project" and that of al-Hariri only intensified. Hizballah's insistence on maintaining its special status as an armed militia has exposed the fact that its "resistance" was not only against the Israeli occupation of South Lebanon, but was part of a strategic plan to use the struggle against Israel as a means of placing (Shi'i) Islam and Arabism at the centre of the country's identity, thereby jettisoning the Riviera project. Such a Lebanon would have no room for any hallucinations about age-old, pre-Arab and pre-Islamic cultures, nor would it accept softer versions of these Riviera-like fantasies as espoused by al-Hariri.

An examination of two diametrically opposed projects reveals the difference between Hizballah's and al-Hariri's visions of Lebanon. Both projects—the reconstruction of Beirut Central District (BCD) by Rafiq al-Hariri's firm, Solidere, and the construction of Hizballah's resistance memorial site in Mleeta—were intended to evoke specific memories and a sense of heritage. Since 1994, Solidere has been in charge of rebuilding downtown Beirut, an area that was largely destroyed during the civil war, with the aim of restoring its previous glory as a tourist and financial centre (tourism and finance being the two largest profit-making sectors in Lebanon) of Lebanon and even the entire Middle East. In this project, which was endorsed by the Lebanese Ministry of Tourism, not only was the impact of the civil war almost entirely obliterated from the reconstructed landscape (paradoxically, it was the devastation caused by the war that enabled the reconstruction project), but amid the reconstructed buildings, archaeological sites have been excavated and preserved as open-space exhibits. These sites expose the ancient Phoenician, Hellenic and Roman eras of Beirut (while ignoring other eras), presenting them as Lebanon's national and historical heritage. Just south of BCD, Lebanon's national museum, also part of the post-civil war reconstruction project, conveys a similar message about Lebanon's national heritage through exhibits that emphasize these ancient eras and downplay other historical eras. Thus, the urban landscape of BCD presents an image of Lebanon as a modern, Western-inspired society whose historical legacy goes back to these ancient

Mediterranean civilizations. This image of Lebanon, which for decades had been associated with exclusively Lebanist, Maronite-inspired nationalism, has been promoted by Solidere, a company controlled by Sunni urbanites who embraced the broader historical and cosmopolitan narrative because it serves their financial and political interests.[5] Needless to say, the post-civil war reconstruction project of Beirut completely ignores the predominantly Shi'i neighborhoods in southern Beirut.

Conversely, Hizballah's Resistance Tourist Landmark in Mleeta, which like BCD has been sanctioned by the Lebanese Ministry of Tourism, focuses on entirely different memories and heritage. Constructed in a predominantly Shi'i region south east of Sidon in South Lebanon, where major hostilities took place between Hizballah and Israel during 1982-2000, the site serves as a museum commemorating the armed resistance against the Jewish state.[6] As Mona Harb and Lara Deeb argue, Mleeta's resistance memorial is part of Hizballah's effort to establish a Shi'i Islamic milieu (*al-hala al-Islamiyya*) in Lebanon, which they define as "the physical and symbolic spaces within which pious Shi'a live out a particular 'state of being,' the public sphere where its norms and values are debated and shaped, and the 'state of being' itself with its continually shifting moral norms."[7] This site (like other cultural projects of Hizballah such as the museum of Al-Khiam prison, which Harb and Deeb also analyze) aims to educate Lebanese and foreigners about a different history and evoke utterly different memories from the ones Solidere promotes. As the homepage of Mleeta's website states,

> Being the first of its kind, this place carves the memory of a continual stage in the history of Lebanon. This is a natural museum, surrounded by the captivating nature and mountains. Its aim is to preserve the places where the Mujahideen lived, giving people the chance to be acquainted with the style of the unique experience of the Islamic resistance against the Israeli enemy, since its occupation of Beirut in 1982.[8]

The hundreds of thousands of tourists who have visited the Mleeta resistance memorial since its inauguration on 25 May 2010, the tenth anniversary of Israel's withdrawal from South Lebanon, are not only exposed to the history of the *Islamic* resistance, but are also encouraged to continue their support for the unremitting struggle, which will only end with the destruction of Israel.

In the struggle between the "Hanoi" and the "Hong Kong" camps, Phoenicianism as a non-Arab national identity for Lebanon has fallen out of grace. The rising influence of Shi'i and Sunni Islamism in the country has reinforced the drift away from any narrative that negates Arabism and Islam as essential elements in Lebanon's national identity.[9] Nonetheless, there are Lebanese who still toy with the Phoenician project in a bid to challenge the political and cultural trajectory toward which these Islamist movements aspire to take Lebanon. In recent years modern science was recruited for this cause. Like other national movements that have resorted to DNA and genetics research to demonstrate their age-old existence as viable national communities,[10] some Lebanese have invoked the science of genetics, arguing that the ties between modern Lebanese and the ancient inhabitants of their land, the Phoenicians, are not only historical or cultural, but also biological. Lebanese scientists from the Lebanese American University joined the much-publicized global project conducted by National Geographic to study genetic imprints of indigenous populations around the world.[11] They collected blood samples from men in Lebanon, Syria, Malta, Tunisia and other areas where the ancient Phoenicians once dwelled, and they concluded that Phoenician DNA imprints could still be found among residents of these locales. Such DNA studies in Lebanon or elsewhere may have a scientific aura,[12] yet they also reflect a strong political agenda as they are never carried out innocently for the sake of pure science, but rather in order to justify specific arguments with regard to the nation's ancient pedigree. The Lebanese DNA study has gained significant attention in Lebanese, Arab and international media,[13] bringing back to the fore the endless "are we Arabs or Phoenicians?" debates, which are always more politically driven than historiographically or scientifically based. To be sure, neither Hizballah's "Islamic milieu" nor the Sunni Islamist circles in Tripoli and elsewhere in the country take part in these debates. For the latter, the question of Lebanon's identity has been sealed; it is clear and undisputed.

Since the start of the Arab uprisings in December 2010, the Middle East has entered a new era that will undoubtedly transform the political, social and cultural makeup of the region. Islamist parties throughout the Middle East are gaining ground, some through democratic procedures, others through violence. At the time of writing, Syria is torn in a vicious civil war whose end and outcome are not yet clear and Lebanon is gradually drifting into the chaos of its neighbour. The Islamist elements of the Syrian opposition are growing stronger by the day and Lebanese Shi'i and Sunni Islamists are being drawn into the conflict as well, supporting the two opposing sides of the war in Syria. Lebanon's viability as a nation-state has long been disputed, and similar questions now surround Syria, with the possibility that in the post-Asad era it will not be able to sustain itself as a united polity. Should Syria disintegrate, it is likely that Lebanon would be drawn even further into the fray. In such an atmosphere and political state of affairs, reflections about the ancient history of Lebanon (or Syria) and its relevance for the country's current national identity become not only a luxury but practically irrelevant. What might remain is nostalgia for a Middle East that existed not too long ago, when religious extremism and xenophobic nationalism were the exception rather than the rule. In fact, this wave of nostalgia had already begun even before the outbreak of the Arab uprisings. The Levant as a geographical and cultural unit of analysis has been central to this wave of nostalgia for the old Middle East. Books were written,[14] journals were launched,[15] conferences were held and centres were established,[16] all focusing on the Levant, the eastern Mediterranean that roughly includes contemporary Egypt, Israel/Palestine, Lebanon, Syria, Turkey and Greece. These scholarly and popular initiatives focus on the cosmopolitan lifestyle that dominated this region until the 1950s and in which Beirut, Alexandria, Haifa, Aleppo, Istanbul, Smyrna and other cities were linked in a web of multi-ethnic, multi-religious and multi-lingual communities whose boundaries were more flexible and permeable than they are today. The ancient civilizations of the Mediterranean Sea are a salient aspect of this Levantine awakening, which seeks to challenge contemporary national historiographies that present the region as homogenous and unitary (Arab nationalism), or that are exclusive and militant (Zionism). Although they over-romanticize the Levant and Levantinism, they still offer an alternative to the contemporary Middle East that has been ravaged by multiple predicaments such as the Arab-Israeli conflict, the Sunni-Shi'i divide, religious-secular tensions, gender biases and socio-economic stagnation. Looking ahead to an era of shifting sands, which gives rise to hopes as well as major concerns for the region, romanticism may be seen as escapism, but may also be a reminder that the violent trajectory toward which the Middle East appears headed is not inevitable. *Reviving Phoenicia* tells a story about this cosmopolitan Middle East, and while trying not to overly romanticize that time period, and recognizing its shortcomings, the book does remind us that not too long ago things in the Middle East in general and Lebanon in particular were different. Phoenicia, obviously, cannot be revived, but we should hope that at least some elements of the cosmopolitanism that is depicted in this book could.

Notes

* The printing of this edition was made possible in part by support from the Institute for Scholarship in the Liberal Arts, College of Arts and Letters, University of Notre Dame.
1. Yossi Baidatz, "Lebanon: Between Hong Kong and Hanoi," The Washington Institute for Near East Policy, Policy Watch No. 523, March 9, 2001, http://www.washingtoninstitute.org/policy-analysis/view/lebanon-between-hong-kong-and-hanoi (accessed December 28, 2012).
2. Nadim Shehadi, "Riviera vs. Citadel: the Battle for Lebanon," Open democracy, July 2007, http://www.opendemocracy.net/conflict-middle_east_politics/riviera_citadel_3841.jsp (accessed December 28, 2012).
3. Roschanack Shaery-Eisenlohr, *Shi'ite Lebanon: Transnational Religion and the Making of National Identities* (New York: Columbia University Press, 2008), pp. 36-37, 71.
4. Fawwaz Traboulsi, *A History of Modern Lebanon* (London: Pluto Press, 2007), pp. 110.

5. Ghada Masri, "Resurrecting Phoenicia: Tourist Landscape and National Identity in the Heart of the Lebanese Capital," in Robert Maitland and Brent W. Ritchie, eds., *City Tourism National Capital Perspectives* (Cambridge, MA: CABI Publishing, 2010), pp. 225-238.
6. See the website of the museum, http://www.mleeta.com/mleeta/index.html (accessed December 26, 2012).
7. Mona Harb and Lara Deeb, "Culture as History and Landscape: Hizballah's Efforts to Shape an Islamic Milieu in Lebanon," *Arab Studies Journal* (Spring 2011).
8. See the Mleeta website http://mleeta.com/mleeta/eng/definition1.html (accessed May 21, 2014).
9. Robert G. Rabil, *Religion, National Identity, and Confessional Politics in Lebanon; The Challenge of Islamism* (New York: Palgrave Macmillan, 2011).
10. John Entine, *Abraham's Children: Race, Identity, and the DNA of the Chosen People* (New York: Grand Central Publishing, 2007).
11. https://genographic.nationalgeographic.com/ (accessed December 21, 2012).
12. Pierre A. Zalloua et al., "Identifying Genetic Traces of Historical Expansions: Phoenician Footprints in the Mediterranean," *The American Journal of Human Genetics*, Vol. 83, No. 5 (October 2008), pp. 633-642.
13. See, for example, Amitabh Avasthi, "Phoenician Blood Endures 3,000 Years, DNA Study Shows," *National Geographic News*, October 30, 2008, http://news.nationalgeographic.com/news/2008/10/081030-phoenician-dna-genographic-missions.html; LBC program reporting on the research and discussing the question of Lebanese as Phoenicians http://www.youtube.com/watch?v=IoPGLFY1Lxs; DNA legacy of ancient seafarers, BBC News, October 31, 2008, http://news.bbc.co.uk/2/hi/sci/tech/7700356.stm; "Phoenician or Arab? Lebanon non-ending debate," al-Arabia News, http://www.alarabiya.net/articles/2010/06/07/110694.html (all links accessed December 29, 2012).
14. Philipp Mansel, *Levant: Splendour and Catastrophe on the Mediterranean* (New Hampshire: Yale University Press, 2011); William Harris, *The Levant: A Fractured Mosaic* (Princeton: Markus Wiener, 2003 and 2005); Franck Salameh, *Language, Memory and Identity in the Middle East: The Case for Lebanon* (Lanham, Md: Lexington Books, 2010); Amiel Alkalay, *After Jews and Arabs: Remaking Levantine Culture* (Minneapolis: University of Minnesota Press, 1993); Yaakov Shavit, *Mediterranean Anthology* (Tel Aviv: Miskal, 2004) [Hebrew].
15. *Journal of Levantine Studies* http://www.levantine-journal.org/; *The Levantine Review* http://ejournals.bc.edu/ojs/index.php/levantine (links accessed December 29, 2012).
16. Levantine Cultural Center, http://www.levantinecenter.org; Levantine Heritage, http://www.levantineheritage.com/; Conference at Georgetown University, November 2012, "After Jews and Arabs: Remaking Levantine Culture 20 Years Later," http://ccas.georgetown.edu/story/1242690102139.html (links accessed December 29, 2012).

Introduction

> There is much more to the concept of the "nation" than myths and memories. But they constitute a *sine qua non*: there can be no identity without memory (albeit selective), no collective purpose without myth, and identity and purpose or destiny are necessary elements of the very concept of a nation.
>
> *Anthony Smith*[1]

The historical narrative of Lebanon almost invariably begins with the ancient Phoenician seafarers. History textbooks, government publications and full genres of literature and research resolutely follow this path. Lebanon has a history of 6,000 years, they affirm. It begins with the Phoenicians in pre-Biblical times, then proceeds into other eras — Persian, Greek, Roman, Byzantine, Arab, Crusader, Turkish, French — concluding in modern times when Lebanon regains its independence. One of the official websites of Prime Minister Rafiq al-Hariri well reflects this conviction: "We are heirs to a history which spans thousands of years and whose beginnings are lost in the mists of time itself," Hariri writes in his address to his fellow Lebanese, "The alphabet was born in our land. It was from the shores of Sidon and Tyre that sailors ventured to establish the first Mediterranean empire."[2] The assertion that Lebanon's history, even as an Arab country, begins with the ancient Phoenicians has almost become conventional wisdom. Even historians who oppose this narrative fall into its description. As'ad AbuKhalil, for example, in his *Historical Dictionary of Lebanon*, writes in the introduction: "Lebanese ultra-nationalists, who have dominated the official historiography of the country, claim that Lebanon has been in continued existence for over 5000 years and that the present-day country is no more than an extension of the ancient Phoenician kingdom(s). In reality Lebanon is a modern phenomenon; [...]."[3] The book, however, unfolds with a chronological list, beginning with the Canaanite occupation of Sidon and Tyre in 2800 BC and continuing to the Egyptian occupation of the Phoenician coast, the Phoenician expansion towards the sea, the founding of Carthage, the most famous Phoenician colony, and so forth, demonstrating the power of the Phoenician narrative that infiltrated even studies that defy it as a figment of the Lebanese ultra-nationalist imagination.

The present study is an attempt to uncover the social, political and intellectual origins and the development of the phenomenon of Phoenicianism in Lebanon. As in the case of other communities, Lebanese nationalists scrutinized the past to create a narrative that would justify the existence of Lebanon as a viable national community based on age-old historical memories and a proud pedigree. The Phoenician identity was born out of this need, but it soon became one of the major points of contention between and within the different communities, which, since Lebanon's creation in 1920, have been competing with each other to define their country's national identity.

Although this study has nothing to do with the ancient Phoenicians it seems essential to provide a short summary as to who these ancient inhabitants of Lebanon were and why they were so appealing to their modern counterparts. A survey of national movements in the Middle East followed by two brief discussions on selective theories of nationalism and French colonialism provide a general overview and a backdrop for the understanding of Phoenicianism in a broader context. The Introduction concludes with an outline of the study's structure.

Who Were the Phoenicians?

The ancient inhabitants of Lebanon did not call themselves Phoenicians.[4] This term is of Greek origin, appearing for the first time in Greek texts in the 9th century BC; its meaning is still not fully clear. The most accepted explanation, although by no means the only one, is that the Greek word *phoinix*, meaning "red," alludes to the purple textile industry for which the ancient inhabitants of Lebanon were made famous. The Phoenicians actually called themselves Canaanites and their land Canaan, at least until the 1st century AD as documented in the New Testament where it is written that Jesus reached the borders of Tyre and Sidon and cured there a Canaanite woman.[5] The term *Cna'ani* in Biblical Hebrew implies a merchant, which suggests that, as with the Greek word *phoinix*, the name of the country may have derived from the most popular profession of the ancient Lebanese — commerce. These Canaanite-Phoenicians were also often identified according to the city to which they belonged: Sidonites, Tyrians, Giblites and so forth, reflecting the fact that their cities never gained political unity but rather remained independent city-states.

Historians and archeologists tend to mark the beginning of the Phoenician era in the late Bronze Age and the beginning of the Early Iron Age, around 1200 BC. The Phoenician cities were in existence more than a millennium earlier, but around the 12th century, the Near East went through a major socio-political upheaval that reshaped the entire region and forced the Phoenician cities to orient towards the Mediterranean Sea. In just one century, the land of Canaan experienced the arrival of three peoples: the Israelites from the south, who settled in the heartland; the Philistines (or the Peoples of the Sea) from the Greek Islands, who settled along the southern shores of Canaan; and the

Arameans who came from Mesopotamia and settled in the north. These three invasions left no space for the Phoenicians but the coastal range in the northern part of Canaan. Thus, Phoenicia was defined as the small strip of land stretching from the island of Arvad (the ancient Aradus) in the north to Akko (Acre) and Mount Carmel in the south. The eastern border of Phoenicia was Mount Lebanon that runs roughly parallel to the coast, creating a very narrow and clearly-circumscribed territory between the Mediterranean and the Mountain.

From the 12th century BC until the Greek occupation of Phoenicia in 334 AD, the Mediterranean trade routes were practically all controlled by Phoenician seafarers. They established colonies on the major islands in the Mediterranean basin and in today's Greece, Italy, France, Spain and North Africa. The most notable of these was, of course, Carthage (Keret Hadata, New Polis), located in today's Tunisia. Their network of colonies throughout the Mediterranean put the entire basin under one socio-economic system and for the first time in human history it was possible to speak about a "Mediterranean civilization." They perfected the art of sailing and navigating, the use of glass, fabric and many other crafts, which they borrowed from different civilizations in their trade along the Mediterranean. Despite what is commonly believed, the Phoenicians did not invent the alphabet, but they were the last in a line of Semitic peoples to refine it in form and in number of letters and then to export it to Greece. This was undoubtedly their most important achievement and contribution to the intellectual development of humankind.

One of the most intriguing questions about the Phoenicians that preoccupied the modern Lebanese concerned their origin. The Phoenicians were a Semitic people who spoke a Semitic language that belonged to the Western-Semitic family, very similar to ancient Hebrew.[6] Herodotus, who visited Tyre in 450 BC, recounts that the people of the city informed him that they arrived in the region twenty-five centuries earlier from the Red Sea. His account substantiates the popular and polemical thesis that the entire Semitic population of the Near East emigrated from the Arabian Peninsula in endless waves of migration, the last of which was the Arab-Islamic wave in the 7th century AD.[7] This thesis caused some Arab nationalists and demographers to assert that all the ancient peoples of the Middle East were actually Arabs and that the terms "Arab" and "Semite" are, therefore, synonymous. It enabled them to claim that the Arab-Islamic conquest brought a new faith to a land that ethnically was already their own. It is not difficult to imagine what the reaction to this claim was by Lebanese nationalists and other centrifugal forces within the Arab world.

Another interesting scholarly — yet often politically motivated — debate about the ancient Phoenicians (whose history is as lengthy as the tomes of modern research on them and had a tremendous impact on the modern Phoenician-Lebanese view of the past) centers on the question of their influence on ancient Greek civilization. From the 18th century, European intellectuals exhibited a growing interest in ancient Greece, depicting it as the cradle of Western-European civilization and portraying its population as Aryan, the first link in the noble European racial chain. There were, however, a few French scholars who, although they regarded themselves as the legitimate heirs of Plato and Aristotle, still viewed Greek civilization as more than simply the product of a European endeavor. The scholar and journalist Victor Bérard was among the most influential classicists to write about the role of the Phoenicians in the formation of Greek civilization. In his works he demonstrated that, to a large extent, Hellenic religion and mythology were of Semitic origin, more precisely of Phoenician-Egyptian seed.[8] In 1902, Bérard published *Les Phéniciens et l'Odyssée*, in which he described the Odyssey as a travelogue written by a seafarer sitting on the deck of a Phoenician trireme and noting the different events he witnessed along the way. By and large, Bérard's theories were rejected by the Hellenic scholarly establishment, but, as we shall see, they were welcomed with open arms by Lebanese nationalists who viewed them as proof of the fact that they were the ones who should be credited as the cradle of Western civilization. A little more than a decade ago a new and controversial study, *Black Athena*, brought Bérard's ideas back to life arguing that the glory days of the Hellenic world were a direct product of Phoenician and Egyptian — i.e., Semitic — civilizations and that scholars have deliberately ignored this fact because it undermines the very foundations of Western civilization.[9] Whether Bernal, the author of *Black Athena*, was accurate or not, it should be remembered that all scholars agree that the ancient Phoenicians had *some* impact on Greek civilization, by the sheer fact that for 1,000 years they controlled most of the trade in the Mediterranean, which means that even a lofty civilization such as the Greeks could not have ignored their presence and preeminence.

In the millennium that marked Phoenician domination in the Mediterranean basin, the Phoenicians developed and attained a clear sense of being a "people," despite the fact that they never lived in one unified political system.[10] They spoke and wrote in the same language, they worshiped similar gods, conducted similar rituals related to birth, death and burial, and collaborated with each other in their commercial enterprises. Following the Macedonian-Greek occupation in 334 BC, the Phoenician civilization slowly declined and cleared the way for Greek and Roman domination. The Phoenician-Canaanite language was replaced by Greek and Aramaic and, similarly, the Phoenician religion was superceded by Greek and later Roman pantheons. The Phoenicians disappeared as a people not because of a major trauma such as expulsion or plague, but rather by a slow process of adaptation to the new political reality. In Greek and Roman eras, the land of Phoenicia continued to flourish. Beirut-Berytus became one of the world's most important intellectual centers through the Roman School of Law, while Tyre and Sidon continued to prosper in trade, with the entire Roman Empire open to their commercial skills. An indication of the rich Greek and Roman civilizations in Phoenicia can be seen in the archeological sites of that era that are scattered throughout Lebanon, most notably the Temple of Balbeck. Despite the fact that the Phoenician era is clearly circumscribed between the 12th century BC and the Greek occupation in the 3rd century BC, the neo-Phoenicians, who are the focus of this study, held a broader interpretation of the time span of this era. Thus, for example, the city of Ugarit, which prospered in the 16th-15th centuries BC and declined by the 14th century BC, was incorporated into the Phoenician civilization; and the Greek and Roman eras were "Phoenicianized" as well. It was a tendency to view the entire ancient time as one historical unit, separated by different foreign conquests but united through the one gifted people that dwelt in the land of Phoenicia. Some of the modern ultra-Phoenicians claimed that the Phoenician era never ceased to exist and today's Lebanese are as Phoenician as their ancient ancestors.

National Identities in the Arab Middle East

Studies on Lebanon and the Lebanese national movement demonstrated for years continuity between four hundred years of political autonomy in Mount Lebanon and the establishment of Greater Lebanon in 1920.[11] These studies asserted that a certain collective identity was formed in the Mountain since the time of Fakhr al-Din al-Ma'ni (1590-1635), an identity that radiated to the coastal strip and the Biqa' region. By interpreting the history of Lebanon in this way, these works actually claimed that the idea of a Lebanese state in its current borders was, in fact, historically viable. Modern Lebanon was not formed in a vacuum. Its national movement has had its roots deep in the socio-political history of Mount Lebanon. Many of the advocates of this narrative were Lebanese historians who wrote their country's history justifying Lebanon's existence as a national community.[12] This kind of historiography was also a result of genuine belief in the Lebanese political system before the eruption of the civil war in 1975. Even more recent studies, written during and after the civil war, still supported the view that modern Lebanon was founded on a lengthy historical experience of Maronite ethnic cohesiveness in Mount Lebanon which functioned as the basis for the foundation of the Lebanese state.[13]

A recent study by Carol Hakim-Dowek, *The Origins of the Lebanese National Idea, 1840-1914*,[14] persuasively demonstrates that in fact the Lebanist idea was relatively novel and its formation was by no means linear. Hakim-Dowek shows in her work that Lebanism — the idea of an independent political framework with Mount Lebanon as its core — appeared for the first time in 1840. It was raised by Maronite clergy but faded away soon thereafter as a result of the political settlements of the double *Qai'maqamiyya* in 1842 and the *Mutasarrifiyya*, the autonomous region, in 1861.[15] Having been articulated by the Church, Lebanism was envisioned as a Christian conservative political framework, controlled by the Maronite clergy. According to her research, Lebanism reappeared in a laical form only at the beginning of the 20th century as a result of primarily internal social problems within the *Mutasarrifiyya*. Christian Lebanese of the new secular and educated elite, residing either in Lebanon or in various Syro-Lebanese immigrant communities in Egypt and in the Americas, were promoting the idea of an extended autonomous region of Lebanon in a larger Syrian political framework. Their point of departure was a general dislike of the social and political situation in the *Mutasarrifiyya*, which they attributed to the deficiency of the religious establishments. The autonomous region was controlled by the Maronite clergy and the traditional notable families; the new, emerging stratum challenged their authority while at the same time aimed to expand the autonomous territory. At first, Lebanism was not expressed as an alternative to Ottomanism. Its advocates were asking for administrative reforms and border revisions within the context of the Ottoman Empire. It took almost an additional twenty years before these demands turned into an appeal for the formation of an independent Lebanese state, and before the Maronite Church made this Lebanism its official platform and led the movement for the formation of an independent Lebanese state. Thus, Hakim-Dowek depicts a non-linear development of the Lebanist idea demonstrating that Christian Lebanese, in and out of Mount Lebanon and Beirut, held different views about the political solution of the "Lebanese question" until early 1919. Only then did most political forces join together in their demand for the establishment of an independent state.

Lebanism, and Lebanese national sentiments, were born and developed alongside other collective identities in the Arab Middle East, most notably Ottomanism, Syrianism, Arabism and Islamism. For many years, historians of the Middle East gave much weight to the Arab identity as a powerful political force in the Arab provinces of the declining Ottoman Empire.[16] They saw Arabism as a secular movement led by Syro-Lebanese who, equipped with Western education, reacted to the encroaching measures of the Ottomans, first to the oppressing policies of Sultan Abdülhamid and later the "turkifying" attempts of the Young Turks. This interpretation also viewed most of the political developments in the Middle East at that time as *reactions* and *responses* to the increase in Arab sentiments. Thus, the rise of non-Arab sentiments among some Christian Lebanese was also seen as a reaction to the growing strength of Arabism rather than as an independent desire emanating from a socio-political reality within Lebanon.

However, it has been long understood that this kind of interpretation overemphasized the strength of Arabism, under-emphasized the power of loyalty to the Ottoman Empire and almost entirely disregarded local territorial sentiments in geographical Syria. The established narrative today is that Ottomanism remained the strongest focus of allegiance until the end of World War I among the majority of the Syrian population. Arab national sentiments, founded on the writings of Islamic reformists, existed before 1914, but by no means did they win the overwhelming support of the local elite. This elite turned Arabist only with the fall of the Empire, after 1918. Their Arabism was not based on secular ideology, but was actually embedded on Islamic terminology as appeared in the writings of Muslim reformists such as Muhammad 'Abduh, Jamal al-Din al-Afghani and Rashid Rida.[17]

Syrian sentiments before 1920 can be divided into three categories: secular Arab Syrianism, Muslim-Arab Syrianism and secular non-Arab Syrianism. Secular Arab Syrianism existed as a geo-political and cultural identity since the 1860s, interwoven with Ottoman and Arab sentiments. Butrus al-Bustani, who advocated Ottomanism and loyalty to the Sublime Porte, was the one who also set the foundation of this identity.[18] A leading member of the Arabic *Nahda*, or renaissance, movement, al-Bustani generated Arabism through Arabic literature as a cultural identity while at the same time he regarded Syria as his *watan,* or homeland. He defined the inhabitants of Syria (stretching in the north from the Tauros mountains to the Sinai desert in the south, and from the Mediterranean in the west to the Euphrates in the east) as members of one nation who culturally held strong Arab characteristics and who politically belonged to the larger Ottoman Empire.[19] He viewed this identity as secular, and shared by Muslims, Christians and Jews alike. During WWI and after, this kind of Syrianism continued to be expressed especially by Christians from Beirut and Mount Lebanon. The 1916 book of the Greek Catholic Nadra Moutran, *La Syrie de Demain,* to be discussed in Chapter II, arguably encapsulates well this kind of Arab-Syrian secular thought. There were also some Maronites, such as Iskandar 'Amoun and Ibrahim al-Najjar, who cooperated with Faysal in Damascus in 1918-1920. Similar to al-Bustani sixty years earlier they saw themselves as Arab Syrians and they believed that Lebanon should be given a leading role in a Syrian-Arab federation.

The second stream, Muslim Arab Syrianism, added the religious Islamic component to the Syrian identity and viewed Islam and Arabism as its two prime pillars. This stream was best expressed by Rashid Rida, a Syrian-Arab Islamist and a disciple of Muhammad 'Abduh, who called for the establishment of an Arab Syrian nation based on Islam as its prime pillar of identity (more about him in Chapter V). The Arab government of Faysal in 1918-1920 Damascus was in fact the political manifestation of the ideas of Rashid Rida, who envisioned a larger Arab-Muslim state, but viewed geographical Syria as the first step in attaining this greater plan. Hence, he took an active role in Faysal's government and in the Syro-Palestinian Congress of Shekib Arslan in Geneva in 1921.

The third stream, secular non-Arab Syrianism, existed from the beginning of the 20th century, but emerged as a political force during WWI. Chékri Ganem and Georges Samné, with the ever-present encouragement of the French, advocated for the establishment of a Syrian, non-Arab, federation based on principles of democracy, laicism and decentralization. In their vision, Lebanon would be given an eminent leading role in this federation. This type of Syrianism relied heavily on works of French scholars who wrote about the existence of a Syrian nation based on a unity of geography and race. The most notable example of this kind of writing was Elisée Reclus, the French geographer, whose impact on the crystallization of Syrian nationalism was great. In his gigantic work, *Nouvelle Géographie Universelle,* Reclus wrote about the existence of a Syrian race circumscribed within the limits of geographical Syria and utterly distinct from the Arab race. He depicted the civilization of the ancient world as an axle whose two edges were India on the far east, and France and Britain on the far west. Since antiquity, Reclus maintained, Syria, as a well-defined geographic and racial unit, was located exactly at the center of this axle.[20] We shall see in the following chapters that Reclus' theories were used extensively by supporters of the Syrian identity and especially by the Jesuit teacher Henri Lammens who had many disciples among Lebanese nationalists before and after 1920.

It was within this political reality that the Lebanese national idea was formed and articulated. Loyalty to the Ottoman Empire was the strongest force of political identity, whereas regionally most intellectual Lebanese, although conscious of their special political and social status, still perceived themselves part of a larger Syrian framework. Arabism as a national movement was in its seminal stage and, before 1908, the designation "Arab" was still associated with Bedouins and the desert, despite the "awakening" of the Arab literary movement.

Until WWI, most Lebanese intellectuals did not call for the establishment of an independent state and if such claims were made, they were mainly in the context of a Syrian federation. Belonging to a geo-political Syrian framework was the dominant view even among Christian Lebanese who, by April 1919, would become the strongest advocates for the formation of an independent Christian, Western-oriented Lebanon. As we shall see in this study, the preoccupation with the Phoenician past in Lebanon and the identification of intellectuals from Beirut as "Phoenicians" commenced decades before "anti-Arab" sentiments were even a possibility, simply because Arabism was not yet a dominant identity that had to be reckoned with.

Theorizing Lebanese Nationalism?

Despite the obsessive preoccupation in academia with the attempt to theorize the rise of nationalism in the past two hundred years, there has not been — because there cannot be — one homogenous explanation for this phenomenon, which makes "men and women willing to die for their countries."[21] The rise of nationalism, like all political forces with cultural manifestations, is shaped by specific and local social, economic and political conditions. Even the separation between "classical" or "modular" forms of nationalism that appeared in the West and "special" or "deviant" expressions of nationalism that emerged in the East and the South do not provide us with two single explanations for the rise of nationalism. Some theories can help us understand some aspects of different national behaviors, but no one theory (or two) can provide a single explanation for the rise and impact of the most powerful and destructive ideology of the 20th century, continuing consistently into the 21st century.

It is beyond the point of this study, not to say redundant, to provide an overview of the existing theories of nationalism.[22] Likewise, I do not wish to posit this study within these theories in an attempt to find the "proper" matrix for the rise of Lebanese nationalism and its historical narrative. Rather, I selectively chose certain theories and position them alongside Lebanese nationalism in order to clarify some of its notions. I shall start with Anthony Smith who has been labeled, exaggeratedly I believe, as the theoretician closest to the primordialist approach of nationalism.[23] Nationalism, for Smith, cannot be explained as a purely modern phenomenon but neither can it be seen and understood as a primordial "natural" occurrence, existing since the beginning of time and expressed in various cultural and political forms. Modernization, according to him, utterly transformed societies and shaped their identities into the modern concept of "nation" as political unit. Yet, at the same time, some modern nations do rest on foundations of a certain collective identity — the *ethnie* — which he defines as "a named human population possessing a myth of common descent, common historical memories, elements of shared culture, an association with a particular territory and a sense of solidarity."[24] At the core of some national movements one can find an ethnic identity that was in existence centuries before the process of modernization began and that has been used by the local intelligentsia to mobilize the ethnic community into a self-aware national community. In states in which an *ethnie* did not exist it had to be invented for the modern nation to emerge and survive.[25] Smith finds the Maronite community a good example for the concept of *ethnie*,[26] and to a large extent he is right. This community is circumscribed within a well-defined territory — Mount Lebanon. Its historical memories, cultivated by its clergy, are traced back to the 5th century, to Saint Marun, claimed as the father of the Church, and its religious affiliation enhanced its sense of uniqueness not only vis-à-vis its Muslim neighbors, but also vis-à-vis the other Eastern churches. Although the *ethnie* of Smith seems the most suitable to describe the Maronite sense of identity it also fails in ignoring its complexity. It should be remembered that the Maronites, before the 19th century and after, have never been one unified group with one collective will. Often their sense of common identity was weaker than, say, the sense of identity which the Maronite Khazin feudal family shared with other Druze and Sunni feudal families. In addition, as we shall see in this study, the political aspirations of the Maronite church as advocated by its high clergy since the 1840s were not the same as those of lay Maronites who resided in Beirut during the same time. For example, when the brothers Philippe and Farid al-Khazin advocated in Beirut in 1910 the establishment of an autonomous greater Lebanon, they based their claim on a laical historical narrative, beginning with the Druze leader, Fakhr al-Din, and not with a traditional Maronite claim (see more in Chapter II). Moreover, as will be discussed, until 1919, most Maronite intellectuals did not call for the establishment of Greater Lebanon but rather viewed Greater Syria as the solution for the "Question of Lebanon." There has never been one Maronite will. Maronites, just like other sects in Lebanon, operate in the context of intra-sectarian dynamics sometimes even more than inter-sectarian. Thus, despite the fact that the concept of *ethnie* is helpful in understanding the development of the Lebanist idea, it needs to be remembered that the Maronite *ethnies* have always been dynamic, multifaceted and sometimes even invented.

Nationalism is a modern phenomenon in the sense that it created a sentiment of human allegiance that did not exist before it was formed. It is modern also because in order to spread its message widely and effectively it employs modern means of communication, such as radio, museums, printed material, maps and so forth. However, there are more nations and national movements throughout the world that did not go through a modernizing, industrial revolution than ones that did. In this respect, Ernest Gellner, the arch-modernist theoretician, does not help us to understand nationalism in non-industrialized societies. Focusing on material conditions, Gellner holds that the industrial revolution separates between pre-modernity and modernity and that only following a process of modernization, i.e., the rise of capitalism, bureaucracy and secularism, can a nation emerge. "Nationalism," according to his much quoted claim, "is not the awakening of nations to self-consciousness: it invents nations where they do not exist."[27] Nationalism, as Gellner states, invented nations in the Middle East. Or more accurately, to use Sami Zubaida's words, it is the state that created the nation in the Middle East.[28] Yet, these "nations," Lebanon included, were not born in the watershed between pre-modernity and modernity. Societies in the Middle East still await, to this day, their industrial revolution and yet they hold their "nationalism" dearly to the point that they are "prepared to sacrifice their lives for the recognition of their national identities."[29] Moreover, Gellner argues that the nation-state replaces kinship with national identity. However, in Lebanon, as in other Middle Eastern societies, nationalism did not replace kinship, but rather learned to live with it, sometimes in conflict and at other times in agreement.

Modernism and secularism were important pillars in Gellner's theory of nationalism. They were also the prime foundations of Benedict Anderson's book, *Imagined Communities*, which has been the touchstone of most studies on nationalism in the last decade, to the point that the word "imagine" and its derivatives are probably by now the most used terms in studies on national movements. Anderson views nationalism as a modern phenomenon, born out of the rise of capitalism. Yet he also provides an innovative angle for understanding it by defining the nation as an "imagined political community."[30]

It is imagined, Anderson explains, in the sense that its members will never be able to meet, hear or know the vast majority of the other members of the community, and yet they share a strong sense of belonging to this imagined non-tangible community. Such an analysis enabled Anderson to examine national communities not within the context of their authenticity or lack thereof, but rather in the way they imagine themselves. The concept of "imagining" enables us to do the same. Although, as it will become clear in the study, I view the claims for Phoenician descent in Lebanon as nebulous, I still consider the validity of Phoenicianism, or lack thereof, irrelevant to this study. The main thrust here is to analyze how a community imagined itself and not whether this imagining was historically conceivable. In other words, I am concerned with one aspect of the emergence of national consciousness — the national historical narrative — rather than with the rise of nationalism as a social formation in Lebanon.

Anderson's point of departure in his analysis of the rise of nationalism is twofold: the decline of religion (and in this respect he follows Gellner) and the rise of vernacular languages.[31] According to him, religion provided a sense of continuity and enabled people to come to grips with death. The "ebbing of religious belief," a product of the 18th century Enlightenment, did not reduce the need for continuity among humans which had previously been provided by religion. This is where nationalism came in and provided the secular sense of continuity and belonging. As for vernacular languages, Anderson writes that thanks to the new medium of "print capitalism" it was possible for national communities to abandon their written lingua franca (Latin, in the case of Europe) and to use a unified form of their own vernaculars that, through mass production of printed matter, also helped in shaping the national consciousness of the community.

As interesting as these two observations are, they still pose some major problems when applied to the Middle East. It is clear today that the Arab national movement was not born as a secular reaction to the exposure to the West, but actually as a religious Muslim response to the challenges posed by Europe. Similarly, the Lebanese national movement cannot be detached from its Christian religious context. It was the Maronite Patriarch who, in his trip to the Peace Congress in Versailles in 1919, exerted the last necessary pressure on France in favor of the establishment of Greater Lebanon. It was also he who preached in his weekly sermons that "patriotism is a religious practice"(see Chapter I). Moreover, even liberal lay Syro-Lebanese who were in charge of the introduction of Western thought to the region and who cooperated with the Church in 1919 envisioned Lebanon as a Christian dominated entity. Religion was and still is a prime component of all national movements in the Middle East and any attempt to understand nationalism in this region cannot be complete without taking this factor into account.

As for language, it seems that the Middle East actually experienced a different process from that in Europe. The rise of the Arab national movement actually suppressed the vernacular Arab dialects and, instead, revived and glorified literary Arabic as the lingua franca of all Arabs. Even local national movements in the Arab world did not make an attempt, except in marginal cases, to turn the regional dialects into their national language. This reflects the dichotomy in which national movements in the Arab Middle East operate. On the one hand, Arab states share a strong cultural affiliation with each other and an unfulfilled dream of political unity; on the other, local-territorial identities have only strengthened since the formation of the Arab states after WWI, yet not to the point of turning one of their vernaculars into the official national language. Literary Arabic, because of its deep theological weight, has always carried immense power in the Middle East, far more than Latin in Europe. We shall see that this strength caused many Lebanese nationalists to practice exceptional verbal acrobatics in their attempts to reconcile between their assertion that they were not Arabs and the fact that they used Arabic as their national language.

Western-centric theories on the rise of nationalism can sometimes confuse more than elucidate our attempt to explain the rise of nationalism in the Middle East or the Southern Hemisphere. There have been several attempts to provide a theoretical explanation of the rise of nationalism in non-Western societies. I refer here mainly to the works of Partha Chatterjee who added another component to the study of nationalism by claiming that its character changes in colonial settings.[32] Chatterjee holds that national identity in colonized societies can be divided into spiritual and material realms. Anti-colonial movements are deeply affected by the material advantages of their colonizer. Acknowledging its technological superiority, they study its economy, statecraft, science and so forth. However, adopting the "material domain" leads them to cling tighter, even when it requires invention, to the "spiritual domain," i.e.; to a cultural identity that preserves their spiritual culture. In other words, while the state adopts the material Western domain, the emerging nation embraces a national culture that keeps the colonizer out. By presenting this view, Chatterjee actually criticized Anderson who asserted that non-Western societies imagine a Western model of the nation.[33] According to Chatterjee, non-Western nationalists may strive to emulate the material domain of Western nationalism, but they imagine and create a spiritual domain independent of their colonizer.

Lebanon poses an interesting case when trying to juxtapose its colonial experience with Chatterjee's analysis. As we shall see in this study, the national movement that advocated the establishment of Greater Lebanon was a mélange of modern (Beirut's emerging Christian bourgeoisie) and traditional (the Maronite Church) social forces. In a unique historical moment they cooperated and asked to be occupied by France so as to realize their political aspirations and establish an independent state. They based their demand on the assertion that they were part of Western civilization, that they were in fact the French of the Levant and that there were no cultural and political ties between them and their Arab neighbors. After 1920, a large number of Lebanese nationalists continued to look to France as their source of emulation, not only in the material domain, but also in the spiritual. Moreover, French colonial practice was far more intrusive than the British. Thus, France aggressively intervened in an attempt to set the content of the spiritual domain of the society of the fledgling state. In addition, even after most Lebanese nationalists were disillusioned by France's conduct and understood that independence was not underway, they still shared with France their most basic demand: to be a separate entity, not related politically or culturally to the Syrian and/or Arab national movements. This dichotomy prevailed until 1943, the year of independence. The compromise between "Arabs" and "non-Arabs," as manifested in the 1943 National Pact, was less related to the national character of Lebanon and more to the agreement of the Maronite and Sunni political elites to find a *modus vivendi* in a country that became a fact but that lacked a unifying "spiritual domain."

The French Colonial Idea

Before 1870, French colonialism was guided by the notion of "assimilation," which meant that a "colony was to become an integral if not a contiguous part of France with its society and population made over in her image."[34] Yet, the attempts to gallicize the colonized peoples utterly failed and by the time Tunisia was taken in 1882 a new theory of "association" stood behind French colonial conduct. This theory reflected the desire of the colonial circles to have a more realistic and flexible doctrine that would win the cooperation of the natives by means of co-opting the elite with as little direct French involvement as possible. By 1905, the theory of association had become the leitmotif of all colonial bodies in France. It was best practiced by Louis-Hubert Lyautey, a French officer who was in charge of the pacification of indigenous unrest in Tonkin (Indochina), Madagascar, Algeria and who, in 1912, became the first Resident General of Morocco. Lyautey believed that a protectorate, governed firmly but indirectly by France, rather than outright colonial expansion and direct colonial rule, was the best way to establish quick, effective and inexpensive colonial control. This could be done, he believed, through collaboration with the indigenous elites, enlisting the ruling classes into the service of the French Empire.

An important facet of Lyautey's theory was the *politique de races,* which implied emphasizing the ethnic, cultural and racial differences between the various communities in the colonized area. When Lyautey became the Resident General of Morocco he had the opportunity to practice his theory in full scale, in what he called a "moral conquest;" to leave the ruling elite intact and exploit the existence of a large Berber population in order to highlight ethnic and cultural differences between the Berbers and the Arab communities, forging the Berbers into a large collaborative group with French rule. Guided by the theory of Lyautey, French military men and civil administrators worked ardently to separate the Arab and Berber populations. They founded schools in Berber regions with the prime purpose of teaching French instead of Arabic and European and local Berber history instead of Arab-Islamic history, all aimed at encouraging tribal sentiments among the Berber tribes.[35] They created centers for the study of the Berber society and published journals focusing on various aspects of Berber life, proliferating information and data on the Berber population in Morocco.[36] The French constructed a complete myth of origin and ancestry for the Berbers. They were regarded as the indigenous population of North Africa whose racial origins went back to the Indo-Europeans races; some even said that their origin could be specifically traced to the Nordic races of northern Europe.[37] The Berbers were depicted as a powerful but peaceful people with a strong sense of democracy and love for personal freedom. As opposed to their Arab-Muslim neighbors, they did not accept Islam as an authority of the State. In order to maintain these qualities they made the mountains their place of refuge, thus keeping their particular features despite the foreign Arab-Muslim occupiers. With the right guidance, the French believed, it would be possible to strengthen their distinct identity and to stop the process of their assimilation into the Arab-Muslim society.[38]

Morocco, of course, was not the first place where the French met Berber tribes. Already in Algeria the colonizers encountered Berbers and began developing a strong romantic view towards them, considering them perfect candidates for gallicization.[39] Yet in Morocco the Berber policy developed into a coherent program supported by the entire colonial party and executed by the military officers of the new protectorate who became Lyautey's disciples. By the time French forces arrived in Beirut in October 1918, French colonial circles had already gained experience in governing an Arab-Muslim population and attempting to seclude an ethnic group out of the majority population to shape it as a collaborative group of their colonial enterprise.

Molding the Berbers into a collaborative group was not an easy task, for there was a need to instruct them about their self-perception (as seen by the French), to teach them French and to stop the existing process of their integration into the larger Moroccan population. As we shall see below, the same task was much easier to accomplish in Lebanon among the Maronites, whose elite had already mastered French and whose self-perception was very distinct even without the assistance of the French. Three decades ago, R. Robinson called for a new evaluation in our understanding of the process of colonialism by shifting the focus away from Europe towards the colonized societies.[40] He believed that, to a large extent, European colonialism was determined by the collaborative groups, sometimes even more so than by the socio-political forces in the colonizing power itself. Considering this view may help illustrate why it was so important for France, through the medium of its missionaries, geographers, scholars and politicians, to emphasize the distinct features of the Christians in Lebanon and why in the end France succumbed to the demands of Lebanese nationalists and allowed the formation of Greater Lebanon. Collaboration was a key element in French colonial doctrine for their conduct towards the Berbers and towards the Maronites in Lebanon even though it utterly failed with the former and ran into difficulties with the latter.

In conclusion, there were different internal and external forces that set the stage for the appearance of the Phoenician identity at the end of the 19th century: the introduction of nationalism as a new form of identity in the Middle East and the local struggle over the variety of this identity; the increasing power of colonialism in the region; the gradual shift in the social structure of the local societies; and the improvement of education that catered to increasing interest in the ancient civilizations of the Near East among Westerners and local elites alike. The dynamic between these forces in the mid-19th century is the source from which this study begins.

* * *

Before commencing, a quick survey of the study's structure and main premises is in order. The book is divided into three sections. The first section, "Origins," comprising Chapters I and II, covers the roots of Phoenicianism from the mid-19th century to the formation of Greater Lebanon. The second section, "The Mandate Years," Chapters III, IV and V, discusses the mandate years, the formative period of the Phoenician national narrative. The third section, "After Independence and Beyond," including Chapter VI and the Conclusion, addresses the evolution of Phoenicianism after independence from 1943 to the 1990s and offers some concluding remarks and observations about the Lebanese national identity.

Chapter I addresses the origins of Phoenicianism in the 19th century by analyzing the writings of French travelers, colonialists and the Jesuits, on the one hand, and lay Syro-Lebanese and Maronite clergy, on the other. The chapter explores Western interest in the ancient history of Lebanon and its impact on the local population. It also surveys the arrival of the French Jesuit order in Lebanon and its gradual growing domination over local education. The writings of Maronite clergy in the 19th century demonstrate that the Maronite Church did not advocate the Phoenician identity of its flock. It was rather the new stratum of lay Christians, and not necessarily Maronites, who began writing about their "ancestors" the ancient Phoenicians. The chapter illustrates that this was done not in the context of anti-Arab sentiments but rather the contrary, simply because Arab nationalism was not yet an ideology with which Syro-Lebanese had to come to terms.

Chapter II looks at four different locales — Egypt, France, America and Lebanon — that functioned as centers of Phoenician expressions before and during World War I, explaining the reasons why Phoenicianism was used by Syro-Lebanese in these places and in what capacity. The chapter explores the existing political orientations held by Lebanese and their use of the Phoenician past. The chapter also analyzes the way Phoenicianism began carrying its non-Arab stance, to the point that in 1919 the entire movement for the formation of Greater Lebanon was labeled "Phoenician."

Chapter III discusses the development of the Phoenician identity in mandatory Lebanon. It looks at the role the Jesuits and the French High Commission played in the dissemination of Phoenician sentiments, through the education system and other state agents such as archeology and museums. The chapter also illustrates how Lebanese graduates of the Jesuit educational establishment helped in the dissemination of the Phoenician identity in Lebanon. Finally, the chapter analyzes local developments within Lebanese society that led to the entrance of the Phoenician past into the Lebanese national narrative.

Chapter IV discusses major Phoenician streams through the writing of three different advocates, Charles Corm, Michel Chiha and Sa'id 'Aql. Corm and Chiha represent francophone national Lebanese writing in the mandate years. Corm was the prime "preacher" of Phoenicianism until his death in 1963 and any discussion on this identity would not be complete without a thorough evaluation of his work. Chiha has been regarded as the architect of the Lebanese confessional system, and his impact on the political fate of Lebanon was immense. From WWI he was closely associated with the literary circles that advocated the Phoenician identity. He often wrote about Lebanon's Phoenician past and promoted the idea that the Mediterranean basin was the prime source of its identity. Although there has been a tendency to separate his writing from the Phoenician group by asserting that Mediterraneanism was somewhat different, it is my contention that his views of Lebanese identity were one variant of Phoenicianism and therefore should be evaluated in the context of this study. Sa'id 'Aql also became a prime Phoenician advocate in the mid-1930s and remains so to this day. Unlike Corm and Chiha he wrote the majority of his works in Arabic. In addition, whereas Corm and Chiha were born, raised and educated in Beirut, 'Aql's background is from Mount Lebanon. The section on 'Aql focuses on his different social origins and on arabophone Phoenicians in general. Analyzing the writing of these three not only reveals their understanding of Phoenicianism, but also sheds new light on the way this identity was disseminated in mandatory Lebanon.

Chapter V examines four different political groups that opposed the Phoenician narrative of Lebanon: Arab-Muslim, secular pan-Arabs, Muslim Lebanese and Antun Sa'adeh, who headed the Syrian Social Nationalist party. The chapter discloses not only the views of the adversaries of Phoenicianism but it also reveals more about the content and weight of the Phoenician identity in mandatory Lebanon. Furthermore, through this discussion, the chapter also juxtaposes Phoenicianism in a wider regional context of other forces of identity that existed in Lebanon during the first half of the 20th century.

Chapter VI provides an overview of the development of Phoenicianism from 1945 until the end of the civil war in 1990. Unlike the preceding chapters, it does not follow its evolution systematically. Phoenicianism as an alternative to the Arab identity of Lebanon was marginalized in the 1940s with the political integration of Lebanon into the Arab world. Yet, despite this integration, the Lebanese territorial national identity persisted and with it also remained aspects of the Phoenician idea. Thus, Phoenicianism continued to be expressed in two different ways. On the one hand, Christian Lebanese nationalists continued to express their vision of Lebanon as neo-Phoenicia, on the other, after decades of preoccupation with the Phoenician past of the country, a Phoenician "language" was formed that was used by all sects and parties in Lebanon, even by those that defied Phoenicianism as a figment of Christian imagination.

References

1 *The Ethnic Origins of Nations* (Oxford: B. Blackwell, 1986), p. 2.
2 http://www.rafikhariri.net/v1/
3 As'ad AbuKhalil, *Historical Dictionary of Lebanon* (Maryland: The Scarecrow Press, inc., 1998), p. 1. AbuKhalil reiterates four times in the first five pages of the introduction his view that the Phoenician ideal is false. Such a preoccupation with Phoenicianism only reflects, in my view, the strength of this myth of origin.
4 For general information on the ancient Phoenicians and their civilization, see Maria Eugenia Aubet, *The Phoenicians and the West* (Cambridge: Cambridge University Press, 1993); M. Gras, R. Rouillard and J. Teixidor, *L'Univers Phénicien* (Paris: Hachette, 1989); Sabatino Moscati, *The Phoenicians* (New York: Rizoli, 1999). For the interested reader, these works contain lengthy bibliographical lists.
5 New Testament, Matthew, 15: 21-28; Mark, 7: 24-30.
6 The genealogy in the Book of Genesis, Chapter 10, actually refers to the Canaanites-Phoenicians as Hamites by stating that Ham, Noah's son, begat Canaan who begat Sidon. This, however, was an attempt of the Hebrew author of Genesis to separate the Hebrews from the Canaanites, due to the animosity between the two peoples.
7 This thesis was first articulated by the Italian scholar Leone Caetani in his monumental *Annali dell'Islam* (Milan: Hoepli, 1905-1907). Philip Hitti was one of the most distinguished scholars who wrote on and advocated this theory. See his *History of the Arabs,* fifth edition (London: Macmillan, 1953), pp. 3-13; *The Near East in History* (Princeton: Van Nostrand, 1961), pp. 29-33.
8 Bérard's first work that argued this thesis was *De l'Origine des Cultes Arcadiens; Essai de Méthode en Mythologie Grecque* (Paris: Thorin, 1894).
9 Martin Bernal, *Black Athena: The Afroasiatic Roots of Classical Civilization.* 2 volumes (New Jersey: Rutgers University Press, 1987, 1991). Bernal's thesis agitated the whole scholarly world of the ancient civilizations of the Mediterranean

basin and brought numerous critical responses. One of the more recent ones is Jacques Berlinerblau, *Heresy in the University* (New Jersey: Rutgers University Press, 1999). See especially pp. 96-101 for Bérard's thesis and its use by Bernal.

10 See Smith's discussion on the Phoenicians as an *"ethnie"* in *The Ethnic Origins of Nations* (Oxford: B. Blackwell, 1986), pp. 83-84, and 99-100.

11 The most notable examples are the works of Kamal Salibi and Philip Hitti, *The Modern History of Lebanon* (London: Weidenfeld and Nicolson, 1964) and *Lebanon in History* (London: Macmillan, 1957). A similar tendency can be seen in the following works: William R. Polk, *The Opening of South Lebanon, 1788-1840* (Cambridge: Harvard University Press, 1963); Ilya Harik, *Politics and Change in a Traditional Society* (Princeton: Princeton University Press, 1968).

12 On two of these Lebanese historians, Asad Rustum and Fouad Afram al-Bustani, see Chapter III.

13 Meir Zamir, *The Formation of Modern Lebanon* (London: Croom Helm, 1985); Engin Deniz Akarli, *The Long Peace: Ottoman Lebanon 1861-1920* (Berkeley: University of California Press, 1993).

14 Carol Hakim-Dowek, *The Origins of the Lebanese National Idea, 1840-1914* (Ph.D. Thesis, St. Antony's College, 1997).

15 These were the official names of the administrative province on Mount Lebanon created as a result of foreign and Ottoman intervention that put an end to heavy civil clashes among the local population. The 1861 settlement established for the first time a Lebanese political entity dominated by the Maronite community.

16 On the "old narrative," see Israel Gershoni, "Rethinking the Formation of Arab Nationalism in the Middle East, 1920-1945," in James Jankowski and Israel Gershoni, *Rethinking Nationalism in the Arab Middle East* (New York: Columbia University Press, 1997), pp. 5-11.

17 Ernest Dawn, "The Origins of Arab Nationalism," in R. Khalidi, L. Anderson, M. Muslih and R. S. Simon (eds.), *The Origins of Arab Nationalism* (New York: Columbia University Press, 1991), pp. 3-30.

18 Butrus Abu-Manneh, "The Christians between Ottomanism and Syrian Nationalism: The ideas of Butrus al-Bustani," *International Journal of Middle East Studies,* 11 (1980), pp. 287-304.

19 Itamar Rabinovich, "Syria and the Syrian Land: the 19th Century Roots of 20th Century Developments," in Thomas Philipp (ed.), *The Syrian Land in the 18th and 19th century* (Stuttgart: F. Steiner, 1992), pp. 43-54.

20 Elisée Reclus, *Nouvelle Géographie Universelle*, Vol. XI, *l'Asie Antérieure*, (Paris: Hachette et Cie., 1884), pp. 5-6. See especially the map of ethnographic division that separates Syria from the rest of the Arab lands. Reclus was also preoccupied with the ancient Phoenicians themselves and the geographical setting of the Syrian coast which enabled them to construct their impressive civilization. See in Reclus, "La Phénicie et les Phéniciens," *Bulletin de la Société Neuchâteloise de Géographie,* XII (1900).

21 Smith, *The Ethnic Origins of Nationalism*, p. 6.

22 See surveys on existing theories in Geoff Eley and Ronald Grigor Suny, "From the Moment of Social History to the Work of Cultural Representation," in Eley and Suny (eds.), *Becoming National* (New York: Oxford University Press, 1996), pp. 3-37; Yael Tamir, "The Enigma of Nationalism," *World Politics* 47 (April 1995), pp. 418-440.

23 Juan R. I. Cole and Deniz Kandiyoti, "Nationalism and the Colonial Legacy in the Middle East and Central Asia: Introduction," *International Journal of Middle East Studies* 34(2002), pp. 191-192. For a discussion on the primordialist and the modernist schools see Smith himself in *The Ethnic Origins of Nationalism*, pp. 7-13.
24 Anthony D. Smith, "The Myth of the 'Modern Nation' and the Myths of Nations," *Ethnic and Racial Studies* II, no. I (January, 1988), p. 9. See also *The Ethnic Origins of Nations*, pp. 21-46.
25 Smith, *The Ethnic Origins of Nations*, pp. 147, 212.
26 *Ibid*, pp. 36, 86, 168.
27 Ernest Gellner, *Thought and Change* (Chicago: University of Chicago Press, 1964), p. 169; see also *Nations and Nationalism* (Oxford: B. Blackwell, 1983), pp. 48-49.
28 Sami Zubaida, "The Fragments Imagine the Nation: The Case of Iraq," *International Journal of Middle East Studies,* 34 (2002), p. 206.
29 Smith, *The Ethnic Origins of Nations*, p. 1.
30 Benedict Anderson, *Imagined Communities: Reflections on the Origin and Spread of Nationalism*, 2nd revised edition (London: Verso, 1991), p. 6.
31 *Ibid*, pp. 9-36.
32 Partha Chatterjee, *Nationalist Thought and the Colonial World* (Minneapolis: University of Minnesota Press, 1986); *The Nation and Its Fragments* (New Jersey: Princeton University Press, 1993).
33 Chatterjee, *The Nation and Its Fragments*, p. 5.
34 Betts, *Assimilation and Association,* p. 8.
35 Archives Diplomatiques (henceforth AD) Nantes, Maroc, carton DAI-63, Capitane Bertchi, renseignement du cercle des Beni-Mguild, June 15, 1914; M. Bel to Lyautey, au sujet des écoles franco-berbères dans la région de Meknès." September 4, 1915; AD Nantes, Maroc, carton DAI-59, M. Le Glay, Contrôleur civil, Notes contributives à l'étude de la question berbère. Note no. 4 — Comment administrer les Berbères?; Le Sûreté Général au Général Commandant, Général du Sud au sujet de l'organisation judiciaire des tribus berbères. July 30, 1913.
36 AD Nantes, Maroc, carton DAI-59, But d'une enquête sur la société berbère aux points de vue sociologiques et ethnographiques, sa valeur au point de vue politique, No date. About the establishment of Comité d'Etudes Berbères in Rabat and the publication of the review *Archives Berbères* see AD Nantes, Maroc, carton DAI-59, direction du service des renseignements, January 5, 1919 Rabbath. See also a lengthy exchange of letters during 1913 between Lyautey and A. le Chatelier, the General Delegate of the Mission Scientifique du Maroc, carton 17 DAI.
37 A different and more marginal theory about the racial origins of the Berbers claimed that they were actually the descendents of Jewish tribes who immigrated to North Africa as part of the Phoenician expansion in the Mediterranean basin. Nahum Slouschz, *Hebréo-Phéniciens et Judéo-Berbères* (Paris, 1908); Slouschz, *La Civilisation Hébraïque à Carthage* (Paris: E. Leroux, 1911). The works of Slouschz were embraced by some Revisionist Zionists in the 1920s-1930s and later became the basis of the Canaanite movement in pre-Israel. On this, see Ya'akov Shavit, *Me-'Ivri 'Ad Kena'ani* [From Hebrew to Canaanite] (Tel-Aviv: Domino, 1984), pp. 67-93.

38 Robin Bidwell, *Morocco Under Colonial Rule* (London: Cass, 1973), pp. 53-54; Edmond Burke, "The Image of the Moroccan State in French Ethnological Literature: A New Look at the Origin of Lyautey's Berber Policy," in Ernest Gellner and C. Micaud (eds.), *Arabs and Berbers* (London: Lexington, 1973), p. 194; Louis-Jean Duclos, "The Berbers and the Rise of Moroccan Nationalism," *Ibid,* pp. 217-229.
39 Lahouari Addi, 'Colonial Mythologies: Algeria in the French Imagination,' in L. Carl Brown and Matthew S. Gordon, *Franco-Arab Encounters* (Beirut: AUB, 1996), pp. 93-105; Charles-Robert Ageron, *L'Algérie Algérienne de Napoléon III à de Gaule* (Paris: Sindbad, 1980), p. 38.
40 R. Robinson, "Non-European Foundations of European Imperialism: Sketch for a Theory of Collaboration," in Owen and Sutcliff, *Studies in the Theory of Imperialism,* pp. 117-142.

1
First Buds: 1860-1918

The Cedar should be the flag that all Lebanese hold high and that makes them leap with pride and joy when they see it fluttering over the hilltops and in front of their homes, and for which they will sacrifice, if necessary, their possessions and lives.
The Cedar, witness of the past, will be the witness of the present and the future.
The Cedar on a foundation of blue, white and red. This is the flag. French colors. Phoenician colors, too.
The blue, it is the sea that the Phoenicians introduced, through their vessels, to human history, and which they traversed along the maritime routes that civilized the world; it is also the azure of a new sky, a new horizon: the horizon of peace and heaven of liberty.
The white, it is the eternal snow of the mountain; it is also the purity of the principles of justice, faith and loyalty on which the Lebanese have been raised.
The red, it is the purple which gave Phoenicia its reputation and its fortune; it is the blood spilled through the centuries by ancestors to safeguard rights and traditions; it is also the struggle to hold on, the sacrifices made to elevate the fatherland to the rank of the most glorious countries.
Before the flag, all Lebanese bow down, whatever their beliefs. If he [the Lebanese] dies, it is within its folds that he will sleep his final slumber.

Pierre Raphaël (Maronite-born Jesuit)[1]

France in the Levant

On October 21, 1860, the French naval ship *Colbert* set sail from Marseille, the French gateway to the east, bound for the shores of Lebanon. On deck was Ernest Renan, the renowned philologist and orientalist, accompanied by a unit of French soldiers assigned to work with him. Renan was a member of the French expedition force that had been dispatched to Lebanon following the bloody events of the spring and summer on Mount Lebanon. Long years of capitulations and patronage over the Catholic rites in the Ottoman Empire had led France to intervene in favor of its Christian protégés to try and halt the civil war and bloodshed. The inclusion of Renan's scientific expedition in this military and political mission was a natural step that corresponded with France's political agendas. Acquisition of scientific knowledge of areas occupied by France had become a tradition, begun by Napoleon Bonaparte and his "*Savants*" in Egypt in 1798.

Two years before arriving on the Phoenician coast, Renan expressed his desire to excavate in Byblos, one of the Phoenician city-states, thirty kilometers north of Beirut. Following the discovery of a Phoenician inscription at the tomb of Eshmon'ezer (Sidon, 1856), Renan hoped that a thorough excavating enterprise along the Phoenician coast would provide more Semitic texts, similar to those found in Cyprus, Malta and North Africa. During his yearlong sojourn in Lebanon, he excavated in Tyre, Sidon, Byblos and Arados. He also visited Palestine and prepared notes for his book *La Vie de Jésus*. Three years after his return to France, he published his corpulent tome, *Mission de Phénicie*.[2] Renan's work was not the most significant scientific enterprise in the study of ancient Phoenicia, but it was certainly the most popular at the time. His reputation in France and abroad made his work in Phoenicia a most celebrated undertaking. It was the first time that a serious field study had been conducted in Phoenicia itself rather than in its colonies around the Mediterranean basin, laying the emphasis on the Phoenician city-states of the Lebanese coast.

Renan, of course, was not the first scholar to study the Phoenician civilization. The first attempts to critically probe the history of ancient Phoenicia were made in the 18th century by French and German scholars, concomitantly with the beginning of the modern and critical study of the Bible and its civilizations. Jean-Jacques Barthélémy (1716-1795), Arnold Heeren (1760-1842), François-Charles Movers (1806-1856) and others became the founding fathers of the study of the ancient Phoenician world, long before Ernest Renan published *Mission de Phénicie*.[3] For them, just as for Renan, Jerusalem, Bethlehem, Sidon and Tyre were almost equally considered part of the Holy Land.

The attentiveness of the French public to ancient Phoenicia became apparent with the publication of *Salammbô*,[4] the novel by Gustave Flaubert, only a year after the return of Renan's exploratory mission. The novel tells the story of an historical episode of the most eminent Phoenician colony — Carthage. Flaubert depicted the second war between the Carthaginians and the Romans in the latter half of the 2nd century BC and thus introduced the Phoenician world to the average educated French household. Choosing this theme was by no means coincidental on Flaubert's part.[5] With France's growing interest in North Africa, French scholars began studying the ancient civilizations that had lived around the Mediterranean basin. Archaeological excavations in the Levant became intertwined with French Christian missionary work. As of 1867, the historical research of the ancient civilizations in Algeria and Tunisia became inseparably affiliated with the new Bishop of Algeria, Monsignor Lavigerie. He entrusted the excavations in Carthage to the hands of the Pères Blancs and, by so doing, set the example that would be followed in geographical Syria by the Jesuit mission.[6] Lavigerie's archaeological work in North Africa, just like the Jesuits' in Syria, was strongly tied to his Christian convictions. In this missionary enterprise, excavation of the ancient world was perceived as the unearthing of the missioners' own cultural roots. It was a belief shared by most Europeans, lay and clerical alike. By exposing the ancient past of the Biblical world, Rome, and Greece, they believed they were actually excavating and exposing their own progenitors and thus demonstrating their own cultural, scientific and political superiority.[7] For this reason the history curricula of French religious and secular schools focused not only on local or European history but also on the ancient civilizations of the Levant — Egypt, Babylon, Assyria, Canaan and Phoenicia.[8]

European exposure of eastern civilizations almost always resulted in romantic, fantastic attitudes. European travelers had always been attracted to the Orient, but in the 19th century their number increased dramatically, and the character of the journeys changed as well. If previously they embarked on their journeys as private adventurers, then as the 19th century progressed they often came in official expeditionary delegations with a clear agenda of unearthing what they perceived as their own history and tradition. Shipping their finds to Europe was the next natural step. Paris, London, and Berlin became huge warehouses of these finds. Thus was the Egyptian Obelisk displaced from Luxor and installed in Paris, at the Place de le Concorde, in a pompous ceremony orchestrated by French King Louis Philippe; and the tomb of Eshmon'ezer, the Phoenician king, was taken from Sidon, where it had rested untouched for 2,600 years, to be laid, with due respect, at the Louvre.[9]

The indigenous populations often came under scrutiny as well, much like the mute archaeological sites. If a European arrived in Jerusalem to search after King David under the debris of the Old City, he would then often look for David's progeny among the contemporary inhabitants of the city. The same applied to visitors to Mount Lebanon and the surrounding areas. An example of such an approach, chosen out of numerous books written by European travelers, is that of Louis Lortet, the Dean of the Faculty of Medicine of the University of Lyon. The University had acted as a patron of Université Saint Joseph in Beirut since its establishment in 1875. The Jesuit order of Lyon and the University of Lyon became two of the most important factors in shaping the character of the Jesuit University. The following description is quoted from Lortet's account of his visit to Beirut, where Université Saint Joseph had been recently established:

Dans les rues, en moins d'une heure, on peut voit les descendants de tous ces peuples divers: voici un Égyptien aux membres grêles, aux yeux taillés en amande, au profil de sphinx. A côté de lui s'avance un guerrier semblable à ceux des palais de Khorsabad et de Ninive; les membres de l'Assyrien sont épais et robustes, les épaules larges, carrées, fortement musclées; la taille est petite, la barbe épaisse est frisé en tire-bouchons serrés et sympathique, comme l'étaient celles des terribles conquérants des bordes de l'Euphrate. Ici passe le successeur de l'ancien Phénicien: Sa face est fine, distinguée, son nez aquilin, ses lèvres minces, il est grand et souple dans ses mouvements; ses beaux yeux noirs pétillent de feu et d'intelligence. N'exiger cependant de lui aucune autre aptitude que celle nécessitées pour le commerce; il est âpre au gain, quelquefois économe jusqu'à l'avarice, entreprenant, et n'hésitera jamais à vous tromper pour gagner une somme modique [...] Ce sont les dignes fils de fameux marchands de Tyr, Sidon et Aradus dont les flottes puissantes trafiquaient dans les contrées les plus lointaines.

So, the streets of Beirut in 1880 were bustling with descendants of ancient peoples: Egyptians, Assyrians and Phoenicians. The latter have distinct facial features and, of course, they excel in commerce. The Arab, Lortet informs us, is:

... pur sang, fort, vigoureux, infatigable, au teint basané, bien musclé est néanmoins souple et agile; ses jarrets sont d'acier; cavalier accompli, sa vie passe à cheval. Il a un front largement développé, des lèvres plus épaisses que celles du Phénicien, un nez moins aquilin [...] Il estime aussi avant tout commerce, le trafic, mais il est pourtant passionné pour les luttes du corps, pour les exercices violentes de la guerre et de la chasse. Son imagination est vive et enjouée, il adore les contes merveilleux, les poésies d'Antar, les récits des *Milles et une nuit*.[10]

These images were prevalent in many of the travelogues published throughout the 19th century and were shared by the leading intellectual Europeans of the time. The scents of the Orient intoxicated the Europeans, who began seeing what they had wished and dreamed of witnessing. The ancient world was revived, and an impoverished peasant in Upper Egypt, the Galilee or Mount Lebanon suddenly became a descendent of an ancient and imposing lineage.

One of the last French sojourners in the Levant who wrote a travelogue in the tradition of the time was Maurice Barrès, whose name will resurface repeatedly in this study. Barrès, the speaker and thinker of the French radical right after the French defeat by Germany in 1870, visited the Levant on the eve of World War I and published a two-volume book depicting his impressions. By 1914, he was a person of great fame, and his trip created as much enthusiasm among the local intellectual elite as it did among the French missionaries who welcomed and facilitated his journey. The book is saturated with romantic images of the Levant and very strong sympathy for the Christian Syrians and the French missions. His visit to the Ibrahim River, named Adonis in antiquity after one of the Phoenician deities, inspired him to write the following passage:

> [...] rien ne m'attire plus que cette vallée de l'Adonis, dont nos maîtres ont fait le paysage romantique par excellence. L'embouchure de l'Adonis est un endroit charmant, que l'antique Phénicie a chargé de mythes. Le fleuve y coule au fond d'un abîme. Un bouquet de trembles le surplombe et fraîchit dans son courant d'air. Je m'y suis assis, sous une tonnelle pour boire un verre de cette eau sacrée, surgissant des profondes déchirures du Liban. Adonis est-il mort? Une petite église sur la côte l'atteste. Elle surveille les lieux où débouchait, il y a dix huit siècles, à son retour d'Afaka, le cortège des flagellants, des hurleurs, des danseurs, des mutilés volontaires, des pleureuses et des prêtres.[11]

Barrès' enthusiasm with the ancient Phoenician sites in Lebanon caused him to reflect upon the influence of the ancient world on the present religions in Lebanon:

> Le vieux culte qui, jadis, attira ici tant de pèlerins, a-t-il été anéanti sous les ruines du temple? Les dieux de Byblos ont-ils coulé au fond des âges, sans laisser de ride sur l'abîme? Ces vives sources sont-elles aujourd'hui complètement desséchées? La racine des sentiments et des mythes qui, durant des siècles, fleurirent auprès d'Afaka, a-t-elle été arrachée? Qui le dira? Pour moi j'ai peine à croire que le Christianisme ait transformé les Libanais jusqu'au fond de leur être, jusqu'au sanctuaire intérieur où naissent les songeries.[12]

For Barrès there was no question that the ancient cults of Adonis and the gods of Byblos could still be found in the Christian traditions of Mount Lebanon. Just like other European travelers to the Orient, he truly believed that the imprints of the ancient world could be detected in his own time. Barrès applied this perception first and foremost to France itself. He believed that French Roman Catholicism was inseparably intertwined with ancient Celtic traditions. This conviction deeply influenced Christian Lebanese national thinkers. They were looking for a "nationalism" to emulate, and found it in the Barrèsian national idea, a point that will be explored later in this study.

Maurice Barrès died in 1923 shortly after the publication of *Une Enquête aux Pays du Levant*, his last book.[13] In the concluding remarks of his travelogue he reflected upon the ties between France and the inhabitants of the Orient:

> Comment approprierons-nous l'enseignement occidental à nos élèves orientaux, de telle manière qu'au sortir de nos collèges ils restent commerçants, propriétaires, fonctionnaires, au milieu des leurs, pareil aux leurs, encadrés dans les expériences de leur race, et cependant, grâce à la langue et à la culture, de moins en moins séparés de nous? [...] Il s'agit de susciter dans ces peuples étrangers le goût de maintenir, *quoi qu'il advienne un jour de leurs destinées nationales*, [emphasis in original text] le contact avec notre intelligence.

How could we teach our Oriental students, Barrès asked, to remain attached to their national destinies and at the same time, through our language and culture, stay firmly connected to us? This was the prime objective of the French *mission civilisatrice*, and in Lebanon the Jesuit Order would take this task upon itself to fully implement it.

Franco-Maronite Relations

The French attachment to Syria and to the Maronites did not begin in 1860 with their intervention following the civil war on Mount Lebanon. Both French and Maronites like to assert that Frankish Crusaders found the Maronites to be faithful allies in a hostile Muslim environment during the Crusade era of 1099-1291. Probably this is a late-19th century projection of their relationship, but even so, this view is indicative of the close Franco-Maronite ties in modern times. What is unquestionable, though, is that the Maronite Church became affiliated with the Vatican in Rome, becoming the first Uniate church in the East.[14] In 1584, a Maronite Seminary was established in Rome, reinforcing those ties. The mission to establish the seminary was given to an Italian Jesuit monk named Eliano Romanero. Thus was the link established between the Jesuits, whose order was founded in 1534, and the Maronites.[15] The Roman-Maronite connection strengthened the Vatican's influence over the latter. Maronite children were sent to Rome where they spent their formative years acquiring religious education and foreign languages; they returned to Mount Lebanon as clergymen with knowledge of Latin and Italian.[16] With the entry of the French Jesuit order into Syria in 1831, however, French language and culture took over all other foreign influences.[17] Since the Capitulations Agreement was signed with the Sublime Porte in 1535, France had considered itself to be the guardian of the Catholics in the Ottoman Empire.[18] In 1860, following the massacre of thousands of Christians in Mount Lebanon during the sanguineous civil war, it was only natural that France would intervene on behalf of its longtime and beloved protégés.

French travelers to the Levant who visited Mount Lebanon have always written in remarkably warm terms about the Maronites. One, who passed through just after the bloody events of 1860, emphatically wrote about the Maronites the following words:

> Il y a pourtant là un peuple dont il est utile d'étudier le caractère; il y a pourtant là un peuple qui vit, qui pense, qui progresse comme nous; et si peuple mérite notre sympathie; c'est certainement celui lui; il y a là un peuple dont toutes les traditions sont des témoignages de notre ancienne chevalerie; il y a là un peuple qui sème le grain, fait pousser les mûriers, et voit mûrir la ligne et les orangers sur le sol qui fut le berceau sanglant de la noblesse des premières maisons de France; il y a là un peuple qui sait mourir pour les mêmes idées que nous défendons; mourir, non comme nos soldats d'Europe, avec la mâle consolation que chaque goutte de leur sang qui tombe est une perle pour la couronne de gloire que l'Histoire leur réserve, mais mourir martyr et ignoré, sous le yatagan du fanatisme. Ce peuple, c'est le peuple maronite.[19]

Words in this spirit had become commonplace in the relationship between the Maronites and the French. The idea that the Maronites were in fact "*les Français du Levant*" was a wish made by both sides – the Maronites, who entrusted their hopes to the French, and the French who, on the one hand, had sincere feelings for the Maronites and, on the other, aspired to find a perfect collaborator for their colonial aspirations in the region.[20] The affection of the French towards the Maronites and the genuine belief in France's protective role were important pillars of the latter's policy in Syria and Lebanon. French officials, from 1860-1920 and beyond, cultivated the idea that the Maronites were as close as one could get in the Orient to a civilized and noble culture.[21] Only with the formation of the mandate regime over Syria and Lebanon were mythical notions confronted with reality. Until 1920, and in the few years after the creation of Greater Lebanon, French officials in the *Métropole* and in Beirut, the domicile of the High Commissioner, were taken by such sentiments.

Once Greater Lebanon was formed, the French worked ardently to turn it into a Western-oriented stronghold, for it precisely matched their colonial doctrine. By establishing a collaborative state, it was believed that it would be far easier to control the rest of the mandated territories of Syria. Robert de Caix, the first secretary of the High Commissioner, was one of the most influential persons to set French policy in Syria and Lebanon during the first five years of the mandate. An active member of numerous French colonial circles and colonial ventures, de Caix had worked tirelessly in Morocco, along with General Gouraud, especially in forming the "divide and rule" policy between the Berbers and the Arabs.[22] When he and Gouraud were transferred to Syria, de Caix brought with him similar ideas to implement in the newly acquired territories. He envisioned a complete separation of Syria and Lebanon — the first belonging to the East, the latter to the West:

Enfin ce qui me parait maintenant le plus important c'est de bien assurer la séparation du Grand Liban d'avec la Syrie, l'un doit évoluer autant que possible vers l'occident, et l'autre nous donner un terrain d'accès sur le monde oriental. Je me suis d'accord avec le Général sur ce point [...].[23]

De Caix himself was a very religious person, who was well suited for the first five years of the French mandate in Lebanon, years that were characterized by a very strong French pro-Christian orientation. Nor was the selection of General Gouraud to the post of High Commissioner coincidental. Gouraud was also a devout Catholic, whose faith tremendously influenced his policies. The two, like many other French, regarded the Christian Lebanese, in general, and the Maronites and the Greek Catholics, in particular, as brothers of the same faith. Indeed, this notion dramatically influenced the colonial psyche of France in Syria and Lebanon. It was the only colonial setting in the French empire where a colonized group shared the faith of the colonizer without any process of proselytizing.

The religious affinity between Christian Syro-Lebanese and the French cannot be regarded casually. For the French, colonizing was not only an economic and political enterprise, it was a *Mission civilisatrice*, a mission to civilize. France, as the embodiment of a superior civilization that believed it absorbed its grandeur from the Roman Empire and Christian creed, could not simply colonize a territory without spreading its lofty civilization among the natives. Gabriel Hanotaux, the French foreign minister from 1894-1898, who worked tirelessly to revive France's interest in colonialism, was one of the officials who determined the French colonial idea of the Third Republic. After retiring from politics, he turned to historiography and edited a multi-volume study on French colonialism. In a sub-chapter entitled "*L'expansion doit-il être religieuse*" he wrote:

> La véritable question est de savoir si l'expansion sur les terres lointaines peut se justifier si elle n'offre pas un idéal de civilisation supérieure, et si cet idéal lui-même ne doit pas être soutenu par une croyance religieuse?
>
> Logiquement, toute action prolongée d'un peuple sur l'autre suppose un bien fait offert dans les mœurs, dans la direction sociale, non moins que dans la prospérité matérielle. Il n'y a de conquête excusable que si elle conserve, protège, élève les peuples qu'elle se soumet.
>
> Pour toute puissance civilisée, fille de la civilisation méditerranéenne, l'expansion aboutit donc, logiquement, *à une extension de la morale chrétienne* [emphasis added, A.K.] puisque celle-ci est à la base de toute la civilisation moderne. Et il se trouve, en fait, que toutes les puissances qui ont exercé ou exercent une influence extérieure ont eu et ont des missionnaires. En fait également, il s'est trouvé que les populations

occupées, colonisées, ou seulement entraînées dans un courant civilisateur, n'ont pu s'adapter au bien fait qui leur était présenté que par un moment plus au moins marqué de leur part vers la pensée supérieure qui animait les peuples expansionnistes. Si par suit d'un esprit farouche de résistance, ou, au contraire, par suite d'une trop cruelle exigences des maîtres, cette amélioration ne se produit pas, ou bien les populations conquises retournent à la barbarie, ou bien elles persistent faute d'adaptation.[24]

Christianity, for Hanotaux, was the foundation and the moral justification of expansion, especially for France as a Mediterranean power. Such a view was normal and even conventional among colonial circles in those days; but in this context Lebanon poses an intriguing situation. Maronites who had for centuries regarded themselves associated with Catholicism, and who shared the same Mediterranean Sea with their guardian angel, did not need this civilizing mission, for they were already civilized and well behaved.

Romanticism aside, the Maronites, of course, were not actually treated on equal terms by the French, yet they did constitute a special case in their empire. One example that illustrates this special status is the idea of transferring the Maronites to Algeria, which was raised twice by French colonialists — first after the 1840-1845 events in Mount Lebanon and again following the 1860 civil war. The desire to help their "Christian brothers in a sea of Islamic hatred" led Frenchmen to come up with this proposition, for it was believed that in Algeria they would be able to live safely and prosper, thus meeting the interests of both the Maronites and the French.[25] When this idea was proposed, France was just beginning to recreate its overseas empire. The Maronites, the colonialists believed, were good farmers and good merchants, they spoke French and, most important of all, they could help France rule Algeria more easily. In fact, they were like the Berber Kabyles, only better — they were Christian. The initiative was never realized, but it illustrates how the French regarded the Maronites in the context of their colonial venture: a well-loved collaborative group that could only facilitate the process of colonization.

The Jesuits in Syria and Lebanon

From the time of the establishment of the Maronite College in Rome in 1584, the Jesuit Order was strongly involved in geographical Syria. Jesuits always considered education the best means of attaining their religious ends. They aspired not only to influence Christian character and education but also to have a deep and lasting impact on society at large and on the elite strata in particular. To achieve this objective, they established chains of schools and educated children from a very young age according to a strict curriculum.[26] It is not without reason that the telling phrase "give us a child of seven and we have him forever" is attributed to the Jesuits. In their activities for the Church, Jesuit priests have often appeared to be opportunists, changing their dispositions due to their subtle understanding of politics, willing to change their methods and activities in line with the circumstances of time and place. The College in Rome became an important channel through which Jesuits left their mark on Maronite students, who, indeed, were often not more than seven years old. When these students returned to their parishes in Mount Lebanon, the Jesuit experience remained imprinted on their spirits.

In 1739, the Vatican replaced the Jesuits with the Lazarist Order to run the Catholic establishments in Mount Lebanon. The Jesuits, however, returned to the scene in 1831, and this time it was French Jesuits, from Lyon, who became involved in the missionary work in geographical Syria.[27] Their arrival in Beirut that year was in large part the Vatican's response to the activities of the American Protestant mission in the region, which had started operating there in 1823 and caused much anxiety among local Catholics.[28]

Slowly but surely the new Jesuit mission set up educational institutions in Mount Lebanon and the surrounding areas. Soon, their superior position in education became incontestable. Surpassing the position of the American mission, it was only a matter of time before French became the dominant foreign language in Syria. The Jesuits spread their famous educational web and, like a well-oiled machine, were preoccupied with dogmatic instruction of the Order's principles, Christianity and French language and culture. Other French orders followed suit, contributing to the domination of the French language in Syria. Indeed, religious schools were the spearhead in propagating French culture in Syria and by the late-19th century at the tip of the spear, stood Université Saint Joseph.

The first French institute of higher education to be established in Mount Lebanon was the college in 'Aintoura, founded in 1734 by Lazarist priests. In 1843 the Oriental Seminary in Ghazir was inaugurated by the Jesuits and became the leading French missionary school in Syria. By the 1870s, the Seminary was no longer large enough to satisfy the needs of the mission. Université Saint Joseph was founded in 1875 to meet the mission's expanding needs and as a response to the establishment of the Syrian Protestant College (after 1920, known as the American University of Beirut, or AUB) only a few years earlier by the American Protestant mission.[29]

Université Saint Joseph was founded with firm links to France and its culture. Money flowed from the French government and the university enjoyed wide political and academic patronage. Academic ventures, political considerations and commercial interests were often intertwined in the Jesuit missionary enterprise in Syria and Lebanon. Paul Huvelin is an example of such an amalgam. He was the dean of the Law Faculty of the University of Lyon and the head of La mission économique française en Syrie, and he had strong and warm ties with High Commissioner Gouraud.[30] In January 1919, the city of Marseille hosted the "Congrès français de la Syrie". The participants were all economic, political and religious interest groups attempting to pressure the French government to take full control of Syria. Among those attending the congress were representatives of the University of Lyon and the Lyonnaise Jesuit Order. Huvelin, in an address to the conference, stated:

> La France est devenue en Syrie indiscutablement souveraine. La Syrie est pénétrée jusqu'à la moelle d'influence française. Son instrument d'action le plus puissant est l'école. Tous les gens cultivés, musulmans et chrétiens, parlent et pensent français ... Grâce aux écoles françaises, le français est devenu pour un très grand nombre de Syriens la langue maternelle ... Il y a là quelque chose d'admirable. Je ne sais pas si l'histoire nous fournit un autre exemple de la conquête pacifique d'un pays par une langue ... Il faut remercier profondément, il faut saluer très bas les bons artisans de cet effort généreux ... Je salue en premier lieu nos missionnaires français. Sans eux, la France ne serait rien là-bas, Ils ont accompli une oeuvre admirable ... Le patriotisme des congrégations françaises dans le Levant est pur, jaloux, ardent. Leur enseignement est purement chrétien et ouvertement français; français d'abord, chrétien ensuite.[31]

Huvelin's words should be read, of course, in the context of the time and place they were articulated. He had many reasons to highlight the success of the French missions in Syria in disseminating French domination. His speech, nevertheless, reflects the fact that the French missions were indeed penetrating the fabric of the local society and leaving a lasting impact, especially among the urban upper-middle class in Beirut.

As the 20th century unfolded, Université Saint Joseph was already composed of the Oriental Seminary (transferred from Ghazir to Beirut) and the departments of medicine, pharmacology, theology, and philosophy. In 1902, the Faculté orientale was inaugurated, offering courses in classical Semitic languages, epigraphy, local ancient history, archaeology and geography.[32] By 1905, the Faculty represented the university at international conferences and in 1906 its monthly review, *Mélange de la Faculté Orientale,* was launched.[33] The Oriental Faculty of Université Saint Joseph was by now the quintessential center for the study and teaching of the ancient Near East. Many of its teachers were eminent scholars in their fields and some would play an instrumental role in the dissemination of separatist, non-Arab, Syrian and Lebanese ideas. Names like Henri Lammens, Louis Jalabert, Sébastian and Louis Ronzavelle, Louis Cheikho and others embellished the faculty and elevated it to the highest standards of scholarly work.

Even before the formation of the Oriental Faculty, scholars from the university began publishing works at the Imprimerie catholique, setting forth the history of Syria before the Arab conquest. In the 1880s, the Jesuit teacher

Father Pierre Martin wrote *Histoire Générale de la Syrie,* the original of which did not go to print;[34] but in 1889 Rashid al-Khuri al-Shartuni translated it to Arabic and published it as *Tarikh Lubnan,*[35] thereby launching the historical, archeological and geographical series of the Imprimerie catholique. Martin's manuscript was a detailed three-volume work dealing with the ancient history of Mount Lebanon and the surrounding regions. The first volume begins by placing Lebanon as part of the Promised Land. Then, Martin moves to define, very generously, the geographical limits of Lebanon, from Hamma in the north to the Gilad Mountains in the south. He gives a detailed account of the Phoenician city-states — their origin, expansion, rulers, religion, mythological stories and various crafts — and delves into a discussion of the historical sources on the Phoenicians and the extent of their credibility. Martin depicted the Phoenician cities as one independent and magnificent civilization. He made no attempt to link the ancient Phoenicians directly to the modern inhabitants of Mount Lebanon, but his work represents a new phase in the study of ancient Lebanon by its depth and extent. When the Maronite Bishop of Beirut, Yusuf al-Dibs, wrote his eight-volume tome, *Kitab Tarikh Suriyya* [The Book of Syrian History], to be discussed later, it was the Jesuit Father Martin who served as his major source of reference.[36]

Pierre Martin may have been the first Jesuit scholar to write extensively about the ancient history of Syria while emphasizing Mount Lebanon and the coast. It was, however, Henri Lammens who made the most significant contribution to the dissemination of the pre-Islamic history of Syria.[37] Lammens was actually a student of the early Islamic era, where he obtained his world fame — and infamy.[38] He wrote, though, about the ancient history of Syria as well and turned out to be the most important scholar to supply supporters of separatist Syrian and Lebanese national movements with scholarly ammunition for their arguments. He extensively published articles about Lebanon and its ancient past in the journal of Université Saint Joseph, *al-Mashriq,* based on lectures he presented between 1898-1906. In 1906, these articles were bound into a two-volume book entitled *Tasrih al-Absar fi ma Yahtawi Lubnan min al-Athar* [Panorama of Archeological Inventory in Lebanon].[39] The first volume concentrates on the archaeology and ancient history of Lebanon; the second is preoccupied with its geography and ethnography, and contains the substance of many courses Lammens led at the Oriental Faculty during 1904-1905.

Lammens made a substantial contribution to Saint Joseph, serving for years as the administrative director of the university's curriculum. He learned and taught the history and geography of Syria, embracing this mission with an enthusiasm that was only comparable to the strength of his contempt for Islam. Even before the publication of his famous book, *La Syrie; Prècis Historique,* Lammens' writings provided Christian Syro-Lebanese with scholarly explanations for a separatist Syrian collective identity. He also perfected the theory of "*l'asile du Liban.*" According to this theory, Mount Lebanon was a region that, along the course of history, had become a refuge for oppressed minorities. In this way, although threatened by the Arab-Islamic occupation, the authentic character of Syria was preserved. In the same book he widened the definition of the separatist Syrian nationality, based on a national Syrian consciousness and a Syrian race going back as far as the Phoenician seafarers. Lammens claimed that ancient Phoenicians were actually full-fledged Syrians; that the Syrians, from the days of the Phoenician city-states, were a homogeneous nation; and that the Syrian national idea had, even back then, begun to materialize in the subconscious of the Syrians. Lammens may have been one of the first visionaries of separatist Syrian nationalism. As early as 1904 he wrote about the importance of geography in shaping Syrian nationalism.[40] Despite his support for a Syrian, non-Arab, national consciousness, Lammens' contribution to Lebanese separatist ideas was even greater. He enriched the research (albeit very subjectively) and assisted in the consolidation of the Lebanist idea. He was the first to connect the success of the ancient Phoenicians in commerce to liberal economy, a concept that later would be used by the neo-Phoenicians. Most importantly, Lammens was the first to cite, use and restore to life the 1861 French map of Lebanon, drawn by the French expedition. This map included, in addition to Mount Lebanon, the coast, the Biqa' and Jabal 'Amil and was used in 1919 as a major card in the Maronites' demands for the establishment of Greater Lebanon.[41] The weight of Lammens can be viewed in almost every book written by Syro-Lebanese from the turn of the 20th century until the 1940s. They all refer to his works as academic proof of the existence of a unique Syrian or Lebanese national community. His name became inseparably associated with Université Saint Joseph and with the pro-Christian policy of France in Lebanon. The Maronite Lebanese historian, Youakim Moubarak, rightly defined Lammens as a person who occupied the triple vocation of a scholar, a missioner and a militant, partisan of the Christian Catholic orientalism.[42] Lammens will reappear often in this work, since, almost without exception, all the champions of the "Phoenician plot" used him as their scholarly pillar.

As important as Lammens was for the circulation of pre-Islamic Syrian history, he was not the only person at Université Saint Joseph or in Lebanon to write on the country's ancient history. In 1918, shortly after the end of WWI, a very important study — *Lubnan; Mabahith 'Ilmiyya wa Ijtima'iyya* [Lebanon: Scientific and Social Studies] — was published in Beirut.[43] The initiator of this publication was Isma'il Haqqi Bey, the governor of Beirut. In July 1915, the Ottoman government formally abrogated the *Règlement Organique* and appointed a Muslim governor, instead of the *Mutasarrif* who was a Christian Ottoman subject. In May 1916, Isma'il Haqqi Bey was appointed by the Ottoman government as governor of Mount Lebanon, a position that he held for a year. He was then assigned to be the governor of Beirut and remained so until the entrance of the Allied forces to the city in October 1918.[44] Although Haqqi was not of Lebanese origin, he demonstrated great interest in the country. He was in office in Lebanon no more than two years, but he left in his wake one of the most important scholarly projects on Lebanon at the time. It was a social, economic, historical and geo-political study of "Lebanon and Phoenicia" [sic] that was considered, well into the 1960s, a major source of information about the region. One thousand copies of the book were printed in Beirut in 1918 and distributed to all administrators of the *Mutasarrifiyya*. The introduction of the first edition stated that the book was published so that the Lebanese administrators would learn about themselves and about the country they administered. The Jesuit fathers Antun Salhani and Louis Cheikho (the former of Syrian descent and the latter from Kurdistan, Turkey), from Université Saint Joseph, headed the project. Non-clerical Lebanese, such as Bulus Nujaym, Albert Naccache, 'Isa Iskandar al-Ma'luf and others, contributed articles to the book.[45] Although the project makes no claims for the establishment of a separate Lebanese political entity, it portrays a strong awareness of a unique Lebanese consciousness, with its own historical memory connecting the Mountain and the coast. A detailed account, by Salhani, of the physical geography of wider Lebanon, opened the book. Cheikho wrote a chapter on antiquities in Lebanon, focusing on the Phoenician and Roman eras. He also wrote on "Ethnicities in Lebanon and their Religious Beliefs." Al-Ma'luf wrote on "Lebanese Characteristics and Costumes," surveying in detail the distinct Lebanese way of living, shared by local Christians, Muslims and Druze. Naccache contributed a chapter on the economic situation in Mount Lebanon. And there is a chapter on the history of Lebanon from antiquity until WWI, co-written by Cheikho and Nujaym.

In Cheikho and Nujaym's lengthy chapter, the appellations "Lebanon" and "Phoenicia" appear next to each other, the first denoting the Mountain and the latter the coastal range. The Phoenician coast is described as an inseparable part of Mount Lebanon, from the Litani estuary in the south to Tripoli, Arwad and the 'Akkar in the north.[46] The historical survey begins with a clear statement that Lebanon has never been an independent entity, but rather has been attached to Syria since the beginning of time. We should remember that in 1918, when the book was written, there were a few Lebanese who advocated a separate Lebanese entity (mainly activists of the *Alliance libanaise* in Egypt).[47] Lebanon, even as an autonomous region, was perceived as part of a larger geographical Syrian sphere, and Cheikho and Nujaym only expressed the prevailing view on this issue.

Although geographically, the project differentiates between Phoenicia (the coast) and Lebanon (the Mountain), the two names are often used interchangeably.[48] Thus, a sentence such as the one that follows is often found in the book:

> If we unveiled our ears to Phoenician traditions which were collected by Sanchoniathon, the Beiruti historian, in the fourth century before Christ and that Philo of Byblos, Istephan of Byzantium and Usapyus

the Caesarian carried (to future generations), we would claim that Lebanese history begins with the creation of the two first humans.[49]

The work, in its entirety, provides a very strong sense of continuity between the ancient civilizations in Lebanon and the modern Lebanese. The extensive historical survey follows very closely the different occupiers and political vicissitudes from antiquity to modernity in Phoenicia and Lebanon. When writing about the Arab occupation, the message is clear. Arabs first arrived in Lebanon and Phoenicia in 631 AD with the Islamic conquests, but they had not been successful in entering the Mountain, at least not until the Fatimid occupation. Even then, the Arabs did not enter the northern, Christian, districts of the Mountain.[50]

There is a very detailed account in the book of the different races and ethnic groups that have composed the population of Phoenicia and Lebanon. Cheikho's chapter, "The Ethnic Groups ('anasir) in Lebanon and their Religious Beliefs," portrays the population of Lebanon and Phoenicia as a mélange of races, starting with the Canaanites, the Arameans and going through all the different peoples and occupiers that shaped the population of the region. The Canaanite race, according to the book, remained dominant in Phoenicia until the time of Jesus. This argument is based on the New Testament, which tells that Jesus visited the Phoenician coast and cured a Canaanite woman in the area of Tyre and Sidon.[51] It is a significant point because it links the Canaanites with the birth of Christianity. Thus, a continuous narrative is suggested between the Canaanite Phoenicians and Christianity, a point that will be used to full advantage by the neo-Phoenicians.

This work, sponsored by Haqqi, is clearly not a Phoenician manifesto. Some studies in the book are not even favorable towards the ancient Phoenicians. In the chapter on Lebanese ethnicities and their religious beliefs, Cheikho uses derogatory terms to describe Phoenician paganism. Monotheism was the basis of their religion, he claims, but later Phoenicians subverted this monotheism and increased the number of deities in their pantheon, giving them wives and worshiping natural phenomena. The pagan nature of Phoenician civilization was always a problem with which Christian Lebanese had to grapple. It is one of the prime reasons why the Maronite Church could not possibly advocate for a kinship between the ancient Phoenician faith and Christianity.[52] There was a need for non-clerical Christian Lebanese to make this correlation between the ancient and the new civilizations, as indeed would occur.

The significance of *Lubnan; Mabahith 'Ilmiyya wa Ijtima'iyya* lies in the knowledge it conveys and in the writers who participated in its writing. Leading Jesuit scholars along with local Lebanese, administrators of the *Mutasarrifiyya* and teachers from the Syrian Protestant College, joined forces and wrote this comprehensive study, which radiates a unique historical awareness of "Lebanon and Phoenicia." A reading of it shows us that by 1918 the full knowledge of ancient Phoenicia was already available for local Syro-Lebanese, and not necessarily in the context of anti-Arab sentiments. Phoenicianism in Lebanon expressed as anti-Arabism would indeed surface, and not too long after the publication of this book, but WWI had to terminate; the Ottoman Empire had to disintegrate, and the Arab government in Damascus had to be established before Phoenicianism became associated with anti-Arab notions.

Maronite Clergy and the History of Syria and Lebanon

The contemporary historiography of modern Lebanon takes it for granted that Phoenicianism is a Maronite ideology, born and promoted by the Maronite Church. Meir Zamir, for example, in his important book, *The Formation of Modern Lebanon*, notes that the Maronite Church, through its clergy's historiographic writings, preserved the community's faith, unity and identity. These writings, Zamir asserts, emphasized the ethnic uniqueness of the Maronites and the claim that Phoenician ancestry originated with them.[53] However, as I shall demonstrate below, this was not the case. There is no doubt that the Maronite Church served as a major force in the construction of the Lebanese national consciousness. It provided a kind of pole around which a distinct sense of identity was constructed. From the early 19th century the Church became a crucial player in the politics of the region as its power increased. It served as far more than a religious establishment for the Maronites. It was the source of their distinct identity, which separated them from the rest of the communities in the region. For centuries, Maronite clergy have been preoccupied with writing the annals of the church, its saints, leaders and institutions.[54] Yet, a close look at these writings reveals that the historical horizons of Maronite chroniclers went back only as far as the beginning of Christianity and not before. These writers were concerned more with the Church and its flock than with the history of the land on which both resided. An issue that was of major concern was the question of Maronite loyalty to the Vatican. The preoccupation with this point only grew in the 19th century with the increasing exposure to Europe. Maronite clergy obsessively tried to prove the Roman Catholic adherence of the Maronites from the first days of the Church's existence.[55] Two of the most important books by Maronite clergymen in the 19th century, Nicolas Murad and Abbé Azar, are a case in point.[56] The teleological narrative in both books begins with the rise of Christianity, and not before. Azar's work is a chronology of Christianity in general and the Maronites in particular in Lebanon, written in a traditional historiographical manner. The Maronites, for him, were the Chosen People of God who have preserved Catholicism since the beginning of Christianity. They have never knelt before Ba'al, who, for Azar, symbolized heresy.[57] This view of Ba'al, the leading God in the Phoenician pantheon —

considered in the Bible an abhorred deity — was only understandable in the context of Maronite religious writing of the time. We shall see in the following chapters the way other Maronites, not affiliated directly with the Church, related to this idol.

Far more than Azar, the importance of Murad's book cannot be exaggerated. It is the first book written in French by a Maronite demanding a separate political entity for the Christians in Mount Lebanon. Moreover, arguably, this is the first work that voiced the Lebanist idea.[58] It is, therefore, crucial to note that the historical narrative, which Murad detailed in his plea to French authorities, began with the birth of the Maronite Church. "La Nation maronite," Murad firmly stated at the outset of the book, "tire son origine d'un saint anachorète appelé *Marone*, lequel existait vers la fin du IVe siècle, et dont le nom était en grande vénération au Liban et dans toute la Syrie."[59] Murad attempted throughout the book to demonstrate, first, the Maronite alliance with Catholicism and, second, the attachment to France. Maronite francophilism and Catholicism served for him as justification to ask assistance from France in the formation of a political entity for the Maronites in Mount Lebanon. All this is without mentioning, even once, either Phoenicians or any pre-Christian historical notions.

Towards the end of the 19th century, the content of writings by Maronite clergy on Maronite identity slowly changed. Religious history still dominated, but as a result of the expansion of scientific knowledge about the region, other details were added to the origins of the "mountain people." Yusuf al-Dibs, the Maronite archbishop of Beirut, is a case in point. His series, *Kitab Tarikh Suriyya* [The Book of Syrian History], is a good example of the slow change of emphasis in the historiography of the Maronites. His major sources of reference were works completed by Jesuit teachers from Université Saint Joseph and particularly Father Martin. Al-Dibs noted in his introduction that until now there had not been a single book in Arabic which dealt with the "history of our nation Syria" (*tarikh watanina Suriyya*).[60] His work, he continued, is addressed to the clerical and lay reader alike. This eight-volume project is constructed as a pyramid. The first volumes portray a wide picture of geographical Syria from biblical times through the Persian, Greek and Roman eras. The historical recounting, however, narrows as the volumes progress, and focuses on the history of the Maronite Church and other Eastern Christian denominations. The lion's share of the first volume concentrates on the Phoenician past of the Syrian coastal range. Al-Dibs deals with the origins of the Phoenicians, their commercial skills, their colonies, crafts, the invention of the alphabet and other subjects that later, over the 20th century, became the basis for the assertions of the new Phoenicians of their rich past and their invaluable contribution to human civilization.[61] Al-Dibs made no direct link between the ancient dwellers of Lebanon and the current inhabitants, but he created a continuous chronological narrative from the ancient Phoenicians to the present inhabitants of Mount Lebanon. Later this description would be adopted and extended by Lebanese who were reconstructing the history of their emerging nation.

The last Maronite clergyman I would like to draw attention to is Patriarch Elias Hoyek (Huwayyek) who led his community from 1899-1931, during one of the most decisive eras for the Maronites and for Lebanon alike.[62] Hoyek was the first to use communiqués as a means to address his community on occasions or dates of importance. These communiqués were read by the local priests at Sunday gatherings in church. It was the first time the Maronites were able to listen to the same message from their leader, simultaneously, throughout Lebanon.[63] Religious convictions, in particular the Maronite union with Catholicism, patriotism and education are the three most discussed subjects in the communiqués, which are imbued with a very strong sense of a Maronite collective consciousness. As for patriotism (*hubb al-watan*), Hoyek believed that there cannot be a separation between religion and love of nation (*hubb al-watan min al-din*).[64] His patriotic horizons, however, never exceeded the beginning of Christianity. Even when he spoke about "our ancestors" (*ajdaduna*),[65] he always referred to the founders of the Maronite Church and never to anything that occurred before the birth of Christian faith. Influenced by romantic nationalistic ideas, he believed that every nation had a mission to the world. The mission of the Maronites was to spread Christianity, especially in the non-Christian Middle East. The role of the civilizing mission of Lebanon since antiquity was an important pillar in the construction of the Lebanese national consciousness, but for Hoyek this mission had no secular, non-Christian, denotation.

The Maronite Church, parochial in nature, could not preach in favor of the non-Christian, pagan adherence of its ancestors. Even al-Dibs, who wrote extensively on ancient Phoenicia and whose work is indeed impressive in its depth, could not write about the pagan Phoenician ancestry of his flock. The Church indeed provided the foundation for a separate ancestry and a distinct ethnic cohesiveness, but it was among non-clerical intellectuals (who were the product of years of exposure to European education in Syria, Egypt and other emigrant communities of Syro-Lebanese), many of whom were not Maronites, that the Phoenician myth of origin would surface.

Lay Syro-Lebanese and the Ancient History of Syria

The extensive exposure of Syrians, most of whom were Christians, to Western education created a new type of local intellectual strata. If previously education was in the hands of the various local churches, the foundation of foreign missionary schools offered an alternative that challenged the old political power of these churches. The missionary schools, of course, were not the only factor that brought this change. The weakening of the Ottoman Empire, the subsequent reform efforts (the *Tanzimat*) and increasing emigration all assisted in the creation of a new type of Syrian who began questioning the long-lived clerical domination of all aspects of life in Syria in general and Mount Lebanon in particular.[66]

Dissemination of modern scientific knowledge was one facet of this change. As we have seen, the writing of history or chronicles was mainly restricted to clergy who were preoccupied only with traditional, religious annals of their communities. The 19th century marked a change in perspective. Perhaps the first to write in a secular form on the history of Mount Lebanon was Tannus al-Shidyaq (1794[?]-1861). He was born into a distinguished Maronite family strongly influenced by the exposure to Western missions and education. One of his brothers converted to Protestantism, a phenomenon directly related to American missionary influence, and another became one of the pillars of the Arabic literary movement, the *Nahda*. Tannus al-Shidyaq wrote several books of history, but his most celebrated work was *Kitab Akhbar al-A'yan fi Jabal Lubnan* [The Book of Information about Notable Families in Mount Lebanon], written in Beirut in 1857-1859. Scholars have noted that this book demonstrates the shift from the traditional style of historical clerical writing to secular historiography.[67] It surveys the chronicles of distinguished families, many of whom were not even Christian and the general atmosphere of the book is, by and large, secular. Al-Shidyaq opened this book by defining the limits of Mount Lebanon and reviewing the different sects residing on the Mountain. Then, in a chapter entitled *"Mudun Lubnan al-Finiqiyya"* [The Lebanese Phoenician Cities], he described the eight principal cities of the Phoenician coast and provided a short historical account of each.[68] He referred to the Mountain and the coast as an integral part of historic Lebanon and, in doing so, came closer than any other writer of his time to defining the borders of Greater Lebanon. He asserted that a Lebanese entity had existed since time immemorial, not only as a religious group or a familial estate but as a self-conscious society. The fact that al-Shidyaq's book begins with a historical survey of the Lebanese people starting with the ancient Phoenicians is very important for understanding the development of the Phoenician idea in Lebanon. It shows us that, even before Renan's celebrated mission to Lebanon, a lay Maronite wrote about the Phoenicians in a history book, although he stopped short of describing the dwellers of Mount Lebanon as direct descendants of the ancient Phoenicians.

Tannus al-Shidyaq died in 1861, about the same time as Renan conducted his scientific mission to Phoenicia and as the Arab literary renaissance movement, the *Nahda*, was in a moment of ascendancy. The *Nahda*, whose center was in Beirut and whose leading personalities were associated with the American Protestant mission, did not only strive to revive Arabic language and culture. Its leading protagonists aspired to use Arabic as a vehicle for the formation of a secular identity in the territory they defined as geographical Syria. They did not present Arabic as the holy language of the Quran, but rather as a secular unifier of all Arabic speakers. For the same reason, the group of people who led the Arabic *Nahda* also initiated interest in the ancient pre-Arab-Islamic era of the region. It was a social group that broke away from the old socio-political system of Mount Lebanon seeking new avenues of knowledge, and viewed history in a more challenging way. One of the prime platforms where *Nahda* members first presented their historical worldview was the Syrian Society for the Acquisition of Sciences. Formed in 1847 in Beirut by American missionaries and some of their local Christian students, the society manifested, probably for the first time, the term Syria in such a context.[69] Its activists strove to spread the message of the importance of education in the region. Some of the lectures given in the Society's gathering focused on the history of Syria, from the Phoenician era to modernity. These lectures often radiated a sense of pride in the Phoenician legacy of the region and a desire to revive the glory days of that ancient Syrian epoch.[70]

There is no better illustration for the mindset of this literary group than *Da'irat al-Ma'arif,* the Encyclopedia of Butrus al-Bustani and his four sons, written between 1876-1900. This encyclopedia contained the available body of knowledge that existed in Syria in the late-19th century about numerous subjects, from nature to technology to history. The publication of *Da'irat al-Ma'arif* was discontinued after the Arabic letter "*'ain,*" which meant that the crucial entries for this study about the Phoenicians, the Maronites and Lebanon were never written. Nevertheless, it is easily seen that the preoccupation with the pre-Arab-Islamic era was equal to the preoccupation with the post-7th century AD.[71] Moreover, in several entries there are direct references to the Phoenicians as the forefathers of the modern Syrians. In the entry "commerce" (*Tijara*), for example, al-Bustani presented a chronology of commerce in Syria from the Phoenician era, describing the residents of Beirut as the descendents of the Phoenician merchants.[72]

Al-Bustani, the Syrian, the Arab, the Ottoman loyalist harmonically integrated all these identities into one self-identity. Equally, he saw no contradiction in asserting that the ancient Phoenicians were the forefathers of the 19th-century Arab Syrians. Al-Bustani and his peers were interested in the advancement of knowledge and this was exactly what they did in their literary activities. It was left for the following generations to select their preferred parts of history and construct them according to their own biases and historical propensities.

An important aspect of the Arab literary revival was the foundation of numerous journals, reviews and newspapers that brought the tidings of the new winds coming from Europe. At first Beirut was the center of this activity, but with the change of policy of the Ottoman Sultan Abdülhamid, from apparent liberalism to strict autocracy, Cairo, situated out of his reach, became the hub of the Arab cultural renaissance movement.[73] In the 19th century, Egypt had become the home of many Syrian emigrants, and it now absorbed a new wave of Syrians who found in Cairo and Alexandria havens where they could pursue their cultural and journalistic activities.

Of the numerous publications printed by Syro-Lebanese, first in Beirut and later in Cairo and Alexandria, *al-Muqtataf* and *al-Hilal* were the most celebrated. The first was launched in 1876 in Beirut and the latter in 1892 in Cairo. *Al-Muqtataf* was founded by Ya'qub Sarruf and Faris Nimr, two Protestant teachers (converted from Maronitism) of the Syrian Protestant College, who moved to Cairo in 1884 and continued to issue their journal in the Nile Valley. *Al-Hilal* was founded by Jurji Zaydan, a graduate of the Syrian Protestant College. Zaydan, a Greek Orthodox, became one of the key figures constructing the *Geschichtebild* of Arab history through his journal and the romantic novels he wrote about Arab history. *Al-Muqtataf*, "a magazine for science, craft and agriculture," was primarily preoccupied with the popularization of scientific information, from astronomy to zoology. It nevertheless also provided some information on historical subjects, such as the history of the ancient Near East.[74]

The first articles to mention the ancient Phoenicians appeared in *al-Muqtataf* in 1882-1883.[75] Reading through the journal, it is easy to see that in the 1880s-90s information in Arabic about the ancient Phoenicians reflecting current scholarly knowledge was readily available. From 1882-1900, twenty articles dealt with the ancient Phoenicians. The number is not high, but combined with the "readers' questions" section, it indicates that the subject was already in the public consciousness. In the questions section, readers expressed interest in the Phoenicians and some asked the editorial board to elaborate further on the subject.[76]

The expanding knowledge about the ancient Phoenicians, and its availability to the general public in popular forms such as journals, facilitated making the connection between the ancient and modern worlds. In 1889, *al-Muqtataf* articles, written by Syro-Lebanese, claimed for the first time to have some kind of genealogical relations with the biblical Phoenicians. The journal reported on the annual meeting of *Jam'iyat Shams al-Birr* in Beirut, at which Najib Efendi al-Bustani, the third son of Butrus al-Bustani and the last editor of *Da'irat al-Ma'arif*, lectured on "Phoenicia and the Phoenicians." In the introductory notes to his lecture he explained why he chose this topic:

> My subject tonight is 'Phoenicia and the Phoenicians.' There are several reasons why I chose to discuss this theme: the bond of descent between us and them; the characteristics that they bequeathed to us; the archeological proofs of their strength and fame that they left behind; we are part of them and Beirut is one of their famous cities. I thought that the best for me would be to address to your thoughts a summary of the story of our ancestors the Phoenicians [...][77]

Jam'iyyat Shams al-Birr was founded in 1869 as the Beirut branch of the British YMCA and many of its members were students of the Syrian Protestant College. Faris Nimr, the co-owner and editor of *al-Muqtataf*, was one of the association's two founders and Jurji Zaydan was one of its members.[78] Thus, in a cultural gathering, in the heart of the Protestant Mission in Beirut, a leading local intellectual plainly stated that he and his audience were direct descendents of the ancient Phoenicians. Browsing through the pages of *al-Muqtataf*, it is possible to observe similar thoughts in other contexts. For example, the journal reported on an annual party of the Greek Orthodox school in Beirut. The writer congratulated the students on their celebration and requested that they acquire knowledge in order to re-gain the glory of the ancient Phoenicians.[79]

Al-Muqtataf catered mostly to a Syrian audience, reflecting the situation within the Syrian community in Egypt and its scope of interests.[80] Jurji Zaydan's journal, *al-Hilal*, first issued in 1892, enjoyed a larger audience. Zaydan was more interested in social sciences and humanities and this is reflected in the content of *al-Hilal*'s articles. Zaydan, a Greek Orthodox, used his journal to popularize Arabic and Islamic heritage through historical articles and short stories, all stressing the Arab pre-Islamic and Islamic civilization. Nevertheless, even for Zaydan, the identity issue of the Syrians was still ambiguous. In the first issue of *al-Hilal*, in an article entitled "The Origins of the Arabs of Syria and Palestine,"[81] the writer (denoted as "a Syrian") attempted to trace the lineage of the Syrians. He claimed that the residents of Syria at the beginning of history were Semitic nomads. They were followed by the Phoenicians (or the Canaanites) and the Philistines [in Arabic: *filastiniyun*]. Then came other peoples: Egyptians, Persians, Greeks and Romans. Syria became Arab with the Islamic occupation, especially with the establishment of the Umayyad Caliphate in Damascus. Some of the Syrians converted to Islam; others preferred to pay the *jizya*. A group of the latter escaped to Lebanon, which evolved to be an asylum for Christian minorities. The writer explained that it is impossible to know exactly what the origins of the Syrians are because of the multitude of peoples and occupiers who crisscrossed and settled the country. Rulers and ruled mixed up to form one nation — a Syrian nation.

Also in that first issue of *al-Hilal*, another article, "The Syrians in Egypt,"[82] discusses why the Syrians preferred to immigrate to Egypt. "The Syrians are natural-born merchants," the article explains. They are raised in a nation (*qawm*) whose origins go back to the ancient Phoenicians. Syria is a land of commerce; the coast dwellers particularly excel in business; and they have always mastered languages. These qualities are fully realized in Egypt. There, in the Nile Valley, they find the perfect place to practice their commercial skills. As if to continue this theme, the second issue of *al-Hilal* ran a detailed article on "The Phoenicians and Commerce,"[83] that provides an account of the markets with which the ancient Phoenicians traded. Naturally, major emphasis is given to the exchange of trade between Egypt and Phoenicia. These articles also demonstrate the fact that Zaydan, as a new Syrian immigrant in Egypt, was trying to link his old and new homes into one historical unit. In order to do so, he fused the ancient histories of the two countries into one narrative, starting in antiquity and continuing to the present.

The picture that arises from these articles is quite interesting. First, the notion of a "Syrian" is as strong as that of an "Arab" and stronger than that of a "Lebanese." Second, Syria, in the first article, is a mélange of ethnicities and in the second article the Syrians, especially the coast dwellers, are direct descendants of the merchant Phoenicians. Significant to our point is the fact that Zaydan, who later sharpened his "Arab notions" and contributed to the crystallization of the Arab historical consciousness, published articles in the first two issues of *al-Hilal* in 1892-93 that made a linkage between modern Syrians and the ancient Phoenicians. For Zaydan, just as for Sarruf and Nimr, "Syria" was a wide geographical term, and "Syrian" denoted specific and unique cultural expressions, different from those of the other Arabic-speaking communities of the Ottoman Empire.

Fifteen years after the publication of the first issue of *al-Hilal*, Jurji Zaydan tried again to answer the question, "Who are the Syrians?"[84] It was a year after the outbreak of the Young Turk revolution, and the Arab national movement was in a more progressive stage. Syrian and Lebanese sentiments were also more clearly defined than before. Zaydan attempted to answer questions posed by many readers as to whether the Syrians were Arabs. As in 1892, he still believed that it was difficult to know exactly the origin of the Syrians. In ancient times Syria was populated by Semitic people who immigrated to the region and overpowered its former residents. The geographical centrality of the land made it a locus of invaders of the ancient world. All the occupiers left their mark on the region. The presence of the Greeks was more significant along the coast. In the hinterland the Arab race had been very dominant since the 4th century, three centuries before the Arab-Islamic conquests. Despite that mixture of races, the Semitic race managed to maintain its hegemony in Syria.

The Syrians today, Zaydan continued, are divided by their origin into two groups: Muslims and Christians. Most of the Muslims are Arabs. As for the Christians, the majority are descendants of the Arameans, the Arabs and the Greeks. The Arameans were the original inhabitants of the land, then came the Greeks from the West, followed by the Arabs, the Ghasanis, who came from the Hauran in the hinterland. In short, Christian Syrians are not genealogically Arabs, even if there is some Arab blood flowing in their veins. Yet they are considered Arabs because they speak Arabic, they procreate in an Arab land and they live according to Arab morals. Thus, Syria became an Arab country after the Islamic occupation.

Zaydan's views as to who the Syrians were had clearly changed since *al-Hilal* first appeared, a change that reflected the general transformation of the entire region and the development of Arab and other national identities. From a Syrian nation founded on a mixture of races, Zaydan moved to define Syria as an absolute Arab nation: by race for the Muslims, and by language and historical experience for the Christians. In the 1890s, *Al-Muqtataf* and *al-Hilal* were far from being proponents of non-Arab or anti-Arab sentiments; they only reflected the reality of the time. Arab national sentiments were in a seminal stage and Syrian notions were much stronger than those of any other ethnic identity. Mount Lebanon was in a stage of "long peace"[85] and very few Lebanese, if any, challenged the authority of the Ottoman Empire or the geopolitical situation according to which Lebanon belonged to the wider geographical sphere of Syria.

What is significant to this study is the fact that these journals reflected a growing interest of Syro-Lebanese in the ancient, pre-Islamic past of their country. Moreover, the preoccupation with the pre-Islamic past of Syria was not exclusive to Christians. Ahmad 'Arif al-Zein, for example, the owner and editor of *al-'Irfan*, a Shi'i newspaper from Sidon, is a case in point. Al-Zein and his journal were by no means marginal in Lebanon. His paper was a major source of information of Jabal 'Amil, South Lebanon, and al-Zein himself was regarded as one of the leading intellectuals of his region.[86] In 1913, he published a book, *Tarikh Sayda (The History of Sidon)*,[87] which reviews the history of the city from antiquity to modern times. He described at length the scholarly works on the origin of the Syrians, who according to him were a mélange of races, of which the Phoenician-Semitic race was the first. The latter received much attention from al-Zein who described in detail their cities, commerce, colonies, religion, politics and governmental centers. He presented the city of Sidon and its inhabitants, from the Phoenician Sidonites to the modern Lebanese, dedicating more than a third of his book to the pre-Arab Muslim eras. Al-Zein wrote a teleological story providing a continuous narrative from the ancient to contemporary world. His sources of reference were articles from *al-Muqtataf*, *Da'irat al-Ma'arif* and *Kitab Tarikh Suriyya* of Yusuf al-Dibs, the Maronite Bishop of Beirut. They were all written in Arabic and, except for al-Dibs, associated with the Protestant College in Beirut rather than the Maronites and the Jesuits.

All these examples indicate that even before Université Saint Joseph became a major center for the dissemination of separatist Syrian and Lebanese ideas, Syrians, other than Maronites, in Beirut and in Egypt began writing and deliberating about the ancient, pre-Islamic past of their country. Moreover, graduates and teachers of the Syrian Protestant College, who were not products of the Jesuit missionary system, were among the first Syrians to record the ancient Phoenician past of the Syrian coast.[88] Butrus al-Bustani and his "*Nahda* peers" aspired to construct a secular identity based on culture, history and geography. Arabic provided the cultural component and Syria, from time immemorial to modernity, provided the historical and geographical axis of this identity. Thus, for the first time Phoenicia was resurrected. In doing so, by no means were they expressing anti-Arab sentiments. It was a time when Arab proto-national sentiments were barely in the incubation stage and writing about the pre-Islamic past of Syria was merely an expression of a secular worldview, influenced by similar European attempts to trace their progeny as far back as possible in ancient history. Only later, the association between Phoenicianism and Maronite political aspirations developed, crystallizing around the years of WWI.

To round out the discussion on Syrian lay intellectuals who began addressing the ancient past of their country, I shall proceed to Maronite circles, for they were the ones who, during and after WWI, made Phoenicianism their prime ideology. As important as al-Bustani and his peers were, they remained a tiny minority within the small Syrian elite that deliberated about its identity and its historical consciousness. Moreover, the fact that a large number of people of this group converted to Protestantism, Islam or abandoned religion altogether marked a rupture from their past and a break from their social milieus.[89] The majority of the Christian elite in Mount Lebanon and Beirut would not turn their back on the past and would work within the context of their environment of birth.

From the early 20th century Maronite intellectuals would strive to change the political and social situation in Mount Lebanon and Beirut. Displeased by the domination of the Maronite church and the traditional notables, they attempted to challenge their supremacy by calling for internal reforms. More important, they believed that the economic distress in Mount Lebanon could be resolved by expanding the territory of the autonomous region, including therein the coast cities and the Biqaʿ. This group of primarily Maronites, but by no means exclusively, were deeply influenced by long years of foreign education and by internal developments related to economic recession and political stagnation. They were also influenced by new "liberal" ideas coming from emigrant communities who left the Mountain to the New World but continued to have a major impact on their communities of origin. We shall see in the next chapter the influence two of these communities, in America and in Egypt, had on the political fate of Lebanon. This stratum was engaged in free professions such as journalism, medicine and law. At the same time many of them continued to be preoccupied with business ventures as mediators of all sorts. Thus, it was this group of people who revived the interest in the Lebanist ideal, first introduced by the Maronite church in the 1840s, but which subsided as a result of the political agreements of 1845 and 1860 in Mount Lebanon. Having been articulated this time by lay Western-educated people and not by the Maronite Church the idea acquired secular tones. If religion was no longer the overt reason for the establishment of a wider entity in Lebanon (even if it remained the covert reason) a new rationale had to be articulated. Thus, in addition to the economic need, Christians in Mount Lebanon and Beirut started for the first time to introduce history and geography as reasons for the formation of a greater autonomous Lebanon.

One of the leading personalities of this stratum was Bulus Nujaym, whom I consider the archetype, perhaps the most articulate, of the new lay Maronite intellectual around the turn of the century.[90] Nujaym was born in 1880 in

Junieh, a town on the Lebanese coast north of Beirut. He studied at the Lazarist college in 'Aintoura, and completed his education in Paris, where he received a doctorate in law and political science from the Law Faculty of the University of Paris. He returned to Mount Lebanon and became the director of the office of foreign affairs of the *Mutasarrifiyya* under the *Mutasarrif* Yohanes Pasha. In 1914, at the outset of WWI, he was deported by the Ottomans from Lebanon to Jerusalem where he spent the war years. After the establishment of Greater Lebanon, Nujaym was assigned to be the General Prosecutor of the newly established state. In the late 1920s he moved back to Paris, where he died in 1931.

Nujaym's biography reflects a new kind of Syrian. Educated as a child and adolescent in a foreign missionary schools and then acquiring his higher education in Paris, he was intimately familiar with French and European culture. Indeed, he was a Maronite, but his worldview extended far beyond the Mountain and the Maronite Church. He belonged to this new stratum of Syro-Lebanese who were exposed to, and influenced by, Western values and to whom the socio-political situation in the region in general and in Syria in particular was displeasing. Nujaym's political views were born in the meeting place between the old Uniate-Maronite notions of self-consciousness in Mount Lebanon that evolved around the Maronite church and the modern European education he acquired through the French missions.

In 1908, Nujaym published *La Question du Liban* under the pseudonym M. Jouplain. In the book he drafted a proposal for the solution to the Lebanese question in the wider context of the region. In his eyes, only the establishment of an autonomous entity in a Greater Lebanon, within a Syrian larger framework, under the aegis of France, would bring a solution to the question of Lebanon. He envisioned geographical Syria being completely rehabilitated from its state of stagnation and he bestowed the leading role in this project to the Lebanese within a wider Syrian political framework.[91] In a way, Nujaym preceded many scholars in his analysis of Lebanon. He saw the Maronite Church as the pole, the axle, around which a Lebanese nation should crystallize.

The first chapter of Nujaym's book, *Les Origines Historiques de la Syrie et du Liban*, is basically a historical survey of Syria and Lebanon from prehistory to 1908. From the outset, Nujaym exposes his convictions about the powers that determine historical phenomena:

> L'histoire de la Syrie et du Liban est assise sur les caractères géographiques du pays. Deux faits géographiques en déterminèrent l'histoire et l'ethnographie, premièrement sa constitution en une bande de terrains resserrée entre la Méditerranée et le désert, deuxièmement sa nature montagneuse.[92]

It is geography that determines fates, Nujaym affirms. Geographical determinism, according to the school of thought of Elisée Reclus,[93] to whom

Nujaym constantly referred, is reflected in his words. In order to hone his point about the importance of geography in the physical and human history of Syria and Lebanon, he elaborates extensively on this subject. The Phoenicians themselves could not have ascended, had it not been for the unique geography of the region that enabled them to excel in commerce. The mountains protected them from the east and the Mediterranean basin to the west was wide open for the practice of their talents. Nujaym adhered to the theory that the Mediterranean was "phoenicianized" and civilized from east to west, from the Syrian coast to the Atlantic Ocean. He emphasized in detail the Phoenician contribution to Western civilization. They invented the fabrication of glass; they perfected goldsmithing, metal work and dye-works, including creating the color purple; and they developed the art of navigation, math and writing. Needless to say, they invented the alphabet and introduced it to Greece. In fact, it was the Phoenicians who civilized Greece and brought it onto the path of progress. They had a similar impact on the Gauls, the Italians and the Spaniards.

Writing about the Arab-Islamic occupation of Syria, Nujaym makes a very interesting point. He claims that the Arabs and the Syrians have shared racial affinities. In fact, thanks to the Arab occupation in the 7th century, the Semitic race regained its dominance in Syria after long years of Hellenic occupation. The Syrians, he asserts, regarded the new occupiers as brothers of the same race and welcomed them, because they had never accepted the Hellenistic presence in their country. Thanks to the Arab invasion:

> Une civilisation sémitique allait se développer, profondément indigène, s'inspirant des particularités du pays et des ses races, véritable héritière de cette vieille civilisation orientale que les Phéniciens, les Juifs et d'autres peuplades syriennes avaient illustrée.[94]

At first the Arab occupation was tolerant and accepted the existing faiths in Syria. But with time it changed and oppression prevailed. Mount Lebanon had always demonstrated a strong sense of independence and became the bastion of opposition to the Arabs. Along the Phoenician coast resistance to the Arab occupation was the strongest. More than in the Syrian hinterland, the coastal population maintained strong ties with Greece and Constantinople through its maritime commerce. After the coast was occupied by the Arabs, many inhabitants escaped to the Mountain and continued their struggle, after joining other refugees coming from Syria. It was during that period that Nujaym placed the origins of the Maronites. This was the time when Lebanon began functioning as an asylum for Christians.[95] Mount Lebanon has served since then as a sanctuary for minorities, but its mountainous population remained attached to the urban communities on the coast. Their openness to the coast, and to the Mediterranean cultures beyond, furnished the mountaineers with an open spirit and exposed them to ideas coming from the

West. They developed a culture of commerce, and many of them became industrialists.[96]

In 1908, when Nujaym wrote his book, Henri Lammens was already an authority in the field of the history of Syria. Throughout the chapter on history, Nujaym used Lammens' works to support his arguments. He proposed the existence of a Syrian national framework since the ancient Phoenicians and argued that Lebanon and the Lebanese should play a leading role in this setting. Like the Piedmontese in Italy, Nujaym thought, the Lebanese should be the vanguard of Syrian unification.

Some interesting observations arise from Nujaym's historical analysis of Syria and Lebanon. First, he was not intolerant to Arab ethnicity to the point that he believed there were racial affinities between Syrians and Arabs. This is yet another indication that anti-Arab notions among Christian Lebanese nationalists only emerged later after WWI. Second, indeed he called for the establishment of a Greater Lebanon, but in the context of a larger Syrian framework. This view of Nujaym is important because it reflects the stance shared by the majority of Christian Lebanese who, in 1908, could not envision a Lebanon entirely separated from its surroundings. In 1919, Nujaym published an article in Charles Corm's acclaimed *La Revue Phénicienne* suggesting a different agenda for Arabs and Lebanese independence. We shall return to this article in the next chapter and follow the development and change of his ideas.

Nujaym was not the only Lebanese to write in such a vein in 1908, he simply wrote the most elaborate and well-articulated book. Reading his work and those of others[97] it becomes apparent that a notion of some kind of a Lebanese political framework, based on historical and geographical justifications, was in existence at least from 1908. It developed parallel to, and not in opposition with, Syrian and even Arab notions. The total separation between Syrianism, Lebanism and Arabism would occur later, around the end of WWI. Meanwhile, these national movements were just making their first hesitant steps, and like all national movements, regardless of time or place, they were scrutinizing the past in search of a golden age to cling to and draw on as a model for emulation.

The ancient Phoenician seafarers were a perfect choice for this role.

References

1   Pierre Raphaël, *Le Cèdre du Liban dans l'Histoire* (Beirut: Imprimerie Gédéon, 1924), pp. 221-222.
2   Ernest Renan, *Mission de Phénicie* (Paris: Imprimerie Impériale, 1864); see also René Dussaud, *L'Oeuvre Scientifique d'Ernest Renan* (Paris: P. Geuthner, 1951), pp. 51-76. Renan's book was reprinted in 1998 in Lebanon in *Éditions Terre du Liban*, marking the ongoing interest in his work there.

3   M. Gras, P. Rouillard, J. Teixidor, *L'Univers Phénicien* (Paris: Arthaud, 1989), pp. 13-15.
4   Gustave Flaubert, *Salammbô* (Paris: M. Lévy Frères, 1862).
5   Flaubert himself traveled to the Levant in July-October, 1850 and spent over a month in Lebanon. See Hoda Adra, *Flaubert et le Liban* (Beirut: Université libanaise, 1985), especially pp. 205-235, on the influence of Lebanon on his writing. French interest in Syria can also be seen through the number of French publications concentrating on Syria. See Paul Masson, *Éléments d'une Bibliographie Française de la Syrie* (Paris, Marseille: Champion, 1919). Masson noted 4, 534 entries from the 15th century to 1919. Of this figure, 3, 699 publications were printed after 1860, the year of Renan's expedition to Lebanon.
6   Lavigerie also visited Lebanon after the bloody events of 1860. See his book, *Souscription Recueillie en Faveur des Chrétiens* (Paris: E. Belin, 1861).
7   Neil Asher Silberman, *Between Past and Present* (New York: Anchor Books, 1989), p. 2.
8   M. l'Abbé Gagnol, *Histoire Ancienne des Peuples de l'Orient* (Paris: Poussielgue, 1889), p. 274; V. Duruy, *Histoire de l'Orient* (Paris: Hachette, 1896), pp. 235-248; Désiré Blanchard et Jules Toutain, *Histoire Ancienne des Peuples d'Orient* (Paris, 1901); Emile Segond, *Histoire Ancienne de l'Orient* (Paris, 1920), p. 9.
9   By 1900, the Louvre Museum had a large Phoenician exhibition containing 475 artifacts. See E. Ledrain, *Notice Sommaire des Monuments Phéniciens du Musée du Louvre* (Paris: Libraries-imprimeries réuines, 1900).
10 Louis Lortet, *La Syrie d'Aujourd'hui; Voyages dans la Phénicie, le Liban et la Judée, 1875-1880* (Paris: Librairie Hachette et Cie, 1884), p. 77. An Arabic version of this book was printed in 1993 in Beirut under the title *Ard al-Dhikrayat*, yet another indication for the interest in such writings in Lebanon.
11 Maurice Barrès, *Une Enquête aux Pays du Levant* (Paris: Plon-Nourrit, 1923), pp. 51-52.
12 *Ibid*, p. 102.
13 When the news of Barrès' death reached Beirut memorial services were held at the Latin church of the city and at Université Saint Joseph. The Jesuit university eternalized his memory by dedicating a hall in his name, engraving on a memorial plaque a sentence from *Une Enquête aux Pays du Levant*: "Liban terre de souvenirs, et pleine de semences ..." Henry Bordeaux, *Voyageurs d'Orient* (Paris: Librairie Plon, 1926), pp. 254-255; *Bulletin de l'Association Amicale des Anciens Élèves de l'Université Saint Joseph* (Beirut: Imprimerie Catholique, 1925), pp. 16-17.
14 The Uniate Churches are the churches of Eastern Christendom, which are in communion with Rome yet retain their rites, languages and laws, in accordance with the terms of their union. In addition to the Maronite Church, five other Uniate churches were formed as a result of Catholic missionary activities: the Syrian Catholic (1662), Chaldean Catholic (1672), Greek Catholic (1724), Armenian Catholic (1724), and Coptic Catholic (1741). See Joseph Hajjar, *Les Chrétiens Uniates du Proche-Orient* (Paris: Éditions du Seuil, 1962).
15 Sélim Abou, *Le Bilinguisme Arabe-Français au Liban* (Paris: Presses universitaires de France, 1962), pp. 179-180. A very detailed and documented description of the commencement of the Maronite ties with Europe can be found

in the two volume work of Nasser Gemayel, *Les Echanges Culturelles entre les Maronites et l'Europe 1584-1789* (Beirut: [s.n.], 1984).

16   M. Jullien, *La Nouvelle Mission de la Compagnie de Jésus en Syrie* (Paris: Imprimerie A. Mame et Fils, 1899), p. 41, p. 152; see also Abou, *Ibid*, pp. 180-189.

17   Georges Samné, *Les Oeuvres Françaises en Syrie* (Paris, 1919), p. 9; Jullien, *La Nouvelle Mission*, pp. 47-65.

18   John Spagnolo, *France and Ottoman Lebanon; 1861-1914* (Oxford: Ithaca Press, 1977), p. 4; Nasri Salhab, *La France et les Maronites* (Beirut: Dar el-Machreq, 1997), pp. 43-44.

19   Alfred d'Ancre, *Silhouettes Orientales* (Paris, 1869), p. 203.

20   See, for example, René Ristelhueber, "Les Maronites," *La Revue de Deux Mondes* (January 1, 1915), pp. 198-212.

21   The warm attitude of the French towards the Maronites can also be seen in the introduction to Renan's *Mission de Phénicie*. Renan thanks Yusuf Bey Karam, the Maronite Patriarch and his network of priests in the various Maronite churches, for helping him in conducting the excavations. He then moves to discrediting the Muslim and Shi'i "half savage and stupid [...] inferior races," who disrupted his scientific work in Phoenicia. *Ibid*, p. 14.

22   Edmond Burke III, "A Comparative View of French Native Policy in Morocco and Syria, 1912-1925," *Middle Eastern Studies*, 9 (May 1973), pp. 178-179.

23   MAE Paris, Papiers Robert de Caix. P11203 PA-AP 353, Vol. 3, pp. 311-316, de Caix to Kammerer. Beirut, May 16, 1921.

24   Gabriel Hanotaux et Alfred Martineau, *Histoire des Colonies Françaises et de l'Expansion de la France dans le Monde* (Paris: Plon, 1931), p. XXXIII. And see Vol. III, "La Syrie," by Robert de Caix.

25   E. Vayssettes, *Sauvons les Maronites par l'Algérie et pour l'Algérie* (Algeria: Bastide, 1860); A similar idea was first articulated in the book of Louis de Baudicour, *La Colonisation de l'Algérie* (Paris: Lecoffre, 1847), pp. 234-239; see also Sarkis Abu Zayd, *Tahjir al-Mawarina ila al-Jazai'r* [The Emigration of the Maronites to Algeria] (Beirut: Dar Ab'aad li-al-tiba'a wa al-nashr, 1994), pp. 33-64.

26   See the following books written by Jesuit priests: François Charmot, *La Pédadogie des Jesuites* (Paris: Spes, 1951); John W. Donohue, *Jesuit Education* (New York: Fordham University Press, 1963).

27   M. Jullien, *La Nouvelle Mission de la Compagnie de Jésus en Syrie*, p. 41.

28   A.L. Tibawi, "History of the Syrian Protestant College," *Middle East Journal*, Vol. 21 (1967), pp. 199-212.

29   *Ibid*, pp. 47-65.

30   MAE Paris, Vol. 207, November 11, 1919. A report of an honorary reception to Gouraud at the University of Lyon.

31   Chambre de commerce de Marseille, *Congrès Français de la Syrie* (January, 3-5 1919), pp. 7-8.

32   The Jesuit Archives at Vanves, file no. RPO 52. Curriculum of the Oriental Faculty, 1904-1905, 1906-1907.

33   Université Saint Joseph, *Les Jesuites en Syrie 1831-1931*, Vol. VI, "Les Oeuvres de Presse" (Paris: Les Éditions Dillen, 1931), pp. 59.

34   *Ibid*, p. 60.

35 *Ibid.* Pierre Martin, *Tarikh Lubnan* (Lubnan: Matba'at al-Abaa al-Yasu'iyyin, 1889). Note the easiness in which the names Lebanon and Syria are interchanged.
36 Martin's work was used as a source of reference in many other cases. Michel Ma'luf, a Greek Catholic from the Biqa' wrote in 1890 *Histoire de Ba'albek,* and used Martin's book extensively in his Arabic translation. Ma'luf's book is interesting in and of itself, as it demonstrates the local interest in the ancient history of Lebanon, especially the Phoenician and Roman eras.
37 Lammens was actually Belgian, but for all practical matters he was part of the Lyonnais French Jesuit Order. On Lammens, see Kamal Salibi, "Islam and Syria in the Writings of Henry Lammens," in Lewis and Holt (eds.), *Historians of The Middle East* (London: Oxford University Press, 1962), pp. 330-342; See also Youakim Moubarac, *Recherches sur la Pensée Chrétienne et l'Islam dans les Temps Modernes et à l'Époque Contemporaine* (Beirut: Université Libanaise, 1977), pp. 177-205.
38 Henri Lammens published hundreds of articles about early Islam. See a list of his publications in *Mélanges de l'USJ* (1938).
39 Henri Lammens, *Tasrih al-Absar fi ma Yahtawi Lubnan min al-Athar* [Panorama of Lebanese Antiquities] (Beirut: Imprimerie Catholique, 1906). In 1914, the Imprimerie catholique, the Jesuit publication house, printed the second edition of this book. It was reprinted twice, in 1982 and 1996, in Dar al-Ra'id al-Lubnani, reflecting the ongoing interest in Lammens' writing.
40 Henri Lammens, *La Syrie et Son Importance Géographique* (Lourain, 1904). See also Levantine H. (pseudonym of Lammens), "Le Liban et son rôle géographique en Syrie," *Études* 116 (1908), pp. 487-505.
41 Henri Lammens, "Rasm Khara'it Lubnan," [Record of Lebanese Maps] in *Tasrih al-Absar,* pp. 98-105.
42 Youakim Moubarac, *Recherches sur la Pensée Chrétienne et l'Islam dans les Temps Modernes et à l'Époque Contemporaine,* p. 177.
43 The references to the book are drawn from its 1968 edition, edited by Fu'ad Afram al-Bustani, another important protagonist in the "Phoenician plot." We shall discuss him and his role further in Chapter III. *Lubnan; Mabahith 'Ilmiyya wa Ijtima'iyya,* 2nd Edition (Beirut: Université Libanaise, 1968). Henceforth: *Lubnan; Mabahith.*
44 Kamal Salibi, *The Modern History of Lebanon* (London: Weidenfeld and Nicolson, 1965), pp. 116-117; Engin Deniz Akarli, *The Long Peace, Ottoman Lebanon, 1861-1921* (Berkeley: University of California Press, 1993), p. 199.
45 Albert Naccache was a close friend of Charles Corm and a staunch supporter of the Phoenician identity in Lebanon. Al-Ma'luf continued to write on the history of Lebanon and contributed to the construction of the Lebanese historical consciousness. See his book *Tarikh al-Amir Fakhr al-Din al-Ma'ni al-Thani* [The History of the Prince Fakhr al-Din II], (Junieh: Matba'at al-Risala al-Lubnaniyya, 1934). This book was in fact a collection of several articles that al-Ma'luf himself published in a journal he owned and edited in Zahle, *al-Athar,* between 1911-1914. See Ahmad Beidoun, *Identité Confessionnelle,* p. 516. On Bulus Nujaym, see below in this chapter.
46 *Lubnan; Mabahith,* p. 262. Salhani himself circumscribed the "natural borders" of Lebanon from the south in the Litani River to the north in Nahar al-Kebir and from the west in the Mediterranean sea to the east in the Biqa'.

47 About the *Alliance Libanaise*, see Chapter II.
48 The geo-political distinction between Phoenicia and Lebanon was often blurred. See for example Pierre Raphaël, the Jesuit teacher from USJ of Maronite descent: "Lebanon is an integral part of Phoenicia, says a well known orientalist" [Henri Lammens in *Tasrih al-Absar* Vol. II, p. 228. A.K.] Phoenicia and Lebanon, two names of the same country. Phoenicia, it is the Lebanese coast; Lebanon, it is the Phoenician mountain." *Le Cèdre du Liban*, p. 1.
49 *Lubnan; Mabahith*, p. 263.
50 *Ibid*, p. 244.
51 *The New Testament*, Matti, 15, 21-28. Marcus, 7, 24-30.
52 This situation would change with time. Maronite clergymen would become increasingly involved in the dissemination of Phoenicianism in Lebanon, especially in the 1970s, as a result of the civil war that radicalized all groups within the Lebanese society.
53 Meir Zamir, *The Formation of Modern Lebanon* (London: Croom Helm, 1985), p. 7.
54 Kamal Salibi, *Maronite Historians of Mediaeval Lebanon* (Beirut: American University of Beirut, 1959).
55 The Maronite Church has tried to demonstrate that it has always followed Catholic Orthodoxy. Matti Moosa, in his *The Maronites in History* (New York: Syracuse University Press, 1986), pp. 217-232, presents an angry reproach against the Maronite attempts to demonstrate their "orthodoxy" since the Church's inception. Pierre Dibs, in his *Histoire de l'Église Maronite* (Beirut: La Sagesse, 1962), demonstrates the opposite approach. In any case, this topic left the theological field and evolved into a purely political issue long ago.
56 Nicolas Murad, *Notice Historique sur l'Origine de la Nation Maronite et sur Ses Rapports avec la France* (Paris: Adrien le Clere, 1844); Abbé Azar, *Les Marounites d'après le Manuscrit Arabe du R.P. Azar* (Cambari: F Deligne et E Lesne, 1852). For other works written in a similar vein, see Yussuf Debs [sic], *Lettre de Mgr Debs Touchant le Patriarche des Maronites, 30 December 1893* (Amiens, 1894); Mgr Emmanuel Pharès, *Les Maronites du Liban* (Lille: Imprimerie de la Croix du Nord, 1908); Bernard Ghobaira al-Ghaziri, *Rome et l'Église Syrienne Maronite d'Antioche, 517-1531* (Beyrouth: Khalil Sarkis, 1906).
57 Abbé Azar, *Les Marounites*, p. 7.
58 See Carol Hakim-Dowek, *The Origins of the Lebanese National Idea*, p. 86; Iliya Harik, *Politics and Change in a Traditional Society* (Princeton: Princeton University Press, 1968), pp. 139-142.
59 Murad, *Notice Historique*, p. 11.
60 Yusuf al-Dibs, *Kitab Ta'rikh Suriyya* (Beirut: Imprimerie Catholique, 1893), Vol. 1, p. 4.
61 *Ibid*, pp. 255-365.
62 See Samawil Bulus, *The Maronite Patriarch Elias Butrus al-Howayyek and the Establishment of Greater Lebanon* (Hebrew). (MA Thesis, Haifa University, 1987), pp. 16-22.
63 These communiqués were made possible through the introduction of mass print, which only strengthened the sense of a (imagined) community among the Maronites. See Anderson, *Imagined Communities,* pp. 37-46. In 1931, the communiqués were compiled into a book, *Al-Dhakha'ir al-Saniyya* [The Splendid

Treasures] (Junieh: Matba'at al-Mursalin al-Lubnaniyin), by Filib al-Samrani, in honor of the Patriarch's 32nd year in office.
64   *Al-Dhakha'ir al-Saniyya*, p. 587.
65   See, for example, his sermon on the occasion of the end of the War. He thanks the two factors that brought about the successful end: the Europeans, mainly the French, and "our ancestors," the first Maronites. *Ibid*, pp. 487-509.
66   Carol Hakim-Dowek, *The Origins of the Lebanese National Idea*, p. 270. The socio-political changes in 19th-century Lebanon were the subject of several works, most notably William R. Polk, *The Opening of South Lebanon, 1788-1840* (Cambridge: Harvard University Press, 1963); Iliya Harik, *Politics and Change in a Traditional Society Lebanon, 1711-1845* (Princeton: Princeton University Press, 1968); Samir Khalaf, *Persistence and Change in 19th Century Lebanon: A Sociological Essay* (Beirut: American University of Beirut, 1979).
67   See: Kamal Salibi, *Maronite Historians of Medieval Lebanon* (Beirut: AUB, 1959), pp. 161-233; Hourani, *Arabic Thought*, p. 58, pp. 97-98. Harik, *Politics and Change*, pp. 145-147.
68   Al-Shidyaq, the scholar, was by no means oblivious to the biggest archeological discovery in Lebanon of his time. In 1856, a year before he began writing his book, the great sarcophagus of Eshmon'ezer, the Sidonite king of the 5th century BC, was discovered and generated waves of excitement among Western savants. See: James B. Pritchard, *Archaeology and the Old Testament* (Princeton: Princeton University Press, 1958), p. 95.
69   Fruma Schreier-Zachs, *From Communal to Territorial Identity: the Emergence of the 'Syrian Concept' 1831-1881* (Hebrew), Ph.D. Dissertation, Haifa University, September 1997, p. 130.
70   *Ibid*, pp. 140-147.
71   See, for example, the entries: "Adunis," Vol. 3, pp. 713-714; "Ba'al," Vol. 5, pp. 493-496; "B'albak," Vol. 5, pp. 496-501.
72   Schreier-Zachs, *From Communal to Territorial Identity*, pp. 142-143.
73   Donald J. Cioeta, "Ottoman Censorship in Lebanon and Syria, 1876-1908," *IJMES*, Vol. 10 (May 1979), pp. 167-181.
74   Ami Ayalon, *The Press in the Arab Middle East* (Oxford: Oxford University Press, 1995), p. 53.
75   "The Phoenicians and their Religions," *Al-Muqtataf*, 7 (1882), p. 602, p. 749; "The Expansion of Phoenician History" 8 (1883), p. 245; "An Important Discovery in Phoenicia," 9 (1883), p. 35; see also in 12 (October 1887), pp. 321-328."The Phoenicians and their Glorious Deeds," 12 (1888), p. 321.
76   See for example *Al-Muqtataf*, 8 (August 1883), p. 245.
77   *Al-Muqtataf*, 14 (October 1889), p. 729.
78   Thomas Philipp, *Gurgi Zaidan; His Life and Thought* (Beirut: Franz Steiner, 1979), pp. 22-23.
79   *Al-Muqtataf*, 12 (October, 1887), p. 578.
80   For more information, see L. M. Kenny, "East Versus West in Al-Muqtataf, 1875-1900," in Donald P. Little (ed.), *Essays on Islamic Civilization* (Leiden: E.J. Brill, 1976), pp. 140-154.
81   *Al-Hilal*, 1 (1892-1893), pp. 219-222.
82   *Ibid*, pp. 359.
83   *Al-Hilal*, 2 (1893-1894), pp. 354-357.

84 *Al-Hilal*, 17 (1909), pp. 425-429.
85 Engin Akarli, *The Long Peace; Ottoman Lebanon 1861-1920* (Berkeley: University of California Press, 1993).
86 Tarif Khalidi, "Shaykh Ahmad 'Arif al-Zayn and *al-'Irfan*," in Kemal Karpat, *Political and Social Thought in the Contemporary Middle East*, Revised Edition (New York: Praeger, 1982), pp. 110-123.
87 Ahmad 'Arif al-Zein, *Tarikh Sayda* (Sidon: Matba'at al-'Irfan, 1913).
88 This point is especially interesting in light of the vehement attacks of Louis Cheikho, the editor of the Jesuit journal *al-Mashriq*, against *al-Hilal* and *al-Muqtataf*, because of their Protestant background and their affiliation with the Freemasons. See: Robert Bell Campbell, *The Arabic Journal, Al-Mashriq: Its Beginning and First Twenty-Five Years under the Editorship of Père Louis Cheikho, S.J.* Ph.D. Dissertation, The University of Michigan, 1972. pp. 2-3; pp. 165-169.
89 Jean Fontaine, *La Crise Religieuse des Écrivains Syro-Libanais Chrétiens de 1825 à1940* (Tunis: IBLA, 1996).
90 Biographical notes about Nujaym are taken from the introduction to the second edition of his book: M. Jouplain [Bulus Nujaym], *La Question du Liban; Étude d'Histoire Diplomatique et de Droit International* (Paris: A. Rousseau, 1908). See also Marwan Buheiry, "Bulus Nujaym and the Grand Liban idea 1908-1919," in L.I. Conrad (ed.), *The Formation and Perception of the Modern Arab World. Studies by Marwan Buheiry* (New Jersey: Darwin Press, 1988), pp. 575-595.
91 Hakim-Dowek, *The Origins of the Lebanese National Idea*, pp. 297-301.
92 Nujaym, *La Question du Liban*, p. 1.
93 On Reclus, see the Introduction.
94 *Ibid*, p. 7
95 *Ibid*, pp. 12-34.
96 *Ibid*, p. 35.
97 For example: Ferdinand Tyan, *Sous les Cèdres du Liban, la Nationalité Maronite* (Montligeon, 1905). Unlike Nujaym, the reason behind Tyan's appeal for an establishment of an independent political entity in the Mountain was strictly religious. In the Middle East, he asserted, nations are formed around their faith. Therefore, the Maronite nation is entitled to have its own political entity. Following this theme, Tyan did not exceed beyond Christianity in his historical narrative.

2

Before and After the War

At the foot of these majestic mountains, which have been the strength of your country and remain the impregnable stronghold of its faith and freedom; on the shore of this sea of many legends that has seen the triremes of Phoenicia, Greece and Rome, that, in subtle spirit, carried through the world your fathers, skilled in commerce and eloquence. Now, by a happy return, this sea brings you the confirmation of a great and ancient friendship and the blessings of French peace. In front of all these witnesses of your wishes, of your struggles and of your victory, it is in sharing your joy and pride that I solemnly salute Greater Lebanon in its glory and its force from *Nahr al-Kébir* to the gates of Palestine and to the crest of the Anti-Lebanon mountains

General Henri Gouraud's proclamation of Greater Lebanon, September 1, 1920

By the early 1910s many voices in the Middle East were calling for transformation of the political system shaped by the Ottoman Empire. Syrianism, Arabism, Ottomanism, Islamic revivalism and Lebanism (in Mount Lebanon and the coast) were all competing to put their mark on the political and cultural fate of the region. Inspired by the Young Turk revolution and its aftermath which unleashed unprecedented desire for change in the Arab Middle East, between 1908-1914, some twenty associations were established advocating reform. Paris, Cairo, Alexandria and immigrant communities in the New World, out of Ottoman reach, became the hubs of this political activity. The difference between the various political streams, however, was not at all evident. Notions of Arabism were often intertwined with Syrian consciousness, and vice versa. Most Lebanese, who after April 1919 were calling for the establishment of an independent Greater Lebanon, still saw Lebanon as part of a larger Syrian framework, even if only as an autonomous enlarged region. Advocates of a clear Syrian non-Arab identity were, in 1913, still participating in Arab associations. Islamic revivalists were often associating the attainment of their objectives with Arab and Syrian notions of identity. Last but not least, Ottomanism, albeit in demise, was still considered a viable option for the majority of the Syro-Lebanese.

The 1908 revolution in Istanbul, then, provoked much turmoil in the political structure of Mount Lebanon. The Western-educated stratum that emerged in Mount Lebanon and Beirut from the end of the 19th century sought to use the momentum of the liberal winds blowing from Turkey to transform the socio-political system in the Mountain. Pro-Ottoman tendencies became prevalent among many members of this new group. Some were hoping to be elected to the Ottoman parliament as delegates from the Mountain; others even supported full attachment to the Young Turk movement. Lebanese pro-Ottoman associations were formed in Paris and in Egypt.[1] The common denominator of this activity was the desire to transform the old, worn out, stagnant political situation in the Mountain and join the new spirits of progressiveness blowing from Istanbul.

A counter-reaction to this activity was quick to surface. The Maronite Church and the old notables did not wish to change the existing system and relinquish the special status of the Mountain. And once the centralizing attempts of the Young Turks were revealed, secular, liberal Lebanese joined forces with the Church. Now the opposition was not only unwilling to abandon the privileges of the autonomous region of the Mountain, but also aspired to expand them, especially in light of the centralizing attempts of Istanbul. Thus, following the 1908 events and the successive hopes, disillusionments and reassessments, the first Lebanist associations were formed. They did not share an identical platform, but they all supported the existence of a somewhat independent political framework in Lebanon, either as an autonomous region of the Mountain or as part of a greater Syrian political setting. They also called for a re-examination of the Organic Law (*Règlement organique*) of 1861, adapting it to the needs of the time. These associations did not yet have a clear national agenda. Yet, the fact of their formation bore witness to the rebirth of the Lebanist idea: the conception of an extended Lebanese political framework embracing the various communities residing in the Mountain, the coast, the Biqaʻ in the east and Jabal ʻAmil in the south, into one political community.

Once the Lebanist idea came back to the fore, there was a need to support it with historical justification. If there should be a Lebanese entity, then there should also be a historical reason for its existence. Philippe and Farid al-Khazin, two important Lebanese journalists, published in 1910 a manifesto, "Perpétuelle indépendance législative et judiciaire du Liban depuis la conquête ottomane en 1516,"[2] in which they emphasized the continuous existence of an independent Greater Lebanese political entity and demonstrated its viability since the days of Fakhr al-Din al-Ma'ni in the 16th century. There is no reference in this famous pamphlet to any Phoenician past of Lebanon. Clearly, knowledge about ancient Phoenicia was available, but the authors chose not to use it. Rather, they limited the historical horizon of Lebanon to the 16th century. The reference to Fakhr al-Din as the founding father of modern Lebanon became one of the foundation myths in Lebanon. It reflected the laical worldview from which the two Maronite brothers were writing: Fakhr al-Din was a Druze, but still a founder of modern Lebanon.[3]

Philippe and Farid al-Khazin belonged to the new liberal Western-educated stratum that emerged in Beirut and in Mount Lebanon towards the end of the 19th century. Some of their peers were already speaking about the Phoenician past of Lebanon. In 1910, as we have seen, Phoenician expressions were not yet uttered in any political context (meaning Phoenicianism as an expression of national aspirations of one kind or another). It is possible that this was the reason the Khazins did not use the Phoenician past in their pamphlet. Considering their socio-political background, there are many reasons to believe that, had they not been executed by the Ottomans in 1916,[4] they would have become pillars of the new Lebanese state and most likely, as their peers did, would have supported, if not advocated, the Phoenician narration of Lebanon.

While the Khazin brothers published their pamphlet, other Lebanese were active in similar initiatives. However, as a result of the Young Turks' coercive measures the center of the political activity moved out of Mount Lebanon into Paris, Cairo, Alexandria and other Syro-Lebanese emigrant communities in the Americas. There, the Ottomans could not curtail separatist political activity. These communities were not only struggling to define their identity in the context of their countries of origin, but also vis-à-vis the societies to which they had immigrated and in which they lived. Only by the end of WWI did the center of the political activity return to Beirut. By that time the Ottoman Empire was out of the equation and a new world order was emerging.

The Syro-Lebanese Community in Egypt

Syrian emigrants began arriving in Egypt by the end of the 18th century. They sought refuge from the Ottoman system and found it in the Nile Valley under the relative independent regime of the Mamluk Beys.[5] By the mid-19th century a steady stream replaced the small trickle of Syrian émigrés. The reign of Muhammad 'Ali in Egypt opened the country to Europe and, particularly, to the European economic system. A desperate need emerged for skilled professionals to administer the burgeoning Egyptian economy. The Egyptians themselves, lagging behind in their level of education, could not meet this need. Syria, however, had begun producing more and more graduates of European missionary schools who were exposed to Western thought and knew foreign languages. This new educated stratum was looking for sources of livelihood, which it could not find in Syria, but found in abundance in Egypt. Cairo and Alexandria attracted thousands of Syrians, Christians mostly, who found these cities to be safe asylums and islands of stability in a precarious region. Muhammad 'Ali and his heirs knew how to use the Syrians and their skills. Modernization, becoming the mark of the Khedive family, necessitated cadres of administrators, technicians and clerks, positions the Syrians filled with joy. The fact that they mastered Arabic and at least one or two foreign languages gave the Syrians an advantage in the local market. The ambitious plans of the Khedive Isma'il to make Egypt a part of Europe opened up ample options for the educated, and the Syrians took full advantage of these opportunities. The following testimony of the time well illustrates this:

> In certain offices which have been remodeled according to foreign ideas, or in which technical knowledge is required, there is a sprinkling of foreigners; and standing half way, as it were between the Europeans and the Egyptians, are a number of Syrian Christians, who have been educated in the French schools of their native province, and who have come to make their fortune in a country not yet overstocked with a men of their own type. The young Syrian is becoming, indeed, a common and rather conspicuous typical figure in this section of Cairo society.[6]

The landing of Napoleon's *Armée d'Orient* in Alexandria in July 1798 was a watershed event for the entire Middle East. Napoleon, just like the French expedition sixty-two years later in Lebanon, had in tow a group of scholars (the *savants d'Egypte*) who launched a scientific survey of Egypt.[7] One of the most important subjects they explored was the pharaonic past of the country. The French scholars mapped the country (as they would do in Lebanon in 1861) and conducted archeological excavations, which led, among other things, to the discovery of the Rosetta Stone that would later help decipher the Egyptian hieroglyphs. French Egyptomania was underway.

Paradoxically, the Egyptian exposure to France was only strengthened with the departure of Napoleon's army in 1801. Muhammad 'Ali used many Frenchmen in his ambitious plans to develop Egypt into a modern state. His heirs followed suit and were helped by French specialists in their projects. Cairo, and more so Alexandria, evolved to become cities imbued with strong European influence. The latter developed as a typical Mediterranean cosmopolitan city, home to many Levantine communities. For the Alexandrians, "whether they were great merchants or middling shopkeepers or humble artisans, whether Greek or Italian or French or Syrian or Maltese in origin, Egypt was a land of opportunity and Alexandria a new home."[8]

The city accommodated a Levantine society with a unique culture, in many aspects shared by other Mediterranean cities such as Smyrna, Salonika, and later Beirut. Although in each the socio-political backgrounds of the communities and their class divisions differed, many cultural realms were shared. It was a world where at least three languages were spoken, commercial ties were drawn and strong geographical mobility was prevalent. It was not uncommon to see families with branches around the Mediterranean basin: one brother in Alexandria, another in Beirut and a third in Smyrna.

By the turn of the century, Alexandria and Cairo were hubs of a vibrant Syrian community. Three factors shaped the political proclivities of the Syro-Lebanese residing in Egypt: the cosmopolitan lifestyle (in Alexandria in particular), the rising Egyptian national movement, and the socio-political vicissitudes in Syria and Lebanon. The Syro-Lebanese knew how to use the Mediterranean basin and the Ottoman system to their own advantage. The mobility the Ottoman Empire provided between the different Mediterranean cities enabled them to conduct commerce with much success. The city of Alexandria, as a commercial center located on an important trade route, provided access to markets both in the east and the west. In a way, Alexandria, even after the British occupation in 1882, was a world with no borders. The city was part of one large financial system in which the Syrians excelled, not so much because commerce was imprinted in their blood, as they often seemed to believe, but because of several cultural and political configurations. To begin with, they were better educated than the average Egyptian. Second, they spoke French and often another foreign language as well, possibly English or Italian. These qualities were also shared by the European communities in the Levantine cities. The Syrians, however, also knew Arabic and were part of a larger Arabic-speaking world. This fact gave them an edge over the other foreign communities and opened many more horizons in their financial transactions. This border-less world treated them well, and many Syrians who lived in Alexandria wished to preserve it.[9] Lord Cromer, the British High Commissioner in Egypt, described this situation well:

> When the demand for employés was felt, the supply of Europeanized Egyptians was insufficient, and further, the Europeanized Egyptian was often a less useful agent than his social and political kinsman, the Syrian. The Syrian's opportunity, therefore, came, and he profited from it. He possessed all the qualifications required. Arabic was his mother tongue. He was generally familiar with French, having been educated at some French college in Syria. He was versatile, pushing, and ambitious. [...] He possessed in no small degree the talent, which was particularly useful in a cosmopolitan society, of being all things to all men.[10]

Local socio-political developments were also crucial in shaping the political agenda of the Syro-Lebanese in Egypt. Long years of exposure to the West bore fruit; a new stratum of educated Egyptians was formed that challenged Syrian dominance in Egyptian administration. The use of national claims became more and more frequent as a justification for the demand to overthrow the Syrians from their positions and statures. Of the foreign communities in Egypt, the Syrians were the first to be attacked by the rising Egyptian nationalism.[11] The British occupation in 1882 diverted the anti-Syrian tendencies in the Egyptian national movement, and the Syrians became even more powerful under the British than they had been in the days of the Khedive Isma'il. This, however, was only temporary. The rising Egyptian intelligentsia aspired to have control in exactly the fields in which the Syrians were dominant: journalism and public administration. To demonstrate the frustration of the Egyptians against the Syrians, I shall again use the words of Lord Cromer:

> For the more intelligent Moslem, when he gradually woke up to what was going around him, said to himself: The Englishman I understand; I recognize his good qualities; he brings to bear on his work, not only knowledge, but energy superior to my own; I do not like him but I understand that he means well by me, and I see that he confers certain material benefits on me, which I am very willing to accept; but what of the Syrian? Am I not as good as he? If native agents be required, why should not my kinsman be employed rather than this alien, who possesses neither the advantages of the European nor those of the Egyptian.[12]

By 1908, the year of the Young Turk revolution, there was little doubt that the Syrians had no place in the rising Egyptian national movement. Integration into the state was no longer an option. When new Syrian émigrés arrived in Egypt from 1908 onward, their center of attention remained in their country of origin.

Syrian emigrants have always remained in very close contact with their communities at home. Those in Egypt retained even stronger attachments because of the geographical proximity of the two countries. Only a two-day sail separated Alexandria and Beirut and even less time was required for a train ride, once this option was available. When WWI broke out, Egypt became the major location of refuge for many Syro-Lebanese who escaped the oppressive measures of the Ottoman government. Alexandria, over Cairo, was the preferred place of sanctuary perhaps because of the similarities between this city and Beirut. Hundreds of Lebanese found refuge in Egypt during the war, including numerous personalities who would play a crucial role in the formation of modern Lebanon: Emile Eddé, Béchara al-Khoury, Michel Chiha, Jacques Tabet, Gabriel Trad, Choucri Cardahi, Béchara Tabbah, Gabriel

Yared, Daoud 'Amoun and others.[13] The local Syro-Lebanese community embraced them with warmth. Many of the newcomers even had branches of their own families who had resided in Egypt for a generation or two — the 'Amouns, the Naccaches, the Tabets, the Klats, the Trads, the Sursuks, the Doumanis. These families belonged to a strong, bourgeois urban class in Beirut as much as in Alexandria and Cairo. They were engaged mainly in commerce and they further augmented their ties through financial interests and intermarriages that crossed sectarian lines.[14] By no means were they exclusively Maronites. Greek Orthodox, Greek Catholic, Protestants, Maronites and Urban Sunnis cooperated in this world that revolved around commerce. Intermarriage, however, existed only between the Christian communities. As of 1920, this class would become the backbone of the Lebanese state. In fact, it could be said that they were the *raison d'être* for the formation of Greater Lebanon. Lebanon as a "Republic of Merchants" was shaped in their image.

The Syro-Lebanese community in Egypt was tied to the political developments in Lebanon. The numerous societies formed in Egypt by members of this community between 1908-1919 reflected their deep involvement in the political process in Syria and Lebanon in those years. One of the first and most important of these societies was the *Alliance libanaise*. Its Cairo branch was established in February 1909, followed by the Alexandria branch a year later.[15] The *Alliance* expressed steadfast support for the re-evaluation of the *Règlement organique* and, towards the end of the war, for the formation of Greater Lebanon as an independent state. The Alexandria branch became largely identified with its secretary, Yusuf al-Saouda, one of the most prolific and vocal Lebanese advocating for the "Phoenician idea" in Lebanon well into the 1970s.

Al-Saouda was born in 1891 in the village of Bikfaya. He acquired his primary education at the Maronite *École de la sagesse* (*Madrasat al-hikma*). From 1900-1907 he studied at USJ. He then moved to Alexandria to study law at the *Faculté français de droit*, after which he worked at the mixed judicial courts (*Tribunaux mixtes*) for foreigners and locals, a position he could hold thanks to his bilingual skills. His family was not part of the Beirut bourgeoisie and his social milieu was always associated more with the Mountain than the city. He knew French,[16] but preferred to write his books in Arabic, marking him conspicuously as an *Arabic* writer in a generation of francophone Lebanese nationalists.

Having studied at the Oriental Faculty under teachers such as Henri Lammens, Antun Salhani, Gabriel Levenq and others, he must have been well informed of the pre-Islamic past of Lebanon.[17] In early 1919, when the peace conference was underway in Paris, he published *Fi Sabil Lubnan* (For the Sake of Lebanon). In writing this book, al-Saouda's aim, as he himself testified many years later, was to chronicle the 5,000-year history of a Lebanon portrayed as "the lighthouse of civilization and a fortress of freedom."[18]

The book is divided into three parts: the history of Lebanon from the Phoenician city-states until 1860; the status of Lebanon in international law; and Lebanon after the *Règlement organique* of 1861.[19] The first chapter begins with the following statement:

> Every nation has a strong desire to return to its roots by drawing from the well of its past to its present the glory of its pedigree. Italy is proud to be the heir of mighty Rome with its triumph, its glory and its banner. The Greeks glorify in their lineage to the important dynasty of personalities of the Iliad with its poets and philosophers. The civilized world thanks Italy and Greece and respects their descendants and the greatness of their forefathers. [...] The same as a nation is proud of its roots and draws its good virtues from its good progeny, so is Lebanon proud to remember and remind all that it is the cradle of civilization in the world. It was born on the slopes of its mountain and ripened on its shores, and from there, the Phoenicians carried it to the four corners of the earth. Just as Europe must be committed to Italy and Greece, it also has to be committed to a land that is the teacher of Rome and the mother of Greece.[20]

Al-Saouda was a prolific writer, although too often quantity interested him over quality. He left us, therefore, several books, all advocating a separatist, Lebanese, non-Arab (if not anti-Arab) identity. Prolific as he was, there were many other Lebanese who wrote in a similar vein in Egypt between 1917-1920. One of these was Auguste Adib Pasha. Born in 1859 in Deir al-Qamar to a Maronite family, he studied with the Jesuits, first at the Oriental Seminar in Ghazir and then in 1875 at the newly founded USJ. In 1885 he moved to Egypt where he soon integrated into the state administration. He spent thirty-five years in Egypt before returning to Lebanon in 1920.[21] The positions he occupied upon his return attest to his high status in his homeland: in September 1920 he was appointed Lebanon's first director of finances; the following May he became the first general secretary of Greater Lebanon; and in May 1926 he had the honor of being the first prime minister of the Lebanese Republic.[22]

In his book, *Le Liban après la Guerre*, Adib Pasha wrote about his solution to the Lebanese problem after the war. Following the official stand of the *Alliance libanaise,* of which he had been president since 1918, he was in favor of the establishment of a Greater Lebanese state with the assistance of the European powers.[23] Like all books at the time, his work provides a historical précis as a foundation to the political demands that follow. The ancient Phoenicians occupy a large portion of this chapter with a clear message that modern Lebanese are actually descendants of the ancient Phoenicians and, therefore, are not part of the larger Arab world.[24] In July 1919, Auguste

Adib Pasha published an article in Charles Corm's *La Revue Phénicienne* entitled, *"Aperçu historique sur le Liban depuis les origines jusqu'au début de la grande guerre,"* declaring it was "à l'usage des jeunes Libanais qui feront la Patrie de Demain."[25] Beginning with the ancient Phoenicians he explained what had made the Lebanese race so unique. First were the Phoenicians, thereafter other nations came and went, and thus a mélange of races was created in Lebanon. "[...] c'est de cet amalgame de races," Adib Pasha concluded," où prédomine le sang phénicien, qui sont sortis les habitants actuels du Mont Liban et du littoral qui l'avoisine."[26]

The significance of Adib Pasha to this study lies not so much in the quality of the Phoenician expressions he uttered, but in the generation he represents. Having been born in 1859, he was part and parcel of the Ottoman system. He studied under the Jesuits even before USJ had been founded. He was much older than Charles Corm and his peers, to whom I shall refer in greater detail later. Corm's generation was born in the last decade of the 19th century and underwent the "Jesuit experience" in the Oriental Faculty in the first decade of the 20th, under the supervision of Lammens, Cheikho, Jalabert and others. Adib Pasha belonged to an older generation for whom the Ottoman world was part of reality. It is clear that his exposure to Phoenician-Lebanist ideas were entirely an outcome of life and experience in Egypt. Living for so many years in the Nile Valley, he must have been exposed to and influenced by the burgeoning Egyptian national movement that had put its emphasis on separatist Egyptian-Pharaonic characteristics. Upon his return to Lebanon he did not join the "Phoenician circles," most likely because of the generation gap. He was an administrator in Egypt and remained so in Lebanon. He nevertheless adopted the Phoenician plot, seeing Lebanon and the Lebanese as direct descendants of the Phoenician seafarers.[27]

Yusuf al-Saouda and Auguste Adib Pasha were part of the emigrant community that had resided in Egypt before WWI. One member of this community, actually born in Alexandria, was Hector Klat, one of the most prolific francophone Phoenician poets right up until his death in 1973. The Greek Orthodox Klat family hailed from Tripoli and had branches in Alexandria and Cairo. Hector was born in 1888 and spent all his school years in French missionary educational establishments in the city, *Collège Ste Catherine* and *Collège des Frères des écoles chrétiens*.[28] Klat reflects even more than al-Saouda and Adib Pasha the importance of the atmosphere in Alexandria on the political and cultural trends of the Syro-Lebanese community in Egypt. Born and raised in Alexandria, Lebanon was not part of his day-to-day reality, except in the context of nostalgia and family anecdotes. The schools he attended instructed him in French history, religious practices, civil studies and, of course, language.[29] By the time he graduated from college, he was completely immersed into French culture. He visited Europe twice before the war, in 1909 and 1912, to pursue his art education.[30] His family, coming from

Tripoli, the Sunni-dominated city, was not even part of the Mountain experience. Yet he evolved to be a firm supporter of the Phoenician narrative and of the Lebanist idea.

Klat began writing poetry at a fairly young age and published his works in local Egyptian literary magazines. In 1910, he published "*Mots français*," one of the first poems that carried his reputation all the way to Beirut. Klat testified that when Maurice Barrès landed in Alexandria in 1914, the French ambassador asked him to read this poem before the distinguished French intellectual. Later, when Barrès arrived in Beirut he mentioned, in passing, a certain Syrian poet who recited to him a poem about the love of France.[31] Because of the length of the poem I will quote here only the first verse, which sufficiently illustrates Klat's cultural world.

Mots français, mots du clair parler de douce France;
Mots que je n'appris tard que pour vous aimer mieux
Tels des amis choisis au sortir de l'enfance;
Mots qui m'êtes entrés jusqu'au cœur par les yeux,
Ceux du berceau m'ayant conquis par les oreilles;
Mots qui m'avez du monde enseigné les merveilles;
Mots sur qui j'ai pâli; mots par qui j'ai pleuré,
Soit que l'on me grondât, petit, de vous mal lire,
Soit que l'on m'applaudît, plus tard, de vous mieux dire;
Mots par qui j'ai connu le vertige enivré
De vous goûter, savants, poètes, philosophes
Et d'apprendre, dans vos systèmes ou vos strophes,
La force de la prose ou la grâce des vers;
Mots qui, par vos vertus fécondant mes études,
Avez ouvert mes yeux cillés sur l'univers,
Mot français, tous les mots, les doux, les forts, les rudes,
Les mièvres, je vous aime, Ô Mots avec ferveur.[32]

Hector Klat gave a very warm account of his Alexandria experience in his memoirs. He described the city's Lebanese community and its vibrant cultural activities. He depicted at length the arrival of the Lebanese political refugees who escaped troubled Lebanon at the beginning of WWI and found shelter in Alexandria. The image derived from his and al-Saouda's descriptions is that of a close circle of Lebanese, living side by side through the war years, crystallizing their ideas concerning Lebanon's cultural and political future.[33] Shortly after al-Saouda's *Fi Sabil Lubnan* was released, Hector Klat, Béchara al-Khoury and Michel Chiha decided to translate it to French. By the time Klat finished the translation of the first chapter, Chiha and al-Khoury had returned to Lebanon. Later, according to al-Saouda, al-Khoury, back in Lebanon, asked Charles Corm to translate the rest of the book.[34] Poetry writing and exchanges of dedications also characterized the literary cooperation of this group in Alexandria. Michel Chiha, then twenty-four years old, wrote the following poem in Alexandria and dedicated it to Klat. I present it here in its entirety as it provides an excellent illustration of the writer's cultural references. The architect of the Lebanese confessional system and the driving and financial force behind Béchara al-Khoury, with whom he had close familial ties, Chiha's role in the fate of Lebanon throughout the 20th century cannot be exaggerated.

> Toi que la Muse latine
> Qui Lutine,
> Tous les fols, fous de rimer,
> Sut aimes;
>
> Fils de la côte fleurie,
> Ma patrie,
> Jadis royaume des Francs
> Conquérants;
>
> Toi qui fais de la musique
> Symphonique,
> En sertissant les beaux mots,
> Ces émaux;
>
> Ivre du parler de France
> Dès l'enfance,
> Et de son rythme obsesseur
> Et berceur,
>
> J'aime ta voix sérieuse
> Ou rieuse,
> Voix d'un pâtre de vingt ans
> Au printemps.
> Lorsque ta lyre résonne,
> Je frissonne.
> Mes yeux revoient, éblouis,
> Mon pays,
>
> Elle évoque, douce et fière,
> Notre terre,
> Le parfum oriental,
> L'air natal.

La cité de la "lointaine"
Souveraine,
Mélissinde, que Rostand
Aima tant;

Béryte, cette amoureuse
Langoureus,
Fraîche du baiser amer
De la mer;

Héroïnes d'épopées,
Éclopées,
Tyr, la ville de Didon
Et Sidon:

Paysage noble et triste
Où persiste
L'ombre immense d'un passé
Effacé ...

Et les vieux Cèdres sublimes
Et les cimes
- Roches roses au front blanc-
Du Liban.

C'est la divine allégresse
De la Grèce,
Le ciel le plus bleu, l'azur
Le plus pur
Et c'est la brune Italie
Si jolie,
La Sicile et ses vergers
D'orangers;

C'est surtout ce coin de France
La Provence
Où croît, près du clair vivier,
L'olivier.

Car le laboureur agile
De virgile
Et le sillon ancestral
De Mistral,

L'Hellade de Théocrite
Qui s'agite
A l'appel mélodieux
De ses dieux:

Tout se trouve en ma patrie
Si chérie ...
-Aussi passionnément
Son amant,

Tu vas à l'heure héroïque.
Gesteé pique,
Ceindre le front des guerriers
de laurels.

A very strong affection towards Latin culture and Mediterranean societies, especially France, surfaces in the poem.[35] Tripoli, on the northern part of the Syrian coast, is mentioned in the play of Edmond Rostand, *La Princesse Lointaine*,[36] Beirut is ancient Béryte, the Phoenician port city, and Tyre is referred to through Dido[n], the legendary Tyrian princess who founded the Phoenician colony of Carthage. The sea, the cedars, the blue skies, the oriental perfume all blend into a remarkably romantic image of Lebanon.

Michel Chiha and Hector Klat cooperated in Alexandria on the publication of a short-lived literary magazine, *Ebauches*.[37] Klat claimed that he was the editor in chief and Chiha remained behind the scenes. The friendship between the two was clearly warm, according to accounts by both.[38] In the 1930s the political map of Lebanon was harshly divided between the camps of Béchara al-Khoury and Emile Eddé. Chiha was squarely in the al-Khoury camp and Klat, upon his final return to Beirut in 1932, became identified with Eddé. Thus, WWI saw strong ties being built between individuals who were now becoming political rivals. And yet Chiha, for example, as we shall see, never abandoned the literary activity led by Klat and Charles Corm, even though politically the two were associated with Eddé.

Chiha's significance in the dissemination of the Phoenician myth of origin in Lebanon is far beyond what scholars have attributed to him. I shall return to this point in Chapter IV. For now, it is sufficient to say that Chiha, as *the* architect of the Lebanese confessional system and one of the few political philosophers Lebanon has produced, had enormous power in the Lebanese political arena. His Phoenician-Mediterranean beliefs were far more significant to the spread of the idea than those of Klat, al-Saouda or even Corm, whose impact on the shape of Lebanese society was minimal.

Returning to Alexandria, among the many Lebanese who found refuge in the city during the war was Jacques Tabet (1885-1956), himself a strong advocate of the Phoenician identity in Lebanon. The Maronite Tabet family was one of the richest in Beirut, gaining its wealth primarily from real estate deals. As with many other Lebanese families, a number of Tabet relatives lived in Alexandria and Cairo. Jacques Tabet arrived in Alexandria at the outset of WWI, escaping troubled Beirut. In 1915 he wrote a book, *La Syrie*,[39] urging the creation of a Syrian federation wherein Lebanon would hold a leading role. This Syrian federation, he proposed, would be comprised of one nation — the Syrian nation — which draws its origins from the ancient Phoenician seafarers. Like Bulus Nujaym, he based his assertion on the theory that history is a result of geographic circumstances and that politics derived from geography are the kind that determine destinies. In his own words:

> La Syrie est syrienne et phénicienne comme son histoire et sa nature géographique l'indiquent, elle aspire désormais à redevenir elle-même et vivre de sa vie indépendante et personnelle.[40]

Both Jacques Tabet and Bulus Nujaym drew their references largely from Lammens' works on Syrian, Phoenician, non-Arab identity. In fact, Tabet's book almost repeats word-for-word Lammens' ideas about Syrian nationalism. Through the examination of history, ethnography, religion, language, geography and economy, Tabet elaborated on the uniqueness of the Syrian-Phoenician nation, which is utterly different from the Arab race. For example, outlining the different faiths which have been practiced in Syria he naturally began with the Phoenician religion. Indeed it was a pagan religion, but it was a tolerant one, he contended. Tabet even offered a correlation between the Phoenician paganism and the monotheist religions that followed.[41]

Like many other Lebanese, Tabet also attempted to come to grips with the issue of whether language is an essential, or inessential, ingredient in national consciousness. Phoenician for him was clearly the "national language" of the ancient Syrians, although they did speak many other languages throughout history. He expressed regret that this language was not revived, but he insisted that it did not diminish the validity of Syrian nationalism. The Arabic spoken in Syria since the Arab occupation evolved to be a Syrian dialect different from other Arabic dialects.[42] Arabic language, therefore, was not a factor in determining the national identity of Syria. "It is the character of the people, a natural product of the country, that had an influence on the language, and not the language on the character of the people."[43] In other words, language is not a factor in shaping collective identities. It is only the natural setting of the land that serves as a cast from which the nation is shaped. In the concluding notes of the book, Tabet located the reconstruction of ancient Phoenicia in a broader historical picture:

> Il est un moment où les peuples sortent de la longue léthargie où les plongent d'épuisants efforts, et réclament leur héritage tombé entre les

mains des nations. L'Italie rêve aujourd'hui de reconstituer l'Empire Romain; Athènes et les Etats Macédoniens se disputent le sceptre d'Alexandre; la chute de l'Empire Turc va redonner le jour [...] aux royaumes d'Alyatte, de Cyrus et des Pharaons. Le pays de Cadmus et de Hiram a sa place toute indiquée dans ce concert oriental, et c'est naturellement à la France, la plus généreuse de toutes les nations [...] qui revient la tâche d'aider à sa résurrection. La reconstitution de la Phénicie sur des bases larges et solides s'impose donc pour le présent comme pour l'avenir; elle est une nécessité géographique et politique, une arme très précieuse dont la France ne saurait méconnaître la valeur, en même temps qu'un gage d'équilibre et de paix pour le monde occidental et oriental.[44]

Tabet raises some intriguing observations. His social background corresponded well with his "Phoenician peers." Born in 1885 to a wealthy Maronite family in Beirut, he was part of the bourgeoisie that emerged in the city from the second half of the 19th century. Naturally, he studied at the Jesuit University under the supervision of Henri Lammens, who left a lasting impact on him.[45] When the war broke out, he fled to Alexandria where he met his future wife, Anna Karameh. Her familial biography can serve, in and of itself, as a reflection of the Levantine world in which she and her family lived. She belonged to a branch of the Maronite Karameh family that emigrated to Alexandria in the last third of the 19th century. Her mother was a member of the flourishing Greek community that dominated the city.[46] Jacques and Anna Tabet were a very wealthy couple. Alexandria, Beirut and Paris were their cultural circles. Reading through the archives of the French Mandate in Syria and Lebanon and the French Ministry of Foreign Affairs, Jacques Tabet's name surfaces time and again. He often visited Paris, wrote articles for French journals and was invited to parties and receptions given by French officials.[47] He frequently wrote to French officials expressing his views, and they in turn approached him for his opinions. Shortly after his return to Beirut he launched a project for the construction of the Lebanese National Museum.[48] Through this initiative he became one of the most important persons in the dissemination of the Phoenician past in Lebanon. Like many other Lebanese, after the formation of Greater Lebanon he abandoned his Syrian tendencies.

In Alexandria and Cairo there were many more Syro-Lebanese who, like Tabet, were advocating the formation of a greater Syrian, non-Arab, state. The *Comité central syrien* of Chékri Ganem (Ghanim) and Georges Samné had branches in Egypt named *Le comité libano-syrien*,[49] which enjoyed financial and other support from French officials. The Maronite vicar in Egypt, Monsignor Darian, was one of the founders and an active member of the *Comité*. Later analyses have tended to attribute Greater Lebanese tendencies to the Maronite Church, yet Monsignor Darian, the highest Maronite official in Egypt, was active in societies that supported the Greater Syria option and at the same time wrote about the Phoenician origin of the Maronites.[50] This is especially interesting because, as a Maronite clergyman, Darian stands out by the fact that he explicitly connected the ancient Phoenicians with the Maronites. It seems to be directly related to the fact that he was residing in Egypt and was strongly influenced by the Phoenician claims made by the Lebanese community there. Darian, whom the French considered a francophile, was even assisted financially by the Quai d'Orsay.[51] The French government supported and financed his trip to New York to the Syro-Lebanese community residing along the American East Coast, so that he could promote the French "Greater Syria" position there.[52]

To conclude the discussion of Egypt, it is no wonder that the Nile Valley was a center of Syro-Lebanese political activity. It is possible to find among members of this community opinions from the entire political spectrum, from pan-Islamic notions[53] through pro-Arab tendencies, all the way to Syrian and Lebanese non-Arab inclinations. The number of Syrians in Egypt reached a critical mass, at which point the community was felt in various levels of regional politics.[54] Just like elsewhere, until April 1919 the majority of the Syro-Lebanese community in Egypt supported the formation of a Syrian secular federation, granting Lebanon a leading role therein. The *Alliance libanaise* was the only group that from the start advocated the formation of an independent Greater Lebanon.

As a result of its physical proximity to Syria and Lebanon, there were close contacts between this community and its lands of origin. Egypt — Alexandria in particular — provided a door to the world, which many Syro-Lebanese enjoyed and utilized. For many of them, the Phoenician idea was a tool through which they expressed their desire to be oriented towards the Mediterranean rather than the Arab Orient and they looked to the pre-Islamic history of Syria to locate their roots as far back in time as possible. Egypt itself was going through a similar process simultaneously. The Syro-Lebanese could not participate in the Egyptian national movement and they certainly could not claim to be descendants of the Pharaohs, as many Egyptian intellectuals began to allege about themselves. Persons like Michel Chiha, Jacques Tabet, Hector Klat, Béchara al-Khoury, Emile Eddé, Yusuf al-Saouda and many more formed a cohesive social group that worked together for the betterment of their political and socio-economic future. Later on, in Lebanon of the 1920s-30s, some of them would become bitter rivals. But in their Alexandria days, the political skirmishes that characterized the mandate period did not yet exist.

Syro-Lebanese in America

Syro-Lebanese immigrants began crossing the Atlantic Ocean in relatively large numbers in the 1880s. They were overwhelmingly Christian from Mount

Lebanon and they almost all came from lower social classes.[55] Although many immigrated to Latin America as well, this part of the study will be limited, with the exception of a few references, to the United States. For it was in North America, until the closing of the immigration gates in 1924, that the majority of the Syro-Lebanese immigrants built their new homes.

The Syro-Lebanese immigration can only be understood within the larger context of immigration to the new world.[56] The arrival of this group in America in the 1880s coincided with the large waves of immigrants from elsewhere who had left their countries as a result of socio-economic and political centrifugal dynamics — the "push forces" — and were attracted to the thriving economy in America — the "pull forces."[57] These millions of new arrivals triggered what became to be known in America as the "Immigration Problem."[58] The mass immigration from Eastern Europe, Southern Europe and the Mediterranean menaced the hegemony of the Anglo-Saxon Protestant American majority, who quickly developed a strong dislike towards the newcomers. Erroneous sociological and anthropological studies encouraged these fears. Pseudo-scientific research provided a social ladder of the human race in which the Anglo-Saxon and Nordic races were at the top, followed by the Eastern Europeans, Mediterraneans, Asians and finally the other races that were classified as low on the human scale.[59] Quite a few voices in America called for rejecting these inferior races lest they impair the high standards of American society. Indeed, many Americans perceived their country as "the highest, best civilization in the world,"[60] and the desire to constrain the masses of immigrants was often stronger than the recognition of the positive economic ramifications of immigration to America.[61]

The preoccupation with immigrants and their impact on American society manifested itself in the printed press and in the House of Representatives and the Senate. Many sessions were spent discussing these issues, expressing concern about the uncontrolled waves of new aliens.[62] As part of an attempt to have better control over them, several bills were legislated between 1889-1913, all attempting to filter the waves of immigrants and select a better pool of people, more "constructive" to American society. In 1891, an article in the new immigration law obliged the commanding officer of every vessel bringing in aliens to report to the inspection officers the name, nationality, last residence and destination of each one.[63] In 1907 an amendment to the bill was added and the immigrants had to answer additional questions concerning their identity — name, sex, age, marital status, occupation, level of literacy, nationality, race, last residence and expected residence in the U.S.[64]

The questions concerning nationality and race are of major importance for this study, for they demonstrate a collision between two different concepts of identity. On the one hand, there was the modern American concept that divided the world according to races and nations; on the other, there was the traditional (Syrian, in our case) concept in which the identity realms were more local and limited: the family, village, church and so forth. This clash between modernity and tradition existed throughout the world, in all colonial settings, wherever "West" encountered "East." Syrians, arriving at Ellis Island, must have answered the questions as to "who they were" for the first time in their lives. It is practically impossible to find their responses, but we can imagine that the few educated Syrians, students of the foreign missions, better understood these questions and could answer them with Western terminology, whereas the vast majority of the Syrian newcomers had no idea as to the race to which they belonged, or the nationality of which they were a part.

The American Immigration Bureau, for its part, defined the Syrians as "Turks from Asia" or as "other Asians" until 1899. Only at the turn of the 20th century did the term "Syrian" begin to appear in Bureau reports.[65] The American public, however, continued to use the appellation "Turk" to define all immigrants hailing from the Middle East, often confusing Turks with Arabs and with Muslims, or referring to all three definitions as one, despite the fact that the majority of those disembarking on Ellis Island were Christians from Mount Lebanon.[66]

The image of the Turk in the eyes of the American was not too encouraging for the arriving Syrians. Most Americans were totally ignorant of the Ottoman Empire, its Arab provinces and inhabitants. When the first wave of Syrians came to America, there was no knowledge whatsoever as to who they were. Only a few Americans who had been involved in missionary work in Syria had some idea who the Syrians were.[67] Turks were perceived by the average American as the most inferior ethnic group in America, bar the Blacks.[68] Even the Chinese, who were excluded from immigration to America by law, were higher on the social ladder than the Turks. A 1924 survey stated that the Turk "ranks among the highest in the racial antipathy column of Americans and among the lowest as far as any direct personal experiences of Americans are concerned."[69]

The "Immigration Problem" continued to preoccupy the American public until well into the 1920s. Due to the general ignorance of both the American populace and politicians as to the immigrants' identity and racial origin, the Immigration Commission of the House published in 1911 a *Dictionary of Races or Peoples*, "to promote a better knowledge of the numerous elements included in the present immigrant movement."[70] The dictionary enables us to see what the official standpoint of the American government was vis-à-vis the groups that concern us: the Syrians and the Arabs.

The Syrians, the dictionary tells us, are the native Aramaic race or people of Syria. They are not Arabs, although they do speak Arabic and a considerable number of Arabs live in Syrian territory. Of the estimated three million residents of geographical Syria the majority is Syrian Christian and not Arab. Elaborating on the various groups of the Syrian population, we are told that the descendants of the ancient Phoenicians, who are closely related to the Syrians if not of the same blood, reside along the coast.[71] The entry on the

Arabs tells us that we should not confuse them either with the Turks who belong to the Mongolian race, or with the Syrians, who are Semites like the Arabs but are mostly Christian.[72]

These interesting entries mark two facts. First, official American documents in 1911 made a distinction between Syrians and Arabs and referred to the inhabitants of the Syrian coast as descendants of the ancient Phoenicians. Second, America, as a developed national collective society, provided its Syrian newcomers with an identity of their own to cling to. If a villager from Mount Lebanon who immigrated to America did not know in 1910 "who he was," the American modern national consciousness, assisted by scientific research,[73] provided an answer for him. This does not mean, of course, that the Syrians learned they were Phoenicians from the American Immigration Bureau, but it is impossible to ignore the fact that an American official document "phoenicianized" the Lebanese and differentiated between Arabs and Syrians.

Once they had undergone the immigration inspections that defined them, as of 1899, as Syrians, the immigrants from Mount Lebanon had to confront additional obstacles of identity. An example comes from Birmingham, Alabama.[74] One of the more industrialized burgeoning centers in the U.S. around the turn of the century, Birmingham drew many immigrants searching for sources of livelihood. The Alabama Legislature, aspiring to attract desirable immigrants, passed laws encouraging newcomers to move to the state and establish their homes in the heart of the American South. In section 8 of the Act of 1907, Alabama State Law, it is clearly stated that "be it further enacted that immigrants shall be sought from desirable white citizens of the U.S. first and then citizens of English-speaking and Germanic countries, France and the Scandinavian countries, and Belgium, as prospective citizens of this State [...]."[75] The Alabama State Legislature had no qualms about clearly declaring the preferred kind of immigrants.

Still, some Syro-Lebanese trickled into Birmingham — into this white-supremacy reality — and a small community took shape. Between 1899-1910, 270 Syro-Lebanese arrived in the city,[76] most originating from the city of Zahle and its surroundings in the Biqa', making them predominantly Maronite and Greek-Catholic. The ethnic hierarchy in Birmingham clearly gave a superior place to white Protestant Americans, who constituted the majority throughout the American South. The immigrants found themselves in the midst of a racial struggle, which forced them to ask themselves questions of identity as to who they were and to what race they belonged.

The struggle of the "whites" in Birmingham against the "non-white" immigrants who infiltrated the South allows us to observe an interesting development in the Phoenician identity of Syro-Lebanese in America. A congressman from South Carolina, E. J. Burnett, who was a member of House Immigration Commission, aspired to limit the number of undesirable aliens to the

U.S. through legislation. Following a trip of the Immigration Commission to Europe and the Ottoman Empire to study, up close, the reasons for the mass emigration, Burnett drafted a bill that was supposed to "cut out 50% of the South Italians and more than 35% of the Greeks, Poles and Syrians and other undesirable classes"[77] from the immigrants to the U.S. His anti-Syrian inclinations were already stated in a lecture he gave at the Birmingham Commercial Club in the fall of 1907. Among the many anti-immigration issues he raised, he named the Syrians immigrants in the U.S. "a Phoenician curse." In response, a Lebanese resident of Birmingham, Dr. El-Khoury, wrote in a local paper that the Syrians were actually of the Semitic race and therefore belonged to the larger white Caucasian race. The Semitic Phoenicians, he continued, made an invaluable contribution to white-Western civilization: the invention of the alphabet, the perfection of navigation and so forth. What surfaces from the attack against the Syrians and the response that follows is the fact that House Representative Burnett charged the Syrians as "Phoenicians," which provides a clear indication that in 1907 in America, there were Syrians who were defined as such (even derogatorily), and a Syrian defended his Phoenician-ness by asserting that, first, the Phoenicians were Semites and therefore Caucasians and, second, these ancient Phoenicians should be evaluated according to their contribution to Western civilization.

In light of their racial and religious marginalization in white-Protestant Birmingham, the Syro-Lebanese in the city clung strongly to each other and to their community. In addition to the two Maronite and Greek Catholic churches that functioned as social and cultural centers, they also established a meeting house, named "The Phoenician Club," which evolved into a community cultural center.[78] In the community school at the St. Elias Maronite Catholic Church, established in 1915, Lebanese children learned about their Phoenician heritage and studied Arabic and the history of Lebanon.[79]

The encounter with American society clearly escalated the process of identity searching among the Syro-Lebanese immigrants. Syrian immigrants in America were asking themselves questions concerning their identity a decade before similar questions preoccupied their relations in Syria. Obviously, the problem of identity did not preoccupy the entire Syrian community in America. The majority was more concerned with daily survival and had no time to engage in the "luxury" of identity issues. For the educated minority, however, who were asking these questions, the Phoenician identity was a valuable option. As the first wave of Syrian immigrants began arriving in America in the 1880s, the Phoenician past began to be excavated in Lebanon and, as we saw in Chapter I, some Syrian intellectuals were already elaborating about their ancestors the Phoenicians. Upon settling in the New World, the label "Phoenician" came to the fore as an attempt to define their identity in a society that, on the one hand, despised them as Arabs or Turks and, on the other, forced all immigrants to be labeled according to nationality and race.

By the 1920s many Phoenician clubs had been established in Lebanese communities throughout the U.S., addressing the American and the Lebanese populace.[80] It was an expression of their support for the existence of Greater Lebanon as a non-Arab state and their attempt to define themselves in the American social ladder higher than the Arabs or the Turks and equal to the Caucasian majority.

Two notable examples of this process are Na'um Mukarzal and Philip Hitti, two Maronites who made America their home, although they remained in intimate contact with Lebanon, and through their respective fields of occupation — journalism and historiography — had an impact on Lebanon's political and cultural fate. Na'um Mukarzal's biography concurs with many other biographies of Maronites who originated from Mount Lebanon.[81] He was born in 1864 in Freiké (Furayka),[82] a village twenty kilometers northeast of Beirut. His father, Antun, was a Maronite priest. He acquired his education at the Maronite *Madrasat al-Hikma* in Beirut under the supervision of Bishop Yusuf al-Dibs and at USJ where he mastered Arabic and French. After graduation, he moved to Cairo and taught Arabic for a year at the school of the Jesuits. An unexpected illness caused him to return to his village in Lebanon. In 1890, he immigrated to America to try his luck in the land of opportunity. He found work as a French teacher at the Jesuit school in New York and later turned to journalism. In February 1898, he began publishing *al-Hoda*, first as a bi-weekly in Philadelphia and then, from 1902, as a daily in New York. In 1910, he left the running of the paper to his brother Salum and immersed himself in political activity for Lebanon. The following year, he established the Lebanese League of Revival, a sister association of the *Alliance libanaise*. He participated in the 1913 Arab-Syrian Congress in Paris representing his League and in 1919 he was in France again, calling for the establishment of Greater Lebanon as a non-Arab state at the peace conference in Versailles. His political convictions were almost identical to those of the *Alliance libanaise* branch in Alexandria. In fact, had he remained in Egypt and not returned to Lebanon he probably would have integrated perfectly within the leadership of the *Alliance* in Egypt along with Auguste Adib Pasha, Yusuf al-Saouda and Daoud 'Amoun.[83]

Philip Khuri Hitti, the reputed historian of the Middle East, was born in 1886 in Shimlan, a village south of Beirut. Unlike the Maronite villages in the northern part of Mount Lebanon that were heavily influenced by the Jesuits, Shimlan's proximity to Beirut and its location at the heart of a predominantly Druze region opened the village to additional currents. This explains how Hitti, although a Maronite, acquired his secondary and higher education in American Protestant educational institutions, first in the American High School of Suq al-Gharb and later at AUB where he graduated with honors in 1908. After teaching at AUB, Hitti moved to New York in 1913 to pursue his studies at Colombia University. He received his Ph.D. in Oriental languages and literature in 1915 and for the next five years taught the history of the Near East at Colombia. As part of his involvement in the life of the local Syrian community, Hitti founded the Syrian Educational Society in New York in 1916.[84] In 1920, he returned to AUB as a professor of oriental history. In 1926, he moved to America permanently after being offered a position at Princeton University where he spent the remainder of his long and distinguished academic career.

Mukarzal and Hitti do not represent the average Lebanese immigrant to America because of the extent of their education. They were far more learned and well-informed than the majority of the Syro-Lebanese community. When Mukarzal landed at Ellis Island the "immigration problem" was just beginning and Syrians were still defined as "Turks" or "other Asians" by the Immigration Bureau. When Hitti first crossed the Atlantic Ocean, in 1913, America's relations with its immigrants were at a different stage — and so was the political situation in the Ottoman Empire. Twenty-three years separate their respective arrivals to America, but, as we shall see, Hitti's writings indicate that the Syro-Lebanese in America were facing similar absorption problems in the 1910s to those they had faced in the late 19th century.

Mukarzal used *al-Hoda* not only as a news source but also as a tool through which he tried to shape the collective agenda of the Maronite community in America. *Al-Hoda* became the voice of two seemingly different streams. On the one hand, Mukarzal shaped the paper in his image and made it a staunch Maronite publication and an advocate of the Lebanist idea.[85] On the other hand, living in America, Mukarzal used the paper almost from its inception to defend the idea that the *Syrians* were part of the white race and, therefore, the Immigration Bureau and American society should not label them either as Asians or Turks.[86] As we have seen, this duality between Syrian and Lebanese identities was prevalent in the first two decades of the 20th century and even beyond. In America it was sharpened in the context of the identification of all immigrants from greater Syria as Syrians. From 1910, the commencement of Mukarzal's political activity for the Lebanist idea, he honed his Lebanese inclinations through the Lebanese League of Revival. He expressed similar ideas to Yusuf al-Saouda about Lebanon and its non-Arab identity.[87] Al-Saouda and Mukarzal, in a time difference of fifteen years, went down the same track: the Maronite Madrasat al-Hikma, the Jesuit college and thereafter immigration to Egypt. Interestingly, the two developed the exact same views about Arabic, seeing it as the sole Lebanese national language.[88] Their origin from the Mountain rather than the city and the impact of the parochial Maronite school may have caused them to refer to Arabic as they did, different from the Beirut francophile milieu.

In Hitti's first sojourn in New York, from 1913-1920, Syro-Lebanese continued to arrive in large numbers in America. Their identity problem was not fully resolved, as is reflected in Hitti's writings about them. During these years Hitti contributed several articles to *al-Muqtataf* concerning his experiences as an Oriental in America.[89] In 1917, he penned "The Colonization of the Syrians between Two Eras,"[90] which recounts the story of Syrian emigration from antiquity to modernity, beginning with the Phoenicians, who, according to Hitti, were as Syrian as their modern counterparts. The ancient Phoenician-Syrians had a lasting impact on the countries to which they immigrated, he explained. Their impact on the Roman Empire, for instance, was very significant, for they actually revitalized the Roman Empire and restored its strength.[91] Like many other Lebanese who wrote about the Phoenician heritage in Lebanon Hitti demonstrated, in a lengthy elaboration, the invaluable contribution of the Syrians to Western civilization. Using *al-Muqtataf* as a stage for his articles was not coincidental. As noted in Chapter I, this journal addressed primarily the Syro-Lebanese community in and out of Egypt and it publicly supported an exclusive, non-Arab identity for the Syrians and Lebanese.[92] While the competing journal, *al-Hilal*, was active in the construction of Arab-Islamic past, *al-Muqtataf* clearly provided an alternative to Jurji Zaydan's pro-Arab inclinations.

For Philip Hitti in 1917, the Syrians were clearly descendants of the ancient Phoenicians and Lebanon and the Lebanese were part of a larger Syrian political framework. In 1924, four years after his return to Beirut, Hitti continued to write in the same vein of thought, referring to the Phoenician origin of the Syrians. In *The Syrians in America*, addressed to an American audience, he elaborated more on the origin of the Syrians. The book is an attempt to incorporate the Syrians into mainstream America and it demonstrates the fact that the identity problems the first Syrian immigrants faced at the turn of the century were similar to those in 1924. In contrast to what Americans believe, Hitti explains, the Syrians are neither Turks nor Arabs. They are Semitic Arabic-speaking Syrians. Arabism is a linguistic rather than ethnic designation. The Syrians spoke Aramaic for most of their history and adopted Arabic only with the rise of Islam.[93]

So who are the Syrians?

> The modern Syrians are the remnant of the ancient Phoenician-Canaanite tribes who entered Syria about 2500 B.C. and the Arabs who have drifted, and still drift in, from the desert and gradually pass from a nomadic to an agricultural state. With this Semitic stock as a substratum the Syrians are a highly mixed race of whom some rightly trace their origin back to the Greek settlers and colonists of the Seleucidae period, others to the Frankish and other European Crusaders, and still others to Kurdish and Persian invaders and immigrants.

The fact that the Syrians carry some Arab blood does not have an effect on their race, Hitti explains, because "after all, culture, and not a strain of blood, is the determining factor in the identification of a race."[94] As in the aforementioned article on Syrian emigration, Hitti provided a sense of continuity between ancient times and modernity. Thus, the Syrian immigration to America began, according to him, not in the mid-19th century, but rather with the Phoenician seafarers who were the first Syrian immigrants to the American continent.[95] The idea that the ancient Phoenicians had crossed the Atlantic was a view shared by many Lebanese and supported by dubious scholarly work.[96] It reflected the attempt made by Syro-Lebanese, advocates of the Phoenician identity, to illustrate their contribution to Western civilization since time immemorial. In the American context, it was an attempt to make evident that the Syro-Lebanese were actually more American than Americans. The ancient Phoenicians arrived to the American continent in their pursuit of commerce and well-being and their descendants, the modern Syrians, were simply emulating their forefathers' conduct. Hitti's continued use of the term "Syrian" in 1924 is another example of the American context from which he wrote. Although he was a professor at AUB in 1924, and a strong supporter of the Lebanist idea, he wrote his book using terms understandable to the Americans.

By the 1950s, Hitti was regarded as one of the most distinguished historians of the Middle East. There is no doubt about his empathy toward the subject of his studies, the Arabs. This extended to his politics too, expressed in his support of the Arab cause against the Zionist movement.[97] Nevertheless, his academic writing continued to promote the unique cultural features of Syria and Lebanon. In 1951, he published the first edition of *History of Syria, Including Lebanon and Palestine*. In 1957, when Lebanon was believed to be stepping forward into a bright and promising future, Hitti published another book in the same vein, *Lebanon in History,* which had a lengthy narrative that began with the Stone Age and followed, of course, with the ancient Lebanese, the Phoenicians, and their contribution to Western civilization.

Philip Hitti was a very important factor in the dissemination of the Phoenician myth of origin in Lebanon. Through his studies on Lebanon he provided the Lebanist idea a thoughtful scholarly mantle. Students in the Lebanese educational system learned about their country's historical legacy through his books that were always translated into Arabic.[98] His work on Arab civilization and Islam reflected his worldview, seeing the Arab-Islamic occupation as just another event in a region with a history of 5,000 years. Thus, equal attention should be given to ancient pre-Islamic civilizations that left their ethnic and cultural mark on the region, in some places — like Lebanon — even more than the Arab-Islamic civilization.[99] It should be remembered that Hitti was never considered a staunch Phoenician or an anti-Arab.[100] This fact only helped in the dissemination of his views about the history of Lebanon because he was accepted in circles otherwise closed to Mukarzal and his peers.

Phoenicianism in America, as elsewhere, was more than an intellectual enterprise of a few individuals. It was a kind of an abstract code shared by many Syrians and Lebanese who attempted to construct their national narrative. In America it meant that not only did they participate in the political and cultural debate of their country of origin but they also emphasized to their American neighbors that they were part and parcel of the Western world and equal members in the American melting pot. The need to define their identity led them to use the Phoenician past as a political tool before this was done in Lebanon or Egypt. There was strong interaction between Syro-Lebanese immigrants and their communities of origin. It was manifested not only in a constant flow of moneys but also in the flow of ideas. When Hitti arrived in New York in 1913, there were not yet Phoenician clubs in Beirut but such clubs were already operating in various Syrian communities in North and Latin America.[101] By 1920, when he returned to Lebanon, the Phoenician view of the past was already completely identified with the Lebanese national movement.

Between Paris and Beirut: 1913-1919

For many Middle Easterners, Paris has always been the gateway to the West. Since the early 19th century, the French capital attracted numerous Levantines, who were often enchanted by French society and culture.[102] As a result of the political vicissitudes in the Ottoman Empire, Paris also evolved to be an asylum for political dissidents and for intellectual freethinkers who could not express themselves freely in the framework of the Empire. When the 1908 Young Turk revolution erupted, it was only natural that Paris would become a center of political activity for a great number of associations and secret clubs, formed as a reaction to the turmoil in Istanbul. Syrians like Ganem, Samné and Khairallah Khairallah, who made Paris their home, worked vigorously, along with others, on shaping the fate of their countries of origin. Unlike in either America or Egypt, the Syro-Lebanese who resided in France prior to WWI were not integrated into a large-scale community. They were, for the most part, educated professional individuals who did not live in a closed community, as did the Syrian emigrants elsewhere. The political activity in Paris, therefore, was characterized not by the mass presence of a Syrian community, but rather through the activity of a few individuals. The French, naturally, had a clear interest in encouraging and controlling such activity, for it enabled them to manipulate and play a better hand in the political game concerning the fate of the Ottoman Empire. Some Syro-Lebanese were even on the Quai d'Orsay's payroll — Chékri Ganem and Georges Samné are the most notable examples — and French impact on their opinions was evidently great. Nevertheless, despite the fact that they were "French mercenaries," their views reflected the convictions held by many Syro-Lebanese at the time, and should, therefore, be assessed seriously.[103]

In the following section I shall examine the Syro-Lebanese political activity in Paris through three different angles: the Arab-Syrian Congress, the *Comité central syrien* (CCS) and the post-war peace conference. These three themes provide a good spectrum of the political changes before, during and after WWI. The Arab-Syrian Congress gives a good perspective of the political convictions held by many Syrians before the war. The CCS reflects the opinions shared by many Syro-Lebanese during and after the war; and the peace conference in Versailles mirrors the change of the political conviction of most Syro-Lebanese regarding the fate of their country. In discussing the peace conference I shall digress from Paris to Beirut and elaborate on the American King-Crane Commission and the reactions it stirred in Syria and Lebanon.

Between 1908-1919, many Syro-Lebanese who had lived in America, Egypt and Syria arrived in Paris at various times to participate in political gatherings of clubs and associations which used Paris as the center of their activity. One such entity, formed mainly by Syrians demanding the decentralization of the Ottoman Empire, was the Arab-Syrian Congress, convened in June 1913 in Paris. The Congress, an umbrella organization for several societies with different agendas, was composed of twenty-three members: eleven Christians, eleven Muslims and one Jew, twenty-one Syrians and two Iraqis. Twelve delegates were Lebanese in the sense that they either lived in what would become Greater Lebanon or had emigrated from the region to a different overseas locale. The organizers set the agenda to focus on the national existence of Arabs in the Empire and their rights, demanding reform and decentralization. However, because of internal rivalries and ideological disagreements between the participants, the statements issued by the Congress were often confused and mixed with Arab, Syrian, Lebanese and Ottoman convictions.[104]

Looking at the names of the delegates, the picture presented reflects the complexity and lack of unanimity of the political orientation of many Syro-Lebanese in the pre-war era. Of the twenty-three members there were at least five who later, in one way or another, would not consider themselves part of a larger Arab ethnicity. For example, Ayyub Tabet (Protestant) from Bhamdoun who would become Emile Eddé's right hand in the 1920s-1930s and an eminent politician in his own right.[105] From 1917-1920 he called for the establishment of non-Arab Greater Syria through a society he established in New York, where he spent the war years. Na'um Mukarzal (Maronite), the emigrant from New York, who, as we saw above, was one of the more vocal voices in favor of the Phoenician narrative. Chékri Ganem (Maronite), president of the CCS from April 1917 and one of the leading personalities behind the idea of the formation of non-Arab Greater Syria. Charles Debbas (Greek

Orthodox), a supporter of the Western, non-Arab orientation of Lebanon who would become, in 1926, the first Lebanese president. Khairallah Khairallah (Maronite) who, unlike most Lebanese, from the early 1910s was consistent in his Greater Lebanese leanings. He would later publish national poetry using Phoenician symbols to extol Lebanon.[106] I do not mean here to attribute Phoenician tendencies to all these five individuals, although Mukarzal clearly saw himself a neo-Phoenician. I only wish to demonstrate, again, that in 1913, expressing or writing about the pre-Islamic past of Lebanon or Syria did not yet imply a complete separation between races: Arabs on the one hand and Lebanese (or Syrian) Phoenicians on the other. Muslims, Christians and Jews could participate in such a conference since they shared the same agenda — improving the status of the Arabic-speaking communities within the context of the Ottoman Empire. In addition, in 1913, being an "Arab nationalist" meant a different thing from being one in 1919, after the war. Arabism was mainly focused in the Syrian lands and was not associated with Arabia, an association that in 1918-1919 would alienate many Christian Syro-Lebanese. Though beginning to take shape as a political manifestation, it was still predominantly a cultural movement asking for a larger share within the Ottoman Empire.

Nadra Moutran, another participant in the Congress, represents this kind of Arabism that dominated the Christian participants of the Arab associations in Syria. A Greek Catholic and a graduate of USJ,[107] Moutran should have seemingly endorsed either a Syrian or a Lebanese rather than an Arab solution. However, a longtime Syrian activist, Moutran advocated the formation of a Syrian-Arab political entity that included Lebanon. In 1916, he wrote a book, *La Syrie de Demain*, stressing his political convictions concerning the fate of Syria. Primarily an ardent pro-French and vehement anti-Turk work, the book enables us to observe the available knowledge regarding identity issues from an oppositional angle to separatist non-Arab tendencies in Syria and Lebanon. Moutran saw the Syrians as outright Arabs, descendents of the glorious Umayyads, and he viewed France as a "Muslim power" that should assist the Syrians in forming their own political framework.[108] The Franco-Syrian alliance began, he claimed, in the 8th century with the cooperation of Harun al-Rashid, the Abbasid Khalifa, and Charlemagne, the Frankish leader. Maronites tend to trace the beginning of the Franco-Maronite friendship to the Crusader era, giving it a Christian setting, rather than Muslim. Moutran, though a Christian, interpreted history through Arab-Muslim eyes. Lebanon, according to him, had always been an integral part of Syria and had never enjoyed any form of political independence.[109]

Moutran's large Greek-Catholic family was from Zahle, the capital of the Biqa', the valley between Mount Lebanon and the Anti-Lebanon mountain range. Nadra was not part of the Christian Beirut milieu. He did, however, graduate from USJ, making his educational background similar to the francophone, bourgeois environment in that city. As a result, his book draws on the same sources that many Syro-Lebanese graduates of French missionary schools used.[110] Referring to the origin of the Maronites, he states that while some tended to see them as descendents of the Assyrians, who emigrated from Mesopotamia to Lebanon, others claimed that they were descendents of the *Marada*, the Christian tribe of the 7th century, that was thought to have fought the Muslim occupation. There is also a belief, he wrote, that they are the offspring of the ancient Phoenicians.[111] He acknowledges that none of these hypotheses can be proved today. It is clear, however, that the Maronites became a well-defined community only around the 8th century. When describing their characteristics, he states clearly: "Les Maronites ont toutes les qualités viriles des habitants des montagnes, et commerciales des descendants des Phéniciens."[112] Greek Orthodox and Greek Catholic Syrians, according to him, were Arabs through and through. Moutran traces their origins, and for that matter his own, to the Arab Ghassani tribes that entered Syria centuries before the Arab Islamic conquests. These tribes adopted Christianity shortly after their arrival in Syria, and many of them continued to cling to their faith after the Islamic occupation.[113]

The fact that he mentions several times the possibility of a Phoenician descent of the Maronites, as opposed to an Arab descent of the rest of the population, reflects the beginning of a change in emphasis in the Phoenician myth of origin in Syria and Lebanon. Although Moutran was an opponent of Lebanese irredentism, he acknowledged ethnic differences between the Maronites and the rest of the population — Christians and Muslims — in Syria. We clearly see a gradual shift in the emphasis on Phoenician expressions. If previously one could be simultaneously an Arab, a Syrian and an heir to a Phoenician pedigree, then by 1916, phoenicianism began to be associated with Lebanon and Maronite separatist demands.[114] It is possible that Moutran's origin from the Biqa', the buffer zone — an important link between Mount Lebanon and the Syrian hinterland — had an impact on his political convictions. His hometown, Zahle, was predominantly Greek Catholic, but overall the Biqa' was principally Muslim. The Zahliotes developed a strong Arab collective identity and a historical narrative beginning with the Ghasani Arab pre-Islamic tribes. Growing up in a city whose population was conscious of its Arab identity, Moutran may have reflected in his book these Arab convictions shared by many Zahliotes, proud of their Arab Bedouin origin.[115]

Moutran died in 1917, soon after publishing his book, and it is of course impossible to know what his political convictions might have been after WWI, the occupation of Syria by Britain and France, and the struggle for the formation of an independent Lebanon. At around the time he died, the CCS was established in Paris by two of his colleagues at the Syrian-Arab Congress, Samné and Ganem. Between its formation and the establishment of Greater

Lebanon in September 1920, the CCS had become one of the most dominant societies in Paris. Ganem, as president, and Samné, its secretary, ardently advocated the formation of Greater Syria under the aegis of France. They perceived the Syrians, the Lebanese included, as a full-fledged nation, utterly different, ethnically and culturally, from the Arabs.[116] Their activity was coordinated with the French government and supported by the colonial circles in Paris. Georges Samné was particularly active in literary and journalistic activity promoting the CCS's themes. A Greek Catholic from Damascus, living in Paris for more than twenty years, Samné perceived the Syrians as a nation whose ethnic roots go back to the Aramaic people who occupied the Syrian hinterland in Biblical times. He believed the Syrians were also culturally different from the Arabs. They were closer to the Mediterranean Greek-Latin culture and were not associated with the Arab desert culture.[117] He strongly disapproved, even more than Chékri Ganem, of the separation of Lebanon from Syria, a conviction, which he continued to hold even after 1920, when Greater Lebanon was already a *fait accompli*.[118] Following the arrival of Faysal in Damascus in October 1918 and the formation of the Arab-Syrian Government in the city, Ganem and Samné sharpened their advocacy for a non-Arab Greater Syria. Samné's *Le Chérifat de la Mecque et l'Unité Syrienne*,[119] was written exactly for this purpose. This booklet explains that Arabia had never been connected either by race or by customs with Syria. The Arabs in Arabia, Samné claimed, are pure Arabs. In Syria, by contrast, any Arabs who crossed this land may have merged with the many other peoples who traversed Syria, forging one nation, the Syrian nation. Faysal's takeover of Syria is, therefore, unjust for historical, ethnic, cultural and national reasons.

Neither Ganem nor Samné advocated the Phoenician narrative publicly to Syria. They did, however, open their journal, *Correspondance d'Orient,* for Syrian Phoenician expressions. Jacques Tabet, for example, published Syrian nationalistic poems with Phoenician symbols in this journal.[120] Ganem participated in Charles Corm's *La Revue Phénicienne*, as we shall see below, and Corm corresponded with him in April 1919, expressing his support of Ganem's activity. The CCS, however, did not become a "Phoenician" society. Advocating the establishment of Greater Syria, the CCS may have been more attuned to the multitude of communities residing in Syria, especially Muslims, to whom Phoenician expressions would not have been comprehensible. It is also possible that the fierce rivalry between the CCS and the *Alliance libanaise* in Egypt generated the different historical positions the two societies embraced. Each evolved to stand on a separate, opposite conviction: the former, supporting the formation of Greater Syria with the assistance of France, and the latter promoting the formation of Greater Lebanon with the aid of the European powers in general, and not specifically France. The CCS was supported and financed by France and the *Alliance libanaise* evolved to be a strong anti-French society. It would appear that the two societies also developed two different historical narratives to support their respective solutions.[121] The CCS, particularly Georges Samné, referred to the Arameans, the inhabitants of biblical Damascus, as their ancestors, whereas the *Alliance libanaise*, and especially Yusuf al-Saouda and Auguste Adib Pasha, referred to the ancient Phoenicians whose center was the coast.

The CCS was very active in the political bargaining of the Versailles peace conference, relentlessly calling for the formation of a Syrian federation under the aegis of France. The conference evolved to be a new diplomatic battlefield between the victorious powers over the fate of the Ottoman lands. The U.S., against the wishes of Britain and France, demanded to send a commission to the disputed region to examine the dispositions of the indigenous populations. A commission was eventually sent, composed only of two American delegates, Henry King and Charles Crane. The King-Crane Commission, which arrived in Beirut in June 1919, may have been a nuisance for France and Britain, but it created much enthusiasm throughout the Syrian lands. The Syrian and Lebanese elites took the commission ever so seriously and lined up to stress their political convictions. Politicians, religious leaders, businessmen and journalists met with them to express their desired political solutions. By that time the Greater Syria option had begun to be identified with the Arab government of Faysal in Damascus, and as a result many Christians from the Mountain and the coast no longer called for the establishment of a Syrian federation but rather reverted to the Greater Lebanon option. Thus, for example, a petition, one of many, from a Beirut Christian delegation stated that the need to separate Lebanon from Syria was supported by history, mores, racial affinities, geographical considerations, language, legislation and common intellectual thinking. Syria and Lebanon were simply two different civilizations, because "the coast, which has turned towards the Occident since the days of the Phoenicians, cannot consciously consent to let itself drown in an intrusive and planned pan-Arabism."[122] The petition's signatories were Michel Tuéni (Greek Orthodox), Alfred Mussa Sursock (Greek Orthodox), Pierre Trad (Greek Orthodox), Emile Achou (Greek Orthodox), Chécri Arcache (Greek Catholic), Phillipe de Tarrazi (Syrian Orthodox), Michel Namé Trad (Greek Orthodox), Michel Chiha (Chaldean Catholic). This list of personalities indicates again that the vision of Lebanon as a Western-oriented state, supported by a historical narrative beginning with the Phoenicians, was prevalent in Beirut among the Christian bourgeoisie and was not confined to the Maronites.

Calls for the recognition of Lebanese (or Syrians) as non-Arabs reached the American Commission from many Christian communities throughout geographical Syria. In the hinterland, the petitions focused on Syrian ethnicity as separate from Hijazi Arab ethnicity. On the coast, the calls often added the Phoenician angle to the Greater Lebanese demands, as the following petition demonstrates:

Nous demandons la justice et l'égalité entre tous les habitants, et que cette paix, cette justice et égalité soient dispensées dans ce pays qui appartient, par hérédité, à nous, descendants des Phéniciens sous l'égide d'un gouvernement chrétien et démocrate, dont le passé et le présent sont le meilleur gage de bonheur pour nous et nos enfants tant opprimés, et pour notre pays qui a stupéfié le monde entier par ses dons naturels et par le vertu d'assimilation de ses enfants.[123]

Clearly, by July 1919 the term "Phoenician" bore a definite political weight, implying non-Arab, non-Syrian, pro-Western orientation. There were still a few Syro-Lebanese, however, such as Jacques Tabet, who used the term in the wider context of Syria. The employment of the designation "Phoenician" in a context of claims for age-old historical roots was so prevalent that even some advocates of Arab identity began using it. In the Syrian-Arab journal *al-Kawkab*, edited by 'Abd al-Rahman al-Shahbandar, the future eminent Arab-Syrian leader, the following statement was made: "We Syrians, we obtain Arab blood and traces of Phoenician blood. The [Turkish] conquest modified our social character, but the unity of language unifies us as much as living in the same fatherland."[124] Shahbandar was, of course, a Syrian-Arab nationalist with strong Arab convictions, but in his attempts to demonstrate the long-lasting Greater Syrian-Arab nationality, he did not mind using the term Phoenician. By doing so he began a trend that would continue among the adversaries of the Lebanese-Phoenician idea: attempting to expropriate the Phoenicians from the Lebanese national movement and arabize them.

The second Lebanese delegation, headed by the Maronite Patriarch Elias Hoyek, arrived in Paris in August 1919 to present its platform before the delegates of the peace conference. By that time, Phoenician expressions were totally identified with the Greater Lebanon camp. Charles Corm in Beirut had just published the second issue of *La Revue Phénicienne,* and in Egypt, al-Saouda, Adib Pasha and other longtime supporters of the Greater Lebanon idea were publicly identified as "Phoenicians." What Hoyek could not state before his own community — that their ancestors were the pagan, idol worshiper Phoenicians — he had no problem proclaiming to the delegates of the Western powers. In the memorandum he submitted to the peace conference on October 23, he demanded independence of Lebanon in its natural, historical and geographical borders, under the aegis of France. He inserted Phoenician notions in his words:

Par une conception abusive de la notion de la langue, on a voulu confondre le Liban et la Syrie. C'est là une erreur. Sans remonter à leurs ancêtres Phéniciens, les Libanais ont toujours constitué une entité nationale, distincte des groupements voisins par sa langue, ses mœurs, ses affinités, sa culture occidentale.[125]

Demanding that France should become the mandatory power over Lebanon, again Hoyek used the ancient Phoenicians. Historical ties bound the French and the Lebanese. The Frankish Crusaders who arrived in Lebanon in the 12th century were actually the descendants of the Phoenicians. Hoyek explained that the French cities, from which these cavaliers left, heading to the Levant, had been actually founded by the ancient Phoenicians, making these cities and their inhabitants Phoenicians as well.[126] In Paris, before a Western audience, Hoyek did not see any dilemma in highlighting the Phoenician origin of the Lebanese. He did not, however, use the Phoenician past of Lebanon before his flock in his frequent communiqués, not even in 1919-1920. Possibly the reason, as I have previously noted, was that he could not preach in Maronite churches, before Maronite believers, about the pre-Christian past of the country and its people.

In the three months Hoyek and his delegation spent in France, the Maronite claims for the establishment of Greater Lebanon became strongly identified with the Christian assertions for a Phoenician pedigree. An American journalist in Paris, unfamiliar with the Middle East, reported on the "Lebonites" in the context of their political aspirations as expressed before the peace conference. He visited a Sunday mass at the Maronite church in Paris on rue d'Ulm and learned from those present that these "Lebonites" were divided into different religious groups but united politically. They had a historical connection to the Phoenicians, and Tyre and Sidon were their outlets to the sea. They were zealous of their autonomy and wished not to be swallowed up by the Muslims.[127] This report of the American journalist is of course somewhat shallow, but it indicates the prevailing atmosphere created by the Lebanese delegation as to the cultural and political orientation of all Lebanese.

Another case that demonstrates the Phoenician atmosphere exhibited by the Lebanese delegation in Versailles is that of Ibrahim Salim al-Najjar. Al-Najjar was a Maronite political activist and journalist who, by 1919, opposed the Greater Lebanon idea and put his trust in the Arab cause and Faysal in Damascus.[128] His paper, *L'Asie Arabe*, became the voice of Faysal in Paris in 1918-1919. Writing counter to the Maronite claims for independence based on their ethnic differences from the Arabs, al-Najjar criticized the Phoenician tendencies of the Christian Lebanese as expressed by the Lebanese delegation to the peace conference. He called for Christian recognition of the reality of the Arab-Muslim region in which they lived.[129] As a Maronite whose political convictions supported the Arab identity in Syria, al-Najjar reflects the fact that there was no absolute homogeneity in the political orientation of the Syro-Lebanese. By July 1919, most Maronites did support the formation of Greater Lebanon as an independent pro-French entity with historical roots beginning with the ancient Phoenicians. There were, however, others, like al-Najjar, who opposed this solution. Sometimes the division cut across familial lines. The eminent 'Amoun Maronite family, for example, had two of its sons in different camps. Daoud 'Amoun was a strong advocate of the Greater Lebanon idea and Iskandar 'Amoun joined the Arab government of Faysal in Damascus.[130]

By 1920 the fate of Syria and Lebanon was determined when France finally decided to fully support the establishment of a Christian Western-oriented state in Lebanon and to assume direct control over Syria at the expense of Faysal's regime. By then, there was neither space nor point in having societies such as the CCS that would advance a Syrian option. Indeed, by the time Greater Lebanon was formed in September 1920, the CCS had been dissolved. Chékri Ganem, disappointed by the formation of Greater Lebanon, wrote in Georges Samné's book, *La Syrie*, an ill-fated prophecy. He claimed that within a few years Greater Syria would be established and Greater Lebanon or Phoenicia [sic] would dissolve. In referring to the supporters of Greater Lebanon he was very clear in naming them Phoenicians, as if to say that the entire Greater Lebanon movement was Phoenician.[131] A few years later, Ganem changed his convictions and supported the Lebanist idea, presumably also embracing its national historical narrative, beginning with the ancient Phoenicians.

Beirut 1919: Charles Corm and *La Revue Phénicienne*

> Everything in him is charm, his hair is black, his eyes are wide, his look is sharp. His name fills the world. Who does not know about Charles Corm [...] but nobody knows who he is, because he wants to keep it a secret. Where was he born, where did he study, and what did he do before the world learned about him as an inspired genius poet? This is a secret he keeps and does not wish anyone to inquire about. Even when the oriental and occidental journals wrote about the master of the "Diwan" *La Montagne Inspirée*, the lengthy columns, the multitude of chapters, they could not find a thing about the past of Charles Corm. They had to settle with the study of his brilliant poetry.[132]

In 1934, Charles Corm underwent a radical transformation. From being a businessman, preoccupied with operating a large and successful firm, he became a poet, an *homme de lettres*, a thinker "at the service of his country."[133] He liquidated his business and wiped out his past. The quotation above suggests the mist Corm himself cast upon his literary rebirth.

So who was Charles Corm, the person inherently associated with the Phoenician idea in Lebanon?

Born into a francophile Beirut family, Corm's life started out on an anticipated trajectory. His father, Daoud Corm (1852-1930), was born in the village of Ghousta, but his family soon moved to Ghazir. The physical proximity to the Jesuits of the Oriental Seminar in Ghazir introduced Daoud to the Jesuit mission up close. Jesuit priests were the first to notice his painting talents and used his skills in their churches and schools. At the age of eighteen, after spending a considerable number of years next to the Oriental Seminar, Daoud left Ghazir and traveled to Rome to study drawing at the Institute of Fine Arts. He returned to Lebanon five years later, settled in Beirut and married Virgine Naʻman. He began painting portraits of important personalities and church interiors throughout Syria. His works were exhibited at the Exposition Universelle in Versailles in 1889 and in Paris in 1901.[134] Daoud and Virgine Corm lived in a social milieu remarkably exposed to the West. Beirut, with its cosmopolitan communities and its role as the Mediterranean port of the Syrian hinterland, became their city. Charles, their first of four sons, was born in 1894 into that environment; the rural and bare life of the dwellers in Mount Lebanon was far-removed from his day-to-day reality.

Charles Corm must have had an impressive and charming personality. His name is always couched in affectionate terms, with repeated references to his alluring nature. He was born in the burgeoning, Levantine city and spent the majority of his childhood and adolescence in Jesuit establishments. Between 1906-1911 he studied at the Oriental Faculty of the College of Saint Joseph. In the last year of his studies he wrote his final thesis: "Quelle est la fin de l'éducation et quel y doivent jouer les idées religieuses."[135] Maybe this was an indication of his future religious inclinations. He won the highest honorary award for this paper and also earned from his father a trip to Europe and New York. He traveled for a year, probably establishing initial connections with the Ford Motor Company, of which he later became the sole representative in all of Syria and Lebanon. Shortly after his return to Beirut, he founded the *Association des arts* which was short-lived due to the outbreak of WWI. At that point the Corms left Beirut and moved to the Mountain, only returning to the coast when the cannons stopped their roar. Already by then Charles was leaving memorable impressions on people who had encountered him. He helped the French rehabilitate Beirut, in particular the buildings of USJ, and Gontaut-Biron, the French official, took the trouble to personally thank him for his assistance.[136]

In February 1919, shortly after the first Lebanese delegation to the peace conference arrived in Paris, Charles Corm established *l'Association nationale de la jeunesse syrienne*, advocating "indissolvable Syrian unity, equitable conciliation between all parties and disregarding all consideration of ritual or religion."[137] The association supported the formation of Greater Syria as a non-Arab state, disassociated from the Arab movement of the Hijaz. The association's members gave public lectures on the different social and intellectual questions that concerned Syria.[138] Corm also planned for the association to open an evening school for the study of French and Arabic and to establish a Syrian academy of fine arts.[139] In the closing words of the mission statement of the association, Corm wrote:

Nous ne doutons pas que c'est d'un tel foyer d'activité et d'énergie nationales, que doivent sortir un jour les hommes qui mèneront les destinées de *la plus grande Syrie* [emphasis added, A.K.]. Tous nos encouragements et toute notre confiance leur sont acquis.[140]

Clearly, in early 1919 Corm supported the formation of Greater Syria, like many other Lebanese. They all wished to form an extended political framework oriented towards the West, separated from the Arab movement.[141] Only when Faysal's Arab movement slowly took over the Syrian national movement and identified it with Arab-Islamic causes did this group change its orientation and begin calling unequivocally for the establishment of Greater Lebanon. The British-French rivalry also contributed to the separation between the Syrian (and Lebanese) and the Arab national movements.[142] At the end of March 1919, Corm wrote to Chékri Ganem, president of the CCS, supporting the Committee's stand and entrusting him to represent the Association's view in Versailles.[143] Corm also asked Ganem to join his Association, which the latter honorably accepted.[144] By the time the American King-Crane Commission arrived in the region in June 1919, Corm had already changed his views and supported the formation of a Greater Lebanese state.[145] The *Association nationale de la jeunesse syrienne* did not last too long. The last records of its activity are dated July 1919.[146] The transformed views of Corm and many other Lebanese no longer left room for the existence of a pro-Greater Syrian association.

In July 1919, Charles Corm began issuing his most celebrated journal, *La Revue Phénicienne,* from his father's printing house *Editions maison d'art.* Only four issues appeared: July, August, September and December. *La Revue Phénicienne* became, however, one of the most renowned publications of the time, and Charles Corm attained his eminence thanks to it. It is very possible that French officials, and especially Robert de Caix, Gouraud's general secretary, helped finance the review's publication.[147] De Caix, who, as noted in Chapter I, aspired to turn Lebanon into a Western-oriented, pro-French bastion, had many reasons to support such a publication. Corm gathered around him a group of francophile businessmen, lawyers and administrators, all writing about socio-political, economic and historical issues concerning Syria and Lebanon. The unadulterated francophilism of its writers can be encountered in every note and letter in Corm's review. The anti-Arab inclinations are just as evident. Although about forty people wrote for the review, the final product was the fruit of Charles Corm's personality and creativity. He wrote several articles in each issue, under various noms de plumes: "Caf Rémine," standing for the Arabic (or other Semitic) letters of his last name: Caf, Ra, Mim; "Chinalef Relame", standing for the letters of his first name: Shin, Alef, Ra, Lam; "Sanchoniathon," referring to the Beirut historian who wrote the annals of the city in 1000 BC; "Ariel Caliban," a reference to the two images from Shakespeare's *The Tempest* and probably also to Ernest Renan's *Caliban: Suite de la Tempête*; and E. Le Veilleur, meaning the guardian (of Lebanon?).

Participating in the review, Phillippe de Tarrazi and Joseph al-Gemayel each contributed a series of four articles, one to each issue. Michel Chiha, Jacques Tabet and Emile Arab each contributed three articles. Albert Naccache, Ibrahim J. Tabet, Abdallah Kheir and Auguste Adib Pasha each wrote two. Many others contributed one article; among them were Elie Tyane, Chékri Ganem, Hector Klat, Paul Nujaym and Henri Lammens. *La Revue Phénicienne* also inaugurated the publication of francophone poetry by Lebanese poets composing "national poetry" saturated with Phoenician symbols.[148] Hector Klat, Elie Tyane, Michel Talhamé, Emile Coussa, Georges Corm, Alfred Naccache, Michel Chiha and Jean Corm were the first to publish their poetry in Corm's forum.

If we take the first issue of *La Revue Phénicienne* and examine the articles and their writers, we get a good picture of the atmosphere that surfaces in its pages. Of the twenty essays, Charles Corm wrote six, one in his own name and the rest under different pseudonyms. One deals with a current political issue, the American King-Crane Commission, and the other five are literary pieces underpinning, on the one hand, the immense love and devotion of the Lebanese to France and, on the other, the disassociation between Lebanon and the Arab national movements.

Five articles are preoccupied with economic issues of Syria and Lebanon. Albert Naccache, a close friend of Corm, opened the issue with an article entitled *"Notre avenir économique."* Using economic rationale, he justified separating Lebanon from Syria. Joseph Gemayel, a tobacco industrialist and the owner of a large pharmacy in Beirut, commenced with a series of articles entitled, *"La culture du tabac au Liban."* Amin Mouchahwar, the future inspector of finances in Lebanon, wrote *"Nos resources agricoles, industrielles, minières et commerciales."* Fouad al-Khoury, a member of Corm's *Association nationale de la jeunesse syrienne* wrote about the hotel industry in Lebanon. Under the pseudonym D.C.F. (denoting *David Corm et Fils)*, Daoud Corm sealed the first issue with an essay on *"Le movement commercial,"* discussing the necessary steps to revitalize commerce in Lebanon.

Two articles deal with Lebanon's ancient past. The first was by Jean Jalkh who wrote about ancient Béryte (Beirut) being the major city of law of the Roman Empire.[149] Surveying the famous jurists the city produced and the Roman Codex of Law written in Béryte in the second century AD, Jalkh offered a link between the ancient center of jurisprudence and the modern French Faculty of Law at USJ:

> Mais comme la Phénicie avait jadis attiré les yeux de Rome sur ses ressources intellectuelles, nous avons depuis 6 ans, une Faculté de droit à Beyrouth, qui avec le code romain, qui lui a été inspiré par nos pères

[the ancient Beiruties, A.K.], nous enseigne les principes de droit incomparable de la "Justice française.[150]

The second article was written by Jacques Tabet and entitled, *"Ce qu'était notre patrie (9 siècles AC)."* It explored the religion, culture and accomplishments of the ancient Phoenician cities, giving them credit even for social achievements:

> Il était dit que le petit peuple phénicien qui, le premier avait fait connaître au monde les bienfaits du commerce, devait aussi entrer le premier dans l'ère des revendications sociales; et cela au moment où la société chez ses puissants voisins, Chaldéens, Égyptiens et Grecs, se contentait encore de lois à demi barbares.[151]

Three articles are political in nature. Chafic Halabi, magistrate of the Beirut Court of Appeals, wrote on *Les bases de l'état: équilibre, nationalité, plébiscite*. Auguste Adib Pasha wrote *Constitution politique du Liban administratif*, analyzing the negative repercussions of the *Règlement organique* of 1861 on Lebanon. The third article, written by Charles Corm as Caf Rémine, focused on the American Commission and called for instituting a French mandatory regime over Lebanon.

There is also an article by Dr. Emile Arab, a lecturer at the Faculté française de médecine at USJ and a member of Corm's Association, pertaining to health issues in Lebanon. Elie Tyane contributed *"Le symbolisme dans la littérature française."*[152] Several articles in the four issues of *La Revue Phénicienne* surveyed literary trends in France. They all illustrate the extent of knowledge and intimacy with France and its cultural currents possessed by Corm's social milieu.[153] Philippe de Tarrazi embarked on a series of essays entitled *"Nos grands hommes,"* dealing with famous literary, Lebanese personalities. Lastly, Corm published a letter dated April 29, 1919 from Chekri Ganem thanking Corm for asking him to be an honorary president of the *Association de la jeunesse syrienne*.

Corm authored five additional articles, in his own name and under pseudonyms, which enable us to determine his own worldview in July 1919. Although by that date he already supported the formation of Greater Lebanon, it is still possible to see his Greater Syrian inclinations. Moreover, he hosted, in his Review, persons who were still strong advocates of the Syrian option, such as Jacques Tabet, Henri Lammens (in the December issue of the Review) and of course Chekri Ganem. The opening essay of the July issue is entitled, how else, *"Phénicia."* It is a short exposition of the contribution of the ancient Phoenicians to humanity. The second one, penned by Corm — *"L'ombre s'étend sur la montagne"* — calls for the establishment of Greater Lebanon in its natural borders, casting Lebanon as a shining light[154] and the Arab movement coming from Asia as threatening darkness: "Nous avons toujours été, malgré l'adversité, le rempart de la civilisation, dressé contre les Ténèbres de l'Asie. L'ombre ne doit plus escalader la montagne éclatante. L'ombre ne doit plus étouffer la lumière."[155]

Under the pseudonym Cédar, Corm also wrote "*Les impressions d'un jeune phénicien d'aujourd'hui*,"[156] which seems to be based on his personal experiences during WWI in Lebanon. It tells the story of a young man who remained in Lebanon through the war but fled to the mountains where he waited for the French to arrive. When the French landed in Beirut he was filled with bliss. He returned to the city to be among the first to welcome them. The article is imbued with words of admiration for France and its culture. "Nous sommes plus francophiles que les français! ... Seuls, les français ne sont plus francophiles! ...," the "Young Phoenician" Cédar tells us.

Then, as Chinalef Rélame, Corm wrote another piece which, it seems, is also partly autobiographical.[157] In the form of a screenplay he recounts the story of a bourgeois family in Beirut and the way they relate to the arrival of the French army. The characters include a man and his wife, a son and a niece. The teenagers, bearing the French names of Jean and Henriette (most likely named after Ernest Renan's sister whose remains are buried in Amchit, a few kilometers north of Byblos), are very excited about the arrival of the French soldiers. They run off to the bustling streets and cheer them on; M. Jabali,[158] the boy's father, meanwhile, is troubled by the political fervor that has caught everyone. Risking his life, Jean had left the Mountain seven months earlier to welcome the first French soldiers at the port of Beirut. Jean and Henriette wish to introduce *"la vrai Syrie"* to the French through the publication of a journal called *La Jeune Syrie* or *La Syrie nouvelle*. Returning from the streets, Jean brings home a French captain who speaks French badly, corrupted by military slang. The Jabalis decide to re-teach the French soldier his own language. Henriette informs the captain that many Syrians, especially activists of *l'Association nationale de la jeunesse syrienne*, write French poetry. Their source of inspiration, she says, is France and the *patrie*. As the plot unfolds, it turns out that Henriette has been corresponding with the captain for the last three months, not realizing who he was. The play terminates, as expected, with Henriette and the captain falling in love and with the promise of marriage, symbolizing the cultural and political wedlock between France and Lebanon.

In another literary effort Corm wrote the first essay in a series entitled "*Variations sur le mode sentimental*,"[159] describing personal encounters with different Lebanese women who enchanted him. This essay was written under the pseudonym Ariel Caliban, an interesting name in and of itself for it enlightens us to Corm's cultural world. As noted above, Ariel and Caliban are two contradictory characters in Shakespeare's *The Tempest*, which is set on a Mediterranean island. The former is a spirit with high moral standards; the latter is an earthly deformed servant who lacks any moral values. The appellation Ariel has become identified over the years with highly poetic imagination. Caliban, even more than Ariel, has been a significant cultural reference since Shakespeare conceived him in the early 17th century. The only native on the island taken by Prospero, the Duke of Milan, Caliban has evolved to represent anti-colonial movements and the struggle of the indigenous against the white European imperialist. Ernest Renan, a cultural reference himself for many Lebanese, wrote in 1878 his own sequel to Shakespeare's masterpiece. In the final act of *The Tempest* the grotesque Caliban remains alone on the island while the rest of the play's characters return to Italy; however, in Renan's sequel Caliban leaves the island with the group. In Milan, according to Renan, he learns manners and becomes civilized, eventually becoming the city's ruler. Interesting as it may be, it is beyond the scope of this study to elaborate more on this issue. It is only important to remember that Corm was, by no means, oblivious to the multiple cultural layers of Ariel and of Caliban. By fusing them into one nom de plume, perhaps he demonstrated his own duality: the spiritual Ariel and the materialistic Caliban; the savage Caliban of the island and the civilized, elitist Caliban of Renan after his translocation to Milan. We shall see in Chapter IV that this duality served as a central theme in Corm's epic *La Montagne Inspirée*.

The other three issues of *La Revue Phénicienne* resemble the first. About a third of each issue features articles preoccupied with economic themes. Another third contains political articles on the preferred solution for the Lebanese question. The remaining essays are literary or historical pieces highlighting their authors' Western cultural orientation. It is obvious that the participants in Corm's review were from the urban commercial elite in Lebanon. Some were more Westernized than others, but they all shared a close commercial interest. From Michel Chiha, who, upon his return to Lebanon in 1918, became involved in managing his familial bank, to Jacques Tabet the real estate landlord, to Albert Naccache the engineer who worked in the French-financed Kadicha electric power plant; all wished to preserve the world that enabled them to be affluent. At first, many of them believed that an enlarged Syrian political framework would provide the means for them to maintain this world. As 1919 unfolded, it became more and more evident that the Syrian idea had been taken over by Faysal and his movement. This change is crystal clear in *La Revue Phénicienne*. Bulus Nujaym, for example, who in 1908 wrote in favor of the formation of a Greater Lebanese autonomous region, but in a larger Syrian framework, wrote in the August issue of the Review about the Lebanese nation which, jealous of its independence, does not wish to be attached to Syria.[160]

Charles Corm, Bulus Nujaym, Hector Klat, Emile Eddé, Alfred Naccache and others from the same social milieu were intimately familiar with Western cultural references. They may have been numerically marginal in the Lebanese society of 1919, but they had a non-marginal political role in determining the fate of Lebanon in the post-war period. Arguably, Michel Chiha is one of the most outstanding examples of this social and cultural environment.

Chiha has long enjoyed his reputation as the father and thinker of the Lebanese confessional system.[161] He was the major architect of the 1926 constitution and of the 1943 "National Pact" and the vigorous engine behind Béchara al-Khoury's camp for more than twenty years. Although the Chihas originally came from Iraq, Michel adopted Lebanon as his land and wrote extensively about its national culture. He wrote three essays for the Review, under the banner *Entretiens de Patrice,* which are imagined conversations between himself and a person named Patrice. There is no etymological connection between the name Patrice and the word *patrie,* but the visual association is unmistakable. In the first conversation Chiha and Patrice sit in an Athenian setting gazing at the *patrie* from across the Mediterranean Sea and reflecting upon its current situation. We are lacking an ideal, Patrice says, we think on a small scale:

> Nous nous réclamons des Phéniciens: que nous reste-t-il de leurs vertus? Ils donnèrent la pourpre[162] à Rome! Impavides, ils allaient sur la mer furieuse portant comme une torche, l'idée! Et nous?

We have become a nation of petty merchants, Patrice concludes. "This is why the bones of our fathers are warmer than our lives." Chiha's criticism of the Lebanese merchant characters is actually quite interesting, especially considering his own background as a businessman. Given his future writings, I can only assume that Chiha had visions of a larger scale for Lebanon, beyond a country of petty merchants. In the same essay, Chiha harshly disapproves of the idea that the United States might become the mandatory power in Syria and Lebanon. Interestingly, he employs cultural reasons to reject this idea. We Lebanese belong to the Mediterranean Latin culture through our past, our traditions, our morals and our language, Chiha affirms. It is this identity of spirit and thought that ties us with the Latin Occident. We should not enable the Anglo-Saxon iceberg to penetrate the warm waters of the Mediterranean, concludes Patrice-Chiha. Three quotations embellish Chiha's essay and expose his cultural realm: the first by Victor Hugo, the second from *The Odyssey* and the third from *Anthinéa* by Charles Maurras, the radical right French thinker.

In 1919, Chiha was part of Charles Corm's intimate circle. Politically he changed his views in the 1920s, even more so in 1930s, and differed from Corm in his ideas about the integration of Lebanon in the Middle East. Nevertheless, socially and artistically he never left this circle. Even in the heyday of the political rivalry between Béchara al-Khoury and Emile Eddé that found Corm and Chiha in two different camps, the two men did not loosen their literary ties, as we shall see later.

Phoenicianism in 1919 was no marginal phenomenon; it was one of the foundations of the Lebanist idea. Adib Pasha, Chiha, Mouchahwar, Nujaym and others all turned out to be leading political and administrative figures in

Lebanon after 1920. Charles Corm, Joseph Gemayel and Jacques Tabet were prominent businessmen, representing the urban commercial backbone of Lebanon. There is no need to elaborate on the gravity of the Maronite Patriarch Elias Hoyek, whose report about his trip to Paris with the Lebanese delegation to the peace congress appeared in the December issue of the Review. Habib Pasha al-Sa'ad, the President of the Administrative Council of the *Mutasarrifiyya*, Emile Eddé and Michel Bey Tuéni participated in Corm's extra-journalistic activity.[163] Corm turned out to be a pivot around which the Phoenician idea was expressed in Beirut of 1919, but the entire socio-political milieu that supported the formation of Greater Lebanon was "Phoenician" in a way. Chékri Ganem, still defending the Greater Syrian idea, wrote in 1920:

Dans vingt ou trente ans quand on demandera à un musulman, à un chrétien de n'importe quel rite, qu'êtes-vous? il répondra: je suis Syrien et non pas ce qu'il répondait dans le passé, ou bien dans les années de début: je suis Phénicien (grand Libanais), [sic]ou Damascain, ou Alépin ...[164]

Ganem repeated this analogy between Phoenicianism and Greater Lebanon several times, as if to say that one who supported the creation of Greater Lebanon also supported the Phoenician idea. Referring specifically to Corm's Review, Ganem said:

Je lisais il y a quelques mois, dans une Revue syrienne qui se publiait à Beyrouth, "La Revue Phénicienne", des articles qui auraient fait figure dans n'importe quelle grande Revue de Paris. Elle avait pour directeur M. Charles Corm qui avait réuni autour de lui une pléiade de jeunes écrivains, tous syriens [...] On me dit que cette Revue ne paraît plus. Je le regrette. Les Syriens et ceux qui viennent de prendre en main la destinée de ces pays s'honoreraient en encourageant de telles publications.[165]

Indeed, the December 1919 issue sealed the publication of *La Revue Phénicienne*. The six months that passed between the publication of the first and last issues witnessed a crucial change in Syria and Lebanon. If, in July, the fate of Lebanon was not at all clear and France was still deliberating as to what its policy should be in Syria and Lebanon, then by January 1920, especially with the governmental change in Paris, France decided to fully side with the Maronites' demands.[166] It is not clear to me why Corm discontinued publication of the Review. In the September issue, he hinted to some financial difficulties, and that could be a possible reason.[167]

In the academic year of 1919-1920, Charles Corm was registered as a student at the French Faculty of Law at USJ.[168] The following year he did not return to school but completely immersed himself in business. He established a company, *La société générale industrielle et commerciale Charles Corm et Cie*,[169] that served as the sole agency of the Ford Motor Company in Syria and Lebanon. By 1923, he must have been very wealthy: forty-five percent of all cars traveling on the French mandatory roads were Ford vehicles.[170] The reputation he had gained in 1918-1919 as a "Lebanese patriot" opened doors within the French mandatory regime.[171] He ceased, however, his literary activities only to resume them years later, in 1934.

Corm did not invent, nor was he the first to express, Phoenician ideas. Yet, his alluring personality shaped Phoenicianism in the Lebanon of 1919-1920. It is often the character of the right person showing up at the right time that molds an ideology in the person's image. Such was the case with Charles Corm. In the 1930s, when he resumed his literary and artistic activity, Lebanon would be at a different stage of development — and so would the Phoenician narrative of the past.

References

1 Carol Hakim-Dowek, *The Origins of the Lebanese National Idea; 1840-1914*, pp. 312-319. Eliezer Tauber, *The Emergence of the Arab Movements* (London: Frank Cass, 1993), pp. 70-71.
2 The pamphlet can be found in MAE, Paris, NS Turkie, Vol. 113, or in *l'Asie Française* (September 1911), the journal edited by Robert de Caix.
3 On the historiographical debate about Fakhr al-Din's role in the formation of modern Lebanon, see Ahmad Beydoun, *Identité Confessionnelle*, pp. 513-565.
4 The Khazins were executed in the central square of Beirut along with fourteen other Lebanese. All sixteen became national mythical figures in Lebanon. The central square in Beirut, Place des Martyres (*Sahat al-shuhada*), is named for them.
5 Albert Hourani, "Lebanese and Syrians in Egypt," in Hourani and Shehadi (eds.), *The Lebanese in the World* (London: Centre for Lebanese Studies, 1992), pp. 498-499; Thomas Philipp, *The Syrians in Egypt* (Stuttgart: Steiner, 1985), pp. 1-24.
6 O.M. Wallace, *Egypt and the Egyptian Question* (London, 1883), p. 143, cited in Thomas Philipp, *The Syrians in Egypt,* p. 99.
7 On Napoleon's infatuation with antiquity, see Jean Charles Assali, "Napoléon et l'antiquité," in Michel Ganzin (ed.), *L'Influence de l'Antiquité sur la Pensée Politique Européenne (XVI-XX siècles)* (Aix-en-Provence, 1996), pp. 423-431.
8 Michael J. Reimer, *Colonial Bridgehead; Government and Society in Alexandria, 1807-1882* (Boulder: Westview Press, 1997), p. 12.
9 The affection towards this Levantine world is especially apparent when reading Michel Chiha's political writing in the 1930s-1940s. I shall discuss this point at length in Chapter IV.
10 Earl of Cromer, *Modern Egypt* (London: Macmillan, 1908), 2nd Vol. p. 215.
11 Philipp, *The Syrians in Egypt*, pp. 100-101.

12   Earl of Cromer, *Modern Egypt*, p. 216.
13   See more names in Yusuf al-Saouda, *Fi Sabil al-Istiqlal* [For the Sake of Independence] (Beirut, [n.s.] 1967), p. 66. Henri Lammens also found refuge in Alexandria during the war. See in Université Saint Joseph, "In Memoriam, Le Père Henri Lammens," *Mélanges de la Faculté Orientale* (1937-1938), p. 335.
14   On the sectarian relations, see Leila Fawaz, *Merchants and Migrants in Nineteenth Century Beirut* (Cambridge: Harvard University Press, 1983), pp. 103-120.
15   Yusuf al-Saouda, *Fi Sabil Lubnan*, (Alexandria: Matba'at madrasat Freir al-Sina'iyya, 1918), p. 25. See also al-Saouda, *Istiqlal Lubnan wa al-Itihad al-Lubnani fi Iskandariyya* [Lebanese Independence and the Alliance Libanaise in Alexandria] (Alexandria: Matba'at al-Hilal, 1920), p. 8.
16   MAE, Nantes, Syrie-Liban, carton 930. Renseignements, December 1924. See also Jurj Harun, *Yusuf al-Sawda* (Beirut: Kaslik, 1979). The entire book is one lengthy homage to al-Saouda's Phoenician inclinations. See p. 131 on his use of Arabic. Not surprisingly, the book was issued by the publishing house of the Maronite Université Saint Esprit, in Kaslik.
17   Association amicale des anciens élèves, *Livre d'Or* (Beirut, 1949), p. 25. Louis Cheikho, *Souvenir des Noces d'Or, de l'USJ de Beyrouth* (Beirut, no date); *Bulletin Annuel de l'Association Amicale des Anciens Élèves de l'USJ* (Beirut, 1907), p. 50.
18   Al-Saouda, *Fi Sabil Lubnan*, p. 183.
19   Al-Saouda claimed that the book reached the hands of the administrative council and the Patriarch who were influenced by it. See *Fi Sabil al-Istiqlal*, p. 184.
20   Yusuf al-Saouda, *Fi Sabil Lubnan* (Alexandria, 1919), p. 15.
21   Information taken from MAE, Paris, Syrie-Liban, Vol. 630, p. 20. Notes biographiques.
22   Meir Zamir, *The Formation of Modern Lebanon*, pp. 214-215; Kamal Salibi, *The Modern History of Lebanon*, p. 170; Meir Zamir, *Lebanon's Quest* (London: I.B. Tauris, 1997), p. 45.
23   St. Antony's College, Yale papers, Report no. 12. January 28, 1918. William Yale was an American officer who served the American consulate in Egypt. When the American Commission arrived to the region in July 1919 he worked as its special advisor. See also Auguste Adib Pasha, *Le Liban après la Guerre* (Paris: E. Leroux, 1918), pp. 161. According to the author's note the book was written in April 1917 with the assistance of Henri Lammens.
24   *Ibid*, pp. 46-49.
25   *La Revue Phénicienne* (July 1919), pp. 136-141.
26   *Ibid*, p. 136.
27   Auguste Adib Pasha sent a copy of the article he published in *La Revue Phénicienne* to the High Commissioner in Beirut. See MAE, Nantes, Syrie-Liban, carton 1561.
28   For biographical information on Hector Klat, see his semi-autobiography, *Feuilles Mortes* (Beirut: Ghorayeb, 1970); *Who's Who in Lebanon* (Beirut, 1963-1964); *La Revue du Liban et l'Orient Méditerranéen*, No. 36 (January 1936), p. 16; Rachid Lahoud, *La Littérature Libanaise de Langue Française* (Beirut: [n.s.], 1945), pp. 60-64.
29   The curricula in the French Jesuit schools throughout the Levant were similar. See *Association Amicale des Anciens Élèves des Pères Jésuites en Orient; Alexandrie, Beyrouth, le Caire* (Cairo, 1929).

30 Klat, *Feuilles Mortes*, pp. 25-26.
31 *Ibid*.
32 Hector Klat, *Le Cèdre et les Lys* (Beirut: Éditions de la Revue Phénicienne, 1935), p. 6. See also his poem "Notre Dame des opprimés", in *La Revue Phénicienne* (August 1919), pp. 125-126.
33 See also Béchara al-Khoury's testimony about his Alexandria experience in *Haqa'iq Lubnaniyya* [Lebanese Facts] (Beirut: Awraq Lubnaniyya, 1961), pp. 78-85.
34 al-Saouda, *Fi Sabil al-Istiqlal*, p. 380.
35 The Catholic extraction of Chiha should be remembered in this context. As Robert Haddad wrote in his *Syrian Christians in Muslim Societies* (Princeton: Princeton University Press, 1970), pp. 51-52: "...the Uniate Melkites were the most 'westernized' Arabic-speaking community in Syria (and Egypt) and the most alienated from indigenous traditions and values." Chiha was a Chaldean Catholic, but Haddad's words can also be applied to his church.
36 Edmond Rostand was a beloved author among many Syro-Lebanese. His hero, Cyrano de Bergerac, became a national symbol in France. The French saw in him the soldier, the daring and gentleman of spirit, the embodiment of all the positive national characteristics they needed so badly at the end of the nineteenth century. Rostand wrote this play in 1895. It tells a love story of a desperate French troubadour and an Oriental princess, the Countess of Tripoli. See many other references to Rostand, some in a Phoenician context, in Hector Klat, "Edmond Rostand: Poète de guerre," *La Revue Phénicienne* (August, 1919), pp. 92-104. In a separate article in the Revue, Henri Lammens also refers to Rostand's "La Princesse Lointaine," *La Revue Phénicienne* (December, 1919), p. 196.
37 Klat, *Feuilles Mortes*, p. 86. p. 110. The first issue of *Ébauches* appeared in May 1916. The review lasted no more than a year. Another indication of the Jesuit connection emerges from Klat's description. He writes about an exchange of poems with Chiha while the latter was recuperating in the "Maison des campagne des pères jesuites" out of Alexandria. p. 110.
38 Al-Saouda, *Fi Sabil al-Istiqlal*, especially pp. 373-380.
39 Jacques Tabet, *La Syrie* (Paris: A. Lemerre, 1920). According to the author's note, the book was written between 1915-1920.
40 *Ibid*, pp. 28-29.
41 *Ibid*, p. 105.
42 This idea would be adopted and used in the 1930s-1940s by Lebanese poets with Phoenician tendencies such as Sa'id 'Aql, Rushdi Ma'luf and Salah Labaki. See more about them in Chapter IV.
43 Tabet, *La Syrie*, p. 151.
44 *Ibid*, pp. 301-302.
45 On May 1922, Jacques Tabet wanted to set up a foundation that would offer an annual essay competition on the history and geography of Syria and Lebanon for local students taking the French *baccalauoréat*. He presented this idea to Robert de Caix and Henri Gouraud, suggesting that the essays be based on Lammens' book, *La Syrie; Précis Historique*. Tabet conditioned this initiative with the request that the history and geography of Syria and Lebanon become recognized subjects in the *baccalauoréat*, a condition that neither de Caix nor Gouraud could approve,

since the matriculation exams, they responded, could only be changed by Paris. The two officials also wrote him that such an initiative should be based on more than one book. Tabet then defended Lammens' book, arguing that it was the only study that fulfilled the national needs of Syria and Lebanon. This initiative of *"Prix Jacques Tabet de l'histoire et de la géographie syrienne"* never materialized. MAE, Nantes, Syrie-Liban, Carton 14, de Caix to Tabet, May 9, 1922; de Caix to Tabet, May 30, 1922; Tabet to Gouraud, June 14, 1922. In the same year, Tabet published a lengthy novel, *Helissa*, that told the story of the Tyrien princess who founded Carthage in the 8th century BC.

46 I would like to thank Carol Hakim-Dowek for providing me with this valuable information on Jacques and Anna Tabet.

47 MAE, Paris, Syrie-Liban, Vol. 57, pp. 123-124, notes de presses, December 30, 1920, a report about a party in Paris thrown by Henri Gouraud. Jacques and Anna Tabet were invited along with other distinguished Syrians and Lebanese, among them Charles Corm, "the well-known Lebanese patriot." See also the participation of the Tabets in organizing social-academic events, in René Moutèrde, "Le congrès archéologique en Syrie, April 8-7, 1926," *Études* (April-June, 1927), pp. 564-570. Yusuf Ahmad al-Zein, the owner of *al-'Irfan*, also helped in the preparation of the congress along with the wife of Alfred Bey Sursuk. (Note the confessional cooperation: a Maronite [Tabet], a Greek Orthodox [Sursuk] and a Shi'i [al-Zein]). MAE, Paris, Syrie-Liban, Vol. 209, pp. 75-82, Tabet to the French Prime Minister, August 26, 1924; MAE, Paris, Syrie-Liban, Vol. 531, p. 13, Revue de la Presse, August 30-September 5, 1937.

48 MAE, Paris, Syrie-Liban, Vol. 252, pp. 34-44. Rapport sur la Situation de la Syrie et du Liban (Paris, 1924). See also the 1928 report to the League of Nations: MAE, Paris, Syrie-Liban, Vol. 253, pp. 89-91. See also http://www.lebanon.com/where/lebanonguide/nationalmuseum.htm

49 See the books of two activists of the Committee that emphasize the non-Arab identity of the Syrians and Lebanese, referring to their Phoenician ancestors: Edgard Tawil, *La Syrie* (Alexandria, 1919). 'Abdallah Sfeir Pasha, *Le Mandat Français et les Traditions Françaises en Syrie et au Liban* (Paris, 1922). Edgard Tawil was the secretary of the Alexandria branch of the Committee and 'Abdallah Sfeir was president of the Cairo branch.

50 See the review in *al-Muqtataf* (July 1917), pp. 84-86, of a pamphlet Darian wrote, entitled *Nubdha Tarikhiyya fi Asl al-Tai'ifa al-Maruniyya wa Istiqlaliha bi-Jabal Lubnan* [A Historical Note about the Origin of the Maronite Community and its Independence in Mount Lebanon]. The review elaborates on Darian's attempts to demonstrate the Phoenician descent of the inhabitants of Mount Lebanon. Darian wrote this book in response to Nadra Moutran's book in order to prove the unique and separate identity of the Maronites. See in Cedar of Lebanon, *Syria Reborn* (Alexandria: Molco, Petrini & Co., 1919), p. 28.

51 The French regularly allocated money to Monsignor Darian (50,000 FF a year). MAE, Paris, Syrie-Liban, Vol. 110, p. 36, MAE to Lefevre-Pontalis, Ministre Plenipotentiaire, September 3, 1918. See also Béchara al-Khouri, *Haqa'iq Lubnaniyya*, Vol. I, p. 84; al-Saouda, *Fi Sabil al-Istiqlal*, pp. 79-82.

52 MAE, Paris, Syrie-Liban Vol. 110, June 14, 1918, MAE to Jusserand, the French ambassador to the USA, asking him to allocate funds for Darian's visit to America because "it is in the best of our political interests."

53 The most famous is of course Rashid Rida. We shall discuss his stand vis-à-vis the Phoenician myth of origin in Chapter V.
54 Thomas Philipp provides the following figures of Syro-Lebanese in Egypt: 10,000 Greek Catholic; 6,000 Maronites, 5,000 Greek Orthodox. *The Syrians in Egypt*, p. 86.
55 The 1911 U.S. census recorded 56,903 Syrians emigrants who arrived in America between 1899-1910. Philip Hitti, in his *The Syrians in America* (New York: Georges H. Doran Company, 1924), p. 65, estimated that around 200,000 Syrians lived in the U.S. at the end of WWI, of whom 95% were Christians. The sectarian division he provides is as follows: 45% Maronites, 43% Greek Orthodox, 5% Catholic, 2.5% Protestants, and 4.5% Druze and Muslims. On the social class of the Syrian immigrants, see Magelssen to Loomis, 12 September 1904, US GR 84, Miscellaneous, Beirut, quoted in Charles Issawi, *The Fertile Crescent 1800-1914, A Documentary Economic History* (New York: Oxford University Press, 1988), p. 71; See also Philip M. Kayal and Joseph M. Kayal, *The Syrian-Lebanese in America* (Boston: Twayne Publishers, 1975), p. 74.
56 See Roger Owen, "Lebanese Migration in the Context of World Population Movements," in Hournai and Shehadi, *The Lebanese in the World*, pp. 33-39.
57 For more information on the socio-political reasons that "pushed" the emigrants from Mount Lebanon to the Americas, see Samir Khalaf, "The Background and Causes of Lebanese/Syrian Immigration to the United States before World War I," in: Eric J. Hoogland (ed.), *Crossing the Waters* (Washington D.C., Smithsonian Institution Press, 1987), pp. 17-35; Said Himadeh, *Economic Organization of Syria* (Beirut: American Press, 1936), pp. 14-20; Charles Issawi, "The Historical Background of Lebanese Emigration 1800-1914," in Albert Hourani and Nadim Shehadi, *The Lebanese in the World* (London: I.B. Tauris and The Centre for Lebanese Studies, 1992), pp. 13-32; Najib Saliba, "Emigration from Syria," *Arab Studies Quarterly* 3, No. 1(1981), p. 61.
58 See Jeremiah Jenks & Jett Lauck, *The Immigration Problem* (New York: Funk & Wagnalls, 1911).
59 The leading thinkers of these theories were: Gobineau, *Essai sur l'Inégalité des Races Humaines* (Paris, 1853-1855); H.S. Chamberlain, *The Foundations of the Nineteenth Century* (London: J. Lane, 1910); C. Woodruff, *The Expansion of Races* (New York: Rebman Company, 1909); G.V. Lapouge, *Les selections sociales* (Paris: A. Fontemoing, 1888-1889).
60 Jenks and Lauck, *The Immigration Problem*, p. 1.
61 See, for example, William Ripley, "Races in the United States," *Atlantic Monthly* (1907). The writer, a distinguished professor at Harvard, wrote against the absorption of inferior Mediterranean races to America. "We have even tapped the political sinks of Europe and are now drawing large numbers of Greeks, Armenians and Syrians. No people is too mean or too lowly to seek asylum on our shores."
62 Congress, House, Reports of the Immigration Commission, *Immigration Legislation*, 61st Congress, 3rd session, 1911, p. 38.
63 *Ibid*, p. 40.
64 *Ibid*, p. 63.
65 Congress, House, Reports of the Immigration Commission, *Abstracts of Reports of the Immigration Commission* (Washington, D.C. 1911), p. 96. In 1899, the

year in which the term "Syrian" began to be used, 3,708 immigrants registered themselves as Syrians and only 28 as Turks. See in *The Immigration Problem*, p. 667.

66 See Philip Hitti, *The Syrians in America*, pp. 19-20; Michael W. Suleiman, "Early Arab Americans: The Search for Identity," in Hoogland, *Crossing the Waters*, p. 42

67 See, for example, the case of Louise Houghton, an American missioner, who returned to America and wrote about the Syrian immigrants mentioning the Phoenician blood that flows in their veins: Adele L. Younis, *The Coming of the Arabic-Speaking People to the United States* (New York: Center for Migration Studies, 1995), p. 174; Helen McCready Kearny, *American Images of the Middle East, 1824-1924: A Century of Antipathy* (Ph.D. dissertation, University of Rochester, 1976), p. 310.

68 Helen McCready Kearny, *Ibid*, pp. 6-8.

69 *Ibid*, p. 15; p. 18. A different study conducted in 1928 among undergraduate students of the University of Chicago had similar results, making the Turk only better than the Negro. See *Ibid*, pp. 300-302 for many examples of negative reactions to the arrival of Arabs and Syrians to America.

70 Congress, House, Reports of the Immigration Commission, presented by Mr. Dillingham, *Dictionary of Races or Peoples* (Washington, D.C. 1911), p. 1.

71 *Ibid*, p. 139.

72 *Ibid*, p. 16.

73 See *Ibid*, pp. 9-12 for the bibliographical list used to write the Dictionary. Elisée Reclus' *Nouvelle Géographie Universelle* stands out, yet again, on this list. In addition to Reclus, other works consulted on the subject "Geography of Races" were: *Stanford's Compendium of Geography and Travel* (London, 1983-1899); Hugh R. Mill (ed.), *The International Geography* (London, 1909); and Alfred Hettner, *Grundzüge der Länderkunde* (Leipzig, 1907).

74 The example of Birmingham, Alabama is primarily based on the following fascinating project: Nancy Faires Conklin and Brenda McCallum, "Final Report: Greek School, Holy Trinity-Holy Cross Orthodox Cathedral, and Lebanese Arabic School, St. Elias Maronite Catholic Church, Birmingham, Alabama;" in *Project on Ethnic Heritage and Language Schools in America*, 1982. I would like to thank Jim Hardin from the American Folk Life Center at the Library of Congress for providing me with this study.

75 Congress, House, Immigration Legislation, 61st congress. 3rd session. doc no. 758. p. 519. About the racial discrimination in Birmingham, see also Hitti, *The Syrians in America*, p. 89.

76 Congress, House, Reports of the Immigration Commission, *Abstracts of Reports of the Immigration Commission* (Washington, D.C., 1911) p. 106: Table: destination of immigrants admitted to the U.S. between 1899-1910; See also Kayal & Kayal, p. 83.

77 Congress, House, Report No. 851. 62nd Congress, 2nd Session. June 7, 1912.

78 Nancy Faires Conklin and Nora Faires, "Colored and Catholic; The Lebanese in Birmingham, Alabama," in: Eric Hoogland (ed.), *Crossing the Waters*, pp. 69-84.

79 Conklin and McCallum interviewed a Maronite elder who testified that as children they studied their Phoenician heritage in this school. "We started learning. We

started navigation. We started accounting. Just name it and it was started by the Phoenicians." Conklin and McCallum, "Final Report," pp. 238-239. In a telephone interview I conducted with Mr. Hardin from the American Folk Life Center at the Library of Congress, he recalled Phoenician vessels decorating the history textbooks used in this school.

80 Alixa Naff, *Becoming American*, p. 310.
81 Biographical information about Mukarzal is taken from Henry Melki, *Al-Sahafa al-'Arabiyya fi al-Mahjar wa 'Alaqatuha bi-al-Adab al-Mahjari* [Arabic Press in the Diaspora and Its Ties with the Diaspora's Literature] (Ph.D. Thesis, Georgetown University, 1972), p. 56; *Tarikh Jaridat al-Hoda wa al- Jawali al-Lubnaniyya fi Amrika, 1898-1968* [The History of the journal al-Hoda and the Lebanese communities in America] (New York, 1968), pp. 5-12. The author defined Mukarzal as a Phoenician by ancestry, a Maradite in his carriage, an Arab by his pride, a Crusader through his sacrifice, and above all a Lebanese.
82 See in Chapters IV and V about another son of Freiké, Amin al-Rihani, who developed a different worldview from Mukarzal's.
83 Mukarzal also wrote history books supporting the historical validity of the existence of Lebanon since antiquity. See, for example, *Qissat Yusuf bek Karam* [The Story of Yusuf Bey Karam] (New York, 1909) and *Tarikh Hanib'al* [The History of Hannibal] (New York, 1924). Both were published in al-Hoda Press. Hannibal was a hit among many Lebanese nationalists. See also Farid Haddad, *Sirat Hanib'al Shi'iran*, [The Epic of Hannibal in Poetry] (Alexandria, 1925).
84 See his *Educational Guide for Syrian Students in the United States* (New York: The Syrian American Press, 1921).
85 *Al-Hoda* became the voice of the Maronite community in America, often with fierce opposition to other Syrian communities, especially the Greek Orthodox in New York. See Henry Melki, *al-Sahafa al-'Arabiyya*, p. 56.
86 Mary Mokarzel, *Al-Hoda, 1898-1968* (New York: [n.s.], 1968), p. 7; see also *Al-Hoda*, January 17, 1914.
87 Eliezer Tauber, *The Arab Movements in World War I*, pp. 223-230, p. 256.
88 Mukarzal, like al-Saouda, loved and mastered Arabic. In the platform of Mukarzal's league, he called for Arabic to be the official language of Lebanon. French, although he knew it very well, is not mentioned at all. The platform of the Lebanese League of Progress appeared for ten consecutive days on the front page of *al-Hoda*; July 10, 1919. Like al-Saouda, Mukarzal vehemently opposed the CCS of Chékri Ganem and Georges Samné. See *al-Hoda*, August 12-13, 1919. The French, for their part, regarded Mukarzal a Francophobe, just as they viewed al-Saouda: MAE, Paris, Syrie-Liban, Vol. 4, p. 62.
89 Hitti, *Amrika fi Nadhar Sharqi* [America in the Eyes of an Oriental] (New York, 1919).
90 Philip Hitti, "Isti'mar al-Surriyyin bayna al-'Ahdayn," [Colonization of the Syrians Between the Two Eras], *al-Muqtataf* (July 1917), pp. 9-18. Salum Mukarzal, Na'um's brother, published this article in 1919 under a slightly different title: *Muhajarat al-Suriyyin wa 'Isti'imaruhum bayna al- 'Ahd al-Finiqi wa al-'Ahd al-Hadir* [The Emigration and Colonization of the Syrians between the Phoenician and the New Eras] (New York: al-Matba'a al-Tijariyya al-Suriyya al-Amrikiyya, 1919). The Mukarzals also published Hitti's famous *Antuniyus al-Bish'alani:*

Awwal Muhajir Suri ila al-'Alam al-Jadid (Antonius al-Bisha'alani, First Syrian Immigrant to the New World) (New York, 1916).
91   Hitti, *Muhajarat al-Suriyyin*, p. 14.
92   See the political views of Faris Nimr, the owner and editor of *al-Muqtataf*, as cited in *Correspondance d'Orient*, No. 213 (May 15, 1919), pp. 422-423. See also *al-Muqtataf* (July 1917), p. 84, about the strong support of the journal in the establishment of Greater Lebanon, Phoenician or not. On *al-Muqtataf*'s orientation see also Ami Ayalon, *The Arab Press*, pp. 53. Rightly, it seems, Muhammad Kurd 'Ali, the Arab journalist and scholar, accused the editors of *al-Muqtataf* of degrading Arab civilization. See in Kenny "East Versus West," p. 152.
93   *The Syrians in America*, p. 19.
94   *Ibid*, p. 21.
95   *Ibid*, p. 56.
96   See, for example, Le Vicomte Onffroy de Thoron, *Les Phéniciens à l'île d'Haïti et sur le Continent Américain* (Paris: Louvain C. Peeters, 1889). The writer was a Lebanese immigrant who lived in Mexico; see also "Al-Finiqiyyun wa Iktishsf Amrika" [The Phoenicians and the Discovery of America] *Al-Hilal*, 16(1907-1908), pp. 545-547. For more recent studies that deal with the disputed issue of the arrival of the Phoenicians to America see Cyrus H. Gordon, *Before Columbus* (New York: Crown, 1971); Frederick J. Pohl, *Atlantic Crossings before Columbus* (New York: Norton, 1961), pp. 17-35.
97   Hitti, Testimony before the Anglo-American Committee on Palestine (Washington, D.C.: Arab Office, 1946).
98   Kamal Salibi referred to Hitti's role in the dissemination of the Phoenician idea through the history textbooks in Lebanese schools that used Hitti's studies to prove the political and cultural continuity between ancient and modern Lebanon. See in Salibi, *A House of Many Mansions*, p. 174. See also Bassem Khalifah, *The Rise and Fall of Christian Lebanon* (Toronto: York Press, 1997), pp. 100-105.
99   Hitti's writings on the Middle East were widely read in the West and in Lebanon but criticized by many Arabs. See, for example, Shawqi Abu Khalil, *Mawdu'iyyat Filib Hitti fi Kitabihi Tarikh al-'Arab al-Mutawwal* [The Objectivity of Philip Hitti in His Book History of the Arabs] (Damascus: Dar al-Fikr, 1985).
100 Zionist activists in America, for example, considered Hitti a pro-Arab: CZA S25 4549, Tuvia Arazi to the Political Department, April 8, 1945. Yusuf al-Saouda, one of the most ardent Phoenician Lebanese, criticized Hitti's claims that the Phoenicians came from the Arabian Peninsula and therefore were ethnically similar to the Arabs. See Jurj Harun, *A'lam al-Qawmiyya al-Lubnaniyya, Yusuf al-Sawda* (Kaslik, 1979), p. 24.
101 On Syro-Lebanese associations in Latin America and their Phoenician inclinations, see MAE, Paris, Vol. 412. Publications des Syriens en Amerique, p. 34; MAE, Paris, Vol. 525, propagande et presse, p. 277; MAE Paris, Vol. 46, A memorandum of "Union libanaise," Les aspirations des libanais (Buenos Aires, 1919). See also in chapter 5, note 7, an article written by Rashid Rida in *al-Manar*, dated 1914, that attacks the Phoenician inclinations of the branches of the "Lebanese Revival" in São Paulo and New York.
102 L. Carl Brown, "France and the Arabs: An Overview," in L. Carl Brown and Mathew S. Gordon, *Franco-Arab Encounters* (Beirut: American University of Beirut, 1996), pp. 1-31.

103 Georges Samné, in particular, was a very serious and pensive person. His writings and specifically the journal of the Comité central syrien, *Correspondance d'Orient*, which he edited, were far from being French platform but rather sober and realistic, representing the complexities of the political situation.

104 Eliezer Tauber, *The Emergence of the Arab Movements* (London: Frank Cass, 1993), pp. 178-197. Hasan Kayali, *Arabs and Young Turks* (Berkeley: University of California Press, 1997), pp. 137-140.

105 On Ayyub Tabet see MAE, Nantes, Syrie-Liban, carton 455, renseignement au sujet de Eyub Tabet. No date.

106 Eliezer Tauber, *The Arab Movements in World War I* (London: Frank Cass, 1993), pp. 204-205. Khairallah Khairallah, "Le Cèdre, emblème national," *La Revue du Liban et l'Orient Arabe*, (September 1, 1942), p. 6; See also *La Voix du Liban*, No. 1(August 1945), p. 10.

107 Louis Cheikho, *Souvenir des Noces d'Or de l'USJ de Beyrouth*. page number missing.

108 Nadra Moutran, *La Syrie de Demain* (Paris, 1916), p. 48.

109 *Ibid*, p. 97: "Le Liban est une partie intégrale de la Syrie. Au point de vue historique, ethnographique, et commercial, il ne saurait en être distingué."

110 See Moutran's reference to Elisée Reclus in *La Syrie de Demain*, p. 42.

111 *Ibid*, pp. 354-356.

112 *Ibid*, p. 358.

113 *Ibid*, pp. 365-368.

114 As discussed earlier, signs of the identification of Phoenician claims with Lebanese irredentism can already be found in 1907 in the U.S. See also in Chapter V, Rashid Rida's reaction to these claims.

115 Alixa Naff, *A Social History of Zahle, The Principal Market Town in Nineteenth Century Lebanon* (Ph.D. Thesis, UCLA, 1972), p. 2, pp. 109-129. Sai'd 'Aql, another distinguished Zahliote, developed an entirely different identity, as will be discussed in Chapter IV.

116 Comité central syrien, *L'Opinion Syrienne à l'Étranger pendant la Guerre* (Paris, 1918); Comité central syrien, *La Syrie devant la Conférence* (Paris, 1919).

117 *La Syrie devant la Conférence*, pp. 7-8; see also many articles in *Correspondance d'Orient* written in a similar spirit, for example No. 205, January 15, 1919, pp. 1-21; No. 206, January 30, 1919, p. 88.

118 Samné remained faithful to the Syrian idea even after Greater Lebanon was established. In an article in *Correspondance d'Orient*, September 15-30, 1921, he ferociously rejected the establishment of Greater Lebanon, and the division of Syria into four petty states. There is one Syrian people, he stated. There are no Lebanese people. There are many Christians on the Mountain, where the idea of "*foyer libanais*" had emerged, but this does not justify an establishment of a Lebanese state. Samné also uses Elisée Reclus as a reference. We can see again that the scholarly sources were the same for the two camps, the Syrian and the Lebanese. See the pamphlet written by Samné, Comité de l'Orient, *Les Oeuvres Françaises en Syrie* (Paris, 1919). See also Georges Samné, *Vers le Petit Liban* (Paris, 1926), in which he recognizes the existence of independent Lebanon, but calls for reducing its borders.

119 Georges Samné *Le Chérifat de la Mecque et l'Unité Syrienne* (Paris, 1919).

120 Jacaues Tabet, "À la Syrie" *Correspondance d'Orient*, Vol. 209 (March, 15 1919).
121 See about this rivalry in MAE, Paris, Syrie-Liban, carton 313, Dossier 1. Chékri Ganem to Stephen Pichon, the minister of Foreign Affairs, protesting against the Alliance libanaise in Cairo, following an article published in *Le Temps* in March 6, 1918 on behalf of the Alliance libanaise entitled "La question du Liban." See also Comte R. de Gontaut-Biron, *Comment la France S'est Installée en Syrie 1918-1919* (Paris: Plon-Nourrit 1922), p. 188; Tauber, *The Arab Movements in World War I*, pp. 197-199.
122 MAE, Paris, Syrie-Liban, Vol. 43, p. 113, *Le Comité Permanent Exécutif du Groupement Chrétien de Beyrouth*, July 7, 1919. See a report on this group in *Le Journal du Caire* (July 19, 1919).
123 MAE, Paris, Syrie-Liban, Vol. 43, p. 156, Mme Antoine Sassy, présidente du Comité de dames de Saida, July 10, 1919, Memorandum to the American Commission.
124 MAE, Paris, Syrie-Liban, Vol. 4, Annexe à la dépêche politique du Caire, May 16, 1918, a translation of an article entitled "The Future of Syria" as appeared in *al-Kawkab*, May 7, 1918.
125 MAE, Paris, Syrie-Liban, Vol. 266, Elias Hoyek, "Les revendications du Liban." The memorandum can also be found in *La Revue Phénicienne* (December 1919), pp. 236-241.
126 See Georges Samné's report about the Patriarch's visit to Paris in "Le Patriarche maronite en France," *Correspondance d'Orient*, No. 221 (September, 15 1919), p. 125; see also MAE, Paris, Syrie-Liban, Vol. 278, p.28, Patriarcat maronite.
127 MAE, Paris, Syrie-Liban, Vol. 12, p. 257, "Lebanon of the Cedars," by J.C. Walsh, Staff Correspondent of *America* at the peace conference.
128 Al-Najjar began his journalistic activity in *al-Hoda*, the paper of Na'um Mukarzal, the devout Maronite Lebanist, yet another indication for the flexibility in the political orientation of Syro-Lebanese in the 1910s. See Mary Mukarzel, *Al-Hoda, 1898-1968* (New York: Al-Hoda Press, 1968), pp. 9-11. The French attested to al-Najjar's dubious personality. MAE, Paris, Syrie-Liban, Vol. 57, p. 145, Note au sujet de *l'Asie Arabe*, January 26, 1921.
129 *L'Asie Arabe*, 2 (August, 1919); *L'Asie Arabe*, 5 (November, 1919); in *L'Asie Arabe* from November 25, 1919, al-Najjar reports on pamphlets with Phoenician claims, distributed by the Lebanese delegation in Versailles, which he naturally criticizes.
130 Eliezer Tauber, *The Arab Movements*, p. 169, pp. 192-194; Lynne Lohéac-Amoun, *Daoud Amoun et la Création de l'État Libanaise* (Paris: Naufal, 1972), pp. 71-72. Daoud 'Amoun's daughter, Blanche 'Amoun, would become an artist with strong Phoenician tendencies. See more about her in Chapter IV.
131 George Samné, *La Syrie* (Paris, 1920), p. XI.
132 Anis Nasr, *al-Nubugh al-Lubnani fi al-Qarn al-'Ishrin* [Lebanese Genius in the Twentieth Century] (Aleppo: Maktabat al-'Asr al-Jadid, 1938), p. 82.
133 "[...]I left definitively business in order to be able to dedicate myself to my country through speech and writing. I hope my action will succeed in tightening the ties between Lebanon and France [...]." Charles Corm to the Jesuit father Louis Jalabert, the director of the prestigious Jesuit journal *Études*, a former teacher at USJ and the representative of the Faculty of Medicine of the University in Paris. Jesuit Archives, Vanves. Fond Louis Jalabert, May 24, 1934.

134 *Lebanon — The Artists View* (London: The British Lebanese Association, 1989), p. 101. Edouard Lahoud, *L'Art Contemporain au Liban* (Beirut: Librairie Orientale, 1974), pp. 1-9.
135 USJ, *1875-1925, Cinquantenaire de l'Université St. Joseph* (Beirut, 1925), p. 27.
136 Gontaut-Biron, *Comment la France s'est Installée en Syrie*, p. 93. See also Anis Nasr, *al-Nubugh al-Lubnani*, pp. 82-83.
137 *Correspondance d'Orient*, No. 210 (April 1, 1919), pp. 378-379. A report from *Le Journal de Beyrouth*, February 3, 1919.
138 A list of the lectures can be found in *Correspondance d'Orient*, No. 209 (March 15, 1919), pp. 378-379. The bulletin of the Association of July 1919 can be found in the September issue of *La Revue Phénicienne*, pp. 127-128. See also MAE, Paris, Syrie-Liban, Vol. 103, p. 151. A report of the Mission Laïque in Beirut, dated February-April 1919, protests the pro-Christian policy of France in Beirut. The report mentions an incident in a gathering of Corm's Association in which Muslims were thrown out of the meeting while the Christians chanted mocking songs against them. The writer, Paul Deschamps, director of the Mission Laïque, also mentions the Christian-Phoenician versus Muslim-Arab division that dominates Beirut.
139 Alfred Sursock, Albert Masoul and Georges Tabet were the patrons of these plans. Georges Tabet was a distant cousin of Jacques Tabet. He also spent the years of the War in Alexandria where he married Laure Klat, the younger sister of Hector Klat. The social circles are almost always the same. Georges Tabet would become a leading politician in mandated Lebanon and one of the major contestants for the president's seat.
140 *Correspondance d'Orient*, No. 212 (April 30, 1919), p. 377.
141 See a recent attempt of a Lebanese writer, Jamil Jabar, to hide the fact that Corm supported the formation of a Greater Syrian state. Jabar did write about the formation of the association by Corm, but he named it "The National Association of *Lebanese* Youth," instead of the correct name, which, as mentioned above, was the "*Syrian* Youth." Jabar, Sharl al-Qurm (Beirut: Al-Majala al-Finiqiyya, 1995), p. 24. Note that the book was published by the still active publishing house *Éditions de la Revue Phénicienne,* initiated and owned by Charles Corm.
142 Malcolm B. Russell, *The First Modern Arab State; Syria Under Faysal, 1918-1920* (Minneapolis: Bibliotheca Islamica, 1985), pp. 42-66; David Fromkin, *A Peace to End all Peace* (New York: Avon Books, 1989) pp. 315-331, 435-440.
143 MAE, Paris, Syrie-Liban, Vol. 11, p. 141, Corm to Ganem, March 28, 1919. See also *Correspondance d'Orient*, No. 211(April 15, 1919), p. 324.
144 *La Revue Phénicienne* (July 1919), pp. 46-47.
145 MAE, Paris, Syrie-Liban, Vol. 43, p. 111, a petition of Beirut journalists to the American King-Crane Commission, dated July 21, 1919, calling for the establishment of Greater Lebanon with France as a mandatory power. Charles Corm signed the petition as the owner of *La Revue Phénicienne*.
146 *La Revue Phénicienne*, p. 127.
147 CZA S25 10225, a report by Eliahu Epstein (Elath) of a visit to Syria and Lebanon, October 1934. Epstein describes a meeting with Corm and Albert Naccache, two of the founders and activists in the "Young Phoenicians" association. He claims that the association was helped by de Caix and submitted in 1919 a memorandum to the peace conference in Versailles, in which they presented the question of

Lebanon as a separate question from the Syrian one. According to the memorandum, "one cannot consider the inhabitants of Lebanon as part of the Arab world. The Lebanese are descendants of the ancient Phoenicians that were mixed among the Arab speakers." I could not cross reference this information and I suspect that such a memorandum was never sent.

148 This kind of poetry would reach its golden days in the 1930s, again with the assistance of Charles Corm, a point I shall discuss in Chapter IV at length.

149 Jalkh relied on a study conducted by Paul Huvelin, the Dean of the Law Faculty of the University of Lyon that gave the patronage to the Law Faculty of USJ. Fifteen years later Jalkh became an active member of Antun Sa'adeh's PPS.

150 *La Revue Phénicienne* (July 1919), p. 14.

151 *Ibid*, p. 19.

152 *Ibid*, p. 33. Elie Tyane (1885-1957) was one of Corm's closest friends. In the 1930s he published two books with Corm's publication house, *Éditions de la Revue Phénicienne*, which I shall discuss in Chapter IV.

153 See Hector Klat, "Edmond Rostand, Poète de Guerre" (August 1919), pp. 92-104; B. Routhin, "Rieurs Mélancoliques; Villon, Scarron, Molière" (September 1919), pp. 154-165.

154 Illustrating Lebanon as a light to all nations, *Liban lumineux*, will become identified with a different modern Phoenician, Sa'id 'Aql, whom I shall discuss in Chapter IV. See also Nabih Amin Faris, "Lebanon, 'Land of Light,'" in James Kritzek & Bayly Winder, *The World of Islam* (New York: Books for Libraries, 1959), pp. 336-350.

155 *La Revue Phénicienne* (July 1919), p. 13.

156 *Ibid*, p. 30.

157 "Le français tel qu'on le parle: Comédie Pochade en un Acte et en Prose," *Ibid*, pp. 57-58.

158 Jabali, or the Mountaineer, is probably a reference to the origin of the family from Mount Lebanon, an attempt by Corm to create a link between the Beirut bourgeois family and the Mountain.

159 *Ibid*, p. 43.

160 Paul Noujaim, "La Question du Liban, étude de politique économique et de statistique descriptive," *Ibid,* (August 1919), pp. 66-81; especially p. 66.

161 Fawaz, N. Traboulsi, *Identités et Solidarités Croisées dans les Conflits du Liban Contemporain* (Ph.D. Thesis, University of Paris, 1993), pp. 298-363; Traboulsi, *Silat bila Wasl: Mishal Shiha wa al-aydiyulujiyya al-Lubnaniyya* [Michel Chiha and the Lebanese ideology] (Beirut: Riyad al-Rayyis lil-Kutub wa al-Nashr, 1999). See also Khalil Ramiz Sarkis, *Sawt al-Gha'ib* [The Voice of the Absent] (Beirut: Al-Nadwa al-Lubnaniyya, 1956).

162 The new Phoenicians cherished the Word "pourpre" or purple. The radical of the word Phoenicia in Greek meant purple, given to the ancient Phoenicians presumably because of the color of the fabric they traded. It denotes in French also power, imperial distinction. "La Pourpre Romaine" signifies a Cardinal's rank — yet another play on words.

163 In the September issue of *La Revue Phénicienne*, p. 192, Corm published a notice about an essay competition. The jury was composed of Chekri Arcache (Greek Catholic), Michel Chiha (Chaldean Catholic), Emile Eddé (Maronite), Marquise Jean de Freige (Latin), Habib Bey Pharaon (Greek Catholic), Habib Pasha el-

Saad (Maronite), Jacques Tabet, (Maronite), Michel Bey Tuéni (Greek Orthodox) and Charles Corm (Maronite). One could not get higher in Beirut's social echelons of 1919. It stands out that no Muslim is mentioned.
164 George Samné, *La Syrie* (Paris, 1920), p. XI.
165 *Ibid.*
166 Meir Zamir, *The Formation of Modern Lebanon*, pp. 95-96.
167 *La Revue Phénicienne* (September 1919), p. 129
168 MAE, Nantes, Syrie-Liban, carton 2, Ecole Française de Droit, June 7, 1920, a list of registered students.
169 *Proche Orient, Revue Économique et Financière* (Beirut, October 1922), page number missing.
170 *Bulletin de l'Union Économique de Syrie* (Beirut, February, 1923); see also Olivier Dugast, *Automobiles, Chauffeurs et Transports Routiers en Syrie et au Liban pendant la Période Mandataire* (MA Thesis, Université de Rennes II, no date), p. 22.
171 MAE, Paris, Syrie-Liban, Vol. 57, Revue de la Presse, p. 123, A report on a dinner General Gouraud threw in Paris for the local Syro-Lebanese community. Among those present was Corm, who was referred to in the press as "the well-known Lebanese patriot." Jacques Tabet and his wife were also present.

3

The Mandate Years

[...] Lebanon is the meeting place of widely branching roads, struggling nations and various crossing cultures. And just as no power on earth can shut off its western shores — this wide open gate to the Mediterranean — from civilizations and nations which gave unto it and received from it [...] so there is no power in the world that can remove it from this Semite East, whence, since and even before the beginning of history, it received its blood and tongue, its tradition of legend and culture. [...] By nature and by historical decree, Lebanon serves as a means of communication between the East and the West which meet there [...] Possibly the best wares provided by Lebanon are its children, who emigrate to all four corners of the world, who build cities and ships, who compete without being unfair, who are intelligent by nature and work, who are conservative without gloomy gravity, who are new without doing evil, who invented the alphabet in ancient times and who today embrace Arabic; these children carry the cultural mission of Lebanon to the world.

Sunni writer 'Umar Fakhuri[1]

The creation of Greater Lebanon on September 1, 1920 thoroughly transformed the lives of the population in Mount Lebanon and in the territories annexed to the new entity. Much has been written about these fateful days and their impact on the fragile socio-political structure of the fledgling political community.[2] The Maronite absolute majority in the *Mutasarrifiyya*, the autonomous region, was wiped out, and with it the political and cultural justification for the existence of a cohesive national community in Lebanon disappeared. The historical narrative of the Maronites, as a self-conscious community with historical memories that are traced back to the Church's formation in the 5th century, and to the legendary Marada Christian tribe, could not have worked for the rest of the communities in Lebanon. As we have previously seen, in the 1880s the ancient Phoenicians began to be thought as the ancestors of *all* Syrians by lay Syro-Lebanese from Beirut who were seeking a secular identity for themselves and their communities. Phoenicianism, then, did not bear any political connotation. However, during the political strife that led to the formation of Greater Lebanon, the Phoenician identity crystallized and was used by Christian Syro-Lebanese as the historical justification for the existence of a distinct national community, founded on the ethnic and cultural non-Arab similarities of its members. Most of the annexed population, however, could not and would not recognize this identity as their own. Moreover, the Phoenician identity was still an alien concept even for a large number of the inhabitants of Mount Lebanon. Before 1920, Phoenician expressions were strictly limited to the bourgeoisie in Beirut. Thus, Greater Lebanon was founded on a national historical narrative that was not only renounced by the non-Christian population, but was also somewhat foreign for many of the Christian Lebanese, residents of the Mountain and other isolated locales.

The objective of this chapter is not to provide a chronological description of the development of Phoenicianism in mandatory Lebanon. Rather, I explore several subjects that, overall, provide a wide picture of the social, political and cultural forces that helped shape this identity and make it part of the (much disputed) Lebanese national narrative. The first subject I investigate is the French High Commission, which strove to shape the Lebanese society by all possible means. I examine its policy towards education in Lebanon and its approach to archeology in the mandated regions. The second subject is the Jesuits, who, although they were a foreign element within the Lebanese society, evolved to become an inseparable part of the social, political and cultural life there. Thus, their lasting impact on Lebanon was the impact of an insider and, therefore, much stronger than any French colonial force. Third, I look at the period 1936-1937, perhaps the two most turbulent years in mandatory Lebanon, and the role the Phoenician identity played therein. This period saw a concentration of the social and political forces in Lebanon that used this identity to support their political views and challenge the views of their opponents. The chapter concludes with an inquiry of the process that gradually led to the acceptance of Lebanon as a *fait accompli* by all sectors of Lebanese society, most notably the Sunni community. This process also inevitably led to the recognition of a separate Lebanese national narrative, which ushered in an acknowledgement of the Phoenician past, though in a modified, arabized form.

The French Mandate and the Lebanese Educational System

The crucial role of historiography in the process of nation-forging has long been recognized by students of nationalism.[3] Throughout the world, scholars and politicians often collaborated in the dissemination of national sentiments and the crystallization of collective identities by conducting selective historical scientific research, proving the indigenous nature of their nations and demonstrating their ancient and proud pedigrees. Universities, the most powerful institutions of the production and diffusion of knowledge, often served as vital agents in the dissemination of these national sentiments. Using the network of state-controlled schools, the Ministry of Education also evolved as a spearhead in the development of historical national narratives.[4] Keeping all this in mind, there is no surprise in the fact that one of the first steps the French took upon their arrival in Syria, at the end of World War I, was the rehabilitation of the devastated education system and the construction of a wide, French-oriented public school system. They believed that this would best serve their colonial interests and would also befit their *mission civilisatrice*.

Prior to WWI, education in Syria was mainly in the hands of private schools of the various religious communities and the foreign missions that operated throughout Syria but were especially dominant in Mount Lebanon and Beirut. There were also Ottoman state schools, mainly in the large cities of Beirut, Damascus and Aleppo, but only a small number of Syrians attended them and in general these schools were poorly equipped.[5] The two foreign universities in Beirut, Université Saint Joseph and the Syrian Protestant College, were the vanguard of higher education in the Arab provinces of the Ottoman Empire. In addition to functioning as institutes of higher learning, these universities also operated as the basis of a network of schools, from kindergarten through secondary, in their respective missions throughout Syria.[6]

A few days after the entry of the British and French forces into Beirut in October 1918, Colonel Piepape, the head of French troops, issued an act proclaiming the maintenance and rehabilitation of the educational system and the replacement of Turkish with French as the official language of instruction, along with Arabic.[7] At first, this act affected only Lebanon, which was controlled by the French, but in July 1920, General Gouraud entered Damascus and extended the policy to Syria as well. The calamities of the war had left the educational system, like other domains, in debris. The French worked to reconstruct the existing confessional and foreign schools and to construct, almost *ex nihilo*, the public school system. The records of the Office of Public Instruction of the High Commission (that was actually in charge of the private schools as well) are filled with deliberations and reports about the desired curricula in the public state schools. The French authorities were absorbed by the idea that they could use school curricula as an the avenue through which to cast national content into the new petty states they had formed by teaching Syrian, Lebanese, Druze and 'Alawite children French and European Civilization, on the one hand, and selective local history, on the other.[8] This, of course, was not a novel idea for the French, who had already practiced this policy extensively in their colonies, most notably in North Africa. In fact, the majority of the officers who served in Syria during the first decade of the French mandate had previously served in Morocco and were intentionally transferred to Syria so that they could implement the same colonial policy there.[9] French, previously studied only in the private and confessional schools, became a compulsory subject in the public schools as well. After French, history and geography were naturally considered to be the preferred fields through which political messages could be conveyed. The following examples, from the first two years of the mandate, mirror the atmosphere of these deliberations and the educational orientation dictated by the High Commission, particularly from 1920-1924, the terms of the first two commissioners, Henri Gouraud and Maxime Weygand.

In one of the numerous exchanges of letters between the High Commission and its representatives in the mandated regions, High Commissioner Gouraud replied to a report written by Combe, the inspector of public instruction in Aleppo, elaborating on the curriculum in two public schools in the city. Gouraud criticized the content of the curriculum, particularly in the subject of history, and asked Combe to make major revisions. Gouraud wrote that the curriculum did not reflect the shift from Ottoman to French control the region had undergone. It should include courses on the history of Syria instead of on the Arabs. Ancient history prior to the Arab-Islamic conquest should also be taught, Gouraud stated, because there had been other civilizations in Syria before the Arabs and the Prophet. Arab civilization should not be given a place in history greater than it deserved, concluded the High Commissioner.[10] In response, Combe explained that history of the Arabs was studied more than that of Syria simply because the teachers were unfamiliar with the latter. With time, he continued, teachers would learn this new subject and be able to teach Syrian and not only Arab history.[11]

The second example, reflecting the atmosphere in the first years of the French mandate in Syria and Lebanon, pertains to Louis Jalabert, one of the most outspoken Jesuits in support of the Christian Syro-Lebanese and an advocate of the non-Arab identity of Lebanon.[12] Jalabert taught at USJ from 1901-1919, then moved back to Paris to become the editor of the prestigious Jesuit journal *Études* and the representative of USJ's Faculty of Medicine to the Quai d'Orsay. He wrote often to French officials stating his views about political issues in the mandated regions. In a correspondence with Robert de Caix, the secretary of the High Commissioner and the architect behind French policy in Syria and Lebanon, Jalabert explained his ideas on the educational system in Lebanon. He argued that if France wished the mandate to become "*France d'autre Méditerranée*," there was a need to furnish the Lebanese with local, national, and French education simultaneously.[13] Our interest, Jalabert wrote, lies in attaching the thoughts and the hearts of the local elite to France, thus mixing their interests with ours.[14] This goal, he believed, could be achieved by emphasizing secondary and higher education at USJ and AUB. History classes, according to Jalabert, should focus on the Mediterranean and Roman ancient history and on local histories of Syria and Lebanon. Concluding his remarks, Jalabert wrote: "Un programme libanais, syrien, conçu dans cet esprit semblerait devoir donner une satisfaction suffisante à tous les besoins politiques du pays, tout en réservant l'intérêt français."

When Gouraud demanded that the history of Syria should be studied more than the history of the Arabs in public schools, he marked a major change in the historiographical and political focus of the region.[15] Private and confessional schools had already been teaching local history before the establishment of the French mandate, especially in Beirut and Mount Lebanon. Now, with French guidance and a state-controlled educational system, public schools began doing the same, introducing to their primarily Muslim students a new concept of history, one that preceded Muhammad and went as far back as the dark days of the *Jahiliyya* in the pre-Islamic eras. The change did not come at once, for public schools were never too popular in Syria and even less so in Lebanon, but with time, more students attended these schools and naturally were affected by their curricula.

As for Jalabert's ideas regarding the educational system in Syria and Lebanon, they reflect two points. First, they mirror the power of the Jesuits, who felt quite comfortable pressuring the High Commission to follow their desired agenda and, second, they reflect the educational orientation the Jesuits pursued in their schools. The idea of teaching local and Mediterranean history in order to strengthen local patriotism, on the one hand, and to attach the local population to France, on the other, prevailed in Jesuit establishments long before 1920. Jalabert simply wanted to insure that the High Commission would also pursue this policy. The Jesuits, who had been installed in Syria since 1831, and who dominated not only education but also many other aspects of life in Syria and Lebanon, wished to preserve their power also after the formation of the High Commission. This power implied not only the ability to dominate fields such as education, one of the most important in Jesuit dogma, but also other political domains such as state administration and control over local politics.[16] That said, it should not undermine the fact that the French *did* aspire to rehabilitate and ameliorate the education system in the mandated regions. They simply wished, at the same time, to profit politically from this process by creating a curriculum that would best serve their colonial interests.

The schools' curricula continued to preoccupy the French High Commission throughout the Mandate period. Numerous drafts can be found in the files of the *Service de l'instruction publique* in Syria and Lebanon. History and geography, the subjects that concern us, were two of the most sensitive domains in the public school curricula. From the multiple proposals, the picture that emerges of the contents of history and geography classes is of curricula that focused on French and European history and local history beginning in antiquity and chronologically surveying the different eras of Syria and Lebanon. Out of numerous examples, I chose the curriculum of Lebanese state elementary schools, which reflects the curricula of other types of schools. As noted, half of it is dedicated to French and European history, the details of which will not be discussed here. The other half, dedicated to local history, is as follows:

First Section: Syria before the Arab conquest
    First inhabitants of Syria.
    Beginning of agriculture.
    The Syrian race, the tribes, life of the clans.
    The Phoenicians.
    The invasions: Greek, Roman, Byzantine.

Second Section: The Arab conquest
    The Umayyads.
    Society under the Umayyads.
    The Caliphs of Baghdad and Egypt.

Third Section: Frankish Syria
    The Crusades, Saint Louis.
    Organization of the Frankish state.
    Political, social, economic, military and judicial institutions.
    Frankish intellectual movement.
    Architecture, industrial arts.
    The Mamluks.
    Beirut and Lebanon in the XV century.

Fourth Section: Ottoman Syria
    Ottoman conquest, Organization of Ottoman Syria.
    Fakhr al-Din al-Ma'ni.
    The Capitulations, François I, Richelieu, Louis XIV and the Maronites.
    Lebanon in the XVII century, Constitution, The Shihabi family.
    The French Revolution.
    The accords and the Protectorate of the Catholics of the Orient.
    Napoleon Bonaparte in Syria.
    Syria and Lebanon in the XIX century, the Amir Shihab.
    The Egyptians in Syria, Muhammad 'Ali and Ibrahim Pasha.
    Anarchy in Lebanon, the events of 1860.
    The Autonomous government of Lebanon.
    The Third Republic and the French policy in Lebanon.
    Syria on the eve of and after WWI.
    Reorganization of the French mandate in Syria and Lebanon.[17]

The curriculum speaks for itself. First, there is an emphasis on the pre-Arab history of Syria, which for the contemporary reader might seem natural and expected, but for Muslim Lebanese students of the time it was a novel, almost revolutionary, concept. Second, the Arabs receive mention, but as an occupier in a line of occupiers and are represented as "an era" among other eras in Lebanon and Syria, beginning in antiquity and progressing to the Greek, Roman, and Byzantine eras, the Crusades, and so forth. The relations between France and Syria and Lebanon win particular attention. Thus, the era of the Crusades, entitled *La Syrie franque*, reminding the students that Syria was once French, was taught in even more detail than the Arab-Islamic era.[18] There is no particular Phoenician message in this curriculum, but the concepts that it and other state schools' curricula carried unmistakably emphasized Lebanon as a distinct nation with 5,000 years of history, tied to France since the era of the Crusades.

The impact of the public schools on Lebanese society was minimal at first. With time, however, more students, mostly from Sunni and Shi'i lower-class families, began attending, which inevitably facilitated the process of acknowledging the existence of Lebanon as a *fait accompli*.[19] An indication of the growing strength of these schools on the Lebanese educational and political scene can be viewed through the "public school crisis" of 1929. This crisis was triggered as the result of an attempt by Emile Eddé, the new Prime Minister, to close down about a hundred public schools, attended mostly by lower-class Muslims. The Muslim leadership in Lebanon, with bold support from Syrian and other Arab politicians, launched a fierce campaign against Eddé's plan. They saw it as an attempt to force Muslim families to send their children to Christian missionary schools and thus to expose them to Western, anti-Arab, education. As a result, Eddé was forced to resign and the public schools he wanted to close down remained intact. This crisis marked a watershed in Lebanese politics. Eddé was labeled as anti-Arab; his rival, Béchara al-Khoury, overtly cooperated with Muslims against him and for the first time Lebanese Muslims won a major political confrontation against the Maronites.[20] By struggling to maintain a state apparatus, the crisis was registered also as one of the first signs of Muslim acknowledgement in the Lebanese state, a process that would culminate in the 1943 National Pact and the recognition by Muslim-Arab leadership of the right of Lebanon to exist as an independent state.

The Muslims' support of the public schools in Lebanon was motivated more by political causes than educational or ideological considerations. It is true that many Muslims feared sending their children to Christian missionary schools, lest they lose their Arab values in these Western institutions. But it is equally true that many haut-bourgeois Sunni families, which actually led the struggle against closing the public schools, had no misgivings about sending their sons to foreign schools, understanding that this was the key for a better future.[21] Moreover, although Muslims defended the public schools in this political crisis, they, nevertheless, also harshly criticized the curriculum content, especially with regards to the sensitive issues of Arab and Muslim history and Arab culture in Syria and Lebanon. Many complaints by students, parents and politicians as to the way Arabs and Islam were presented in public schools fill the records of the Service of Public Instruction.[22] In December 1932, following ongoing complaints against the public school system, Gabriel Bounoure, the Director of Public Instruction, circulated a note to all public schools in the mandatory regions asking educators and teachers to be extremely sensitive not to offend the oriental students in history classes, especially the Muslims, because French books, used in France and also in Syria, often contained insulting remarks against Muhammad and Islam. The High Commissioner, he recalled, had already discussed this problem in 1924.[23] Indeed, with time, the French learned to be more sensitive to the books and curricula employed in public schools. Thus, for example, the inspector of Public Instruction wrote the Grand Mufti of Lebanon, Sheikh Tawfiq Khalid, asking his opinion about a disputed history textbook. The book (*Le Moyen Âge jusqu'à la Guerre de Cent Ans*, by Charles Aimond) presented Islam in derogatory terms and depicted the Crusades in bright colors. The Mufti rejected the book, and the High Commissioner published an edict prohibiting its use in public schools.[24]

From the records of the Service of Public Instruction, it is apparent that the most sensitive and disputed topics in the public schools were not the ancient civilizations in Syria and Lebanon but rather the way Islam and the Arabs were depicted. The portrayal of the Crusaders was much more problematic and stirred more controversy than the eras that preceded the Arab occupation of Syria and Lebanon. The Crusades symbolized Western and Christian dominance and superiority, and the French spared no effort to present themselves as the new Crusaders. In history classes, as noted, the era of the Crusades was entitled "*La Syrie franque*," semantically stressing the connection between the Crusades and the French. It was the pro-Western and anti-Muslim orientation that agitated Arab-Muslim Lebanese more than the ancient civilizations of the Near East. This was also true for the entire secular Arab movement that did not necessarily view these civilizations as an opposing factor to their national aspirations, so long as they were not used to undermine the Arab culture of the region and were incorporated into the Arab national narrative.

During the first decade of the French mandate, the books used in the public school system were mostly history textbooks written by teachers from USJ. At first, the Service of Public Instruction ordered schools to adopt history and geography textbooks that had been used in the French private schools.[25] From 1920, teachers from USJ began writing new books especially for use in public schools. Henri Lammens, Gabriel Levenq, René Mouterde and Ferdinand Taoutel, all professors at USJ, were the first to publish books on the history and geography of Syria and Lebanon in simple language with clear messages.[26] They all surveyed the history and geography of Syria and Lebanon from antiquity to modernity, demonstrating the Semite, yet not Arab, origins of the inhabitants of Syria and Lebanon and emphasizing their unique physical features. According to these books, the history of Syria and Lebanon began with three major ancient civilizations, Phoenician, Greek and Roman. These civilizations were followed by other occupiers, among them the Arabs, Crusaders, Mamluks and Turks. Thus, the ethnic composition of Syria and Lebanon had evolved to be a mélange of races, forming together a racial mixture ethnically and culturally unique to those lands. Christianity occupies a larger portion than Islam in these works, emphasizing the Christian dominance in the region. These books were not overt Phoenician manifestations (although Lammens, followed by other professors at USJ, clearly supported the Phoenician image of the past in Syria and Lebanon). Yet they began to spread the Phoenician message, first by providing historical narratives of the pre-Islamic and Christian eras and second, by presenting a wide view of historical chronology from antiquity to modernity and by weaving Lebanon and Syria into the history of Europe.

Historical writing on Lebanon was not restricted to Jesuit professors from USJ. Two of the most notable historians of Lebanon were actually Lebanese — Asad Rustum (1897-1965) and Fouad Afram al-Bustani (1906-1995) — who, during the mandate years, became the leading national historians of Lebanon. They deserve the title "national historians" not so much because they wrote about Lebanese nationality, but because they provided Greater Lebanon with a national history of its own, separating it from the history of the Arabs and that of greater Syria.[27] Al-Bustani was a Maronite who acquired his education in USJ and remained a teacher of Arabic and history of the Arabs at the university's Oriental Faculty.[28] Although Arab civilization was his field of specialty, al-Bustani subscribed to the non-Arab identity of Lebanon and often referred in derogatory terms to the Arab-Muslim population of Lebanon. In 1951, he became the first president of the newly-founded Lebanese University and used this influential position to spread his views about the identity of Lebanon.[29] Asad Rustum was born into a Protestant family converted from Greek Orthodoxy. He acquired his education in American mission schools in Lebanon, at AUB, where he graduated in 1916, and at the University of Chicago, where he received his Ph.D. In 1922, he returned to Lebanon and became a faculty member of AUB as a teacher of the modern history of the Middle East.[30] The ancient Phoenicians did not preoccupy the historiographical work of Rustum and al-Bustani. Their contribution to the national historiography of Lebanon lay mainly in their concentration on the eras of the two princedoms of the Ma'nis and the Shihabis, describing them as the political precursors for Greater Lebanon and, specifically, depicting Fakhr al-Din al-Ma'ni as the father of modern Lebanon.

In 1937, following an agreement with the Ministry of Education, Rustum and al-Bustani wrote a series of history textbooks entitled *Tarikh Lubnan* [The History of Lebanon] which included five books at different levels of complexity, designed for different age groups, from elementary to high school.[31] According to these books, the history of Lebanon began with the cave men who were the first Lebanese, followed by the immigration of the Semitic Phoenicians from the Red Sea, who settled on the Lebanese coast and made it their home. Their preoccupation with the Phoenician civilization covers about a third of each of the books: their arrival in Lebanon, their commerce, the maritime activity, the invention of the alphabet, their ties with

Egypt, Greece and Rome, the establishment of Carthage and the military activity of Hannibal. By the time the reader finished the lengthy section on the Phoenicians there was no question as to who were the ancestors of the modern Lebanese. The books continue covering the history of Lebanon in broad strokes, surveying the Arab occupation, the Crusade era, the Ottoman arrival in Lebanon, the *Imara* [princedom] in the days of Fakhr al-Din and Bashir II in Mount Lebanon, concluding with the Lebanese contribution to the *Nahda*, the French arrival and the independence of Lebanon.

The publication of the first edition of *Tarikh Lubnan*, in 1938, stirred sharp controversy concerning the way the authors depicted certain episodes from the history of Lebanon. Yet, as happened previously with disputed books in Lebanese public schools, the sections that upset the Arab-Muslim camp in Lebanon were not about the ancient Phoenicians and their role in the formation of Lebanese national identity, but rather the negative portrayal of the Arabs and the positive description of the Crusaders. A fierce debate ensued in Lebanese papers between supporters and opponents of these books, embellished with exchanges of personal insults between papers such as *l'Orient* and *Bayrut*.[32] The Minister of Education, Khalil Kseib (Kussayb), under whose administrative supervision the books were written, promised to review them and reconsider their use in public schools. Kseib may have reexamined the books, but the fact remained that even after this debate the books were extensively used, right up to 1946, when the sixth edition appeared. These were not easy years for the Lebanese state. Politically, it was struggling on two fronts with France and Syria. Culturally, the country experienced internal strife that practically began with its formation and peaked towards the end of the 1930s, dividing Lebanon between supporters and opponents of its political integrity and cultural uniqueness. In the meantime, in public schools as well as in many of the private and confessional Christian schools, Lebanese students studied the history of their country, beginning with the ancient Phoenicians and concluding with the French mandate, providing them a teleological narrative that justified Lebanon's cultural and political distinctiveness. The history and geography curriculum did not necessarily undervalue the Arab neighbors of Lebanon. In fact, as the following 1946 report indicates, Lebanese students did focus also on Arab civilization and the place of Lebanon therein. This report, conducted by the American Council on Education, explains the objectives of historical studies in primary public schools:

> In teaching history and geography, the teacher is reminded that these subjects are of great use in developing patriotism and national spirit, that the two subjects are intimately related, [...]. History and geography start informally in the first grade [...]. In the second and third years historical pictures and stories about Lebanon and the Arab world are taken up [...] In the fourth grade, early history of Lebanon is brought down to the end of the Byzantine period and the history of the world to

the discovery of America [...]. In the fifth year Lebanese history to the present day is studied including relations with the Arab countries, while modern history takes up to the modern period [...]. In the higher primary course, the history of the ancient peoples having relations with Lebanon is studied, including the Egyptians, the Babylonians, Assyrians and Chaldeans, the Aegeans, Hittites, Hebrew, Persians, Greeks and the Romans; the growth of Christianity and the Byzantine empire. The ancient history of the Phoenicians — the early inhabitants of Lebanon — is then studied with emphasis on their invention of the alphabet, their seafaring and trade, their founding of Carthage and other colonies around the Mediterranean.[33]

The report continues to describe the subjects that Lebanese students study in their schools, following the Arabs, Mamluks, Fatimides, Crusaders, and Ottomans through the 17th century to the establishment of the princedoms of the Ma'nis and later the Shihabis, and concluding with the autonomous region of Mount Lebanon, the arrival of the French and the formation of Greater Lebanon. The picture is very clear. Lebanon is part of a larger geographical Arab region, but it also enjoys a distinct history that begins with the ancient Phoenicians and continues to the present time. This process in Lebanese public schools was one of the strongest forces that led to the inclusion of the Phoenician past into the much-disputed Lebanese national narrative; we shall return to this point later.

Université Saint Joseph and Its Graduates

USJ functioned as a major center of the dissemination of the Phoenician identity in Lebanon, and not only through its curriculum and the history and geography school textbooks its professors had written. The university played a principal role in the formation of the Lebanese state, which enabled the Jesuits to spread their views about the character and identity of the fledgling state. From the first days of French presence in Syria after the war, the Jesuits became involved in the administration of the Syrian territories.[34] Shortly after the formation of Greater Lebanon, an evening school was founded in USJ to train a capable local cadre of state employees that would occupy administrative positions of the state. In addition to the professional classes on state administration, the students of this school were obliged to attend classes on the history and geography of Syria. The teachers were no less than Henri Lammens, René Mouterde and Gabriel Levenq.[35] One does not need to think too hard to guess at the content of these classes. Indeed, USJ evolved to be a quintessential player in the crystallization of Greater Lebanon as a civil and political society. The two following quotes provide two polarized views about the Jesuits and USJ but they also reflect the weight the university carried in the consolidation of the Lebanese state. The first quote is taken from a report written by Gabriel Besnard, the General Secretary of the *Mission Laïque* in Syria, who naturally opposed the worldviews of the USJ Jesuits and struggled against their omnipresence in Lebanon:

> Les Jésuites tiennent tout le clergé maronite; ils agissent sur le Gouvernement local et sur le Haut Commissariat. Rien ne se fait au Liban sans l'assentiment des Jésuites; l'appui que leur donnent les pouvoirs publics explique en grande partie la crainte qu'ils inspirent. Gens aimables et cultivés, ils savent utiliser au plus grand profit de la puissance de l'ordre l'influence réelle dont ils jouissent au Liban. Les Jésuites n'aiment pas la démocratie; ils ne s'en cachent pas; ils ont même été créés pour combattre les institutions qui reflètent plus au moins l'esprit dont elle s'inspire. Et l'on assiste au Liban à ce paradoxe qui serait amusant s'il n'était tragique.[36]

It is tragic, concluded Besnard, because they control the instruction in Lebanon and teach their students their flawed ideas. Besnard's commentary should be read, of course, in the context of the fierce animosity that existed between the *Mission Laïque* and the Jesuit Order in Lebanon. Yet it should be remembered that many Syrians and Lebanese shared his criticism of the Jesuits because of the immense power they wielded in Lebanon. So powerful was their hold that even the High Commission repeatedly complained to the Quai d'Orsay of the Jesuit dominance in Lebanon and tried to curb it, often to no avail.[37]

The second example that illustrates the strength of the Jesuits and their university comes from Georges Naccache, himself a full-fledged product of Jesuit education which he acquired in Alexandria and Beirut.[38] The following quotation is taken from an article he wrote in his newspaper *l'Orient* in honor of the 75th anniversary of the establishment of USJ in 1875:

> Ce serait sans doute une stupidité de dire qu'il n'y aurait pas eu un Liban sans l'Université Saint Joseph; mais il nous serait à peu près impossible d'imaginer quelle aurait pu être l'autre figure de notre destin, si une dizaine de prêtres français, il y a soixante-quinze ans, n'avaient débarqué sur ce littoral de la Turquie d'Asie ... Pouvaient-ils pressentir ici l'extraordinaire aventure? Et quand ils obtenaient d'un vali ottoman l'autorisation de fonder le collège de Beyrouth, voyaient-ils déjà le déroulement précipité qui devait faire de ce petit rocher libanais l'un des centres spirituels — et politique — du monde? Ce fut d'abord une très petite maison, mais qu'habitait une très grande idée. Puis la maison, avec l'idée, a grandi. Et c'est finalement toute l'histoire de notre renaissance intellectuelle et nationale ... C'est là que furent formés les quelques centaines d'hommes — de juristes, de savants, d'ingénieurs

et de médecins, — qui devaient, en trois générations, refaire du Liban un État et une nation ... Nous ne pensons pas qu'il soit exagéré de dire qu'à peu près tout ce qui s'est bâti de valable, au Liban, depuis soixante-quinze ans, est né de cette rencontre.[39]

It is interesting that opponents and supporters of the Jesuits in Lebanon held similar views as to the power they enjoyed in Lebanon; the former simply viewed it negatively and the latter positively. The important point, nevertheless, is that the Jesuits regarded Lebanon as their own front yard and constantly aspired to realize their vision of a Christian-Catholic, Western-oriented society there. They often collaborated with their graduates for the purpose of attaining this goal, as in the case of Maurice Sarrail, the third French High Commissioner (January-November 1925), whose appointment infuriated the Jesuits as well as many of the Christian Lebanese. After two devout Catholic High Commissioners, Sarrail was a dedicated atheist with strong ties to the French anti-clerical left. In his short term as High Commissioner, Sarrail strove to appease the Syrian national movement and the Muslim Lebanese and attempted to curb the immense power of the Jesuits in Mandatory Syria and Lebanon.[40] The Jesuits, who conducted a fierce battle against his policy, both in the mandated regions and in France itself, found a devoted ally in this struggle in the person of Georges Naccache, who ceaselessly wrote against Sarrail and his anti-Jesuit-cum-anti-Lebanese policies in his journal *l'Orient*. Among other things, *l'Orient* reprinted articles from *l'Action française*, the French fascist radical right journal that attacked Sarrail and his anti-Christian policy in Syria. In response, Sarrail suspended the publication of *l'Orient*, accusing Naccache of receiving payments from the Jesuits to conduct this struggle against the High Commission.[41]

As the case of Naccache demonstrates, the Jesuit experience did not cease with graduation from USJ. From 1898, a very active Alumni Association operated in Beirut, functioning as a social club for the USJ graduates.[42] A reading through the various publications of this association reveals the social circles and the social life of these graduates, who used to meet three times a year at the Alumni Association General Assembly at the university, with many of the Jesuit faculty, other dignitaries, and the "who's who" in Syria and Lebanon present. It was a cohesive social class of devout francophones, remarkably influenced by the Jesuit dogma which they experienced during their adolescence and adulthood years.[43] The regular gatherings included speeches by dignitaries, a report of recent achievements of particular graduates and an artistic program.[44] In 1934, the year in which the Oriental Faculty of USJ reopened its gates, the Alumni Association began issuing a new journal, *L'U* (short for *Bulletin de l'Université*), that supplemented the old *Bulletin Annuel de l'Association Amicale des Anciens Eélèves de l'Université Saint Joseph*. Alfred Naccache,[45] then the secretary of the association, opened each issue with a transcript of the speech he had given at the last gathering. In the second issue of *L'U* from June 1934, a third of his speech is dedicated to the recently published *La Montagne Inspirée*, sparing no words to compliment the artistic and patriotic values of Charles Corm, the "*aède phénicien*." Naccache himself never published any work with direct Phoenician symbols but his reference to Corm indicated an unequivocal support of the businessman-poet's Phoenicianism. He ended his praise of Corm with the following sentence: "Le meilleur éloge que je puisse faire de notre ami, c'est que l'émotion qu'il réveille dans nos âmes est de la plus noble qualité et qu'à la lecture de certains passages, j'ai vu perles des larmes dans des yeux libanais."[46]

Two years later, in 1936, Alfred Naccache was still secretary of the Alumni Association. It was a special year for the francophile milieu in Beirut. Emile Eddé ascended to presidency and the pro-Eddé camp had good reason to celebrate. As always, Naccache gave the opening speech to the association's General Assembly. Half of it he dedicated to Eddé's victory, which was seen as the Association's victory and a triumph of the Christian francophone circles in Lebanon. A year earlier, Corm had represented Lebanon in the *Congrès de la Méditerranée* (discussed below), which also received its fair share in Naccache's report. His opening words, in front of the Jesuit teachers, who were always present at these gatherings, and scores of USJ graduates, were as follows:

> S'il est vrai que le soleil est père de la joie, quelle chance pour nous qui sommes du pays de Baal ! Quelle jubilation en cette saison même où la Mer et la Montagne chantent sous la lumière et réveillent dans nos cœurs néo-phéniciens le désir des lointaines évasions![47]

Unlike the mythological *La Revue Phénicienne* or *Phénicia*, *L'U* was not an overt Phoenician organ. It nevertheless reflected the francophone Phoenician circles of Beirut via its writers, who belonged to this clique, and through the atmosphere that imbued its lines. The ambience of *L'U* was recognizable from its front cover. A drawing, depicting a Phoenician vessel with Phoenician seafarers approaching the edifice of the USJ, adorned the bulletin. Parallel to the edifice stood the title, *L'U*, designed as an additional construction. The symbolism was clear: ancient Phoenician seafarers sailing into Beirut docked directly before the walls of USJ and the mansion of *L'U*. Thus, a direct link was formed between the ancient Phoenician maritime navigators and the students of USJ — the "neo-Phoenicians."

Archeology and National Museums

Modern excavations in Syria and Lebanon began, as noted in Chapter I, with the scientific mission of Ernest Renan in 1860. Since then, numerous excavating teams, primarily led by French archeologists, unearthed the ancient civilizations of Syria and Lebanon. The discoveries were either shipped to

Paris and Istanbul or kept in private collections in Syria. The Jesuits accumulated an impressive collection at USJ, and the Syrian Protestant College amassed its own collections in Beirut and Sidon. One of the first administrative measures the French took after their arrival in Syria was to create the Service of Antiquity and Fine Arts that took charge of the administration of excavations and the formation of several museums throughout the mandated regions. On July 1922, the first Lebanese National Museum was inaugurated with the blessing and supervision of the High Commission. It was only a provisory enterprise, and the aim was to later found a larger museum that would bring together under one roof all the archeological collections in Lebanon.[48] In the museum's mission statement, the French authorities made it very clear that the Lebanese National Museum would concentrate on Phoenician archeology, whereas the future museum in Damascus would focus on Islamic and Arab art.[49] The French continued to conduct the policy of archeological division between Beirut and Damascus throughout their mandate in Syria and Lebanon. The 1928 French report to the League of Nations contained a section about archeology and fine arts.[50] The subdivision on archeology in Lebanon was arranged in three different parts, covering Phoenician, Frankish-Crusade and religious-Christian archeology. Muslim Archeology, conducted by l'Institut français d'archéologie et d'art musulmane de Damas, was covered in a different section in the report, reflecting the separation the French made between Syria and Lebanon in the domain of archeology.

Simultaneous with the founding of the museum in Beirut, the Service of Antiquities began issuing its journal, *Syria*, at the publication house of David Corm, the father of Charles. In the first issue of *Syria*, René Dussaud, one of the most distinguished French archeologists in Syria, commented on the Antiquities Service's mission statement. "Notre programme," he explained, "se résume en deux phrases: développer en Syrie le goût de l'art et des antiquités du pays; mieux faire connaître au dehors les arts syriens de toutes les époques. La revue Syria doit servir de trait d'union entre l'intellectualité française et l'élite syrienne en leur fournissant l'occasion d'une collaboration féconde."[51] Befitting the French colonial idea, *Syria* had a civilizing mission to educate the Syrians and to strengthen the ties between Syrian and French intellectuals, with the underlying political agenda of winning the support of the elite to facilitate French control. Moreover, as Benedict Anderson noted in his *Imagined Communities*, there was nothing innocent in the construction of museums and the establishment of national services of antiquities, let alone when these were erected in colonial settings. Anderson named this process "political museumizing" and although his examples for this process were taken from the other, eastern, side of the Asian continent, they elucidate very clearly what happened in any other nation-building processes associated with a colonial power.[52] After France took control over Syria and Lebanon in 1919-1920, it finally had the opportunity to fully manage the archeological excavations of the region. Emulating their own national conduct regarding museums (for what symbolizes French national patrimony and pride better than the Louvre?), the French authorities established "national museums" in Beirut, Damascus, and Aleppo, each focusing on a different theme. The journal *Syria* supplemented the museums with data, tables, illustrations and reports, all to be consumed by the local elite, establishing the triangular connection between ancient local history, its explorer, the French, and its recipient, the Syro-Lebanese. Until 1928, the conservation of the Lebanese National Museum was put in the hands of Charles Virolleaud, Director of the Service of Antiquities, and Philippe de Tarrazi, the Lebanese Conservator of the newly-born National Library.[53] In July 1924, several affluent Lebanese, led by Jacques Tabet launched a committee, *Amis du Musée*,[54] for the construction of a large and respected home for the Lebanese National Museum. They raised money from wealthy families in Beirut and from the Lebanese immigrant communities throughout the world.[55] The process lasted more than a decade, until the completion of the building drew near, and in 1937 the new structure was inaugurated with equal pomp and fanfare.[56]

In 1928, a watershed was crossed in the history of modern Lebanon when Maurice Chéhab became the conservator of the Lebanese National Museum. It was a significant event because it symbolized the beginning of the transfer of archeological management from the French to local Lebanese. Chéhab, scion of the highborn Chéhabi family, was also a product of the Jesuit education system. In one of the USJ alumni bulletins he explained why he chose to be an archeologist. He wrote that he was deliberating over which profession he should choose.[57] The courses he took in local archeology fascinated him. Then, in 1921, Henri Lammens' book, *La Syrie; Précis Historique*, was published and clarified for Chéhab his ideas about the national history of Lebanon. He decided to study archeology, becoming the first Lebanese archeologist to excavate professionally in Lebanon, at the Byblos site. Even more than devout Phoenicians such as Charles Corm and Sa'id 'Aql, Chéhab actually played a tremendous role in the insertion of Phoenician messages into the Lebanese national narrative. Unlike those two, Chéhab was never thought to be a Phoenician thinker. Yet, through his thirty-three years as director of the National Museum and later as the director of the Service of Antiquities, in addition to his numerous publications on Phoenician and Greco-Roman Lebanon, Chéhab was able to spread the word on Phoenicianism more than the best-recognized Phoenician preachers.

Maurice Chéhab is only one example of the fact that by the mid-1930s, intellectual Lebanese were expressing a growing interest in the ancient history of their country. The continuing excavations at various sites in Lebanon, most notably Byblos, Tyre and Sidon, and the sensational discoveries in Ugarit in northern Syria after 1929 added to the growing curiosity about the ancient history of the country.[58] In addition to *Syria,* the Lebanese government began funding the publication of additional archeological journals, such as *Études et Documents d'Archéologie* and *Le Bulletin du Musée de Beyrouth*, first published in 1937 with, on its front cover, a Phoenician vessel. The "political museumizing" that characterized French colonial conduct continued as Lebanon followed the lead of its mandatory power. Imitating the French was not too surprising, for, after all, Lebanon exhibited marked continuity from the French mandate to its independence in many aspects of state and public life, archeology included. In any case, museums are a national educating instrument of the first degree, with or without French influence, and the Museum, through its exhibitions and its *Bulletin,* was a clear Phoenician agent. The *Bulletin*'s mission statement stated its objective plainly:

> Une chronique sera consacrée à l'activité archéologique du Liban. Les documents inédits ou peu connus de nos collections y seront publiés, et ses pages seront ouvertes à toute étude relative à l'histoire et à la civilisation des Phéniciens ainsi qu'aux disciplines connexes.[59]

The Jesuits naturally enjoyed the growing interest in local archeology. In the academic year of 1933-34, the Oriental Faculty at USJ, under the new name of *Leçons des lettres orientales,* reorganized its courses and, for the first time since WWI, offered an organized curriculum and a certified degree in the ancient history and archeology of the region.[60] Charles Dugas, a French professor from Université de Lyon, wrote a special report about the old-new faculty. He praised its director, the Jesuit René Mouterde, for the initiative, but he had two major criticisms of new faculty. He remarked that the theoretical classes required also a practical angle and that there was too much focus on local ancient history. He also averred that a sound education for an archeologist demanded a qualified background in Latin and Greek, not only in Phoenician and other local Semitic civilizations. Still, concluding his review, Dugas wrote that the initiative of opening the *Leçons de Lettres Orientales* deserved all the support possible from the French authorities because at the time of signing the Franco-Syrian and Franco-Lebanese treaties, it was important to win the hearts of these students who find special interest in the history of their county and who, in the foreseeable future, would become history teachers in local schools.[61]

Less than a year after Dugas submitted his report about the *Leçons des Lettres Orientales,* the new Bibliothèque Orientale was inaugurated. This library was one of USJ's finest treasures and its reopening in a smartly renovated building was a joyful occasion for the university. A large fresco, depicting a map of the Near East, welcomed visitors to the new library. Designed by a Jesuit teacher, Father Louis Tresca, it reflected the Jesuit view of the history of the region. Lebanon was located at the center of the map, symbolized by the Mountain and the cedars. Two Phoenician vessels crossed the Mediterranean westwards and one, Jonah, reached the shores of Jaffa. In Egypt, a large image of a Pharaoh stood poised, watching Mesopotamia. An impressive convoy of Crusaders approached the region from Europe, and from the east a huge chariot harnessed to four magnificent horses carried Apollo straight to the heart of the Near East. The image of Jesus was depicted walking along the Phoenician coast. Damascus was represented by the great Umayyad mosque, Jerusalem by a drawing of the Old City and Constantinople by an illustration of the Haghia Sophia. A brochure explained the meaning of the fresco in the following words:

> ... [D]e tout temps, la côte phénicienne en fut la patrie [of the light, A.K.], en particulier ce Liban qui occupe le centre de l'œuvre. L'artiste néglige même de le nommer, tellement la place qu'il occupe montre à l'évidence que c'est vers lui que tout converge. [...]. D'Égypte et d'Assyrie vinrent, avec d'innombrables objets d'art, la science des nombres et les cultes mystérieux qui furent à la base des premières spéculations philosophiques des Grecs. Puis, lorsqu'arriva la plénitude des temps, la Syrie et le Liban durent à leur proximité de la "Terra Domini" de recevoir aussitôt le message de Celui qui vint lui-même un jour "jusqu'aux confines de Tyr et de Sidon." Ce furent alors les siècles de vie chrétienne intense qui précédèrent la conquête musulmane ; puis Bagdad et Damas succédèrent à Byzance et à la "Saint Jérusalem," jusqu'au jour où les Croisés, venus par Constantinople, consolidèrent les résultats de la guerre sainte en fondant le Royaume France de Syrie. Le Levant fait alors la connaissance de l'Occident chrétien comme puissance à la fois politique et spirituelle : main bientôt, dès la fin du Moyen-age, cette influence de l'Occident se réduit au seul élément spirituel. De pays de colonisation, la Syrie devient champs d'apostolat, et la fresque nous rappelle qu'en 1523, Ignace de Loyola, nouvellement converti, s'embarqua pour cette terre d'Orient qu'il désirait ramener tout entière au Christ. Ainsi se trouvait inauguré par le fondateur de la Compagnie de Jésus le travail apostolique auquel, de nos jours encore, ses fils se consacrent ici même. Leur but, en construisant cette nouvelle Bibliothèque Orientale a été de promouvoir le règne du Christ, unique synthèse possible de tant d'influences contradictoires.[62]

This description well outlines the view of history as seen and taught within the walls of USJ in the formative years that shaped Lebanon as a political community. This was the historical baggage with which the graduates of the university departed, which they carried to their posts in state administration, politics, business, instruction and other fields of Lebanese public life.

1936-1937: A Case Study of Phoenicianism and Its Adversaries

On January 20, 1936, Emile Eddé was elected president by the Lebanese Chamber of Deputies. It was the first time the president was nominated by the votes of the deputies rather than by direct appointment of the French High Commissioner. Perplexingly, Eddé won with the support of the majority of the Muslim deputies, whereas his rival Béchara al-Khoury received insufficient votes from the deputies of the Mountain. The results demonstrated the complexity of Lebanese politics. Although Béchara al-Khoury was clearly culturally and socially closer to the Muslim population in Lebanon, he did not win their votes; Eddé, meanwhile, the devout francophile who found it even difficult to converse in Arabic and whose world of reference was the cosmopolitan life of Beirut, did not win the support of the Maronites and instead found his allies among the Sunni and Shi'i deputies. It was an expression of the fact that the Mountain and the ideology it radiated intimidated the Muslim population of Lebanon. Muslim deputies preferred to cast their ballots for Eddé, the "non-Arab" who, as I shall elaborate below, flirted with the Phoenician circles of Beirut, rather than voting for al-Khoury whose power base was less in the city and more in the Maronite fortress of the Mountain. The results of the elections also reflected the fact that the Maronite community was far from united even on its dearest and most important issue — maintaining the integrity of Lebanon and its Christian character.

Eddé's assuming the presidency launched the two most tempestuous years in mandatory Lebanon. From those presidential elections, in January 1936, to the parliamentary elections of October 1937, Lebanon was on the brink of civil war. The streets of its major cities experienced consecutive violent demonstrations, governments rose and fell, major strikes paralyzed the country and Lebanese society seemed on the verge of total anarchy. Internal and external reasons led to this predicament. The Eddé/al-Khoury rivalry continued at full steam and divided the Lebanese social and political scene. In September 1936, the Franco-Syrian treaty was ratified by the Syrian parliament, bringing the Muslim population of Lebanon into the streets, afraid lest their Syrian brothers neglect them. Following the conclusion of the negotiations over the Franco-Syrian treaty, the French began discussing a Franco-Lebanese pact with the Lebanese government. Eddé and al-Khoury cooperated for the talks, but, once the treaty was signed, in November 1936, they resumed their rivalry even more ferociously than before. As a reaction to Muslim irredentist demands and to the growing strength of the Partie Populaire Syrien, Maronite leaders formed the Lebanese Kata'ib in November, marking the establishment of the first well-organized Maronite mass movement within Lebanon. On the Syro-Lebanese front, Tripoli became the major source of contention between the two countries. The Syrians, supported by the majority of the Muslim Lebanese, continued to demand the annexation of the city to Syria. The entire Middle East experienced dramatic shifts in these two years. The Palestinian uprising was underway in Palestine, while in Egypt and Iraq agreements were being signed between Britain and the two local governments. In Europe, the drums of war began pounding, adding to the general sense of insecurity and uncertainty about the future.

The Phoenician identity of Lebanon was by no means at the center of these events, yet often it echoed in the background of the political and social turmoil that characterized 1936-37. Several examples well demonstrate this point. On March 1936, Muslim and Christian leaders[63] convened in Beirut at what was known as the "Congress of the Coast and the Four Districts," responding to the Franco-Syrian negotiations, with two conflicting demands. On the one hand, they demanded that the annexed regions of Lebanon be returned to Syria but on the other, they appealed for a larger and more equal share of Lebanese politics and social life.[64] The Congress triggered a fierce squabble in journals and newspapers in Beirut for and against the demands of the Muslim leadership and their declaration that Lebanon was an Arab country, indistinguishable from its Arab neighbors. The francophone *le Jour* and *l'Orient* shared with the Jesuit *al-Bashir* the view that Lebanon was Lebanese and not Arab, whereas the leading Arabic journals *al-Nahar* and *Bayrut* repeated and supported the demands of the Congress of the Coast.[65] The response of Lebanese nationalists to this Congress often involved the Phoenician angle. Najib Dahdah, for example, a Maronite politician and journalist, responded to the demands of the Conference in an article in the Jesuit journal *al-Mashriq*. There he argued that, geographically, the Lebanese coast had been part of the Mountain since the Phoenician era and, therefore, those who lived along the Mediterranean coast of Lebanon had been Lebanese then just as they are Lebanese today.[66] Similarly, the Beirut municipal elections that took place a month after the Congress ended were also influenced by the claims of the Phoenician identity of Lebanon. Christian and Muslim candidates were divided along Phoenician and Arab lines, increasing the already mounting tension between the two communities.[67] As a reaction to the demands of the Congress of the Coast and to the growing tension in the streets of Beirut, the Maronite Patriarch initiated the formation of a party, *Front national libanais*, headed by Yusuf al-Saouda, one of the most vociferous voices in favor of the Phoenician identity of Lebanon, who used his publication, *al-Raya*, to express his views about the political integrity of Lebanon and its non-Arab identity.[68] Lacking wide popular support, al-Saouda's party did not survive long, but it marked the desire within the Maronite community to establish a popular organization that would confront the Arab and Syrian agitation in Lebanon. This desire was fulfilled at the end of 1936 with the formation of the Lebanese *Kata'ib* by Pierre al-Gemayyel and four other Christian leaders. The vast majority of *Kata'ib* supporters in its first stages were students and graduates of USJ[69] who stormed the streets of Beirut calling for Lebanese integrity and independence; asserting its unique non-Arab cultural and national features. The *Kata'ib* were not labeled as a Phoenician movement, but its leaders often used Phoenician phraseology to explain the non-Arab identity of Lebanon. Lebanon is not Phoenician, it was asserted, in the political meaning, for Lebanon is a relatively new political body dating to the 17th century. It is Phoenician, however, in culture and ethos, bequeathed to the modern Lebanese by their forefathers in ancient times.[70]

The preparations for the 1937 parliamentary elections were also marked by the division between supporters and opponents of the distinct non-Arab identity of Lebanon. Newspapers in Beirut were saturated with accusations and counter-accusations over this disputed national identity. *Al-Nahar*, the journal of the Greek Orthodox Gebran Tuéni, the Arabic paper with the highest readership in Beirut, led the attack against the Phoenician tendencies of the presidency of Emile Eddé and his prime minister, the Sunni Khair al-Din Ahdab.[71] The city of Tripoli, which had always been a center of pro-Syrian agitation, was also doused with the anti-Phoenician mood. A Sunni organization was formed in this coastal city carrying the flag of anti-Phoenicianism, and, as in the case of the Congress of the Coast, the Beirut press used the opportunity to support or denounce this trend.[72] Using the term "Phoenician" in these cases did not strictly mean a recognition of the Phoenician descent of Lebanon in the same way Sa'id 'Aql and Charles Corm understood Phoenicianism. It was more a Christian statement that Lebanon had the historical right of being a political and cultural separate entity. More than anything else, it reflected the fact that in the 1930s Phoenicianism was "in the air," and was used not only by the leading "Phoenician prophets" but also by many Lebanese nationalists, to assert their national identity. So prevalent was the use of the term "Phoenician" that in 1937, when Edmond Rabbath, the Arab-Syrian nationalist, published his book, *Unité Syrien et Devenir Arabe*, he referred to the entire Lebanese national movement as Phoenician and described Lebanese society as split in two camps: supporters and opponents of the Phoenician identity.[73] Similarly, the appearance in January 1938 of *Phénicia*, the literary journal to be discussed below, can only be understood in the context of the political events that preceded its publication. Although Aurore Ougour, the owner and editor of *Phénicia*, clearly stated that there was no political motive behind the journal, only cultural and artistic ones,[74] there is no question that the timing of its appearance, on the heels of two such chaotic years in Lebanese politics, marked a very clear statement by Ougour and her writers — from Charles Corm to Sa'id 'Aql and Michel Chiha — as to their cultural and political convictions about the identity of Lebanon.

Towards Independence

In the week of February 15-21, 1942, the Lebanese Ministry of Education and Fine Arts initiated and organized a series of lectures on Radio Levant (*Idha'at al-Sharq*) entitled, "The Week of Culture in Lebanon." Ramiz Sarkis, the Maronite minister, opened the series with an address emphasizing Lebanon's eminent culture, its esteemed location among its Arab sister countries, and its role in the renaissance of the Arabic language. The lectures clearly supported Lebanon's right to exist as a viable national community, and at the same time they also depicted it as an integral, culturally leading, member of the Arab world. One of the lecturers in this series was presented by 'Umar Fakhuri (1896-1946), a Sunni thinker and writer from Beirut,[75] whose presentation was entitled "Risalat Lubnan al-Thaqafiyya" [The Cultural Mission of Lebanon]. The following quotation reflects its content:

> Since Lebanon's existence, it did not stand still on the shores of this Mediterranean, in front of its ancient and modern civilizations [...]. Its historical and geographical smallness did not prevent it from providing the world, in any era of its civilization, the instrument of ideal communication [the alphabet, A.K.], the methods of preferable worship [monotheism, A.K.] the paths to thought and uprightness. Moreover, possibly this very smallness [...] was what instigated this people (Sha'b), pushing itself with undiminished determination, to seek and find greatness for itself. And thus, we have seen Lebanon spreading by means of ships and towns, gods and temples, expanding the boundaries of handicrafts and thought. From its holy woods they built lofty houses of prayer and ships that sailed afar, and it seemed that because of its limited scope it pursued vengeance on distant parts, and it did not rest until it brought the scattered near, assembled the opposites and united the material and the spirit simultaneously.

These words of Fakhuri could have been comfortably uttered by any Christian Lebanese who supported the idea of Lebanon's unique cultural and special national features.[76] His lecture clearly reflected the long way Phoenicianism had come from the end of the 19th century to the 1940s. By the mid-1930s, there were enough Muslim Lebanese, especially the Sunni haute-bourgeois leadership in Beirut, who were willing to acknowledge the existence of Lebanon as a *fait accompli* as long as Lebanon was recognized as part of a larger Arab world and the Muslim Lebanese were allowed to participate in its national institutions on equal terms. It was a lengthy and rocky process, but recognizing the existence of Lebanon as an independent sovereign state inevitably implied also acknowledging the fact that Lebanon, in its current extended borders, had a separate history that justified its existence as an independent state. Fakhuri's words on Radio Levant were an integral part of this inevitable process. He said not a word about "our ancestors the Phoenicians."[77] Yet, the language he used in his broadcast was based on years of Phoenician terminology recited by historians, archeologists, poets, authors and nationalists. *Al-Adib*, the popular literary journal that published the various lectures of "the Week of Culture," printed them in an interesting format. The top of each page was decorated with drawings of a Phoenician vessel with a woman on each side, dressed in Greco-Roman robes. Thus, "The Week of Culture in Lebanon" conveyed a very clear message that this was an independent country, tied to the Arab world, and simultaneously it also reflected a distinct identity of which one attribute was the Phoenician heritage. Even one of the most francophile journals and a staunch supporter of Lebanon-Phoenicia in the 1930s recognized this transformation in the 1940s. *La Revue du Liban et de l'Orient Méditerranéen*, founded in 1928 in Paris by Ibrahim and Emile Makhluf, was a popular journal with a wide circulation of readers in France and in Lebanon. Almost every issue contained references to the Phoenician descent of Lebanon and included articles about Phoenician archeology, history and civilization.[78] In 1933, the Makhluf brothers founded an organization in Paris for Lebanese émigrés, which they called Nova Phenicia, marking their cultural orientation with this appellation.[79] Yet, in 1939, when they moved back to Beirut as a result of the mounting war in Europe, they continued to publish their journal but with a changed name — *La Revue du Liban et de l'Orient Arabe* — symbolizing their own recognition of change within the Lebanese society.

It is evident that by the 1940s, Phoenician terminology had entered the Lebanese national narrative and become an established part of the story of the formation of the Lebanese nation. Many Muslims and more than a few Christians continued to view Phoenicianism as a foreign, anti-Arab concept, imported by French colonialism, especially in light of the growing strength of the pan-Arab movement in the 1950s.[80] But at the same time, Phoenician symbols, icons and images became an inseparable part of the day-to-day reality of Lebanon. By the mid-1940s the following phrases became conventional wisdom within Lebanon: "Lebanon is a crossroads of civilizations;" "The ancient Lebanese invented the alphabet;" "For 6,000 years, Lebanese have been natural born merchants;" and "Lebanese emigration started with the Phoenician colonies."[81] Younger Lebanese studied about their Phoenician ancestors in school while older ones were smoking Adonis, Byblos and Amir cigarettes, the latter packet decorated with a Phoenician vessel. A Lebanese who used the *Indicateur Libano-Syrien*, the Lebanese "Yellow Pages," encountered a historical précis in the introduction, outlining the history and ethnography of Lebanon, beginning with the ancient Phoenicians.[82] Guidebooks and manuals, written by Lebanese themselves, often with the encouragement of the Lebanese government,[83] played on the Phoenician chord and explained at length the "evolution of the Lebanese nation." The famous series, *Les Guides Verts*, published a handbook *Beyrouth et la République Libanaise*, that opened with an introduction by Philip Hitti and with an essay by 'Abdallah 'Alayli about the history of Lebanon. 'Alayli, a Sunni scholar from Beirut, who acquired his education at al-Azhar University in Cairo, was one of the most important Arabic linguists in the Arab world and no one would dare question his Arab identity. Nevertheless, the history section he wrote carried an unequivocal message that the annals of the Lebanese nation began with the Phoenician navigators. According to him, these Phoenicians were Bedouin Arab tribes that arrived in Lebanon from the Arabian Peninsula and whose contribution to the evolution of the Lebanese stock was immense. Four drawings embellish this section of the guidebook. The first two depict the invention of the alphabet and the construction of Phoenician ships and the other two portray Fakhr al-Din al-Maʻni and Bashir II, demonstrating the three foundational pillars of the Lebanese national history. By "arabizing" the Phoenicians it was possible for him to write a historical essay about the origin and evolution of the Lebanese nation that would not have dishonored any average Christian Lebanese with Phoenician tendencies. ʻAlayli was not the first to refer to the Phoenicians as genuine Arabs. He only reiterated the thesis supported by many Arab demographers who considered Arabia as the human source of the entire population of the Near East.[84] Right or not, if the Phoenicians were believed to be Arabs then a 20th-century Arab nationalist like ʻAbdallah ʻAlayli could take pride in his civilization and its contribution to Arab Lebanon. It would be inconceivable to think that in the 1920s and 1930s, ʻAlayli or ʻUmar Fakhuri would have elaborated on the Phoenician components in the Lebanese collective identity. Yet, in the 1940s, following the gradual process of reconciliation with the existence of Greater Lebanon, these two Sunni intellectuals did glorify the Phoenician past of Lebanon, while at the same time they continued to view themselves as proud Arabs and regard Lebanon as a leading Arab state.

On September 1943, the National Pact, the historic agreement between Béchara al-Khouri and Riad al-Sulh, defined Lebanon as a country with an "Arab face," and simultaneously it also guaranteed the continuation of its traditional links with the West. A year later, Lebanon became one of the founding members of the Arab League. Avid Phoenicians, such as Yusuf al-Saouda, opposed its joining the League.[85] The Maronite Bishop of Beirut, Monsignor Ignace Moubarac, was also one of the most vociferous voices against the inclusion of Lebanon into the Arab fold.[86] Moubarac's views, however, were not endorsed by the Maronite Church. They were more of an independent plea supported by a few Christian intellectuals who remained marginal in 1940s Christian Lebanese society. By and large, the Lebanese population, Christian and Muslim alike, supported the independent, integrationist stream and rejected the vision of a Christian isolationist entity. Even devout, pro-Western Phoenician sympathizers such as Charles Malik and Philip Hitti recognized this. Malik, a well-known philosopher and politician, stood out in his long public career as a sound supporter of Phoenicia-Lebanon. In 1945, he was appointed the Lebanese ambassador to the United Nations and evolved to be the strongest voice in the General Assembly, fighting for the Arab-Palestinian cause and denouncing Zionist ambitions in Palestine.[87] Similarly, Philip Hitti, whose contribution to the diffusion of the Phoenician past into the Lebanese national narrative was immense, also stood out as a defender of the Arab-Palestinian agenda and as an opponent of the Zionist movement.[88] Both Malik and Hitti were avid Lebanese nationalists who simultaneously supported the historical narrative of Lebanon as neo-

Phoenicia and of Lebanon as an active, though unique, member of the Arab world.

The tension between the Christian Phoenician ideal and the Arab-Muslim population of Lebanon never ceased, because the Phoenicianism of some Christian Lebanese remained permanently tied to their assertion that they were not Arabs. Yet the fact remains that, despite this tension, Phoenician expressions did enter Lebanese national consciousness and became an inseparable part of the country's myth of origin. In a way, this kind of Phoenicianism was a return to the first expressions of the Phoenician identity in the 1880s. In a world of "awakening" national communities that were imagining and writing their own autobiographies, the Lebanese were beginning with their distant and invented birth in antiquity.

References

1 *Usbu' al-Thaqafa fi Lubnan* (Beirut, 1942), p. 4.
2 See Meir Zamir, *The Formation of Modern Lebanon*, especially pp. 97-146; Gérard D. Khoury, *La France et l'Orient Arabe* (Paris: A. Colin, 1993), pp. 353-399; Kamal S. Salibi, *The Modern History of Lebanon*, pp. 151-167; Georges Adib Karam, *L'Opinion Publique Libanaise et la Question du Liban* (Beirut: Librairie Orientale, 1981).
3 See, for example, the following works: David, N. Myers, *Re-Inventing the Jewish Past* (New York: Oxford University Press, 1995); Ranajit Guha, *An Indian Historiography of India: A Nineteenth Century Agenda and Its Implications* (Calcutta: K.P. Bagchi & Co., 1988); Bernard Lewis, *History: Remembered, Recovered, Invented* (Princeton: Princeton University Press, 1975); David C. Gordon, *Self-Determination and History in the Third World* (Princeton: Princeton University Press, 1971).
4 Sati' al-Husri, of course, is the most notable example within the Arab world of the use of the Ministry of Education in Iraq for the dissemination of national sentiments. See in William Cleveland, *The Making of an Arab Nationalist; Ottomanism and Arabism in the Life and Thought of Sati' al-Husri* (Princeton: Princeton University Press, 1971), pp. 59-80.
5 For a survey of education in Syria before 1918, see J. A. Babikian, *Civilization and Education in Syria and Lebanon* (Beirut: 1936), pp. 80-87.
6 See more in Munir Bashshur, *The Role of Two Western Universities in the National Life of Lebanon and the Middle East. A Comparative Study of the American University in Beirut and the University of Saint Joseph* (Ph.D. Dissertation, University of Chicago, 1964).
7 Haut Commissariat de la République française en Syrie et au Liban, *La Syrie et le Liban en 1921* (Paris, 1921), p. 106.
8 See, for example, the curriculum that was designed for the 'Alawite state. AD Nantes, Carton 9, Programme d'études, territoire autonome des 'alaouite, 1921. The entire program is focused on the ancient history of the region and on European and French histories. The French were very persistent in their attempt to create a

"nation" out of the 'Alawite region in northern Syria. See, for example, MAE Paris, Vol. 527, Review of the Press, p. 82. May 14-20, 1933, a report of an article written by the Jesuit Louis Jalabert and supported by *l'Orient*, in favor of maintaining the 'Alawite state.

9 See more in Edmond Burke, "A Comparative View of French Native Policy in Morocco and Syria, 1912-1925," *Middle Eastern Studies* (May 1973), pp. 175-186.

10 AD Nantes, Carton 14, Gouraud to Combes, August 10, 1922.

11 AD Nantes, Carton 14, Combes to Haut Commissariat, October 27, 1922. This report stands in sharp contradiction to the situation in USJ and other French private schools where, since the turn of the century, the local history of Syria, together with French history, were the focus of history classes.

12 See some of his articles in *Études* concerning Lebanon and Syria, "L'Amitié Française au Liban," 159(1919), p. 235; "La France Abandonnera-t-elle la Syrie?" 191(1927), pp. 161-182; "Au Pays de l'Amitié Française, à Travers le Liban," 215(1933), pp. 416-435. The publications of Jalabert as a teacher at USJ primarily focused on Phoenician and Roman archeology. See Louis Cheikho, USJ; *Catalogue des Ouvrages, 1875-1925* (Beirut: Imprimerie Catholique, 1925), pp. 18-19. For biographical notes on Louis Jalabert, see Henri Jalabert, *Les Jésuites au Proche Orient*, pp. 420-421.

13 Jesuit Archives, Vanves, Fond Louis Jalabert, Chemise F. A report from Jalabert to de Caix (1922[?]), p. 3.

14 Jalabert made an interesting comparison with Tunisia and Morocco where the majority of the elite opposed French presence. There, he wrote, we do not need the elite in order to control the local population. In Syria and Lebanon, however, because of the high level of the local societies, we do need the elite and therefore we must attach them to us.

15 Henri Lammens recorded in the introduction to his *La Syrie; Précis Historique* that he had written this book at the personal request of Henri Gouraud. It reflects the desire of the French authorities in general and Gouraud in particular to provide Syria with a new local history separated from the Arab history. The book itself became one of the most important textbooks for the supporters of the non-Arab identity of Syria and Lebanon. See more about the use of this book in note 26.

16 Louis Jalabert wrote several times to the High Commission, demanding that more resources be allocated to USJ at the expense of other educational establishments, most notably in Damascus. His explanations were always political, arguing that it serves best the colonial interests of France. See, for example, MAE Paris, Vol. 378 pp. 9-10, Jalabert to the MAE, October 10, 1922. In this letter Jalabert opposes the plans to establish a faculty of medicine in Damascus. Such an act, he wrote, might attract Arabs from the entire Arab world and create anti-French activity in Damascus. Beirut, therefore, should remain the only city within the mandated regions with a school of medicine.

17 AD Nantes, Carton 14, *Instruction publique, programme du brevet élémentaire*, (a certificate of elementary school) 1922-1923.

18 See also AD Nantes, Carton 2, Baccalauréat frano-syrien 1920-21 June 7, 1920; *programme d'étude* 1930; Carton 9, "Certificat d'études primaires franco-syrien," May 1921.

19 A report of "Schools of the Lebanese Republic" of the *Instruction publique* dated 25 April, 1933, gives a detailed list of all schools and registered students in Lebanon. There were 16,706 students in 203 public schools; 52,665 students in 737 private confessional schools; and 38,402 in 420 private foreign schools. AD Nantes, Carton 102, *Table des écoles de la République Libanaise*. The numbers in the public schools were by no means large. Lebanese families continued to prefer to send their children to private foreign or confessional schools. These figures are approximately confirmed in J. A. Babikian, *Civilization and Education in Syria and Lebanon* (Beirut, 1936), p. 214. The attendance in public schools continued, however, to rise steadily. By 1945, Lebanon had 308 public schools with 30,113 students, most of whom were low-middle class Muslims. See Roderic D. Mathews and Metta Akrawi, *Education in the Arab Countries of the Near East* (Washington: American Council on Education, D.C., 1946), p. 422.

20 On this affair, see Meir Zamir, *Lebanon's Quest*, pp. 76-83.

21 The most notable example is that of Riad al-Sulh who graduated from USJ. There were many more Muslim leaders who studied in private foreign schools. Muhammad Jamil Bayhum studied at the schools of the *Mission Laïque* in Beirut and 'Abdallah al-Yafi studied at USJ and completed his higher education in France.

22 See, for example, AD Nantes, Carton 933, Service des renseignement, Tripoli, June 1, 1928, a report of an incident in a school, where a teacher used a French textbook that sharply criticized Islam. Muslim students protested and newspapers followed suit (*Al-Sha'b*, May 26, 1928; *Al-Jawa'ib*, May 28, 1928). AD Nantes, Carton 102, *Instruction publique*, December 1932, a report of a textbook that described Muhammad as a liar. MAE Paris, Vol. 532, p. 197, Review of the press, December 28-March 6, 1938, an argument between *al-Bashir* and *Bayrut* over a history manual entitled, *Histoire du Liban*. *Bayrut* accused the authors of having used only Henri Lammens as their source and ignoring Arab sources. In response, the Jesuit paper *al-Bashir* charged *Bayrut* of harming Lebanese national integrity. For another argument between *al-Bashir* and *Bayrut* over a different textbook and its interpretation of the Koran, see MAE Paris, Vol. 532, p. 60, Review of the Press, February 16, 1938.

23 AD Nantes, Carton 102, a letter from Bounoure circulated to all public schools in Syria and Lebanon, December 29, 1932.

24 AD Nantes, Carton 129, an exchange of letters between Bounoure and Sheikh Tawfiq Khalid, September 17, 18, 19, 1936.

25 AD Nantes, Carton 9, Service de l'Instruction Publique, Monthly Report, September 1921.

26 Gabriel Levenq, *Géographie Élémentaire de la Syrie* (Beirut: Imprimerie catholique, 1920); Henri Lammens *La Syrie; Précis Historique* (Beirut: Imprimerie catholique, 1921); Henri Lammens, Ferdinand Taoutel and René Mouterde, *Petite Histoire de la Syrie et du Liban* (Beirut: Imprimerie catholique, 1924). Ferdinand Taoutel published a similar book in Arabic, *Mukhtasar Tarikh Suriyya wa Lubnan* (Beirut: Imprimerie catholique, 1924). Mouterde republished it under the title, *Précis d'Histoire de la Syrie et du Liban* (Beirut: Imprimerie catholique, 1931, second edition; 1937, third edition). See also Jacques Eddé, *Géographie de la Syrie et du Liban* (Beirut: Imprimerie catholique, 1924); this was essentially a popularization for children of Lammens' work, *La Syrie; Précis Historique* and was used extensively in governmental schools. By 1931 its third

edition was already in print, following a formal decision of the office of public instruction to use it as a formal textbook of the public schools. See USJ, *Les Oeuvres de Presse,* in the series of booklets *Les Jésuites en Syrie 1831-1931,* Vol. VI (Paris: Les Éditions Dillen, 1931).

27 See their joint works that were initiated and financed by the Lebanese Ministry of Education, *Hurub Ibrahim Basha al-Misri fi Suriyya wa al-'Anatul* [The Wars of Ibrahim Pasha in Syria and Anatolia], (Beirut: al-Maktaba al-Bulusiyya, 1927); *Lubnan fi 'Ahd al-Umara' al-Shihabiyyin* [Lebanon in the Time of the Shihabi Princes], (Beirut: al-Matba'a al-Kathulikiya, 1933); *Lubnan fi 'Ahd al-Amir Fakhr al-Din al-Ma'ni al-Thani* [Lebanon in the Time of the Prince Fakhr al-Din al-Ma'ni II], (Beirut: al-Matba'a al-Kathulikiya, 1936). In addition to his historical researches al-Bustani also wrote several books of fiction, some of which focused on the Amir Bashir II. See *'Ala 'Ahd al-Amir* (Beirut: al-Matba'a al-Kathulikiya, 1926); *Limadha* (Beirut: Manshurat al-Da'ira, 1930).

28 *Bulletin de l'Association des Anciens Élèves de l'USJ,* 1928. See also the 1934-1935 curriculum in Jesuit Archives, Vanves, RPO 52.

29 See, for example, his praising remarks on Charles Corm's *La Montagne Inspirée* in the Jesuit journal, *al-Mashriq* (April-June 1934), p. 308-309; and in *al-Ma'rid* (July 2, 1934), p. 15. Al-Bustani became one of the chief ideologues of the Lebanese Forces during the Civil War. See Walid Faris, *Lebanese Christian Nationalism* (Boulder: Lynne Rienner Publishers, 1995), p. 110.

30 For biographical information on Asad Rustum see Ilyas al-Qatar and others, *Asad Rustum, al-Insan wa al-Mu'arikh* [Asad Rustum, the Person and the Historian] (Beirut: al-Maktaba al-Bulusiyya, 1984), pp. 19-34.

31 The five books were *Tarikh Lubnan al-Tamhidi al-Musawwar* [the illustrated preliminary]; *al-I'dadi al- Qassasi* [the preparatory narrative]; *al-Mujaz* [the concise]; *al-Mujmal* [the complete]; *al-Mufassal* [the detailed].

32 MAE Paris, Vol. 532, Review of the Press, p. 101, February 19, 1938; pp. 150-151, February 21-27, 1938.

33 Matthews and Akrawli, *Education in Arab Countries of the Near East,* pp. 430-431.

34 David A, Kerr, *The Temporal Authority of the Maronite Patriarch, 1918-1958: A Study in the Relationship of Religious and Secular Power* (Ph.D. dissertation, Oxford University, 1977), p. 151; See also Iskandar al-Riashi, *Ru'asa Lubnan kama 'Araftuhum,* pp. 220-222.

35 AD Nantes, Carton 2, *École française de droit,* December 1920. The professional teachers of this school were Paul Roubier, Dean of the Law Faculty, Emile Achou, director of *Banque de Syrie,* and Béchara al-Khoury. See also MAE Paris, Vol. 57. Note de presse by Robert de Caix. December 12, 1922.

36 Archives Jesuites, Fond Louis Jalabert, Paquet VII, Chemise GP. M. Besnard, *La Culture française en Orient,* June 1934, p. 6.

37 Meir Zamir, *Lebanon's Quest,* pp. 42-43. Zamir, *The Formation of Modern Lebanon,* p. 84.

38 Georges Naccache was born in Alexandria in 1904. He graduated in 1920 from the secondary school *Collège de Pères Jésuites* in Alexandria and moved to Beirut where he studied at the Engineering Faculty of USJ. He was never involved directly in Phoenician activity, but he used his paper, *l'Orient,* to expound on the non-Arab identity of Lebanon, alleging that along the course of history, a distinct

Lebanese identity had developed which had nothing to do with Arab or Syrian identities. In November 1937, he was one of the founders of the Lebanese *Kata'ib*.

39 Georges Naccache, "Au service du Liban: Les 75 ans de l'Université Saint Joseph," *l'Orient*, 30 April, 1950; Cited in Sélim Abou, *Le Bilinguisme Arabe-Français au Liban*, pp. 203-204. See also Yusuf al-Saouda's reference on the impact of USJ on the formation of his national thought. *Fi Sabil al-Istiqlal* (Beirut: 1967), pp. 11-13.

40 Zamir, The Formation of Modern Lebanon, pp. 159-160.

41 MAE Paris, Vol. 378, p. 46, Herriot to Sarrail, December 27, 1924; MAE Paris, Vol. 286, pp. 176-177, Sarrail to MAE, February 28, 1925; p. 183, Sarrail to MAE, April 21, 1925; pp. 221-223, Sarrail to MAE, May 14, 1925. The ties between certain Lebanese nationalists and the French radical right are an issue that has yet to be studied properly. It is clear that *l'Orient* was infatuated with *l'Action Française*, to judge by the number of articles it quoted. Even the Catholic High Commissioner General Weygand, who was in favor of the pro-Christian policy of France, noted this connection between the two journals. See MAE Paris, Vol. 286, p. 159, Weygand to MAE November 30, 1924. As for the ties between the Jesuits and the French radical right, it is a well-known fact that the former found the latter to be loyal allies in the domains of Catholicism and political conservatism. Thus, in 1941, the Jesuits welcomed the Vichy regime and refused to cooperate with General Catroux, the representative of Free France in the Levant. Chanteur, the Rector of USJ, even encouraged his students to carry prayers for Marshal Petain. See David C. Gordon, *The French Language and National Identity* (The Hague: Mouton, 1978), p. 75.

42 Henri Lammens was the first president of this association. See in *Association Amicale des Anciens Élèves de l'USJ* (Beirut: Imprimerie Catholique, 1949), p. 23.

43 The 1938 *Bulletin de l'Association* listed its active members according to their year of graduation from the university. The list consists of hundreds of names, but there are certain family names that reappear time and again such as Tabet, Eddé, de Tarrazi, Tuéni, Chéhab, Gémmayel, de Freige, Abéla, Sarkis, Hacho, Makhlouf, Gédeon, Hélou, Trad, Tyane, Pharaon, Corm, Haddad, Khayat, Naccache, Cardahi, Chiha, Misk, Yared, Sa'ad, and many more. They were all part of the Lebanese social, commercial and political elite and they formed a distinct social class. Munir Bashshur, writing about the USJ graduates in his study about the two foreign universities in Beirut, stated that "the homogeneity of USJ students in terms of national origin [Lebanese], religion [Christian] and type of secondary education [private Maronite or French schools], makes the efforts of USJ to mold its students in uniform modes of thinking more feasible and acceptable. Consequently, USJ students turn out to be more cohesive in their beliefs and tend to constitute within the Lebanese society, a community of their own." *The Role of Two Western Universities in the National Life of Lebanon and the Middle East*, p. 317.

44 The 1937 report informs readers that the tradition of showing a play at the alumni gatherings was neglected for awhile and renewed that year with the drama *Phéniciennes*, by Georges Rivollet. See *Bulletin de l'Association*, 1938, Nouvelle Série, no. 1.

45 For biographical notes about Alfred Naccache see AD Nantes, Carton 2990, Sûreté générale, info. 1738. April 9, 1932. Naccache was a faithful Christian Maronite and more francophone and francophile than most Lebanese. He was not involved directly in politics until the French themselves suggested him as a possible candidate for presidency.
46 *L'U* (June 1934).
47 *L'U*, no. 6 (June 1936). A speech at the General Assembly, June 7, 1936.
48 MAE Paris, Vol. 380, p. 20, A report of Archeological excavations in Lebanon, July 1922. See also Vol. 52, p. 158-159, Article 14 of the Mandate charter for Syria and Lebanon, July 24, 1922. The document can also be found in Albert Hourani, *Syria and Lebanon* (London: Oxford University Press, 1946), pp. 308-314.
49 *Syrie et Liban, Rapport Mensuel d'Ensemble*, (Beirut, June 1921), pp. 4-6.
50 *Rapport sur la Situation de la Syrie et du Liban* (Paris, 1928), p. 42. See also the 1924 report, pp. 34-44.
51 *SYRIA, Revue d'Art Oriental et d'Archéologie*, no. 1(Paris, 1920), pp. 72-74.
52 Benedict Anderson, *Imagined Communities*, pp. 178-185.
53 AD Nantes, Carton 6, April 18, 1921, letter from Tarrazi to Henri Gouraud. Philippe de Tarrazi was part of the social and cultural circles of Charles Corm and Michel Chiha and on several occasions he participated in Corm's Phoenician activities and even wrote himself about the autochthon-Phoenician origins of his own community, the Orthodox Syrian Church. Filib di Tarazi, *Asdaq Ma Kana 'an Tarikh Lubnan* [The Reliable History of Lebanon] (Beirut: Matabi' Juzif Salim Siqli, 1948), p. 13.
54 The other "Friends of the Museum" were Alfred Sursok, Marios Hanimoglo, Albert Bassoul, 'Omar Daouk, Kamil Eddé, 'Ali Junblat, Henri Faraoun, Georges Veyssié, Assad Younes, Hassan Makhzoumi, Joseph Farahi, Georges Corm, Jean Debs, 'Arif Bayhum and Wafiq Beydoun. See in Yammin Muhsin Edmond, *Lubnan al-Sura: Dhakirat Qarn fi Khamsin al-Istiqlal* (Beirut: Jarrus, Bris, 1994), p. 190.
55 MAE Paris, Vol. 379, Beaux Arts, pp. 22-23; au sujet du musée national de Beyrouth, July 12, 1924.
56 *Bulletin du Musée de Beyrouth*, no. 1 (Paris, 1937). A Phoenician vessel decorates the front cover of the bulletin. Although the museum was inaugurated in 1937, its construction was actually completed in 1941.
57 Jesuits Archives, Vanves, RPO 63, *Association Amicale des Anciens Élèves de l'Université Saint Joseph* (Beirut: Imprimerie Catholique, 1947), pp. 60-61.
58 In 1935, eleven scientific missions were excavating in the mandated territories. See the section on "Service des antiquités" in *Rapport à la Société des Nations sur la Situation de la Syrie et du Liban* (Paris, 1935). See, for example, the various issues of *La Revue du Liban*. Almost every issue contains articles about recent archeological discoveries in Lebanon.
59 *Bulletin du Musée de Beyrouth*, no. 1, p. i.
60 *L'U*, no. 3 (January 1935).
61 AD Nantes, Carton 137, Rapport sur un voyage au Liban, June 5, 1937. Dugas reported that in 1937 eighty Lebanese and Syrian students were registered at the Oriental Faculty.

62 Jesuit Archives, Vanves, RPO 52. A brochure entitled, *La Nouvelle Bibliothèque Orientale,* 1938.
63 The Maronites Salah Labaki and Yusuf Yazbek participated in the Congress; the former represented the PPS and the latter attended as an independent.
64 The discussions and the final statement of the Congress can be found in Hassan 'Ali Hallaq, *Mu'tamar al-Sahil wa al-Aqdiya al-Arba'a* [The Conference of the Coast and the Four Districts] (Beirut: al-Dar al-Jami'iyah, 1983). The Congress reflected the process of gradual recognition of Lebanon as an independent state by Muslim Lebanese. The fact that not all Muslim leaders attended the Congress and that, in conclusion, the participants asked for a larger share in the Lebanese politics marked this change. The conclusions of the Conference of the Coast continued to resonate more than a year after its termination. MAE Paris, Vol. 503, p. 11, The National Muslim Council of Beirut to the MAE July 2, 1937.
65 MAE Paris, Vol. 529, pp. 64-198, Review of the Press, January-October 1936.
66 Najib Dahdah, "Lubnan al-Kabir fi al-Tarikh" [Greater Lebanon in History], *al-Mashriq,* 34 (1936), p. 555.
67 CZA S25 3143 Landman to the Political Department, April 29, 1936.
68 The establishment of al-Saouda's party was also a result of internal Maronite tensions. Tawfiq 'Awad, backed by Emile Eddé, established the *Parti de l'Union Libanais.* The Maronite Patriarch, Arida and the constitutional bloc responded to this initiative by instigating the formation of al-Saouda's party. AD Nantes, Carton 457, Merier to MAE, July 10, 1936; MAE Paris, Vol. 529, Review of the Press, January-October 1936, pp. 198-200, August 7, 1936; AD Nantes, Carton 462, *L'Unité Libanaise, parti national politique,* July 24, 1936. See also *La Revue du Liban,* December 9, 1945.
69 MAE Paris, Vol. 503, p. 238, Information, October 1937.
70 John P. Entelis, *Pluralism and Party Transformation in Lebanon; al-Kata'ib* (Leiden: Brill, 1974), p. 77. We shall see below that Sa'id 'Aql held very similar views on Phoenicianism, interpreting it culturally and not politically.
71 MAE Paris, Vol. 531, Review of the Press, p. 1. p. 4, August 22-29, 1937; p. 13, pp. 24-25, August 30 – September 5, 1937.
72 MAE Paris, Vol. 531, Review of the Press, September 13-19, 1937.
73 See more about Edmond Rabbath in Chapter V.
74 *Phénicia,* no.1 (January, 1938), p. 1.
75 In 1919-1920, Fakhuri cooperated with the Arab government of Faysal, then moved to Paris where he obtained a law degree and returned to Lebanon thereafter, becoming involved in the intellectual and journalistic circles of Beirut until his premature death. See more about his place of eminence in the intellectual circles of Beirut in the introduction to the 1982 reprint of his book *al-Haqiqa al-Lubnaniyya,* first published in 1945.
76 See also the opening quotation in the beginning of this chapter that is taken from the same lecture.
77 See also his *al-Haqiqa al-Lubnaniyya,* pp. 40-41, which contained similar messages.
78 See some examples: Amy Kher, "Complainte d'Astrate," 32(March, 1933); "Les Phéniciens ont crée et répandu l'alphabet," 43 (October, 1934); "Annibal, le phénicien," (March 9, 1942); "Un Peu de mythologie phénicienne: qui est

Adonis?" (March 23, 1942); "Les Phéniciens, ont-ils découvert l'Amérique avant Christophe Colomb?" (August 3, 1942); "Les hommes de l'indépendance: Hiram Roi de Tyr; Byblos pionnier de l'Indépendance; Cadmus" (July-August, 1945)

79 *La Revue du Liban*, 32 (March 1933), p. 23. See also Jurj 'Arij Sa'adah, *Al-Sahafa fi Lubnan* [Journalism in Lebanon] (Beirut: Dar Wakalat al-Nashr al-'Arabiyya, 1965), pp. 165-166. On the front cover of this book there is a picture of a Phoenician vessel made out of pieces of newspaper.

80 Mustafa Khalidi and 'Umar Farukh, *al-Tabshir wa al-Isti'mar fi al-Bilad al-'Arabiyya* [Missionary Activity and Colonialism in the Arab Countries] (Beirut: al-Maktaba al- 'Ilmiyyah, 1953), p. 174.

81 See, for example, the writing of Lebanese who were not necessarily labeled Phoenicians but still used these phrases to describe Lebanon and its national character. Béchara al-Khoury, *Majmu'at Khutab* [Collection of Speeches] (Beirut: s.n, 1951), p. 202; Camille Cham'un, *Marahil al-Istiqlal* [Stages of Independence] (Beirut: Maktabat Sadir, 1949), p. 7. Kamal Junbalat as quoted in *Les Cahiers de l'Est*, no. 1(1945), p. 3.

82 E. & G. Gédéon, *L'Indicateur Libano-Syrien*, (Beirut, 1928-1929) (5th edition).

83 See the brochures "Au Liban, pays des Cèdres," edited in English and French by the Commission de Tourisme et de Villégiature. The authors were Michel Bahout, inspecteur général de services economiques, and Toufic 'Awad, a member of the Commission de l'industrie du tourisme et de l'estivage, AD Nantes, Carton 944, Report of a meeting of the Chamber of Deputies, December 17, 1937. See also *La Revue du Liban* 41(June 1934), p.13.

84 Philip K. Hitti, *A History of the Arabs* (New York: St. Martin's Press, 1970), p. 3.

85 Yusuf al-Saouda, *Étude Juridique sur la Protocole d'Alexandrie* (Beirut, November, 1944).

86 Walid Faris, *Lebanese Christian Nationalism* (Boulder: Lynne Rienner Publishers, 1995), p. 96

87 Sharl Malik, *Sharl Malik wa al-qadiyya al-filastiniyya* (Beirut: Mu'assast Badran, 1973).

88 Philip Hitti, *Testimony before the Anglo-American Committee on Palestine* (Washington, D.C., Arab Office, 1946).

4

Three Phoenician Currents

The Phoenician narrative never developed into an integrated ideology led by key thinkers. There were, however, a few Lebanese who stood out more than others in their support of the Phoenician view of the past. This chapter focuses on three of the Phoenician "preachers" — Charles Corm, Michel Chiha and Sa'id 'Aql — who shaped, to a large extent, the Phoenician narratives and, indeed, the Lebanese national identity(ies). For social and political reasons, these three writers developed different interpretations of the Lebanese identity; the following discussion sheds light not only on their different views but also on the dissemination of Phoenicianism in Lebanon and its many hues.

Charles Corm, the Inspired Maronite Francophone

No small number of Lebanese wrote about Phoenicianism and publicly advocated the Phoenician identity for Lebanon. Nevertheless, it is Charles Corm who became most strongly identified with the Phoenician myth of origin, despite the fact he was neither the most original nor the most articulate "Phoenician." The reasons for this Phoenician fame probably lie in the fact that Corm dedicated his life to the dissemination of his Phoenician message, he was a charming person with abundant charisma, and, no less important, enjoyed abundant wealth which facilitated his mission, especially in Beirut, among the haut-bourgeois Christian milieu.

As noted in Chapter II, in 1934 Charles Corm left a life of business to completely immerse himself in literary and artistic activity with the prime purpose of spreading Phoenicianism in Lebanon.[1] In February 1934, he launched his *Éditions de la Revue Phénicienne*, a publication house that became the major platform for "Phoenician" works in the 1930s-1940s. He also founded *La société des gens de lettre du Liban* and *La société des auteurs libanais de langue française*,[2] loose organizations of Lebanese writers and thinkers who used to meet in his home and discuss literary issues as well as Lebanon's cultural and political orientation.[3] In general, his house became a center of artistic activity and he himself became the patron of leading Lebanese painters and sculptors such as Youssef Hoyeck and Halim al-Hajj who used his studio for their artistic work.[4]

Corm was not a politician nor did he ever participate in any public political activity. He clearly identified, however, with the camp of Emile Eddé, with whom he shared views about the cultural and political orientation of Lebanon. Eddé, similarly, sympathized with the causes of Corm and Albert Naccache, Corm's closest "Phoenician friend," but, as a politician with his two feet planted on the ground, Eddé did not participate in their Phoenician activities.[5] Still, unlike Béchara al-Khoury, Eddé did refer on public occasions to the Phoenicians as the ancestors of modern Lebanese.[6] And Corm, like Eddé, used only French as his means of communication; indeed, the devotion of the two towards France was above and beyond that of most Lebanese to the mandatory power in their land. In November 1943, following the events that led to the eleven-day presidency of Eddé, his loss of power, the rise of al-Khoury to the presidency, and the recognition of Lebanon as a country with an "Arab face," Corm was devastated, fearing that Lebanon was headed toward relinquishing its Christian Western-oriented character.[7]

Charles Corm befriended more than persons like Eddé, who were part and parcel of his socio-political class. Amin al-Rihani, the Lebanese Arab nationalist writer and philosopher, was also a very close friend. Al-Rihani recorded their friendship in his book, *Qalb Lubnan* [The Heart of Lebanon], which he dedicated to "my friend Charles Corm." This beautiful descriptive travelogue about Lebanon gives us interesting insight into Corm's character and temperament. Al-Rihani referred to him as "the Lebanese, Phoenician, French poet [...] one of the legends in the country of legends,"[8] indicating the famed and almost mythical place Corm held in Lebanese society in the mid-1930s. The import of having such a title bestowed on Corm by al-Rihani, another Lebanese legend, should not be overlooked. Al-Rihani made the journey that inspired *Qalb Lubnan* in 1936, one of the most decisive years for Lebanon. It was also a very dynamic time period for Charles Corm. In 1935, his poetic talent won him fame also in France, where he won the Edgar Allan Poe prize for international poetry and the acclamation of numerous French journals.[9] That same year he represented Lebanon at the *Congrès de la Méditerranée* and was also very active at the annual gathering of the *Cercle de la jeunesse catholique de Beyrouth*, a cultural club for young Maronites and other Catholics directed by the Jesuits. Let us not omit the spicy fact that in 1935, Corm, the avid bachelor, finally married Samia Baroudy, Miss Lebanon of 1934 and the winner of fourth place in the Miss Universe pageant of the same year. Alfred Naccache, marking this marriage in *L'U*, defined it as "the prize of poetry marries the prize of beauty."[10] All these deeds of Corm are noted only to confirm the legendary designation with which al-Rihani, who believed that Lebanon and Corm were together in "an inseparable spiritual unity,"[11] crowned his compatriot.

And yet, Al-Rihani, the Arab nationalist, was irked by the fact that Corm's language was French and not Arabic.[12] Al-Rihani viewed Lebanon as an Arab state, politically and culturally tied to the Arab world, and the Western-Phoenician message of Corm could not have appealed to him in its entirety. Thus, for example, al-Rihani scoffed at Corm's tendency to "phoenicianize" every rock and tree in Lebanon. "Corm sees the Phoenicians everywhere in Lebanon," he wrote. "A stone or a worship place? A church? They all go back to the Greek-Roman era, and yes, they are Phoenician."[13]

As part of his travelogue, al-Rihani described a banquet at the house of As'ad Yunis in the village of Laqluq, at which Corm, who accompanied him on this part of the journey, participated. The following illuminating description and critique of Corm's conduct at this banquet gives a good indication of his stature at the time. Al-Rihani told of a vivacious gathering enhanced with the wafting aromas of Lebanese cuisine when suddenly Corm rose and began speaking:

> Charles Corm, the Lebanese who writes poetry in the language of Racine and Molière, to whom Paris abides, extols and honors, does not know the language of his closer forefathers, the Arabs, and does not know to say 'I love you' in the language of his distant forefathers, the Phoenicians, [...] after we were fortunate to know him and were delighted by his love and affection, we enjoyed conversing only in this noble language, the language of the *dad*. [Suddenly] he began saying [in Arabic]: 'You are truly fooling me around.' He did not say this sentence very clearly, but clear enough that we understood it. And this is what he stated: 'Teach me the language of my father and my mother and I will be grateful. And in that night in La'lu' [the colloquial form of Laqluq, A.K.], on the dining table of Yunis, the sun poet[14] stood up, [...] the poet of *La Montagne Inspirée*, the dresser of Lebanon with grandeur and glory, stood and began speaking in Arabic. We were all astonished. He awakened in us feelings of love and awe. Ask me what he said? What does it matter? He spoke in Arabic and that was enough.[15]

Corm's decision to use Arabic and the veneration it generated in al-Rihani and his friends who gathered around the dining table of As'ad Yunis reveals to us the cultural world in which Corm lived. By the 1930s most educated Lebanese were fluent in French as well as Arabic, but Arabic remained their prime means of expression. Corm, however, belonged to a small group of Lebanese for whom the prime medium of communication was French. For him, just as for Eddé, Naccache, 'Ammoun, Chiha and a few others, French was the one and only language in which he felt at home. The fact that he did not speak Arabic, however, did not prevent him from being liked by many Arabic-speaking Lebanese, such as Amin al-Rihani or even the Sunni Taqi al-Din al-Sulh and the Druze Khalil Taqi al-Din who admired his charm and valued his passion for Lebanon, though they criticized his Phoenician ideas.

The Inspired Poet and the Sacred Mountain

Immediately with the resumption of his literary activity in February 1934 Charles Corm published *La Montagne Inspirée*, undoubtedly his most famous book of poetry. It is divided into three sections Corm called "cycles." The first, "Le dit de l'enthousiasme," dedicated to Maurice Barrès, contains a chain of stanzas of which each is a proclamation of joy for the termination of World War I, the arrival of the French and the auspicious future of Lebanon. Needless to say, even the title of *La Montagne Inspirée* is inspired by *La Colline Inspirée* of Maurice Barrès who, as Corm worded it in his dedication, "a su nous comprendre parce qu'il nous a aimés."[16] The second cycle, "Le dit de l'agonie" (dedicated to the Maronite Patriarch Elias Hoyek), depicts horrific scenes and episodes Lebanon has experienced at any given time in its history, alleging that its history is saturated with calamities and atrocities. This cycle, however, concludes with a notion of hope and optimism because, according to Corm, despite its terrible historical experience, Lebanon has never lost its soul and self-respect. The optimistic last verse leads the reader directly to the third cycle, which deals with this soul of Lebanon, with which Corm was so intrigued.

The third cycle, "Le dit du souvenir," occupies three quarters of *La Montagne Inspirée* and is the part that concerns us the most, for it contains the most engaging Phoenician message Corm ever wrote. It is not without reason that Corm dedicated this cycle to Victor Bérard, "qui nous restitua une part légitime de nos contributions au patrimoine de l'humanité."[17] Bérard was one of the most important French scholars to lay the foundation for the Phoenician *Geschichtebild,* and Corm recognized his importance and contribution to the crystallization of his Phoenician worldview. This cycle is brimming with references to Lebanon's history in general and to the Phoenicians in particular, and it would be superfluous to discuss them all. Instead, I chose to review certain themes that are important to understanding Corm's Phoenician worldview. They include the following: the way he perceived the Phoenician-Lebanese mission to the world; his views about faith and Lebanon, and, lastly, the hymn to the Sun that concludes *La Montagne Inspirée*.

"Le dit du souvenir" unfolds with the question that haunts Corm throughout this cycle: Where is the Phoenician language and what has become of it? This is the language that "spread the Idea to the four corners of the earth just as wheat is scattered in the fields and just as God himself sprinkled His purest diamonds in the bosom of profound nights." Corm searches after this language in the local Phoenician sites, on the highest peaks of the Mountain and in the lowest plains of the Biqa', but to no avail. The language and its spirit are absent.

> Je te recherche en vain le long de nos ravages,
> Dans le golfe où la nymphe a baigné Cupidon,

Sur les stèles d'Amrith, et dans les sarcophages
De Tyr et de Sidon;[18]
[...]
Absente, absolument absente de notre âme,
Cette extrême puissance où l'on tombe à genoux,
Pour recevoir des Cieux la rosée et la flamme
Qui descendaient en nous;

Nul ne célèbre plus la splendeur de vos fêtes,
O Baal et Melkhart, El, Ashmoun et Thammour
Qu'invoquaient en tremblant les rois et les suffètes,[19]
Dans vos temples d'amour;[20]

Corm continues in a similar tone for many pages, remarking on the glory days when the Phoenician language was dynamic and its people led the world with their spirit and intellect. The strength of the Phoenicians, which they bequeathed to their descendents, the modern Lebanese, was never expressed in arms and warfare, but rather in intellectual vitality and allure of a great culture. At one point in this long eulogy of the Phoenician civilization, Corm discloses the reason he writes this homage to the language and the role he assigns to Phoenician history:

Si je rappelle aux miens nos aïeux phéniciens
C'est qu'alors nous n'étions au fronton de l'histoire,
Avant de devenir musulmans ou chrétiens,
Qu'un même peuple uni dans une même gloire,
Et qu'en évoluant, nous devrions au moins,
Par le fait d'une foi d'autant plus méritoire,
Nous aimer comme aux Temps où nous étions païens!...
[...]
Langue de mon pays, dites-nous notre histoire,
Dites à nos enfants que tout semble humilier,
Qu'ils peuvent être fiers d'avoir eu dans la gloire,
Des gloires par milliers!

Langue de mon pays, donnez-nous confiance,
Faites-nous croire en nous et nos aïeux,
Gardez-nous notre rang, gardez notre audience
A la table des dieux![21]

Thus, Corm portrays the Lebanese as one people unified in their ancestral past, and he begs this past, represented by "the Phoenician language," to be a bridge for all Lebanese and to teach them — Muslims and Christians — their place of glory in human history. Yet, in a different place in the epic, immediately after Corm praises the Crusaders, the Medieval defenders of Lebanon who found the Christian Lebanese to be their sole allies in the Holy Land, in a sea of Arab-Muslim hostility, he writes perhaps the most famous verse of *La Montagne Inspirée*:

> Mon frère musulman, comprenez ma franchise:
> Je suis le vrai Liban, sincère et pratiquant;
> D'autant plus libanais que ma Foi symbolise
> Le cœur du pélican.[22]

Thus, despite the fact that Corm writes about the history of Lebanon as a unifying factor for all Lebanese, the message of *La Montagne Inspirée* is explicitly and naturally Christian. The images he uses are taken from Christian theology and the majority of the events he mentions highlight Christian moments in the history of Lebanon. Islam, the Arabs and the Arabic language are practically non-existent in *La Montagne Inspirée*.

Christianity was the epitome of perfection for Corm and the ancient Lebanese played a momentous role in its formation and dissemination. Even before Jesus walked in Phoenicia,[23] faith in one god prevailed among these age-old people. Charles Corm was a person of faith and the message of monotheism is an inseparable part of *La Montagne Inspirée*. Already the Phoenician faith, according to him, was somewhat monotheistic:

> Bal-Shamin, Dieu du ciel, Ô Nomen ineffable,
> O seul propriétaire, Ô maître, ô Possesseur,
> Dieu du Temps, Dieu total, Seigneur inconcevable,
> Suprême Créateur;
>
> Toi par qui s'affirmait notre monothéisme,
> Et l'immense unité des cultes phéniciens,
> Avant le grand Moïse, avant le judaïsme,
> Et les platoniciens;[24]

What had begun with the Phoenicians, even before Judaism, continued with Christianity, for "being faithful to God"[25] ties the ancient Lebanese to the modern ones. Viewing the Phoenician faith as monotheistic was, of course, a very liberal interpretation by Corm, but it emanated from a scholarly theory that saw the gradual ascendance to prominence of one supreme Canaanite god from within a group of deities as a forerunner to monotheism.[26]

Numerous geographical and historical locations are described in *La Montagne Inspirée*, but three — the Kadicha Valley, the Ibrahim River and the Temple of Balbeck — receive the greatest attention. These three sites demonstrate Corm's preoccupation with faith and the link he makes between the Phoenicians and Christianity. They also serve Corm in his attempt to locate and define the Lebanese society within its natural landscape. As Anthony

Smith wrote, "holy places of man-made or natural origins are crucial for identifying *ethnie*, both in the past and today, because they evoke forces greater than the individual and induce feelings of awe and reverence by their historic associations and symbolic meaning."[27] Kadicha, the Ibrahim River and Balbeck, three sacred locales, are brought up by Corm to recall dramatic events in the history of the Lebanese nation and "to endow it with foci of creative energy,"[28] energy that emanates from the ancient history of Lebanon and from Christianity.

Kadicha, the Holy Valley, still bearing its Phoenician name, is part of the gorges of the Abu 'Ali River which starts at the highest altitudes of Mount Lebanon and flows down to the Mediterranean sea, emptying not far from contemporary Jbeil, the Phoenician Geval or the Greek Byblos. The majestic atmosphere of the canyon led Byzantine hermits, followed by Maronite monks, to build their monasteries on its magnificent cliffs. The valley, dotted with Maronite villages and churches, evolved to become one of the clearest Maronite strongholds in Mount Lebanon. Paraphrasing Corm, this was Kadicha, a multiple amphitheater where the heart surrenders to the vertigo of the skies; this was the valley where our most humble priests seem to live with God, and which, like Jacob's ladder, may take you directly into the heavens.[29]

If the Kadicha valley symbolizes for Corm the ubiquitous Christian presence in Mount Lebanon, then the Ibrahim River provides the Phoenician angle of faith and history. In ancient times this river was known as the river of Adonis.[30] It was one of the holiest sites for the ancient Phoenicians who used to make a pilgrimage to the source of the river to commemorate one of the greatest love stories of all times: thought to be where Adonis and Astarte ('Ashtoreth in the Hebrew Bible, while in Greek and Roman mythologies it was Aphrodite and Venus, respectively, both descended from Astarte, the Canaanite goddess) first loved and where the most handsome god hunted and died. From Lammartine to Barrès, the Adonis River and its source, Aphaca, today Afka ("the erotic triangle" in Corm's words), also became a pilgrimage site for European travelers who were enchanted by the mythical halo of the place and its extraordinary beauty.[31] The immortal and timeless love story of Adonis and Astarte-Aphrodite provides Corm the backdrop for a very sensual and erotic description of this river, its sources and waters that cut through the deep walls of the canyon "as a virgin in her wedding night is torn by a rapier of happiness."[32] Corm, however, aware of the orgies that occurred at the annual festivals of Adonis, asks the river to mitigate the passion that flows in the veins of the Lebanese:

Ne laisse pas l'ardeur qui domine nos âmes
Jamais dégénérer dans le plaisir pervers;
Fleuve de l'amour pur, ne laisse pas nos flammes
Dépérir dans la chair!

> Que les philtres sans fond, l'ivresse et l'ambroisie
> Dont le sexe étourdit nos assauts triomphants,
> Demeurant, à jamais, générateurs de vie,
> Multiplient nos enfants!³³

The language Corm uses to describe Christianity is different from the language he employs to portray the Phoenicians. The former is always depicted in a spiritual metaphysical manner whereas for the latter he uses physical, tactile terminology, often associated with sex. The two sides of the Lebanese coin complement each other in Corm's world of reference and the earthly and sensuous Phoenicians serve as an appendage to Christian spirituality.

The strongest illustration of the earthly manner Corm perceived the Phoenicians and their heritage for modern Lebanon comes from the hymn to the sun, the penultimate section of *La Montagne Inspirée*. These are engaging verses that begin with a description of the ruins of Balbeck, referring to the masculine character of the famous columns and to the virile message they convey to the Lebanese:

> Il vous importe peu d'être aimée, Ô Virile;
> C'est d'aimer ô Balbeck, corps six fois masculine,³⁴
> C'est de pouvoir aimer, que nous dit l'évangile
> Qui clame dans nos reins!³⁵
>
> C'est d'aimer l'absolu, le divin, l'impossible;
> Et folle du Soleil, d'y tendre éperdument;
> C'est de darder vos fûts vers l'éternel cible;
> C'est d'être un Mâle amant!
> [...]
> Colonnes de Balbeck, vous fûtes les prémices
> De nos virilités;
> Sous vos sceptres d'amour, gardez-nous les délices
> De votre royauté
> [...]
> Car de tous les honneurs que l'homme se partage
> Avec avidité,
> Vous resterez toujours, Balbeck, notre héritage
> A la postérité! ...³⁶

Balbeck, possibly the Lord of the Valley (Ba'al Beqa') or the Lord of the Source (Ba'al Nebek) in its ancient Phoenician name, was a sacred site even before the Greek Seleucid kings erected shrines there and named it Heliopolis, "City of the Sun." Following the Greeks, the Romans began constructing their temples on this ancient holy spot around the 1st century AD, and left for us the most noticeable archeological wonder in Lebanon. The ruins of Balbeck caught the attention of every traveler to Lebanon; all were enchanted by the magnitude of the site, its complexity and architectural uniqueness, which fused classical Roman sanctuaries with Phoenician-Semite shrines. The fact that the temples of Balbeck were erected for the worship of three Roman deities, Jupiter, Bacchus and Venus, did not make this a foreign shrine for Corm, because it was the spirit and concept of Balbeck that made it Lebanese.[37] Furthermore, Greek and Roman mythologies recount that the mother of Bacchus (Dionysus in Greek mythology, the god of wine and vegetation) was Semele, daughter of the celebrated Phoenician, Cadmus King of Thebes, a fact that made Bacchus-Dionysus a Phoenician himself. In one of his numerous trips Bacchus-Dionysus went to Lebanon to visit Aphrodite and Adonis, whose daughter, Beroë, he loved. Indeed, Charles Corm, who intimately mastered Greek and Roman classics, refers only to this god of wine in his verses on Balbeck, possibly because of his Phoenician roots.

The prime message of Balbeck, according to Corm, is clearly the cult of the Sun. This is the Sun that Corm names "the god of my race," to whom he offers himself as a human sacrifice just as his ancestors did more than two millennia earlier:

> Me voici revenu
> Loyal, fidèle et nu,
> Comme tu m'as connu,
> Soleil, mon Souverain!
>
> Reçois ma chair
> Dans ton or clair
> Mon trésor
> Le plus cher
> Et mes formes d'airain!
> [...]
> je m'offre à toi, Soleil au seuil de ton palais,
> Ainsi que tu me veux, ainsi que je te plais![38]

The human sacrifice here evolves into a concrete sexual act. The Sun, just as the city that worships it, is the masculine entity, whereas Corm turns into a frail female:

> Tu es si fort
> Contre mon corps
> Tu es si dur avec ta flamme
> Et portant si subtil
> Que je me sens, moi le viril,
> Devenir, tout à coup, comme une faible femme![39]

This weak woman who was once the poet himself, in turn becomes Mount Lebanon, and it is now the latter that is conducting a passionate penetrating intercourse with the Sun. Thus, Corm's identification with the Mountain comes into completion in this part of the epic. Mount Lebanon is Corm and vice-versa, and both are offering themselves to the Sun, the ancient god of their race. Yet, Corm cannot allow the Mountain and himself to remain weak women, because they have a certain message to convey and this can only be done through powerful physical masculinity:

> [...]
> Que pour te recevoir, il faut que je sois femme;
> Et pour mieux me donner, pour prodiguer mon âme
> Pour accomplir mon but, pour compléter mon somme,
> Il faut en même temps que je demeure un homme;
> Que pareil au foyer de ta forge fumante,
> Je suis cette femelle et ce mâle à la fois,
> Je suis le Mont altier, et la montagne aimante,
> [...].[40]

The cadence of the hymn to the Sun is very rhythmic, like the accelerating beat of drums that leads to the total unification of the Mountain with the Sun. The Mountain, the spine of Lebanon, the Maronite stronghold that symbolizes Christianity, unites with the Sun that represents ancient pre-Christian Lebanon, masculinity and almost primitive and organic manners of the ancient Lebanese.

La Montagne Inspirée does not end with this unification, for Corm has not yet answered the question woven into almost every page — what has become of the Phoenician language, the soul of Lebanon? Corm begins on a pessimistic note:

> Mais tristesse, tristesse, indicible tristesse! ...
> Nos grand-mères parlaient le syriaque à Ghazir,
> Le syriaque où survit la phénicienne adresse
> Et son rude désir
> Mais nul ne songe plus à retrouver l'empreinte
> Des pas d'une grand-mère autour d'un vieux rosier;
> La langue d'autrefois est à jamais éteinte
> Dans nos maigres gosiers.[41]

After this bleak description of the death of the language, he reverts back to a more optimistic tone. The language itself may be dead, but its spirit is still alive in the heart and soul of the Lebanese:

> Nous avons secoué cette planète immense,

Nous avons labouré, jadis, les continents;
Mais notre langue est morte, un soir, dans le silence;
Et nous sommes vivants![42]
[...]
Mais non, vous n'êtes pas, ma langue maternelle,
Un cadavre échoué dans les gouffres du temps,
Puisque j'entends monter votre sève éternelle
Et mon jeune printemps!

Puisque j'entends encor chuchoter dans mon âme,
Et sourdre du passé vos sources de cristal,
Puisque j'entends vibrer votre haleine de flamme
Dans l'air oriental!

Puisque dans le frisson de toute la nature
Qui façonna l'esprit de mes lointains aïeux,
C'est encor votre souffle et c'est votre murmure
Qui passent dans les cieux![43]
[...]
Puisque lorsque j'écris une langue étrangère,
A l'ombre du silence ou dans l'or du discours,
Vous êtes dans ma voix, sainte voix de ma mère,
Chaude comme l'amour!
[...]
Puisque même ces mots qu'aux lèvres de la France
J'ai pris en frissonnant d'un cœur passionné,
Ont un goût, sur ma lèvre, où sourit ma souffrance,

De baisers Libanais![44]

In other words, if the spirit is alive in the landscape and the people of Lebanon, the language itself is also alive. Thus, language *is* a component in Lebanese nationalism, but it dwells in the heart and not on the lips of the Lebanese. The preoccupation with language as a national symbol troubles Corm throughout the epic. Each cycle begins with a statement "translated from Lebanese" to highlight the ultimate fact that the Phoenician language is not dead, it is simply expressed non-verbally but rather in a metaphysical spiritual way. Colloquial Lebanese, let alone literary Arabic, are not the Lebanese languages for Corm. It is an interesting point because at the same time Corm wrote *La Montagne Inspirée*, there were already other Lebanese who began thinking about colloquial Lebanese as the Lebanese national language; we shall see below how two other Phoenicians, Michel Chiha and Sa'id 'Aql, referred to the problem of language and its place in Lebanese identity. For Corm, however, the Lebanese language was ancient Phoenician, but one did not need to revive it because it still lived in the heart of every single Lebanese and, therefore, it could be expressed in French and yet still leave the aftertaste of a Lebanese kiss.

The publication of *La Montagne Inspirée* stirred many reactions in Lebanon. The francophone circles of Beirut celebrated and praised the poetic and nationalistic values of the book. Lebanese journals devoted their literary sections to Corm and his work, glorifying him as *the* Lebanese nationalist *par excellence*. The literary journal of Michel Zakkur, *al-Ma'rid*, dedicated a whole issue to *La Montagne Inspirée*.[45] Zakkur was one of the strongest supporters of Béchara al-Khoury, and his preoccupation with Corm's work demonstrates, again, that Phoenicianism was not limited only to supporters of Eddé's camp but was actually shared, passively if not actively, by the majority of the Christian elites in Lebanon. Most of the articles in *al-Ma'rid* extolled the author and his work with only minute differences between them. Amin al-Rihani contributed an article (to be discussed in the next chapter) with mixed messages about Corm's Phoenicianism.[46] As'ad Yunis praised his friend Corm and apologetically tried to explain that he did not discard Arabism and Islam from the history of Lebanon but that he actually recognized the value of Arab culture and history for the Lebanese society.[47] Taqi al-Din al-Sulh titled his article "al-Jabal al-Ha'ir" [The Confused Mountain] and wrote the only somewhat negative critique of *The Inspired Mountain*. He stated that, like Corm, he recognized Lebanon as an independent national community, but unlike Corm, he perceived the Lebanese identity as part of the larger Arab world. If Corm insisted on the idea that the Lebanese were Phoenicians then it should be remembered that these Phoenicians were actually of Arab descent, and therefore, even if one agreed to Corm's Phoenician claims, it still did not change the fact that the Lebanese had always been Arabs, which made Corm himself an Arab, whether he liked it or not. Al-Sulh's article is the longest of the critiques of *La Montagne Inspirée* and is largely preoccupied with reducing the achievements of the ancient Phoenicians, on the one hand, and affirming the Arab identity of Lebanon, on the other.[48] It reflects the general views of the Muslim community in Lebanon about Phoenicianism, and I shall return to this issue in the next chapter.

La Montagne Inspirée not only focuses on the Phoenician era, but is also imbued with references to the Mediterranean basin. Indeed, Charles Corm's strong Christian convictions tied him to the Mediterranean, which he perceived not only as a Phoenician basin but perhaps even more as a Christian sea. Thus, Lebanon, for Corm, was Phoenician and Mediterranean simultaneously. Nationally and culturally it was Phoenician but it belonged to the wider Mediterranean civilization — a civilization that the Phoenicians themselves, together with the Greeks and the Romans, helped shape in a lengthy historical process that culminated in the birth of Christianity. In November 1935, Corm had the opportunity to expound his views about the ancient Phoenicians and the Mediterranean basin, the two complementary pillars of the Lebanese identity. He represented Lebanon at the Congrès de la Méditerranée in Monaco, where he gave two lectures. The first, "The Description of Lebanon," concentrated on the geography of Lebanon and its Phoenician heritage and identity. The ideas he presented in this lecture were not different from those expressed in *La Montagne Inspirée*. The second lecture, "The Vow of Lebanon," elaborated on the ties between Lebanon and the Mediterranean and the role of Christianity in the formation of a Mediterranean humanism. This humanism, he stated, was based on two foundations: first, a certain altruistic idealism that since antiquity had made the inhabitants of the Mediterranean think about causes higher than themselves, and second, that Christianity was born out of the ancient pagan world and infused a new life to the Greek-Latin civilization, bestowing on it the virtues that, throughout time, have created Mediterranean humanism. This humanistic Mediterranean Christianity, born in the age-old basin, had resided in the hearts of the Lebanese for the last two millennia, forming their character and tying them to the Christian Mediterranean. It provided them their tranquil and peace-oriented nature, because for Corm "to really have christianized a country" (as Lebanon is) "is to have made peace in this country."[49]

Thus, the Mediterranean, for Corm, was another facet in the national and cultural identity of Lebanon. Unlike Chiha, whom we shall discuss below, Corm, the non-politician, had never had to mitigate his straightforward views about the Christian identity of Lebanon. On a few occasions he wrote about Muslim-Christian cooperation under one Lebanese umbrella,[50] but, in general, his views on the aspired identity of Lebanon remained similar to those of the Maronite Church in 1919: a multi-confessional society in theory, but in practice a state dominated by the Maronite community and supported by the French, culturally associated with Europe and financially tied to the Arab east. The Mediterranean provided all the appropriate ingredients for this identity. Geographically it had always served as a bridge between East and West; historically it was Phoenician, Greek and Roman and the northern, better half of it was religiously and culturally Christian and Latin. Indeed, all the required elements were present to form an identity that would divorce Lebanon from its geographical Arab-Muslim surroundings.

New Phoenicia in New York

On July 13, 1939, the Lebanese pavilion of the New York World's Fair opened its gates with great fanfare.[51] The mayor of New York, Fiorello La Guardia, the French ambassador to the United States, René de St. Quentin, other American and French dignitaries and members of the large American Lebanese community attended the opening ceremony. Charles Corm, the commissioner of the pavilion, gave the inaugural speech, expounding in a very flowery tone about Phoenicia-Lebanon and its place and role in human history.[52] It was the culmination of about a year-long process of preparations for this international event, the first at which Lebanon represented itself independently, separate from its mandatory guardian, France. In retrospect, the 1939 New York World's Fair marked the end of an era. The drums of war were already pounding away. It was the last fair before the total collapse of the world system and Lebanon, as a tiny cog in this system, had the benefit of participating in this last world's festival. Within a few years, Lebanon and the entire world would wake up to a new reality and a different world order.[53]

From the 1850s, world fairs had become part of the landscape in Europe and North America. These international expositions were huge extravaganzas, designed to boost the local economy and promote the grandeur of the hosting state. Guest countries, too, considered these fairs important and economically promising for participation granted them an entry ticket to the world's international club. Vast sums of money were invested and immense pavilions were constructed by the greatest architects and designers of the time. The fairs became a sort of a window display of the entire developed world, each pavilion reflecting the way the participating countries wished to be seen. This is the reason why the 1939 New York World's Fair was so important for Lebanon and why the selection of Charles Corm as the planner and commissioner of the Lebanese pavilion is so significant for this study. Analyzing the Lebanese pavilion reveals to us not only Corm's worldview, which in many ways could be foreseen, but more interestingly it suggests the agenda of his senders. It also uncovers for us the Lebanese artistic community and its willingness to cooperate with Corm's Phoenician views.

The preparations for the fair began in November 1938, soon after Corm was assigned to be the commissioner of the pavilion by the Lebanese Chamber of Deputies. The official discussions on the character of the fair and the fiscal allocations indicate that the supporters and opponents of Corm and his Phoenician views cut across other political divisions within the Lebanese government. The Finance Committee supported the plans for the pavilion, although its Muslim members rejected Corm's layout on a budgetary pretext, alleging that they would prefer to allocate such sums to education. Tawfiq 'Awad, a Maronite politician close to the Maronite Patriarch and a supporter of Emile Eddé, opined that the government needed to allocate more money for the fair, lest Lebanon be presented in an undignified way. He nevertheless exploited the moment to attack the Phoenician tendencies of Corm and other Lebanese personalities. The Minister of Finance, Hamid Franjiyeh, defended the project and promised the Chamber of Deputies that the pavilion would not only deal with the Phoenician era of Lebanon but would also portray the Greek, Roman, Crusader, Arab and Turkish times. He emphasized the political and commercial profits Lebanon stood to gain from participating in the fair. Gébran Tuéni, the politician, journalist and a member of al-Khoury clan, rejected the project for financial and personal reasons, disparaging Corm as the commissioner of the Lebanese pavilion. Ayyub Tabet, Emile Eddé's right hand, found an unexpected ally in the image of Béchara al-Khoury, Eddé's bitter foe as both energetically defended the principles of the project.[54] Meanwhile, in a different government session, Corm too found another ally for his plans. Following a debate about the character and predicted expenses of the pavilion, 'Abdallah al-Yafi, the Beirut Sunni prime minister, defended Corm's patriotism and approved the plans.[55] Further indicating the cross-political divisions on this subject, al-Khoury, Ayyub Tabet and 'Abdallah al-Yafi, who could not have agreed on most political issues, professed support for Corm and his project. On the other hand, Tawfiq 'Awad, a staunch supporter of the Maronite-Christian identity of Lebanon, and the Greek Orthodox Gébran Tueni, one of the most vociferous pro-Arab voices in Beirut, shared similar disapproving views about the Phoenician character of the pavilion. Finally, and despite his controversial Phoenician tendencies, Corm was assigned as the commissioner, his plans were approved and the Lebanese pavilion went on its way.

Charles Corm made all possible efforts to portray Lebanon at the New York World's Fair as the new Phoenicia, culturally and ethnically unrelated to its Arab neighbors.[56] The Lebanese pavilion, very modest in size compared with the other pavilions, was arranged into several subdivisions, each focusing on a particular theme: America in Lebanon, France in Lebanon, Arts and Crafts from Lebanon, Lebanese Economy, Intellectual Culture in Lebanon, Archeological Excavations in Lebanon, Lebanon in the Future, and Artistic Work on Phoenician History and Legends. Corm demonstrated the Phoenician identity of Lebanon to the fair visitors through almost every possible artifact. Thus, for example, a large painting, depicting the Galls assisting Hannibal to cross the Alps in his famous journey into the heart of Europe in 218 BC, welcomed visitors entering the "France in Lebanon" gallery. This drawing, Corm explained, was placed there "because, in fact, the great Phoenician of Carthage could not have traversed the Pyreneans, the Rhône and the French Alps, before invading Italy, had he not had a solid alliance with the Gallic tribes." And higher education in Lebanon? Why, its roots lie in the Roman-Phoenician Beirut school of law. Lebanese economic success? It all began with Phoenician trade. Numerous examples can be given that reflect the same ubiquitous tone but it would be superfluous to describe them all.[57]

The ancient Phoenicians took over the Lebanese pavilion, but Corm also referred to other historical personalities and events as long as they did not engage Arab or Muslim presence in Lebanon. Thus, for example, three large statues of Fakhr al-Din al-Ma'ni (1585-1635), Bashir II (1767-1840) and Yusuf Karam (1822-1889) greeted the visitors at the entrance of the pavilion. The first, the father of modern Lebanon as he is exaggeratedly known in Lebanese national narrative and the reviver of "New Canaan," as Corm named him in *La Montagne Inspirée*; the second, the last great *amir* of Mount Lebanon who symbolized the transfer of dominance in the Mountain from the Druze to the Maronites; and the third, the Maronite leader who led a popular revolt against the local government in 1864 and became a mythical figure of endurance and zeal for many Maronites.[58] The Crusaders, as expected, also received their fair share in the historical display in the pavilion. Thundering silence, however, accompanied the almost complete absence of Arabs or Muslims from the display.

Corm recruited almost the entire artistic community of Beirut to partake in the Lebanese pavilion. He prepared sketches of ancient Phoenician drawings, statues and scripts found at excavation sites in Lebanon, and asked the artists to incorporate them into their works.[59] I shall refer here in some detail to the artists and other personalities who cooperated with Corm on this project, because it provides another very good indication of the fact that Phoenicianism in the 1930s was more than a capricious idea of a few dreamers. César Gemayel (Maronite), one of the most important painters and art teachers in Lebanon, depicted the great Phoenician inventions on canvas: the alphabet, navigation, glass and creation of the color purple; Abdel-Wahab Addada (Sunni) drew a series of pictures about the great Phoenician constructions; Mardiros Altounian (Armenian), an architect, painted the important Phoenician maritime discoveries; Blanche 'Ammoun, daughter of Daoud and sister of Charles 'Ammoun, contributed paintings recalling Phoenician diplomatic treaties with the Egyptians, Romans and Israelites;[60] Saliba Douaihi, (Maronite), another legend in Lebanese world of painting, sketched Phoenician, Roman and Christian images to be displayed at the pavilion, as did Georges Coury, who depicted the world-famed Phoenician love affair between Aphrodite-Venus and Adonis; Halim al-Hajj and Yousef al-Hoyeck, the sculptors who worked at Corm's studio in Beirut, contributed medallions and bas-reliefs depicting Phoenician artifacts from the British Museum; Mustapha Farroukh (Sunni), one of the most important Lebanese painters of his time did not provide any Phoenician paintings, but his participation in this Phoenician festival cannot be overlooked.[61] Other Lebanese artists, such as Marie Haddad,[62] Ibrahim 'Abdo Jabbour, Chucri Gabriel, and Maroun Sfeir, appear in the long list of pavilion participants. Clearly Corm managed to turn the project into a joint enterprise of the leading artists in Beirut, who, for their part, must have relished the opportunity to display their art at an internationally acclaimed event.[63]

In addition to the artistic community of Beirut, Corm also engaged the assistance of old Lebanese and French friends. Albert Naccache, perhaps his closest Phoenician friend, prepared a graph of the hydro-electric industry in Lebanon, and French architect Romain Delahalle offered several models of contemporary and future Beirut. Long before the New York World's Fair, Delahalle was infatuated with Lebanon's Phoenician identity. In 1936 he designed an urban plan for Beirut, never to be materialized, reflecting its unique Phoenician and Arab faces,[64] and in 1938 he contributed an article about the art of architecture in *Phénicia*.[65] Jean Dodelle, the French editor of the pro-Christian *la Syrie*, also contributed paintings for the pavilion[66] and R.P. Christophe de Bonneville, the venerable Jesuit from USJ,[67] helped formulate its themes.

Maurice Dunand, the renowned French archeologist who excavated the site in Byblos, headed the archeological gallery of the pavilion and also designed a model of the ancient city of Byblos. Thus, it seems the creation of the Lebanese pavilion of the 1939 New York World's Fair became the joint enterprise of a large number of people, orchestrated by Corm, attempting to exhibit Lebanon as an intellectual, spiritual Western fortress, rooted in the ancient Phoenician past. When Corm returned to Beirut from New York, the Lebanese government decorated him with the celebrated title *"Officier de l'ordre du cèdre"* for his distinguished service as the spearhead of the pavilion, thus giving the official stamp of recognition for his nationalistic activity.[68]

Charles Corm's Phoenicianism was a mélange of several social and political streams of thought. First and foremost, Corm was a Maronite from Beirut, with strong roots in the heart of the Mountain, the village of Ghusta, where the Corm family originated. Beirut was his day-to-day reality, but the Mountain continued to preoccupy his spiritual world of reference. Thus, despite the fact that the cosmopolitan city was his daily reality, his poetry was saturated with allusions to life, nature and landscape on the Mountain and little with Beirut and the coast. Lebanon for him was a Christian country, led by the Maronite community, and his entire political and cultural perspectives emanated from this standpoint. The Phoenicians supplemented the Christian nature of Lebanon by giving it historical depth and a wider cultural and geographical context. They placed Lebanon in the Mediterranean rather than the Arab east and they established the Lebanese-European connection, beginning with the famous Greek-Phoenician myth of Europa, Zeus and Cadmus. Corm viewed the pagan Phoenician world as a precursor for monotheism and Christianity. The ancient Phoenicians worshiped several deities, but they also believed in a one stronger god, Ba'al, a belief that became the antecedent for monotheism and later for Christianity.[69] It is not without reason that Jesus walked in Tyre and Sidon, for there he found a receptive audience for his reverent views. The ancient Phoenicians, according to Corm, were a peaceful people with ample *joie de vivre* embodied in their festivals, wine-drinking, sexual conduct and animated worship of the elements. Christianity mitigated their sensuality but left their joy of life intact. The issue of racial and biological ties between the ancient and the modern Lebanese never bothered Corm. Not once did he refer to blood or genealogy as the generational link of all Lebanese from the beginning of time. For him, it was the immortal spirit of the Phoenicians that remained vital within the hills and trees of Lebanon that united all eras into one Lebanese fate. Christianity perfectly expressed this spirit that had been initiated long before the immaculate conception of Jesus and found its perfect humanistic nest in Lebanon.

Corm remained faithful to France until the last days of the French presence in Lebanon. With the years, most Lebanese francophiles became disillusioned by France and its misconduct in the mandated regions, feeling that the promises it had made to the Christian Lebanese, its devout allies, were not being kept. Corm, however, continued to believe that France should remain in power in Lebanon, even at the price of the loss of independence. His almost blind admiration for France and its culture could be seen from his very first public writings in *La Revue Phénicienne* and continued at the Lebanese pavilion at the New York World's Fair, where France received almost as much attention as Lebanon itself. Corm did not view himself as a "Frenchman of the Levant." He was simply a Maronite Lebanese with enormous affection for France, emanating from his French-Jesuit education, and he continued to put his trust in France, believing that the Christian nature of Lebanon could be maintained only with France's physical presence there.

Corm found enthusiastic allies for his vision of a Western-oriented Phoenicia-Lebanon in the image of the Zionist movement in Palestine. The Zionist Archives in Jerusalem recount a fascinating story of the correspondence between Corm, his friend Albert Naccache[70] and Eliahu Epstein (Elath), the head of the Arab section of the Political Department of the Jewish Agency. Following the publication of *La Montagne Inspirée,* Epstein wrote a glowing review in the Jewish press in Palestine, asserting that Zionism was one of the factors that triggered the Phoenician awakening in Lebanon.[71] Corm and Epstein together sought to establish a "Palestine-Lebanon club" that would gather Lebanese and Jewish scholars, convening in Beirut and Jerusalem, for a series of lectures about the Judeo-Phoenician past and present.[72] The vivid correspondence between the two as to possible cultural cooperation continued through the 1930s, but it appears that none of their mutual cultural projects materialized.[73] When Corm was appointed to head the Lebanese pavilion at the World's Fair, he met in Beirut with the architect of the Jewish pavilion and they exchanged the plans for their respective pavilions. Epstein, for his part, sent Corm letters of introduction to carry with him to New York in order to open doors for Corm among Jewish and Zionist sympathizers.[74] This cooperation between Corm and leading Zionists in Palestine had, of course, a clear political agenda. Yet, it also marked a certain cultural watershed that Corm crossed. It mirrored the fact that, like Emile Eddé, Corm was willing to depart from the eastern geographic and cultural sphere of the region and to ally himself with Zionism, which was perceived not only as a political threat but also as a cultural foreign transplant in the region. In this respect, Corm held a minority position even among Maronites, such as Sa'id 'Aql who disassociated themselves from their Arab surroundings but still viewed Lebanon as an integral part of the eastern tradition of the Middle East.

Charles Corm was not a politician nor was he a political philosopher, as was Michel Chiha. He was a bohemian at heart, with a good sense for business, which he abandoned so that he could immerse himself entirely in the world of art that he loved so much. As an artist-cum-philanthropist he did not have any constituency to which he had to appeal except for, perhaps, the closely knit Beirut haute-bourgeoisie, who overall, even if some ridiculed his Phoenicianism, still agreed with the cultural orientation to which he subscribed for Lebanon. Despite the fact that he was the most outspoken francophone Phoenician in Beirut, his Phoenician views had very little impact on the Lebanese society as a whole. Indeed, large segments of the Beirut population were bilingual, but most still preferred to communicate in Arabic and elaborating in French about the Phoenician identity limited the possibility of its dissemination. Even for the francophone, non-Maronite Beirutis who did read and hear Corm's Phoenician views, his clear Maronite stand hindered the diffusion of his views to a larger audience. In this respect the Phoenician views of Chiha, a non-Maronite whose roots were not planted in Mount Lebanon, were easier to digest.

Michel Chiha, the Merchant Republic and the Lebanese Identity

Michel Chiha, the businessman, politician, thinker, journalist and poet, has long been acknowledged as one of the major architects of the Lebanese confessional and economic systems.[75] His place of eminence in Lebanese politics and society makes him one of the key figures for this study. Chiha has never been labeled as a fervent advocate of the Phoenician identity in Lebanon in the same manner as Corm and Sa'id 'Aql, but his high standing in Lebanese politics and in the upper-class milieu of Beirut made his views about Lebanese identity far more influential than the ideas of the latter two. He has been primarily identified as a supporter of the Mediterranean orientation of Lebanon, viewing it somewhat differently from the Phoenician identity. To the extent that this argument is valid — that Mediterraneanism is not necessarily an integral part of Phoenicianism — Chiha's Mediterranean views were fused with a Phoenician flavor and his arguments for Lebanon's Mediterranean orientation were often founded in Phoenician terminology.

Michel Chiha was born in Beirut in 1891, into a Chaldean Catholic family that originated from Iraq. He acquired his primary and secondary education in Jesuit establishments, most notably at USJ's Jesuit College where he perfected his French and expanded his knowledge of European classic literature.[76] French became his language and Europe his world of reference. As discussed in Chapter II, Chiha spent the years of World War I in Egypt among the Syro-Lebanese who had moved to the Nile Valley. His closest friends from this three-year sojourn in Alexandria were Hector Klat, Yusuf al-Saouda and his future brother-in-law Béchara al-Khoury.[77] This point should not be overlooked, for Klat and al-Saouda became, each in his own way, devout Phoenicians. Chiha maintained a close friendship with Hector Klat although the latter, upon his final return to Lebanon in 1932, aligned himself closely with the Eddé camp, becoming the leader's francophone secretary. The three years Chiha spent with al-Khoury in Alexandria marked the beginning of a forceful friendship between the two, a friendship that determined much in Lebanese politics until well into the 1950s.

In 1919, Chiha participated in Charles Corm's literary circles and contributed articles to *La Revue Phénicienne,* emphasizing the Phoenician past of Lebanon and the Mediterranean cultural orientation of all Lebanese. After the institution of the French mandate in Syria, Chiha formed amicable ties with the High Commission, facilitating his access to the upper echelons of the French administration. In 1925 he was elected to the parliament, to a minority seat, as a deputy from Beirut, and in 1926 he participated in the commission charged with drafting the first constitution of Greater Lebanon. In 1929, he retired from Parliament but remained extremely influential behind the scenes, becoming the financial and ideological force behind the political ambitions of al-Khoury, by then his brother-in-law. In the bitter Eddé-al-Khoury rivalry that dominated the Lebanese political scene from the mid-1920s-1943, it was often Chiha — and not al-Khoury — who set the belligerent tone against Eddé and his camp. Al-Khoury's rise to presidency in November 1943 was Chiha's victory no less than the new president's.

In August 1934, Chiha began publishing the francophone daily *Le Jour*, a journalistic response to *L'Orient*, the daily paper of Gabriel Khabbaz and Georges Naccache.[78] This was the heyday of the infamous rift in Lebanese politics between the Eddé and al-Khoury camps. Naccache and Khabbaz, who supported Emile Eddé, used their newspaper to denounce al-Khoury and his camp. Naccache, the political analyst of *L'Orient*, assertively advocated the non-Arab and Christian identity of Lebanon, attacking the enemies of Lebanon: Syria, the Arab movement and the al-Khoury clan.[79] Michel Chiha, together with other al-Khoury cronies, joined forces and issued *Le Jour* in response. Adjectives such as hypocritical, arrogant, demoniacal and foul embellished Chiha's attacks on Eddé in *Le Jour*, reflecting the personal character of the Eddé-al-Khoury rivalry.[80]

The two papers also differed on certain political issues, such as the relationship with France, the mandatory power, and the issue of the integrity of the borders of Greater Lebanon. *L'Orient*, and for that matter Emile Eddé, supported close ties with France and was willing to yield Muslim-dominated territories to Syria, whereas *Le Jour*, and for that matter Béchara al-Khoury, called for disengaging Lebanon from France's bear hug and sanctified the extended borders of Greater Lebanon. Yet, as far as Lebanon's national identity was concerned, the two newspapers and the two camps did not seem to differ much. Both agreed on the stand that Lebanon should retain its political independence and its unique identity vis-à-vis Syria and the rest of Arab world. They only differed on the means to achieve this end. *L'Orient* supported Christian isolationism whereas *Le Jour* advocated political integration in the region. Later analysis of the political rift in Lebanon from the mid-1920s-1945, especially by al-Khoury and writers on his behalf, depicted Eddé as an advocate of Christian non-Arab Lebanon and as an enemy of the Muslims and the Arab world. Al-Khoury, on the other hand, was portrayed as the opposite — a supporter of co-existence between the Lebanese communities and an opponent of the Christian Phoenician hallucinations.[81] It is clear today that this division was not entirely accurate. In fact, Eddé was the first to find Muslim allies for his political ambitions and, thus, the first to lay the foundation for the Maronite-Sunni cooperation that allowed the formation of the Lebanese confessional system. The following words of Chiha, the chief thinker of the al-Khoury camp, serve as the best illustration of the fact that the leading personalities of the two camps viewed the identity of Lebanon fairly similarly. The time is April 1935, when Lebanon was harshly divided between supporters of the Phoenician and the Arab identities. Moreover, it was the eve of the first free election campaign, which set the Lebanese political system into unprecedented turbulence. A year earlier, Charles Corm began publishing works in his *Éditions de la Revue Phénicienne*, one of which was Chiha's book of poems, *La Maison des Champs*. Chiha's point of departure is indeed Corm's poetic-nationalistic activity:

> Les thèses en présence sont les suivantes: d'une part celle de *la Revue Phénicienne* — dont le titre est un programme — qui se propose, en propageant les 'exploits glorieux des ancêtres,' de favoriser une renaissance patriotique; d'autre part celle d'un jeune avocat syrien, [Edmond Rabbath. A. k.] porte-parole d'une 'certaine élite' qui suit le mouvement avec beaucoup d'intérêt où se mêle une vague inquiétude. Ce jeune avocat (ou cette certaine élite) reproche à *la Revue Phénicienne* de tirer de trop loin les sources de son nationalisme. A une conception du patriotisme qu'il juge trop historique ou trop raciale, il oppose la conception de Renan ou celle, plus récente, de Julien Benda [a famous French essayist (1867-1956)], qui ne veut envisager la formation d'une nation que dans la volonté des habitants d'être cette nation ... Que le principe du libanisme réside dans l'exaltation d'un passé glorieux ou dans celle d'une toute abstraite volonté de cohésion, peu importe pour nous. Nous optons pour les deux points de vue à la fois, ils ne nous apparaissent que comme deux aspects d'une même pensée. En effet l'exaltation du passé peut fort bien — consciemment ou non — aider aux efforts de cohésion nationale. Surtout quand cette exaltation est celle d'un passé assez lointain et assez grand (le passé phénicien par exemple) pour que tous les Libanais actuels puissent s'y reconnaître au-dessus de leurs différences de langue, de mœurs, de religion ou de 'race.' *La Revue Phénicienne* l'a fort bien compris qui proclame qu'en ce cas ... 'la vérité historique repose sur des preuves plutôt morales que matérielles.' Ce qui signifie presque que pour elle, et en cette circonstance, la fin justifie les moyens. Les Syriens devront admettre que ces moyens ne sont que des manifestations de la fameuse volonté d'être une nation.[82]

Some interesting observations arise from Chiha's words. First, the ideological political division he portrays is between Lebanon and Syria but not within Lebanon, and he defends Lebanon's integrity via Corm's Phoenician inclinations. Chiha refers to Syria as the main opposition to Phoenicianism whereas Lebanon is depicted as one ideological camp. Second, Chiha understands Phoenicianism in a functionally conceptual way. For him, it is irrelevant if the ancient Phoenicians were actually the genuine racial and cultural forefathers of the modern Lebanese because the factual validity of national myths is insignificant. What was important for Chiha was that these myths fulfill their function as the adhesive material in the national formation of Lebanon. In this respect, indeed, the end does justify the means; there may be some factual flaws with the claim for Phoenician descent in Lebanon. These flaws, however, do not reduce the strength of Phoenicianism as long as it serves as the common denominator for all Lebanese, regardless of their faith.

Phoenicianism, according to Chiha, agrees with the national matrix set by French thinker Ernest Renan in "Que'est-ce qu'une nation?" Renan's famous wording as to what a nation is, viewing it as a soul or a spiritual principle constituted by two factors, the past and the present, corresponds well with Phoenicianism in Lebanon, according to Chiha. "The worship of ancestors is understandably justifiable," wrote Renan in 1882, "since our ancestors have made us what we are. A heroic past of great men, of glory [...] that is the social principle on which the national idea rests."[83] For Chiha, the Phoenicians serve as the "heroic ancestors" about whom Renan wrote and they provide the modern Lebanese nation with its historical foundation. The present, which, Renan claimed, is "the actual consent, the desire to live together, the will to continue to value the heritage which all hold in common,"[84] is the objective for which the Phoenician past should be used in Lebanon.

Was Chiha, then, a Phoenician? After all, he clearly supported the Phoenician past as the foundation of contemporary Lebanese nationalism. And the ancient Phoenicians certainly played a significant role in the way Chiha perceived Lebanese identity. Yet, unlike Corm, al-Saouda or 'Aql, Phoenicianism for Chiha was not the sole and ultimate identity the Lebanese possessed. Supporting Phoenicianism was a conscious functional decision on his part to find "a past remote enough and great enough" to serve as a common denominator for all Lebanese. Chiha did not refer to any organic or racial ties between the ancient Phoenicians and the modern Lebanese. Every nation possesses "a rich legacy of remembrances," wrote Renan, and so it is that the historical memories of the Lebanese begin with the Phoenicians. Thus, for Chiha in 1935, the Phoenicians were one facet, perhaps the most notable one, of a long Lebanese national history, which made them the foundation of the modern Lebanese identity, but not the only element therein. It is important to keep in mind that Chiha wrote this essay from within the heart of the Khoury camp and that he was not alone there to hold Phoenician views. Yusuf al-Saouda, for example, the staunch Maronite-Phoenician nationalist, was also a member of this camp, and an even more pronounced Phoenician than Chiha.[85]

Chiha professed his views about the identity of Lebanon on other occasions as well. In 1938-1939 he contributed several articles and poems to Aurore Ougour's remarkably francophile literary journal *Phénicia*. One of these articles was an essay from his series "*Entretiens de Patrice*,"[86] which he first published in 1919 in *La Revue Phénicienne*. Now, on the eve of World War II, Chiha elaborated on the calm and soft Mediterranean civilization, of which Lebanon was an integral part, as an alternative to the sinister and hostile winds blowing from northern Europe. In the imaginary conversation between Chiha and Patrice, the author bestows on Lebanon the enormous mission of saving Europe through its Mediterranean personality. This mission, Chiha claims, can be achieved despite the fact that Lebanon is a small country. It may be small, he concludes, but even without getting started on its history, its geography is vaster than that of Homer. Thus, past and present were interwoven in Chiha's words. The Mediterranean, which is omnipresent in Lebanon in all times and eras, intertwined with Homer's ancient Greece that served as an example of the enormity of present-day Lebanon. One should remember, as discussed in the Introduction, that Homer was "phoenicianized" by Victor Bérard. There is no doubt in my mind that Chiha was not oblivious to this nuance. As for the "mission" Lebanon carried, it became a key component in nationalist writings, and we shall see below the impact of 'Aql's ideas on this mission.

"*Entretiens de Patrice*" clearly outlines the Mediterranean identity Chiha subscribed for Lebanon and the weight he assigned to its geographical location. Not a word about "our ancestors the Phoenicians" is uttered in this essay, yet its setting and terminology are undoubtedly "Phoenician." The platform Chiha used for this article was *the* Phoenician organ of the late 1930s, *Phénicia*. Among the regular writers in this journal were Corm, Klat, Elie Tyane and 'Aql. Others included Alfred Naccache, Maurice Chéhab, Marie Hadad, Edmond Saad, to name but some.[87] A picture of an haut-relief, sculpted by Youssef al-Hoyeck, depicting Europa, daughter of Agenor king of Tyre, carried across the Mediterranean by Zeus incarnated as a bull, decorated the front cover of the first eight issues of the journal. The message was unequivocally clear. Most of the articles, essays and poems do not necessarily mention the ancient Phoenicians or the Phoenician identity; the format and the atmosphere, however, clearly mirrored the francophone Beirut milieu that was overall in support of the non-Arab identity of Lebanon and willing to subscribe to the Phoenician narrative. Ougour herself, the owner of *Phénicia*, was a daughter of the affluent Greek Orthodox Trad family. She was married to Joseph Oughourlian,[88] an Armenian businessman, who also wrote for the journal and most likely financed its publication. Thus, collaboration between a Greek Orthodox and an Armenian with the participation of Maronites, Greek Orthodox and Catholics produced *Phénicia* and reflected the wide support of the Phoenician identity among the Christian haute-bourgeoisie in Beirut.

Chiha's participation in this journal, as a distinguished member of this class, was only natural.

In the spring of 1942 Chiha gave a lecture at the *Cercle de la jeunesse catholique de Beyrouth*, entitled *Liban d'aujourd'hui*, which was later published as a book, becoming perhaps Chiha's most famous pamphlet. The Cercle was a club of graduates of Université Saint Joseph, and it was closed to non-Catholics. This was in the midst of World War II, about a year before Lebanon gained its political independence from France and before Béchara al-Khoury and Riad al-Sulh agreed on the famous National Pact. In 1942, Lebanon and the entire Middle East were at a political standstill, awaiting a resolution on the European front. The issue of Lebanon's cultural orientation, however, continued to be a pressing question even in those tempestuous days. This is how Chiha chose to start his lecture:

> Le Liban d'aujourd'hui, vieux de cinq mille ans et davantage, ne s'étonne plus lorsqu'on dit de lui qu'il est jeune. Il en a pris l'habitude. Par-là il justifie son autre nom de Phénicie, s'il est vrai que ce nom est le même que celui du phénix fabuleux, de l'oiseau au plumage de feu qui ne mourait un instant que pour renaître de ses cendres. Et c'est aux Libanais, mieux qu'aux Thébains issus du Phénicien Cadmus, que devrait s'appliquer, de Sophocle, le début solennel d'Œdipe Roi: "Enfants du vieux Cadmus, jeune postérité ..." Pour ce Liban, né d'hier, d'après ce qui se raconte, pour ce Liban tant de fois centenaire, c'est tout juste l'âge de raison qu'on peut paraît-il revendiquer. Le sort a ces ironies.

As in previous instances, Chiha does not claim here that modern Lebanon is the incarnation of ancient Phoenicia and that today's Lebanese are direct descendents of the inhabitants of the Phoenician city-states. The entire text, however, is imbued with paragraphs such as the one above, referring to the eternal existence of Lebanon as a viable cultural entity from the Phoenician era to modern times. Thus, his entire argument regarding the country's national identity is based on identical terminology and argument of the Phoenician idea.

According to Chiha of 1942, one unbroken thread — geographical location — conjoins the ancient Phoenicians with the modern Lebanese. The position of Lebanon as the meeting place of three continents and the interaction between the Sea and the Mountain are the two constant factors that shaped the cultural identity of Lebanon throughout the ages. This is the claim made too by many other modern Phoenician-Lebanese as to their connection with the ancient inhabitants of Lebanon and it is based on the works of Henri Lammens, to whom Chiha constantly refers as the scholarly foundation for his geo-political arguments.[89] Chiha also follows Lammens' theory of Lebanon as a "land of refuge," stating that due to its special geography Lebanon has been a sanctuary for oppressed minorities since time immemorial.

More than geography has defined the inhabitants of Lebanon in all times, according to Chiha. Since the Phoenician era, he wrote, Lebanese have been polyglots, using at least two or three languages, one local and one international. This became the common refrain of Lebanese nationalists attempting to answer Arab nationalists who had defined the Arab nation as any place where Arabic is spoken and Islam is professed.[90] Chiha stretched this argument even further, all the way to the Phoenician era, arguing that even before the invention of the alphabet the ancient Phoenicians were multilingual and the modern Lebanese were simply following the footsteps of their ancestors. Recognizing the sensitivity of this argument, Chiha tried to mitigate it by stating that Arabic is a very important language for Lebanon. But his underlying message — that Arabic is not *the* national language of Lebanon — remains clear.[91]

On other occasions in *Liban d'aujourd'hui*, Chiha used Phoenician terminology to support his arguments for the existence of a unique Lebanese national identity. Just as the ancient Phoenicians immigrated to the four corners of the earth and founded colonies, of which the most notable was Carthage, Chiha explained, modern Lebanese behave similarly: they immigrate and found colonies, the most notable being the Lebanese community in Egypt.[92] This argument was often used to try to explain and justify the enormous human drift that had left Lebanon since the beginning of the 19th century. It was one of Lebanon's greatest problems and by positing it in a historical context it received a certain rationale and justification; we have already seen the way Philip Hitti incorporated it as one of Lebanon's national characteristics.

After establishing his argument as to the crucial importance of geography in the formation of Lebanon's national identity, and the characteristics of this identity, Chiha advanced to define who the Lebanese were. He began by asserting the magnitude of the past in the national identity of the present. "The past never dies," Chiha paraphrased a French author. "Man can forget it, but it remains within him. Whoever he is in any given epoch, man is the product and the essence of all the anterior epochs."[93] The people who lived in Lebanon fifty to twenty centuries ago would recognize in present-day Lebanese their authentic posterity. Their blood, Chiha wrote, could not have completely disappeared from Lebanon. Nevertheless, he believed that it was impossible to know today what the racial composition of the Lebanese had been, and he therefore disagreed with the theses that claimed that the Lebanese bore either Semitic or Indo-European blood. Since the beginning of time, Lebanon had experienced an unprecedented number of peoples and races who had traversed its land and left their ethnic imprint. Thus, Chiha concluded, Lebanon cannot be defined as Semitic, Indo-European, Arab or Phoenician. "The population of Lebanon is simply Lebanese […] it is not more Phoenician than it is Egyptian, Aegean, Assyrian, Median, Greek, Roman, Byzantine, Arab […]. At the most, we say that the Lebanese identity is a Mediterranean variety, probably the least decipherable."[94]

So, according to Chiha, Lebanon is part of the Mediterranean and its national identity is neither Arab nor Phoenician, but simply Mediterranean. What did the "Mediterranean identity" mean for him personally? First and foremost it meant the geographical setting. It was the sea and its climate that from antiquity dictated the national identity of all Mediterranean societies. Thus Egypt, Lebanon, Greece, Italy, France and Spain share one common denominator that makes their cultural identities somewhat similar. The Mediterranean for Chiha was also an exchange of cultures and ideas. It implied openness to other streams of thought and, even more, to financial openness, which since antiquity had made the Lebanese natural-born merchants. All these characteristics connected the modern Mediterranean societies to their roots, far away in the past, in the ancient civilizations of this age-old sea.

The Mediterranean basin also bestowed on Lebanon the connection with the rest of the Latin world. Latin culture for Chiha was associated with warm temperament and temperatures, as opposed to the cold Anglo-Saxon spirit and weather of northern Europe. Latinism was not only a cultural temper but also a religious association. Chiha himself was a Catholic, extremely influenced by French Latin church, and the lecture, *Liban d'aujourd'hui*, was given in front of a young Catholic audience. For this audience, Chiha was more than a politician. He was a mentor who provided them an identity to cling to. In this identity Chiha fused past and present, the former as an ancient sacred past of a religious history, beginning with the passage of Jesus in Phoenicia, and the latter as the Mediterranean which provided a continuous geo-political and cultural link to Europe in the history of Lebanon. The Phoenicians, the foundation, functioned as the past and the Mediterranean, the edifice, was the present at any given moment in Lebanon's history.[95]

The national identity Chiha prescribed for Lebanon was not a rigid ideology, and his political philosophy was not as inflexible as that of other Lebanese nationalists, such as Charles Corm and Yusuf al-Saouda. Chiha constructed Lebanon's identity in the image of the cosmopolitan atmosphere of Beirut. This was the Levantine city of dozens of groups and sects, people who spoke three languages and more, who conducted commercial ties equally with the major Arab cities and with Marseille and Smyrna.[96] Mount Lebanon is omnipresent in Beirut. Its shadow, figuratively and literally, covers the city at dawn. But its message of staunch Maronite nationalism was not part of the city's socio-economic reality. Thus, for example, as much as Charles Corm was a product of Beirut more than of the Mountain, as a second generation Maronite in the city, the ideology of the Mountain still hovered above his national thought. Chiha, conversely, as a Catholic of Iraqi origin, was unrestrained by the confined nationalism of the Mountain. Hence, the literary images he used were related more to the Mediterranean Sea than to the Mountain. His book of poems, *La Maison des Champs*, stands out among the works published by Corm's *Éditions de la Revue Phénicienne*, for it lacks the images about the Mountain that are ubiquitous in the other books. The same applies to Chiha's "*Entretiens de Patrice*," which is entirely oriented towards the Sea and does not mention the Mountain, not even once. This, of course, does not mean that Chiha ignored the Mountain. He named it the spine of the Lebanese state,[97] but mentally and emotionally Paris was closer to Chiha than any age-old village hanging over the rocky cliffs of Mount Lebanon.

Despite the fact that Chiha was *the* leading personality in al-Khoury's camp, he did not see any ideological dilemma in his participation in the literary activities of the Phoenician group that gathered around Charles Corm. Hence, he published his poems with Corm, he contributed writings to *Phénicia*, and he partook in the literary gatherings in Corm's residence.[98] At the same time, Chiha was looking for a common denominator within Lebanon between its different communities and between Lebanon and the rest of the Arab world. He was first and foremost a businessman, a co-owner of one of the largest financial establishments in Lebanon, the Chiha-Pharaoun Bank, and as such he was fully aware of Lebanon's inextricable financial ties with the Arab countries. Having this point in mind, Chiha wrote extensively about the need to form a regional economic and political association for the countries of the Near East,[99] viewing such an association as a potential market for Lebanon and as a warranty for political stability in the region. He even attempted to prescribe the Mediterranean identity to other Arab countries, such as Syria and Egypt. In the 1950s, when the Arab countries were swept up by the wave of pan-Arabism, he wrote against this tendency, begging them to look westwards to the Mediterranean basin and Europe, and not eastwards to Asia and the Third World.[100]

Chiha was a great believer in the British liberal economy and he thought Lebanon could best thrive in a *laissez-faire* financial system. He imagined his country as a commercial passage between the Arab world and the West, and the radicalization of the Arab world against the West upset him as much as the creation of the State of Israel. Zionism disturbed him because it disordered the socio-political system he prescribed for the region. Whereas Corm and Albert Naccache regarded the Zionist movement as a potential ally for the Christian camp in Lebanon, Chiha, who by all means was part of this camp, regarded Zionism as a menace to his grandiose regional plans. One of the steps Chiha took to achieve the financial goals he had assigned for Lebanon was the foundation in 1943, along with other Lebanese businessmen, of a financial club named "The New Phoenicians." It was a group of Christian Beirut entrepreneurs who aspired to return to what they had believed was a *laissez-faire* economy practiced by the ancient Phoenicians, their spiritual forefathers.[101] Thus the appellation "Phoenician" was used simultaneously by Chiha and Corm, who may have agreed on Lebanon's cultural orientation, but definitely differed on its integration in the Middle East and on the political allies Lebanon should acquire in the region.

Although Chiha knew Arabic, he never expressed himself in this language. Unlike his brother-in-law Béchara al-Khoury, who was known for his eloquence in the "language of the *dad*," Chiha's means of communication remained French throughout his public career. This fact, however, did not hinder his views about the identity of Lebanon from being heard and acknowledged by educated Muslim and pro-Arab Lebanese. A non-Maronite Christian without power base in the Mountain, it was easier for other Lebanese to listen to his views about the distinct non-Arab identity of Lebanon without fearing the zealot Maronite nationalism that prevailed in Mount Lebanon.

In 1988, Kamal Salibi, the reputed historian of Lebanon, wrote a soul-searching book, *A House of Many Mansions*, about the Lebanese order, trying to locate the reasons for its disintegration. The book challenged many historical "truths" that Salibi himself, as a Lebanese historian, helped to construct before the civil war, as Lebanon was thought to be stepping into a bright and promising future. One chapter in this book harshly criticizes the Phoenician myth of origin, viewing it as historically fictitious and politically destructive. Paradoxically perhaps, this critique is a good illustration of the impact Michel Chiha left on Lebanese identity and of the Phoenician myth of origin. Salibi recognized Chiha as the most intellectual and articulate mind behind the Phoenician idea. Phoenicianism for Chiha, Salibi wrote, was an impressionist rather than historical idea. He wanted to form Lebanon as "the Phoenicia of the Middle East," a bridge between the Arab East and the European West. Chiha, according to Salibi, considered the ancient Phoenician city-state of Tyre as the prototype of modern Beirut,[102] the "city-state" that was at the center of Chiha's political, social and ideological life.

Yet, after explaining the roots and content of the Phoenician myth and bluntly condemning its validity, Salibi then remarked that urban Lebanese today, who live in the same cities as the ancient Phoenicians did, do not appear to be much different in character than their forefathers. What makes them similar to the ancient Phoenicians, however, is geography and not history. "They live in the same cities along the same Mediterranean shore, and work the same land under the same climate. Geography in some respects can be as important as history."[103] One does not need to go far to notice that this is exactly the way Michel Chiha described the Phoenician identity for Lebanon. Indeed, he had not negated history as Salibi did, but geography for him was still the most important link between the ancient Phoenicians and the modern Lebanese. Chiha would probably agree with Salibi about the historical flaws in the Phoenician identity. But he would dismiss them as irrelevant. Moreover, Salibi even wrote that, in a way, modern Lebanon emerged as a resurrection of ancient Phoenicia by being a kind of a city-state. Beirut, actually annexed to the heart — to the Mountain — became the heart itself and transformed into a modern city-state. This indeed was the Beirut of Chiha, the city that had evolved to lead a state, the modern Lebanese state. Thus, on the one hand, Salibi denounces Phoenicianism but, on the other, he recognizes important aspects of the Phoenician myth as expressed by Chiha. Chiha indeed imagined Beirut as a modern Phoenician city-state, granting it, and not the Mountain, the leading role in the formation of modern Lebanon. All of the above only demonstrates the magnitude of Chiha's thoughts on the national discourse in Lebanon. His views about the Lebanese national identity remained imprinted even among opponents of this identity. Thus, a person such as Salibi who rebuked the historical validity of the Phoenician myth, especially of the Maronite nationalism of the Mountain, approved, perhaps unwittingly, the geographical legitimacy of the Phoenician identity, and the magnitude of the city and not of the Mountain therein, exactly as Chiha articulated.

Sa'id Aql, Arabophones and Maronite Nationalism

This chapter has been primarily preoccupied thus far with Phoenicianism and its francophone manifestations. After all, until the mid-1930s, the most prominent advocates of the Phoenician identity were Lebanese who graduated from French schools, most notably USJ, and who wrote poetry, prose and essays in French about this identity. Despite this francophone prevalence, it should be recalled that from the outset Arabic was also used as a means of expounding on the Phoenician past of Lebanon (and prior to 1920, of geographical Syria as well). We have already seen examples in the journals *al-Muqtataf* and *al-Hilal*, as well as in the works of Henri Lammens who published as many studies in Arabic as in French. The comprehensive study from 1918, *Lubnan; Mabhiith 'Ilmiyya wa-Ijtima'iyya*, sponsored by Isma'il Haqqi Bey, was also an Arabic manifestation of a distinct Lebanese identity starting with the Phoenician era. There were other seminal individual demonstrations of Phoenicianism in Arabic, such as the history textbook *Mukhtasar Tarikh Lubnan*[104] [The Concise History of Lebanon] that clearly elaborated on the uninterrupted historical chain from ancient Phoenicia to the *Mutasarrifiyya* in Lebanon. One should not forget Na'um Mukarzal who, although he mastered and even taught French in Jesuit establishments, still wrote in Arabic in his daily paper, *al-Hoda*, about the non-Arab identity of Syria and Lebanon. Thus, even before public education struck roots in Lebanon and more and more Lebanese children studied in state schools in Arabic about their Phoenician forefathers, there were a fair number of Lebanese who used Arabic, and not French, to elaborate on their Phoenician heritage. These manifestations were not necessarily expressions of a distinct Phoenician, non-Arab, Lebanese identity, but they provided the foundation of what was yet to come around World War I and culminate with the establishment of Greater Lebanon in 1920.

Yusuf al-Saouda was one of the first persons to explicitly record in Arabic about Phoenicianism as an expression of a unique and independent identity of all Lebanese, separated from Arab or Syrian collective identities.[105] In mandatory Lebanon he became a second-rate politician with close ties to right personalities, such as al-Khoury, the Maronite Patriarch Antoine 'Arida and Habib Pasha al-Sa'd, with whom he had familial ties through the marriage of al-Sa'd's niece.[106] By the 1960s, al-Saouda became identified as one of the prime advocates of and speakers on the Maronite nationalism of the Mountain. He published several works supporting Phoenicianism not only as a geo-political and cultural identity, but also as a racial distinction for Lebanon.[107] As noted earlier, al-Saouda acquired his primary education at the Maronite *Madrasat al-Hikma* and his secondary and higher education at Jesuit establishments in Beirut and in Alexandria. Despite this educational background (identical to that of Na'um Mukarzal and many other Maronites), from the outset of his public career al-Saouda wrote all his books in Arabic rather than French. He was born and raised in Bikfaya, twenty-five kilometers north east of Beirut, and felt more comfortable among the arabophone majority of Lebanon than among the small francophone milieu who lived in the affluent Ashrafiyyeh neighborhood in East Beirut. Already in 1922, he rejected the inclusion of French as an official language, asserting that Arabic should be Lebanon's sole official language.[108] Al-Saouda opposed the French mandate in general, and demanded complete independence for Lebanon, a stand that marked him as a francophobe by the French authorities.[109] He argued that the only people to benefit from making French a Lebanese official language would be the francophone Beirutis, whereas the rest of the Lebanese population, who had not mastered French that well, would only be disadvantaged by such a policy. Thus, at the same time that Charles Corm and his associates were elaborating in *French* about the Phoenician identity, first for geographical Syria and from April 1919 for Greater Lebanon, al-Saouda was writing in *Arabic* about the same identity, prescribing it exclusively for Lebanon in its extended borders. From 1916, this was the formal view of the *Alliance libanaise* in Egypt, which publicly called for the establishment of Greater Lebanon as an independent state — in opposition to the opinion of most intellectual Christian Lebanese who were still advocating a greater Syrian federation and including Lebanon therein.

Al-Saouda's Arabic tendencies at the time are also curious as so many of his compatriots, especially those in Alexandria, were publishing books in French about their desired political solution for Lebanon. Evidently, the phenomenon of mastering and cherishing Arabic, on the one hand, and disapproving of Arabs and Arab culture, on the other, became one of the most enigmatic issues within Lebanese society. Na'um Mukarzal, for example, was persistent about the non-Arab identity of Lebanon but, at the same time, he insisted that only Arabic would be the formal language of his country of origin.[110] Fouad Afram al-Bustani wrote most of his books in Arabic, including an Arabic dictionary, taught Arabic and Arab history at USJ before becoming the first president of the newly-founded Lebanese University, and still rejected any cultural ties between Lebanon and the Arab world. Even during the heyday of francophonism in Lebanon in the 1930s-1940s, most

Lebanese preferred to read and converse in Arabic.¹¹¹ It is also clear that many of the Lebanese "non-Arab" arabophones were not born and raised in Beirut, or at least were not part of the francophone haute-bourgeoisie and its ideology. Outside of Beirut, Arabic was still the one and only dominant spoken language, functioning as an inseparable part of the social tissue of the Lebanese society. There were cities and villages that were influenced more than other locales by French (and, to a much lesser extent, English), especially if a foreign school were located nearby, thus having a more direct impact on the local population. But Arabic remained the leading language even in the Maronite villages of the Mountain, where Lebanese separatist nationalism was preached.¹¹² And it was from this reality that al-Saouda emerged, together with Mukarzal, al-Bustani, Anis Freiha and, of course, Sa'id 'Aql, who will occupy the remainder of this section.

We have already seen that Phoenicianism in Lebanon was mainly expressed through poetry and prose, remarkably influenced by French literature. The francophone Lebanese, who were educated in French establishments for so many years, were exposed to the finest and latest expressions of French culture. They frequently alluded to writers such as Charles Baudelaire, Victor Hugo, Edmond Rostand, Paul Valéry and so forth, and to French literary schools, particularly Romanticism and Symbolism,¹¹³ referring to them as their sources of inspiration. Poetry in Arabic, introspecting on the magnificence of Lebanon and its imposing history, was composed in Lebanon long before Charles Corm and his circles began versifying in French. Khalil Mutran, 'Isa 'Iskandar al-Ma'luf, Rashid Nakhla, Shibly al-Malat and others wrote about the splendor of Lebanon when Corm and Chiha were still toddlers in Beirut.¹¹⁴ These writers and poets, however, were still composing in traditional forms and patterns and the inspiration of world's literature on their writings was limited. A new generation of Arabic writers had to rise, writers who were exposed to French education but still clung to Arabic, and allowed these French influences to infiltrate their verse-writing. This indeed occurred around the mid-1930s, especially with the appearance of Sa'id 'Aql onto the literary scene. Thus, just as francophone Phoenician poetry became associated with French schools of literature, especially Romanticism, the same occurred with the French-inspired arabophone literature that used primarily French symbolism to glorify the ancient history and landscape of Lebanon.

'Aql was, and still is, one of the most important Arabic poets of the 20th century, and equally, one of the most controversial personalities in the political and literary circles in Lebanon.¹¹⁵ Born in 1912 in Zahle, the capital of the Biqa' region, his father was a long-time Zahliote and his mother, Adele Yazbek, came from Bikfaya. He studied at the Oriental College of the *Frères Maristes* in Zahle and divided his formative years between Zahleh and Bikfaya. He became known to the Lebanese public as a literary figure in the early 1930s, following the publication of his articles in various journals, particularly his first work, *Bint Yftah*, a tragic play focusing on the biblical story of Jephthah and his daughter. The play highlighted his interest in ancient Biblical eras as a source of inspiration for his writing. Around this time 'Aql briefly flirted with the political views of Antun Sa'adeh and the PPS. Sa'adeh's party was especially appealing to educated Lebanese who were not part of the Beirut francophone circles. Students from AUB were among Sa'adeh's first recruits, but there were also others — such as 'Aql, Salah Labaki, Jean Jalkh,[116] Yusuf Yazbek — who were attracted to the idea of a secular, non-confessional, unified Syria, founded on five millennia of historical experience.[117] This part of 'Aql's biography is very vague, for it seems that he himself made all efforts to cast mist on these days.[118] What is clear is that by 1935, 'Aql had already abandoned the PPS and departed on an independent and very successful literary life, marked by innovative ideas about literature and about the cultural and linguistic interaction between East and West. That year, he translated to Arabic parts of *La Montagne Inspirée* and published them in the Jesuit literary journal *al-Mashriq*,[119] making Corm's epic accessible for readers of Arabic as well.

The publication of the first four books in Corm's *Éditions de la revue phénicienne*[120] was an important event in Lebanese national and literary circles. It provoked enthusiastic responses and led to a series of reviews of the four books. 'Aql himself, a rising star in Lebanese literature, reviewed these books in *al-Mashriq* which reflected the fact that already then, in 1934, he was preoccupied by the problem of the Lebanese national language, an issue that engaged him throughout his career. These were the questions that perturbed 'Aql's mind in his critique:

> [...] Is the Western spring more effective in Lebanese poetic capacity than the Arab spring? Is Lebanon a perplexed country, but still prefers to be oriented towards the west? Is it true that there is a western spirit and an eastern spirit separated from each other? Or, conversely, is it true that Arabic is a higher tool than French in the poetry of the perpetual human spirit? Have some of our Francophone poets realized that, until recently, their Arabic colleagues remained obscured in issues such as innovation, veracity, examination of deep philosophical questions, description of human spirit and the eulogy of the nation? Should we hope, following our French poets, to open a new road to the lines of the world's poets? Are we located now, following the humanistic sections of *La Montagne Inspirée,* at the heart of the human literature? These questions echoed in me as I read Corm, Chiha and their colleagues Tyane and Klat.[121]

'Aql continued to state that in the last century, Arabic poetry had been disconnected from the world's poetic currents. It was only with the Lebanese who learned foreign languages that novel influences were introduced into Lebanese poetry. He recognized the success of the francophone poets and their contribution to the openness of Lebanese poetry to world's currents, but he disagreed with those who claimed that this success was a result of the use of French language rather than Arabic. This was an audacious lie against Arabic, he exclaimed, because Arabic was just as good a language, if not better, for the composition of poetry. Besides, the achievements of these Lebanese francophone poets indicate that poetry is neither Eastern nor Western, for it has one spirit that can be expressed in any language. World literature, 'Aql proclaimed, is not about a Frenchman describing Lebanon or a Lebanese depicting France. World literature is above time and place, it deals with a description of the spirit; and the spirit is one in the entire world. Arabic, therefore, can and should be used the same way that French was used by Corm and his friends, to ask philosophical questions, to express new innovations and to extol the nation — the Lebanese nation, of course.

Although 'Aql wrote about the universality of poetry and the irrelevance of the kind of language in which one composes poems, his words were clearly a defense of Arabic, as a competent and creative language for literary writing. We have seen how sensitive this issue was in the 1930s in Lebanon. Amin al-Rihani, for example, criticized Corm more for the fact that he did not write verse in Arabic than for the Phoenician content of his poems. Similarly, Taqi al-Din al-Sulh dedicated a large portion of his review of *La Montagne Inspirée* to the fact that Corm refused to write in Arabic, and in the following chapter we shall see similar reactions from other adversaries of Phoenicianism. The Beirut that, in the 19th century, produced the most prominent Arabic revivalists also generated in the 20th century the strongest non-Arabic movement within the Arab world, and the above quote by 'Aql should be understood in this context. In his writing in Arabic, 'Aql made an unequivocal statement that this language was good enough for the composition of modern (nationalist) literature and that it was also a flexible language which, with the right pen in hand, welcomed linguistic innovations. He demonstrated this in 1937 in *Al-Majdaliyya* [The Magdalene] and again in 1944, with the publication of his tragic play, *Qadmus (Cadmus)*. He also illustrated in *Cadmus* that Arabic could be "expropriated" from its Arab-Islamic context and used to extol a Christian national movement, which refused to be related to its Arab-Muslim neighbors. When *Cadmus* was published, 'Aql was already toying, along with other Lebanese poets such as Rushdi Ma'luf, with making colloquial Arabic-Lebanese into the formal national language of Lebanon and its prime instrument of literary expression.[122] This effort reached its climax in the 1960s; in the 1940s it was only in its seminal stage. *Cadmus*, however, was written in a highly literary Arabic, often with unusual grammatical configurations, befitting the reputation of 'Aql as an innovative language genius.

'Aql wrote numerous times about the distinct identity of Lebanon, particularly in the 1950s-1960s,[123] but *Cadmus* was undoubtedly his most distinguished Phoenician masterpiece, perhaps the most original Phoenician literary piece ever written in Lebanon. Following its release, he was designated the "architect of Lebanism" and the "soul of Lebanon," becoming the philosopher and teacher of Lebanese nationalism. "Lebanism," he preached, implied that Lebanon was Lebanese (neither Arab nor Syrian nor any other designation), with a clear, explicit and remarkably unique identity — an identity that carries an unequivocal civilizing mission to the world — that, from antiquity to modernity, has survived the vicissitudes of history. According to 'Aql's Lebanism, for 6,000 years Lebanon has been a "land of light" (*balad al-ish'a'* or *Liban lumineux*), radiating its lofty civilization to the rest of the world. There were other Lebanese who spoke in similar terms about Lebanese nationalism,[124] but 'Aql cast into this theory his literary talent and idiosyncratic personality, making it practically his own possession. He began working on *Cadmus* in 1937, when Lebanon was at the height of the struggle over its cultural and national identity, and it is clear that this tragedy was his response and contribution to this debate that pulled Lebanon into competing cultural and national trajectories. Its publication in 1944 coincided with the first anniversary of the November 1943 events and the recognition of Lebanon as an independent, sovereign state with an "Arab face." It was also the year in which the Arab League was formed and into which Lebanon was admitted, a move that stirred many waves within Lebanon, especially among some Christians who absolutely opposed this move.[125]

The prime purpose of *Cadmus* was to extol Lebanese nationalism and to elaborate on the mission Lebanon had been carrying to the world. It contained a didactic message for all Lebanese, attempting to fire their national sentiments by teaching them about what 'Aql believed that civilizing mission was. In case the reader did not understand this message within the plot of the tragedy itself, 'Aql provided an introduction that explained it in plain but powerful words. Its main theme is that Lebanon is an undiminished homeland and the Lebanese are an irrefutable nation, not because of some unique geo-political and ethnic features, but rather because of the distinct spiritual mission Lebanon has borne since the Phoenician era and even before. This mission is embodied in Lebanon as the last capital of truth and tranquility in a world of violence and ignorance (note that this was during World War II). "What is Lebanon? When was it formed and why? What announces it?" 'Aql asks in the introduction, and responds:

> A community of people who live on the eastern shore of the Mediterranean, in an exceptional setting that is neither territorial boundaries, ethnic lineage, phonetic uniformity, nor unity of any history. Rather, it is a conglomerate of efforts in an ascending road from the ignorance of the material to the conscience of reason. Our nation is not a nation in the political sense [...]. By nation we mean a community of capable, illuminated, loving people and we declare that even if Lebanon was not

like that in absolute terms, it is still oriented, more than any other country, towards this direction.[126]

After explaining that Lebanon is a nation not because of conventional Machiavellian socio-political requirements, such as borders and ethnic similarities, but rather because of its spirit, 'Aql moved to outline the capable, illuminated and loving characteristics that made Lebanon a "nation of truth." The Lebanese are a calm and humanistic people, searching for wisdom and addressing the uncorrupted truth in the world. All these characteristics are only highlighted against the atrocities and narrow-mindedness which the nations of the world experience these days. Why and how have we, Lebanese, become like this, 'Aql asks again and immediately replies. It was in Sidon where the first step towards human intelligence was taken. There, in this ancient Phoenician city, man challenged destiny for the first time, using his intelligence to create and then defy fate. After Sidon, there were three other "intellectual foci" that led to the development of human intelligence and civilization. In Jerusalem, Christianity, which meant love, universality and truth, was conceived. In Antioch, this truth was cloaked in Christian dogmas. In Damascus, the fourth focus of intellectual development, a political organization in the shape of the Arab Caliphate took advantage of human development and, for the first time, created an immense political structure based on "the flame of belief." Thus, these four points of convergence — the crux of human intelligence — were based on the first and prime human experience, which began with the Phoenician innovations that defied blind fate. To strengthen this point 'Aql provided a teleological historical description of the development of human intelligence:

From Sidon proceeds a colony to Egypt, founding the most beautiful quarter of Memphis, where a movement of thought provides the education of Moses, the hero of the unity of God. Furthermore, an occupation proceeds to the land of the Greeks, building the city of Thebes, the mother of Athens. And when the star shines on Rome of the order — the heir of Athens of the logic — two of our four cities are opened for Athens and Rome: Athens influences Antioch through Tarsus, and Rome influences Damascus through Byzantine and Beirut. From the nerve of Damascus, Andalusian Cordoba is born, becoming the world's intellectual capital between the years of 800-1000 AD. At that moment, Antioch is completely relocated into Rome of the order, transforming it into Rome of the spirit. From the former, the latter and from Athens, modern Europe is formed, to which we have ceaselessly been attached in the last two centuries through Paris, the spiritual capital of the world and the depositor of its unique intellectual inheritance.

This engaging and historically-arguable description provides some very interesting insights into 'Aql's mind. Lebanon, for him, was the capital of the world's intelligence because it was the ancient Lebanese who planted the seed of human reason and who bestowed monotheism on the world. All of Western civilization emanates from this seed. More than anything else, this patrimony, expressed in wisdom, reason, love and serenity, granted Lebanon its national identity and national validity. Not ethnicity, natural borders or geographic composition, but rather national temper is the one and only important component that makes Lebanon a "nation of the truth." The introduction of *Cadmus* concludes with the following paragraph that summarizes the idea of a *Liban lumineux* and its civilizing mission to the world:

> Out of a powerful luminous and generous heritage, we have thrived at the gates of Asia, in this extension of the patrimony of Europe, a nation of the truth: and we, its people, have publicly declared in the face of the West — that mixture of light and war — that we carry a mission to it, allaying some of its recklessness, enriching its activity and directing its vision far beyond immediate profit. A mission of six thousand years of patience, contemplation, disdain for the material, altruism, aspiration upwards and the consideration of spontaneity before consciousness, a unique mission to the world is vested on us to 'Lebanonize' the world.[127]

It is difficult to overlook the French scent of this *mission civilisatrice* 'Aql prescribed for Lebanon. After all, it is not far from the grandiose and pretentious mission the colonial circles in France believed French culture carried for the rest of the world. For 'Aql, just as for these colonial circles, the civilizing mission was intertwined with Christian faith as the highest expression of a lofty civilization. Yet, whereas France indeed had the power to try to Gallicize the world (even if it ultimately failed), Lebanon barely managed to contain itself and its inhabitants in one political framework. This, though, did not hinder 'Aql and others from writing about the civilizing mission of Lebanon to the world.[128]

The tragedy *Cadmus* is an exemplary illustration of the role of national thinkers, such as 'Aql, in the awakening of ancient (sometimes fictitious) heroes, to remind and teach their nations of their proud and lofty national identity. Many national writers preceded 'Aql and others followed, awakening ancient heroes from the abysses of oblivion to serve as emulating models for their respective nations.[129] Heroes, such as Cadmus, are taken from what is perceived to be the Golden Age of the nation — in the case of Lebanon, the early Phoenician era. These heroes symbolize "a golden age of heroism and glory which, like a shining beacon, furnishes a model for communal regeneration"[130] wrote Anthony Smith. They serve as a point of comparison with the present and assist the nation to reconstruct its ethnic history. In this sense, Cadmus is not much different from, say, Hannibal, Fakhr al-Din al-Ma'ni or

Yusuf al-Karam. All three were depicted by the Lebanese national movement as heroes of an immortal nation. Cadmus simply preceded them and allowed 'Aql to locate the roots of the Lebanese nation in a time period that even predated the events of the Hebrew Bible. Through *Cadmus*, 'Aql wanted to place Lebanon in a specific historical sequence, to direct the Lebanese to behave according to his political beliefs about Lebanon and its place in the Middle East and, finally, he wanted to entertain the reader with a story of a Lebanese hero, perhaps the first Lebanese strongman, a refined form of a *Qabaday*.[131]

Greek mythology recounts the following story of Cadmus and his sister Europa. The young daughter of Agenor, King of Tyre, was playing at the water's edge of the Mediterranean when Zeus fell in love with her. He assumed the form of a white bull and lured her to climb onto his back. Once seated, the bull-Zeus reared to his feet and bounced into the waves, carrying Europa with him to the southern coast of Crete. Zeus succeeded in convincing her of his love and as an expression of his affection he named the continent to which he carried her after his new love. Europa's three brothers, Cadmus, Phoenix and Cilix, set out to find their missing sister. Soon, Cilix and Phoenix stopped their search and founded, respectively, Cilicia and Phoenicia. Cadmus, the most persistent of the three, asked the advice of the oracle of Delphi who suggested that he stop searching, follow a sacred cow and settle down where the cow halts. Cadmus finally settled in Boeotia and founded the city of Thebes. There, he fought and killed a dragon that tried to prevent him from sacrificing the sacred cow to the gods. With the advice of Athene, Cadmus sowed the teeth of the dragon in the ground and from these warriors sprang forth, fighting each other until only five survived. These were the five founders of the city of Thebes. Europa and Cadmus are never reunited in Greek mythology. They have two separate story-lines. In ancient Greece, Cadmus was considered a divine and important figure. The Greeks ascribed to him the discovery of casting metal and the importation of the alphabet. Europa's place in Greek mythology was less significant. It is told that Zeus left her in Crete, but not before she bore him three sons. She later married Asterius, the King of Crete, and that is, in fact, the last reference to her. Thus, her role in Greek mythology is primarily related to Zeus and his relationships with mortal women, of whom Europa was but one.

Four characters feature in 'Aql's tragedy: Cadmus, Europa, Mira their governess, and a blind Greek fortuneteller who symbolizes inevitable fate. Mira serves as the axle of the plot, representing the spirit of the nation. She (how else — a female as a symbol of the nation, Lebanon)[132] also serves as the inner patriotic voice that resides within Europa and Cadmus. She carries the knowledge about the loftiness of Lebanon illustrated by the characters of the two siblings. Whenever Europa doubts the sublime mission she bears from the land of truth, it is Mira who reminds her where she came from and what her message is to the world. The play opens with a discussion between

Europa and Mira. The two are in Greece, after being carried there by Zeus. Europa laments her solitude and her longing for Lebanon. Throughout the play she is torn between her love for Zeus and her love and loyalty to her homeland and her people. Mira, the voice of Lebanon, supports Europa and reminds her of the mission she, as a daughter of Sidon, carries to the continent that will bear her name. In the meantime, Cadmus crosses the seas, searching for his sister. Zeus, fearing that Cadmus might take Europa back to Lebanon, leaves a dragon at the doorstep of Europa to watch after his beloved wife. The dragon, of course, embodies the opposite characteristics of the ones Cadmus bears. The man represents wisdom, tolerance and integrity, whereas the beast stands for ignorance, intolerance and malignancy. Europa, knowing about Cadmus's efforts to retrieve her, fears lest the dragon fight and slay her dearest brother. Through Mira and the blind fortuneteller, Europa tries to dissuade Cadmus from coming to rescue her, but to no avail; fate is stronger than any other power. Cadmus does fight and triumph over the dragon and after this violent struggle, he sets out to save Europa, only to discover that she has already died. Cadmus is filled with agony and sorrow, yet the mission of Lebanon to the world is completed. With her death, Europa resolves the internal struggle between her love for Zeus and her loyalty to Lebanon, with which she was grappling. Her message of love from Lebanon to the world is transmitted. Cadmus himself remains in Greece and builds cities and civilizations with the assistance of Sidonite seafarers and the giants that sprang from the dragon's teeth. Thus, his mission of wisdom is also completed.

More than the plot, it is the underlying message that grants *Cadmus* its major appeal.[133] As 'Aql explicitly explained in the introduction, the main idea behind *Cadmus* was to justify Lebanon's legitimacy as a viable homeland (*watan*) and the Lebanese as a viable nation (*umma*). Responding to those who deny Lebanon's viability, the tragedy *Cadmus* concentrates on the legitimacy of Lebanon and its merit over the nations of the world. 'Aql lets Mira exclaim it directly:

> We shall endure! Whether they like it or not,
> Then, withstand, Lebanon, there is no weakness in you!
> We shall endure! There has to be truth on earth,
> And there is no truth unless we endure![134]

The two leading protagonists, Cadmus and Europa, symbolize two complementary missions Lebanon conveys to the cradle of humanity. Cadmus bears the message of wisdom and Europa the message of love. "Send me tomorrow as a letter of love," says Mira in the name of Europa, "from my country the earth opens up in mercy."[135] Later, Europa declares again her mission:

> I am my country, and Lebanon is a pledge!
> Not a cedar and not a mountain and not a water,

My nation is love, there is no hatred in love
And it is light, it does not go astray: and hard work,
And a hand creating beauty, and wisdom
Do not say: "my nation" and assail the world,
We are a support to human beings and its people![136]

'Aql then allows Mira to define Cadmus's role again: "Cadmus arrived [in Greece] to them, to these ages with writing, with knowledge, and tomorrow they will learn that on the ships we carried the guidance to the world."[137] Elsewhere Cadmus himself describes Lebanon's strength to the blind fortuneteller. Reading the future and fearing the fall of Greece, the fortuneteller asks Cadmus to return to Lebanon. But Cadmus is unwilling to do so before his mission for Lebanon is completed:

I said that we shall embark boldly in sea and land,
We lead conquests after conquests
And from the small land we search the earth
We scatter our villages in all shores
We challenge the world, nations and tribes
And build — everywhere we yearn — a Lebanon.[138]

Just as Charles Corm did in *La Montagne Inspirée*, 'Aql too ties the Phoenician legacy to the world with Christianity. Already in the introduction, referring to the truth Lebanon has been carrying to the West since the time of the ancient Phoenicians, 'Aql explicitly writes:

[…] we know that truth is strength (*Qudra*, which can also mean omnipotence of God. A.K.) and that truth is light and that truth is love. And we know that strength cannot be strength without light and love, and the same for the light without the other two, and the same for love. It has already been said: truth is one, and added - the one is the Trinity.[139]

Throughout the play *Cadmus* it is clear that the messages Europa and Cadmus carry to the West are strength, knowledge (light) and love, and these three attributes, according to 'Aql, reflect, in fact, the three dimensions of the Christian Trinity: the Father, the Son and the Holy Spirit. The Trinity, then, 'Aql explains, was manifested in Lebanon, the land of luminosity, fifteen centuries before the Immaculate Conception of the Virgin Mary. The Father — strength — is the Godhead of the Trinity; the Son — knowledge — is Cadmus; and the Holy Spirit — Europa — is love, God's greatest gift. It could even be said that the death of Europa represents the death of Jesus. Both personages carried a message of love and compassion to humanity and both sacrificed themselves for the benefit of their followers. From this perspective, Europa's death is actually not tragic but victorious. Similar to the mission of Jesus to humanity, Europa transported the Lebanese Eastern spirit of love and beauty to Europe, the land of war and hatred. Thus, despite Europa's death, *Cadmus* actually tells the story of the triumph of Lebanon and its spirit, for just as Jesus was resurrected, so was Europa through her spirit that continued to live in the continent that since then has born her name.

Like Corm and Chiha, 'Aql also believed that Christianity was an inseparable part of the Lebanese identity. Even when he spoke about Lebanon for all Lebanese, Muslim and Christian, he always used Christian terminology to elucidate this identity.[140] He shared with Corm the belief that monotheism was a result of a Lebanese-Phoenician effort no less than a Hebraic-Jewish endeavor.[141] 'Aql believed and preached, as did Corm, that the spirit of Christianity hovered above the shores, hillsides and valleys of Lebanon long before the birth of Jesus. For these two Lebanese nationalists this spirit meant wisdom, peace-searching, universality, and beauty, all residing within Christianity-cum-Lebanon. Of course, Corm and 'Aql did not contrive the link between Christianity and the Lebanese identity *ex nihilo*. Since the 1840s, the Maronite church taught the idea that Lebanism was tied to Christianity, a view that was only strengthened with time and led, finally, to the formation of Greater Lebanon, justified by this very connection. The Lebanist idea, as formulated by 'Aql, the *Kata'ib* and other Lebanese Christian nationalists, was actually a novel variant of this old Maronite Lebanism. 'Aql simply took this idea and extended it to the beginning of human history, where, already then, he claimed, Lebanon and the Christian spirit were synonymous.

Sa'id 'Aql came from an entirely different social background than that of Charles Corm and Michel Chiha. As a Zahliote who always referred to this city as his home, he was removed from the francophones of Beirut. He referred to Corm with great admiration, viewing him as a true Lebanese patriot,[142] but he shared neither with Corm nor with Chiha the comfort the two exhibited within Beirut's French circles. True, perhaps even more than the other two, 'Aql was influenced by French literary schools, especially the writings of Paul Valéry and other French symbolists, to whom he constantly referred as his major source of inspiration.[143] Yet, he clearly felt more at home in Lebanon, in general, and in Zahle, in particular, than in any other Western city, Paris included. Thus, whereas Chiha dedicated a section of his poetry book to Paris[144] and Corm often referred to this city with great affection and admiration,[145] 'Aql's main focus was always anchored in Lebanon. The French language, which he perfectly mastered,[146] functioned as an instrument for him, but never occupied his heart as it did for Chiha and Corm. Zahle, his city, was even more predominantly Christian than Beirut, but its location in the Biqa', a primarily Muslim region, midway between Beirut and Damascus, shaped the identity of its inhabitants and made them highly conscious of their Christian faith and at the same time equally aware of the wide geographic region in which they lived and to which they belonged. The city had always taken great pride in the number of Arabic poets it has produced[147] and probably 'Aql's love, virtuosity, and authority of Arabic emanates from this Zahliote tradition.

Another facet in 'Aql's social background was the village of Bikfaya, his mother's birthplace and where 'Aql himself spent part of his adolescence and where later he also wrote *Cadmus*.[148] This village has been at the center of Christian life in Mount Lebanon for over two centuries. It was the capital of the Christian *Qa'imaqamiyya* in 1845-1860, and it has also been the home of some of the leading Maronite families, most notably the Gemayyels, the founders and leaders of the Lebanese *Kata'ib*. The social origins of the *Kata'ib* are not the subject of this study, yet it is clear that 'Aql, al-Saouda, another son of Bikfaya, and the Gemayyels were products of Lebanon of the Mountain more than Lebanon of the City. Although they spoke about Lebanism as a supra-confessional framework, it was apparent that Maronite nationalism was their prime motive and concern. This nationalism was rooted in the Maronite experience in the Mountain far more than either the cosmopolitan city of Chiha, the affluent Greek Orthodox families from the "Quartier Sursock," the Sunni haut-bourgeois families or, to a certain extent, even Maronites who made Beirut their home, such as the Eddés and the Corms.

Sa'id 'Aql has doubtlessly been the strongest arabophone voice in Lebanon supporting the existence of a viable Lebanese nation, unrelated in any aspect to its Arab neighbors. Nevertheless, when it came to his views about Zionism and a Jewish state in Palestine, he unconditionally rejected both, believing that the Palestinians deserved their own state and that the Zionist movement was threatening the integrity of Lebanon.[149] In the 1970s, when 'Aql became one of the chief ideologues of the Lebanese Forces, he radically changed his views, becoming a strong supporter of the cooperation with Israel against the Palestinian presence in Lebanon. In the 1940s, however, and especially after the establishment of the State of Israel in 1948, 'Aql expressed very strong views against Israel's right to exist at the expense of an Arab Palestine. He shared this view with Chiha, though for different reasons, and he entirely disagreed with Corm on this point. It is an interesting issue, for as a Maronite and a staunch Phoenician, 'Aql was closer to Corm than he was to Chiha, but we can see, yet again, that belonging to one confessional group or another does not necessarily determine one's political views in Lebanon. Although 'Aql rejected any national and ethnic ties with the Arab world, in his manners, language and social worldviews he was still part of the human map of the region and a Jewish Western state was a foreign transplant for him, an intruder in an Eastern region. Corm, on the other hand, sat on the fence, with one leg in the West and the other in the East. Like Emile Eddé, Albert Naccache and others, Corm was able to view a Jewish state as a political and cultural partner of Lebanon, a conception with which 'Aql could not have agreed, at least not before the Lebanese order disintegrated in front of his eyes and, like many other of his compatriots, he had to reevaluate his worldview and adjust it to the changing and painful reality.

The differences between 'Aql, Corm and Chiha surface also in the issue of the national language of Lebanon. In a world of fervent nationalism where language played a decisive role in the definition of numerous national collectives, notably Arab nationalism, many Lebanese felt the need to find a solution to the seeming contradiction between their use of Arabic and their assertion that they were not part of the Arab world. We have already seen the way Chiha and Corm solved this dissonance. The former, followed by many Lebanese, asserted that Lebanon has always spoken one local language and one international language, and today these were Arabic and French; the latter wrote that the Lebanese national language resided in the heart of all Lebanese and it was, therefore, irrelevant what language was used, because, uttered from Lebanese lips, all languages were, in fact, Phoenician languages. 'Aql, conversely, remained faithful to Arabic, but almost from the outset of his literary career he aspired to form a Lebanese language, based on colloquial Arabic Lebanese inscribed in Latin letters according to a simplified system he himself created. There was no coincidence in the fact that such an initiative came from a Phoenician, non-Arab, Lebanese such as 'Aql. The same phenomenon occurred in Egypt when, in 1926, at the height of the Pharaonic wave, Salama Musa, one of the leading Egyptians promoting the Pharaonic identity, called for the latinization of the Arabic characters and the use of colloquial Egyptian as the country's national language.[150] The power of Arabic as a unifying factor for all Arabic speakers was an issue with which any centrifugal force within the Arab world had to grapple. Arabic was never just another national language. It was an adhesive material, tying together tens of millions of people "from the ocean to the gulf," especially in the 20th century as a result of the mass diffusion of literature, journalism, art and ideological streams through the use of what Benedict Anderson called "print capitalism." 'Aql's major effort to transform colloquial Lebanese into his country's national language reached its peak in the 1960s, some two decades after it began. Other Christian Lebanese poets and thinkers, such as Rushdi Ma'luf, Salah Labaki and later Anis Freiha, shared these views. Although each of them spoke eloquent French, they preferred to write and create in Arabic, their prime language. Barring any religious restrictions about this language as Christians, they shared innovative and reforming ideas about Arabic[151] — ideas that many Muslims found difficult to bear. Despite the almost inseparable tie between Arabic and Islam these writers did not see any contradiction between the use of Arabic, on the one hand, and the belief, on the other, that Lebanon holds a unique national identity, unrelated to the Arabs, with roots that can be traced back at least 3,000 years to the ancient Lebanese — the Phoenicians.

Sa'id 'Aql was the spearhead in a literary movement that gathered steam in the late-1930s-1940s. He led a group of thinkers who, using French literary schools, wrote in Arabic about their love for their country, extolling its countryside, people and ancient history. They were not necessarily labeled

"Phoenician" by their allies and foes, but in their poetry they often referred to the Phoenician past of Lebanon. In doing so, they spread the Phoenician message in Lebanese society to corners otherwise neglected. Salah Labaki, for example, who, was briefly the deputy of Antun Sa'adeh and the minister of propaganda of the PPS, was a very important literary figure in the 1930s-1940s. In 1944, he published his book *Min A'amaq al-Jabal* [From the Depth of the Mountain].[152] It is a collection of legendary stories from Greek and Phoenician mythologies, perhaps the most eloquent Arabic attempt to recount mythological stories related to ancient Phoenicia-Lebanon. César Gemayyel, the renowned Lebanese painter, embellished the book with his drawings, demonstrating, again, that one did not have to be marked a Phoenician in order to take a role in a Phoenician literary enterprise. Another example is Rushdi Ma'luf, a poet, teacher and journalist, who published in 1944 a book of poetry entitled *Awwal al-Rabi'* [The Beginning of Spring]. An introduction by 'Aql opens the book, detailing Lebanon's civilizing mission to the world. The first poem is entitled *Biladi* [My Country] and is dedicated to 'Aql and Charles Corm, recognizing their patriotic eminence.[153] The poem recounts, yet again, the contribution of Lebanon to Western civilization since Europa, the daughter of Lebanon, crossed the seas and settled in the continent to which she gave her name.

When the young Sa'id 'Aql came to the literary and nationalistic Lebanese fore, Michel Chiha and Charles Corm were already in their late forties, after more than two decades of intensive political, literary and commercial lives. Corm and Chiha belonged to the generation that made the dream of a Christian Lebanon a reality. But 'Aql's writings were no less fervently nationalistic — perhaps even more so than the writings of Lebanese nationalists in Corm's generation. Corm, 'Aql and Chiha have been among the strongest voices that advocated the Phoenician orientation of Lebanon, each in his own way, and together they spread this Phoenicianism to most corners of the Christian population of Lebanon in the City and on the Mountain. There were hardly any Muslim Phoenician preachers in Lebanon, but the message of this trio also reached parts of the Muslim population, particularly the Sunnis from Beirut, with whom the Maronites shared many political and financial interests. By the 1940s there were already Muslim Beirutis expressing mitigated Phoenician views — a subject I shall explore in the concluding chapter of this study.

References

1 About Charles Corm's metamorphosis from businessman to *"homme de lettres,"* see *La Revue du Liban et L'Orient Méditerranéen*, No. 37 (February 1934). See also Chapter II, note 133.
2 *La société des auteurs libanais de langue française* included in its ranks many francophone Lebanese novelists and poets who wrote about Lebanon and its

ancient heritage. It was not a large circle of writers and they formed a sort of a cohesive social class, as is reflected in their books of poetry; often they dedicated poems to each other or alluded to poems written by their cohorts. The leading names that recur in these organs are Corm, Hector Klat, Elie Tyane, Fouad Abi Zayd, Michel Chiha, Michel Talhamé, Georges Schéhadé, Emile Cousa, Alfred Naccache, Maurice Hajje, Jeanne Arcache, Amy Kher, Joseph Harfouche, Joseph Ayrut, Eveline Bustros, Edmond Saad, Marie Haddad and Blanche Amoun; all were Christian, all had mastered French as if they were indeed *les Français du Levant* and all believed that Lebanon held a unique national and cultural character, different from its Arab neighbors.

3 *La Revue du Liban et L'Orient Méditerranéen,* No. 40 (May 1934), p. 4; CZA S25 10250, a report of Eliahu Epstein, October 1934. Epstein reports that the name of the group that used to meet at Corm's house was "The Young Phoenicians." I could not find any other reference to this name.

4 Youssef Hoyeck is considered to be the father of modern Lebanese sculpture. One of his most famous works was the first monument in Place des Martyres, the central square in Beirut. Halim al-Hajj was another renowned sculptor who tutored many Lebanese art students. Al-Hajj and Hoyeck participated in the 1939 New York World's Fair, on which I shall elaborate below. For more on both, see the British-Lebanese Association, *Lebanon — The Artists View* (London, 1989), p. 128. César Nammur, *Al-Naht fi Lubnan* [Sculpting in Lebanon] (Beirut, 1990), pp. 87-95, pp. 108-113; Edouard Lahoud, *L'Art Contemporain au Liban* (New York-Beirut: Near East Books Co., 1974), pp. 82-88.

5 Eliahu Elath, *Mi-ba'ad le-'Arafel ha-Yamim* [Through the Mist of Time] (Jerusalem: Yad Yitzhak Ben-Tzvi, 1989), pp. 185-186.

6 AD Nantes, Carton 622, Meyier to MAE September 6, 1938. In a report on the inauguration ceremony of Radio Levant on September 31, 1938 Eddé gave a speech, beginning with the Phoenician message Lebanon was still carrying to the world. See also Eddé's opening speech at the Syro-Lebanese pavilion of the *Exposition des Arts et des Techniques* in Paris 1937, where he also elaborated on Lebanon as the political and cultural descendent of ancient Phoenicia. AD Nantes, Carton 461, no date. See too CZA S25 3500, a report of Eddé's speech in Paris, in the Israeli daily *Davar* July 10, 1937. See Béchara al-Khoury's commentary on Eddé's speech at the Paris Exposition in *Haqa'iq Lubnaniyya*, p. 216.

7 Following the November 1943 events, the Zionist emissary in Beirut wrote that "Corm is in a panic" as a result of Eddé's fall, and that he is working with friends to try and reverse the situation. CZA S25 5577 Tzadok to the Political Department December 25, 1943, meetings with Ayyub Tabet, Charles Corm, Pierre Gemmayel and Albert Naccache.

8 Amin al-Rihani, *Qalb Lubnan* [The Heart of Lebanon], sixth edition (Beirut: Dar al-Kutub al-Lubnani, 1978), p. 244.

9 In *La Revue du Liban,* no. 58-59(March 1936), pp. 38-40, there are excerpts of French journals that praised Corm and *La Montagne Inspirée*. About Corm's winning of the Edgar Allan Poe prize of the *Maison de poésie de Paris*, see MAE Paris, Vol. 628, pp. 102-103, p. 108, au sujet de Charles Corm, May 24, 1935.

10 *L'U* (December 1935), p. 89.

11 Al-Rihani, *Adab wa Fann* (Literature and Art), (Beirut: Dar Rihani lil-Tiba'a wa al-Nashr, 1957), p. 106.

12 As part of his travelogue on Mount Lebanon, al-Rihani described a meeting with three well-educated Lebanese women who mastered French but preferred to converse in Arabic because they were "proud Arab women from the heart of Lebanon." They informed al-Rihani that they loved Lebanon in the same magnitude Corm cherished the country, but they were angry at him for using French and not Arabic, the language of Lebanon. Despite their ire, al-Rihani wrote, they were proud of Corm and they admired *La Montagne Inspirée* because it extolled the country they treasured. *Qalb Lubnan*, p. 229.
13 *Ibid*, p. 247. At the same time, as we shall see in Chapter V, al-Rihani also respected parts of Corm's Phoenicianism. In the critique he wrote of *La Montagne Inspirée*, he mainly reproached Corm on two related issues: the fact that Corm used French as his means of expression and the unconditional love of France. The third cycle of Corm's epic which is in fact the Phoenician hymn of hymns, is positively reviewed by al-Rihani. See *Adab wa Fann*, p. 109.
14 A reference to the last section in *La Montagne Inspirée*, the hymn to the Sun.
15 *Qalb Lubnan*, p. 271-272.
16 *La Colline Inspirée* was first published by Barrès in 1913 (Éditions Émile-Paul frères). It tells the story of the three Baillard brothers, Quirin, François and their leader and eldest brother Léopold, who, convinced of the power of Christianity and the national importance of the region of Lorraine to French nationalism, undertook the mission of buying the land and the ruins on the hills of Sion-Vaudémont in Lorraine. Their objective was to establish a new church on the hill, to raise the symbol of Lorraine and to strengthen Christian power. Léopold's dialogue with the forces of the hill preoccupies most of the plot of *La Colline Inspirée*. The hill itself, of course, is a magical place with a lengthy and sacred history. It served as sanctuary for pagan gods before it was Christianized. It radiates enormous energy that feeds the brothers' spirituality. For example, when a hermaphrodite statue of the pagan religion is found in excavations on the site, it fills Léopold with energy and understanding of the power of the old religion. One does not need to imagine why this book of Barrès inspired Charles Corm so much.
17 *La Montagne Inspirée*, p. 39.
18 *Ibid*, p. 42
19 Corm uses the term "*suffète*," the word used in Carthage for "judge," which is similar to the Hebrew biblical term "*shofet*," a magistrate and a political and spiritual leader.
20 *La Montagne Inspirée*, p. 44.
21 *Ibid*, p. 53.
22 *Ibid*, p. 61.
23 New Testament, Matthew, 15, 21-28. Marcus, 7, 24-30.
24 *La Montagne Inspirée*, p. 45.
25 *Ibid*, p. 57.
26 Usually this theory refers to "El" who was the prime god in the Canaanite pantheon and with the development of monotheism became the proper pronoun of the "one and unique God." The fact that Corm chose to relate to Ba'al is interesting, for in the Bible, Ba'al is notorious for being an abhorred deity against whom the prophets fought ferociously.
27 Anthony Smith, *The Ethnic Origins of Nations*, p. 189.

28 *Ibid*, p. 188.
29 *La Montagne Inspirée*, p. 75.
30 The name Adonis is known only in Greek texts. It is derived from the Semitic word Adon or Adoni (my Lord). This Greek-Phoenician god was one of the major sources of pride for the modern Phoenicians, for it symbolized the fact that the Greeks borrowed from their forefathers not only the alphabet, but also some cultural customs, such as the worshiping of Phoenician deities. See the following demonstrations of Lebanese fascination with the cult of Adonis: Habib Thabit, *'Ashtarut wa Adunis: Malhama Shi'riya* (Beirut: Dar Majallat al-Adib, 1948) and Adra Hoda, *Étude Mythique, le Mythe d'Adonis : Culte et Interprétation* (Beirut: Librarie Orientale, 1986).
31 See many references to the Adonis River in the writings of French travelers, as collected in Jean-Claude Berchet, *Le Voyage en Orient*, fourth edition (Turin, Italy: R. Laffont, 1997), pp. 709-801.
32 *La Montagne Inspirée*, p. 76.
33 *Ibid.*
34 A reference to the only six standing columns at the site of the Temple of Jupiter in Balbeck.
35 *La Montagne Inspirée*, p. 84.
36 *Ibid*, p. 85.
37 *Ibid*, p. 83.
38 *Ibid*, p. 92.
39 *Ibid*, p. 98.
40 *Ibid*, p. 99.
41 *Ibid*, p. 101.
42 *Ibid*, p. 103.
43 *Ibid*, p. 105.
44 *Ibid*, p. 106.
45 *Al-Ma'rid*, no. 1022 (July 4, 1934).
46 "Jabal al-Tajalli" [The Mountain of Transfiguration (of Christ)], *Ibid*, p. 9-10.
47 "Al-Jabal al-Mulham, Muharrir al-Arwa'" [The Inspired Mountain, the Deliverer of Wonders], pp. 4-8.
48 It seems there were no hard feelings in Beirut between supporters and opponents of Corm's views. Shortly after the publication of *La Montagne Inspirée*, Corm invited arabophone authors to participate in a new literary association aiming at "strengthening the solidarity between writers in Lebanon." Among the participants were the Muslims Jamil Bayhum and Taqi al-Din al-Sulh and the Druze Khalil Taqi al-Din. The Christian members included Buturs and Salma Sa'igh, Ibrahim Munzar, Habib Thabit, Ilyas Abu Shabka, Karam Malham Karam, Fu'ad Afram al-Bustani, and Amin Nakhla. *La Revue du Liban*, No. 40 (May 1934), p. 4
49 Corm's speeches at this congress can be found in *Études* (January 5, 1936), pp. 74-83; and *al-Mashriq* (January-March, 1936), pp. 94-103. Not coincidentally, I believe, both were Jesuit journals that took the effort to publish the words of Corm. Corm reiterated the same ideas in a speech he gave at the Institut International de Coopération Intellectuelle, quoted in *La Revue du Liban et l'Orient Méditerranéen*, 60 (May 1936), pp. 8-9.
50 In "The Vow of Lebanon" Corm refers once to Muhammad and Islam as contributors to the Mediterranean humanism, but it seems little more than paying

lip service to the Arab delegates from Egypt and North Africa who attended the congress. The message of his lecture is unambiguously and decisively Christian.
51   For general books on the fair see Helen A. Harrison, *Dawn of a New Day; The New York World's Fair, 1939-40* (New York: Queens Museum; New York University Press, 1980); Larry Zim, Mel Lerner, Herbert Rolfes, *The World of Tomorrow; The 1939 New York World's Fair* (New York: Harper & Row, 1988); See also *Official Guide Book, New York World's Fair 1939* (New York: Exposition Publications, 1939).
52   AD Nantes, Carton 1442, French Ambassador to the USA, St. Quentin to Georges Bonnet, MAE, July 20, 1939. In his report to the Quai d'Orsay, the French ambassador described a small incident related to Corm's speech. He reported that Corm read his speech in English and referred to France only in the context of USJ. After returning to his seat, the ambassador continued, Corm realized that he had not said a word about the French government. He, therefore, stood up again and this time improvised in French, thanking the French government and the High Commission, reiterating the familiar words about the Franco-Lebanese friendship. On this incident, see also *al-Hoda*, July 17, 1939.
53   The fair itself was designed with the motto of progress and futurism. Yet, past, present and future were inseparably intertwined in its paths and pavilions. One of the most spectacular and photogenic monuments that garnished the fairgrounds was a huge sculpture of the Greek-Phoenician myth of Europa, daughter of Agenor King of Tyre, carried across the sea by Zeus who had assumed the form of a white bull. No doubt Charles Corm wandered around the plazas and pavilions of the Fair filled with pride over the magnitude, the central location and the attention given to Europa his great-great-great legendary matriarch.
54   AD Nantes, Carton 946, a report of a session of the Chamber of Deputies, November 21, 1938.
55   AD Nantes, Carton 946, a report of a session of the Chamber of Deputies, March 30, 1939. 'Abdallah al-Yafi was a member of the National bloc of Emile Eddé. He acquired his secondary education at USJ and his law degree in Paris. This may explain why he, as a Sunni leader with strong Arab conviction, still supported Corm's patriotism. On Yafi's political views, see AD Nantes, Carton 1365, rapport sur les partis politiques au Liban, December 17, 1942. p. 17. On his activity as an Arab nationalist in his student days in Paris, see MAE Paris, Vol. 381, pp. 61-71, Syrian students in France.
56   CZA S25 1511, The Diary of Bernard Joseph November 6, 1938. Joseph wrote that Eliahu Epstein met with Corm while he was engaged in preparing the Lebanese pavilion. "The entire character of [the] exhibits," he wrote, "will be such as to stress the Phoenician past of the Lebanon. They have been very careful to avoid creating the impression that they are Arabs." About the cooperation between Corm and the planner of the Jewish Palestinian pavilion see below in this chapter. See also Laura Zittrein-Eizenberg, *My Enemy's Enemy* (Detroit: Wayne State University Press, 1994), p. 132.
57   AD Nantes, Carton 924, a report of Charles Corm, "Exposition Mondiale de New York 1939."
58   In the historiographical struggle over the identity of Lebanon, the Lebanism of Karam was confronted with attempts to demonstrate that he was first and foremost an Arab and the revolt he led was a popular Arab uprising. See Sarkis Abu Zaid,

'Urubat Yusuf Karam [The Arabism of Yusuf Karam] (Beirut: Dar Ab'ad lil-Tiba'a wa al-Nashr, 1997).

59 Corm's book, *L'Art Phénicien* (Beirut: Éditions de la Revue Phénicienne, 1940), is in fact a collection of these sketches accompanied by glowing explanations as to what was Phoenician art. This art, for Corm, was closely associated with faith. It is "first and foremost profoundly human. It is also receptive, comprehensive and liberal. Open to all forms of beauty it accepts them with plenty of sympathy as seriousness, and it gives them an accent of gravity, quasi-religious, that does not exist in any art of its epoch. No other object of art gives us the feeling we get in front of certain Phoenician steles. It furnishes a sense of being in front of a man, an honest man that believes in God, a honest man that respects himself and at the same time respects the God that governs him." *Ibid*, p. XIII.

60 Blanche 'Ammoun (who married a French army officer who had served in Beirut) was the first Lebanese woman to graduate from the Law Faculty of USJ, though she never practiced law. Instead, she focused on painting and literature. She published an illustrated children's book, *Histoire du Liban* (Beirut: Éditions "Le Jour", 1937), recounting Lebanon's history through the Phoenician narrative from the Stone Age to the arrival of the French in 1918.

61 Faroukh contributed three paintings, one of the Khalifa Mu'awiyya in Lebanon and the other two depicting societal Lebanese games.

62 Marie Haddad was a Lebanese artist who resided primarily in Paris and became a symbol of Oriental exoticism in the city. She published a book, *Les Heures Libanais* (Beirut, 1937), with Corm's *Éditions de la Revue Phénicienne,* depicting romantic images from Mount Lebanon.

63 The list of participants and their works can be found in AD Nantes, Carton 924, Corm to Abdallah Bey Beyhum, October 23, 1940. Biographical notes about most participants can be found in the following books: Michel Fani, *Dictionnaire de la Peinture au Liban* (Paris: Escalier, 1998); Nammur, *Al-Naht fi Lubnan*; and Edouard Lahoud, *L'Art Contemporain au Liban.*

64 Delahalle, "Pour l'embellissement de Beyrouth," *La Revue du Liban*, 60 (May 1936), p. 20.

65 Delahalle, "L'architecture, élément du bonheur," *Phénicia* (October, 1937), pp. 5-12.

66 Jean Dodelle was the editor in chief of *La Syrie,* the journal of French journalist Georges Vayssié, who was an ardent supporter of Christian Westerm-oriented Lebanon. Vayssié was very active in the artistic community in Beirut. Like Corm and Eddé, he also cooperated with Zionist emissaries in Beirut and often wrote sympathetic articles about the Zionist-Jewish enterprise in Palestine. CZA S25 3143, a report by Eliahu Epstein of a visit of Vayssié in Palestine in 1936, no date. CZA S25 4552 II, Eliahu Sasson to Vayssié, May 28, 1934.

67 Boneville occupied senior Jesuit positions in and out of Beirut. He was the director of the *Cercle de la jeunesse catholique* in Beirut, the rector of USJ (1927-1930), the head of the Jesuit Order in Lyon (1930-1936), in charge of the Jesuit mission in Syria (1936-1937) and of the entire Near East (1937-1939). His participation in the planning of the pavilion demonstrates the close ties Corm maintained with the highest echelons of the Jesuit order in Beirut. On Bonneville, see Henri Jalabert, *Jésuites au Proche-Orient* (Beirut: Dar el-Machreq, 1987), pp. 238-239.

68 CZA S25 4549, Epstein to Corm, June 4, 1940; AD Nantes, Carton 1442 Corm to Gabriel Puaux, the French High Commissioner, May 17, 1940.

69 Corm stretched the connection between the Phoenicians and Christianity in all possible ways. In his *L'Art Phénicien* he wrote that standing in front of the steles of Phoenician gods, one senses that "the god of our ancestors" did not possess the cruelty and the monstrous power of the gods of their neighbors. Moreover, Phoenician religious art already prefigured the purest representations of the Christian art of the Middle Ages. *L'Art Phénicien*, p. XV.

70 According to Epstein, Naccache was married to a Jewish woman whom he met in his studies in Switzerland. Epstein, "Ha-Tziyonut ha-Fenikit bi-Levanon" [Phoenician Zionism in Lebanon] *Cathedra*, 35(1985), pp. 109-124

71 "There can be but little doubt that one of the factors which inspired the new Phoenician aspirations was the Zionist movement which has encouraged them to dream of reviving their own culture and traditions." Epstein, *The Palestine Post*, February 24, 1935.

72 CZA S25 3143, Epstein to Corm, October 24, 1934; Epstein to Corm, October 31, 1934. Corm suggested As'ad Yunis and Amin al-Rihani as possible lecturers who could come to Jerusalem.

73 One of these unrealized projects was related to Nahum Slouschz, a Jewish scholar who wrote extensively about the ancient Phoenicians. Slouschz helped lay the foundation for the historical thesis of the ancient Phoenicians as Hebrews. This theory attributed the achievements of the Phoenicians to the Hebrew civilization and viewed Carthage, for example, as a Hebrew colony. This very unique historical *Geschichtebild* was embraced by certain Zionist Revisionists and later was fully adopted by the Canaanite movement in the *Yishuv* in Palestine. Corm sent Slouschz his *La Montagne Inspirée* and issues of *Phénicia*, and Slouschz was supposed to arrive in Beirut for a series of lectures. However, for unclear reasons, Slouschz's trip never materialized. CZA S25 5581, Corm to Slouschz, February 27, 1938; Corm to Epstein, February 23, 1938; Epstein to Slouschz, March 22, 1938. Epstein to Shertok, no date. On another occasion Epstein tried to accelerate the publication of Slouschz's book, *Otzar ha-Ketovot ha-Fenikiyot* [Lexicon of Phoenician Inscriptions], so that Slouschz could distribute it in Lebanon. CZA S25 4549, Gardon to Epstein, June 17, 1940; Epstein to M. Gardon, July 7, 1940.

74 CZA S25 3500 Epstein to Corm, December 15, 1938; Epstein to Corm, November 14, 1938; Epstein to Corm, February 7, 1939; S25 5581, Epstein to Corm, November 14, 1938; Epstein to Haim Greenberg, May 5, 1939. Greenberg was one of the organizers of the Palestine Pavilion at the World's Fair. Epstein asked him to assist Corm in establishing connections with Jewish and Zionist sympathizers and to use Corm to establish relations with Lebanese immigrants in New York, so that together they could work against their mutual enemy — the pan-Arab movement. Epstein added in the letter that moral support in this respect was given to Corm by Emile Eddé, the Lebanese president, "who is one of our closest friends."

75 On Michel Chiha, see Fawaz Traboulsi, *Identités et Solidarités Croisées dans les Conflits du Liban Contemporain* (Ph.D. Thesis, University of Paris, 1993), pp. 298-299; Traboulsi, *Silat bila Wasl: Mishal Shiha wa al-aydiyulujiyya al-Lubnaniyya* [Michel Chiha and the Lebanese ideology] (Beirut: Riyad al-Rayyis

lil-Kutub wa al-Nashr, 1999); Jean Salem, *Introduction à la Pensée Politique de Michel Chiha* (Beirut: Samir, 1970); Khalil Ramiz Sarkis, *Sawt al-Gha'ib* [The Voice of the Absent] (Beirut: Al-Nadwa al-Lubnaniyya, 1956); Eveline Bustros, *Évocations* (Beirut: Éditions du cénacle libanais, 1956), especially the introduction by Hector Klat.

76 Chiha spent six years at Saint Joseph College (1900-1906), taking classes in the Oriental Seminar of USJ. Jesuit Archives, Vanves, RPO 44. Louis Cheikho, *Souvenir des Noces d'Or de l'USJ de Beyrouth* (Beirut: Imprimerie catholique, 1925).

77 Béchara al-Khoury, *Haqa'iq Lubnaniyya*, (Beirut: Awraq Lubnaniyya, 1961), pp. 78-85; Hector Klat, *Feuilles Mortes*, p. 86, p. 110. Yusuf al-Saouda, *Fi Sabil al-Istiqlal*, pp. 373-380.

78 Zamir, *Lebanon's Quest*, pp. 158-159.

79 See, for example, MAE Paris, Vol. 526, Review of the press, July 17-24, 1932, pp.148-149; September 24-28, 1932, pp. 180-181; November, 20-27, 1932, pp. 222-225. In order to preserve Lebanon's Christian nature Naccache was willing to secede Muslim-dominated territories to Syria in exchange for the transfer of Syrian Christians into Lebanon. See AD Nantes, Carton 411, extracts of *L'Orient*, August 26, 1931; September 10-12, 1931; September 17, 1931.

80 Zamir, *Lebanon's Quest*, p. 158.

81 Kamal Salibi, *The Modern History of Lebanon* (London: Weidenfeld and Nicolson, 1965), pp. 171-174. Michael C. Hudson, *The Precarious Republic* (New York: Random House, 1968), pp. 264-273. Iskandar al-Riyashi, *Ru'asa Lubnan kama 'Araftuhum*, pp. 61-77; compare with pp. 123-160.

82 *Le Jour*, April 24, 1935, Quoted in Sélim Abou, *Le Bilinguisme Arabe-Français au Liban*, p. 356.

83 Ernest Renan, "Qu'est-ce qu'une nation?" in John Hutchinson and Anthony D. Smith (eds.), *Nationalism* (Oxford: Oxford University Press, 1994), pp. 17-18.

84 *Ibid.*

85 On Yusuf al-Saouda's ties with al-Khoury see Zamir, *Lebanon's Quest*, p. 67, p. 75; Béchara al-Khoury, *Haqa'iq Lubnaniyya*, p. 74, p. 78.

86 "Entretiens de Patrice," *Phénicia,* 4 (April, 1938), pp. 1-5, as discussed in Chapter II.

87 Even Edmond Rabbath contributed articles to *Phénicia*. This reflects the ideological flexibility that prevailed in those days. One could be a supporter of the Syrian-Arab national movement and simultaneously write for a Lebanese-Phoenician journal.

88 Aurore shortened her married name to Ougour. I suspect she did so because in the 1930s, an Armenian last name in Beirut would somewhat diminish her social class. Working at the daily *La Syrie,* she became known as the first woman journalist in Lebanon. AD Nantes, Carton 909, "Enquête sur la presse de langue française dans le Proche Orient," *Nouvelles Littéraires*, August 17, 1935. The francophone social circles continued to remain similar. Georges Vayssié, the owner and editor of *La Syrie* and a vocal supporter of Phoenician, Western-oriented Lebanon, employed Aurore Trad-Aughourlian, who, three years later, published her own Phoenician journal and provided another stage for the francophone circles of Beirut to expound their views about Lebanon.

89 *Ibid,* pp. 28-30, p. 39, pp. 42-43.
90 Perhaps the most serious attempt to consolidate this idea into a well-established theory and to incorporate it into the national identity of Lebanon was made by Sélim Abou, the Maronite-born Jesuit from USJ, in his *Le Bilinguisme Arabe-Français au Liban.* This book was a very serious undertaking and still contains a mine of information about the francophone and literary circles in Lebanon. But its underlying agenda — support of the distinct non-Arab identity of Lebanon - is clear.
91 Chiha's realistic worldview surfaces in this context when he states that, unlike the Zionist movement, Lebanon should not try and revive the ancient Phoenician language. There were a few calls by Lebanese ultra-nationalists to revive the ancient tongue, and as we shall see below Sa'id 'Aql actually tried to turn the Lebanese vernacular into the official national language. Most likely Chiha reacted to these attempts. *Ibid,* p. 53.
92 *Liban d'aujourd'hui,* p. 12. Chiha actually compares the Phoenician colony of Carthage with the Lebanese immigrant community in Egypt.
93 *Ibid,* p. 22.
94 *Ibid,* p. 44. As Chiha himself attests, this is in fact a paraphrase of Lammens' words about the identity of Syria, arguing that Syria is simply Syrian, no more no less.
95 *Ibid,* p. 47.
96 "To be a Levantine is to live in two worlds or more at once, without belonging to either; to be able to go through the external forms which indicate the possession of a certain nationality, religion or culture, without actually possessing it." See more of this illuminating and somewhat bleak definition of Levantinism in Albert Hourani, *Syria and Lebanon; A Political Essay* (Oxford: Oxford University Press, 1946), pp. 70-72.
97 *Liban d'aujourd'hui,* p. 13.
98 CZA S25 10255, a report by Eliahu Epstein about a meeting with Albert Naccache and Corm who informed him about literary gatherings they conduct in Corm's domicile with the participation of other Lebanese francophiles, Chiha included.
99 Chiha insisted on using the term "Near East" instead of "Middle East." For him the Near East implied geographical and cultural affinity to the Mediterranean and to Europe, whereas the Middle East was a wider definition, which included central Asia. Lebanon, according to him, along with Syria, Egypt and Palestine belonged to the Near East more than to the Middle East. Michel Chiha, *Variations sur la Mode Méditerranéenne* (Beirut: Fondation Chiha, 1994), pp. 199-201.
100 *Ibid,* pp. 75-76; 99-100; 196-198; 202-204; 230-232.
101 United States National Archives, Scattered Beirut Regional Files, 1930. See also Carolyn L. Gates, *The Merchant Republic of Lebanon* (London: I. B. Tauris, 1998), pp. 82ff.
102 This was the city of Hiram, King of Tyre that incurred the famous prophecy of Ezekiel 27-28.
103 Salibi, *A House of Many Mansions,* p. 178.
104 Lahd Sa'b Khatir, *Mukhtasar Tarikh Lubnan* [The Concise History of Lebanon] (Beirut: Al-Matba'a al-'Ilmiyya, 1914), especially pp. 9-53.
105 See al-Saouda's book, *Fi Sabil Lubnan,* p. 15.

106 MAE Paris, Vol. 500, p. 86, biographical notes on al-Saouda, no date.
107 See especially his *Tarikh Lubnan al-Hadari* [The Cultural History of Lebanon] (Beirut: Dar al-Nahar, 1972), pp. 13-127.
108 MAE Paris, Vol. 127, p. 257, Yusuf al-Saouda, "Note sur le nouveau statut du Liban," Alexandria, May 21, 1922.
109 AD Nantes, Carton 930, Renseignements, December 1924; AD Nantes, Carton 907, Notice sur la presse, no date.
110 See Chapter II, note 88.
111 AD Nantes, Carton 906, Notice sur la presse, 1929. A table of the diffusion of newspapers in Syria and Lebanon. In 1929, three French dailies were published in Beirut, with a circulation of 7,450, in comparison to twelve dailies in Arabic with a circulation of 18,000. These numbers give a strong indication to the fact that Arabic was the preferred language, even in Beirut in the heyday of francophonism.
112 Sélim Abou, in his 1962 *Le Bilinguisme Arabe-Français au Liban*, p. 92, recorded that in the rural areas of Lebanon, twenty percent of the adult population and thirty-six percent of students were bilingual. The figures are certainly high, yet it is clear that Arabic continued to be the dominant language. The Lebanese *Kata'ib*, for example, the most powerful movement born from within the tradition of the Mountain, used Arabic as its prime language to attract the Maronite masses, despite the fact that its leaders were French-educated.
113 The impact of French Romanticism and Symbolism on Lebanese poetry and prose have been the center of many literary studies. See, for example, Salah Labaki, *Al-Tayyarat al-Adabiyya al-Haditha fi Lubnan, Lubnan al-Sha'ir* [Modern Literary Currents in Lebanon] (Cairo: Jam'iat al-Duwal al-'Arabiya ; Ma'had al-Dirasat al-'Arabiya al-'Aliya 1954); Umayya Hamdan, *Al-Ramziyya wa al-Rumantiqiyya fi al-Shi'r al-Lubnani* [Symbolism and Romanticism in Lebanon] (Baghdad: al-Dar al-Wataniya lil-Tawzi' wa al-I'lan, 1981).
114 See their writing and others about Lebanon in Jamil Jabr, *Lubnan fi Rawa'i aqlamihi* [Lebanon According to Its Distinguished Pens] (Beirut: al-Matba'a al-Kathulikiya, 1964).
115 Biographical information about Sa'id 'Aql can be found in Jean Durtal, *Saïd Akl, un Grand Poète Libanais* (Paris: Nouvelles éditions latines, 1970); Naji Salim Nasr, *Sa'id 'Aql, Faylasufan* [Said 'Aql, a Philosopher] (Beirut: N.J. Nasr, 1980).
116 Jalkh was one of the contributors to *La Revue Phénicienne* (January 1919), pp. 13-14.
117 AD Nantes, Carton 2395, Sûreté générale, information no. 266, January 22, 1936, a list of activists of the PPS.
118 In his *al-Sira' al-Fikri fi al-Adab al-Suri*, p. 61, Sa'adeh wrote about 'Aql's short membership in the PPS. He argued that *Bint Yftah* was not Syrian enough for, among other things, it dealt with what Sa'adeh believed was a Jewish story rather than a proud national Syrian story. Sa'adeh also claimed that it was he who gave 'Aql the idea to write about Cadmus, a true Syrian hero.
119 *Al-Mashriq* (January-March 1936), pp. 33-36; (July-September 1936), pp. 354-350.
120 Charles Corm, *La Montagne Inspirée*; Michel Chiha, *La Maison des Champs*; Elie Tyane, *Le Château Merveilleux*, Hector Klat. *Le Cèdre et le Lys*.

121 "Al-Shi'r al-Lubnani bi-al-lugha al-faransawiyya" [Lebanese Poetry in French Language] *Al-Mashriq* (July-September, 1935), pp. 381-393.
122 *L'Orient*, June 10, 1945; June 24, 1945, an interview with the Lebanese poet Khalil Mutran who mentions the experiments of 'Aql to write in colloquial Lebanese, and cautions the latter about these attempts.
123 See, especially, *Lubnan, In Haka* [Lebanon, If It Could Speak] (Beirut, 1960). A collection of essays on the beauty, the nature, the people and history of Lebanon with numerous allusions to the ancient Phoenicians.
124 Already in 1919, Corm described Lebanon as a land of light juxtaposed against the darkness of the Arab civilization. See Chapter II, note 154.
125 See, for example, the pamphlet of Yusuf al-Saouda who wrote against Lebanon's membership in the Arab League. *Étude Juridique sur le Protocole d'Alexandrie* (Beirut, November, 1944); see also *Correspondance d'Orient*, 511(March 1945), p. 31.
126 *Cadmus*, p. 13
127 *Ibid*, p. 24-25.
128 See also the words of Pierre al-Gemayyel about the civilizing mission of Lebanon as quoted in John Entelis, *Pluralism and Party Transformation in Lebanon; al-Kata'ib* (Leiden: Brill, 1974), p. 77-78.
129 See, for example, the book of the Zionist Revisionist leader Ze'ev Jabotinsky, *Shimshon* [Samson], which shares marked similarities with 'Aql's *Cadmus*.
130 Smith, *The Ethnic Origins of Nation*, p. 200.
131 On the Qabadayat, one of the most important Lebanese "institutions," see Michael Gilsenan, *Lords of the Lebanese Marches; Violence and Narrative in an Arab Society* (London: I. B. Tauris, 1996). In Zahleh, 'Aql's city, the Qabadayat and their fantastic stories of strength and wit have always been one of the identifying marks of the local population. See in Alixa Naff, *A Social History of Zahle*, pp. 109-137.
132 Compare with Beth Baron, "Nationalist Iconography: Egypt as a Woman," in Jankowski and Gershoni (eds.), *Rethinking Nationalism in the Arab Middle East*, pp. 105-124.
133 Salah Labaki also noted in *Lubnan al-Sha'ir*, p. 205, that the power of *Cadmus* lies more in the nationalistic content than in its literary form.
134 *Cadmus*, p. 127.
135 *Ibid*, p. 36
136 *Ibid*, pp. 116-117.
137 *Ibid*, p. 38.
138 *Ibid*, pp. 70-71.
139 *Ibid*, p. 18.
140 Joseph Sokhn, *Les Auteurs Libanais Contemporains* (Beirut: Société d'impression et d'édition libanaise, 1972), pp. 25-26; Jean Durtal, *Saïd Akl*, pp. 75-77.
141 See the prayer of Mira to the One God in *Cadmus*, p. 144-146.
142 "Al-Shi'r al-Lubnani bi-al-Lugha al-Faransawiyya," p. 384.
143 See the short-lived literary review *Renaissance*, no. 4 (August 31, 1945). The entire issue is dedicated to the French symbolist poet Paul Valéry. 'Aql introduces and concludes this issue which also includes an article by Hector Klat. See also *l'Orient*, June 3, 1945, a report about a lecture 'Aql gave in Arabic about Thomas

Aquinas, Pascal and Paul Valéry and the physicality and meta-physicality in their work.

144 *La Maison de Champs*, pp. 28-33.

145 See an interview with Corm in *La Revue du Liban*, no. 58-59 (March 1936).

146 'Aql wrote two books of poetry in French, *L'Or Est Poèmes* (Beirut: Éditions Naddaf, 1981), and *Sagèsse de Phénicie* (Beirut: Dergham, 1999). In 1937, he contributed two poems in French to the first two issues of *Phénicia*. On a few other occasions he wrote in French, but in general the vast majority of his writings is either in literary Arabic or in colloquial Lebanese.

147 Joseph Sayegh, *Le Phénomène Poético-Social dans le vallée de Zahleh* (Ph.D. Dissertation, University of Paris), 1964.

148 Jean Durtal, *Saïd Akl*, p. 37.

149 Sa'id 'Aql, *Mushkilat al-Nukhba fi al-Sharq* [The Problem of the Elite in the East] (Beirut: Dar al-Kashshaf, 1954), pp. 14-35. See also Naji Salim Nasr, *Sa'id 'Aql, Faylasufan* (Beirut: [s.n.], 1980), pp. 157-158.

150 Sélim Abou, *Le Bilinguisme Arabe-Français au Liban*, p. 258.

151 See, for example, Anis Furayha, *Tabsit Qawa'id al-'Arabiyya* [Simplification of the Rules of Arabic] (Beirut: al-Jami'a al-Amirkiya, 1952).

152 Salah Labaki, *Min A'amaq al-Jabal* (Beirut: Dar al-Makshuf, 1945). See also his *Urjuhat al-Qamar* [The Moon's Cradle] (Beirut: Dar Rihani, 1955 [1938]), pp. 46-54.

153 *Awwal al-Rabi'* (Beirut, 1944), pp. 17-23.

5

The Adversaries

Sometime ago, a wave of Pharaonism flooded Egypt trying to engulf it. Almost at the same time another wave attempted to mark Lebanon with a Phoenician imprint. Those who preached these two sophisms were liars. Personally, I declare that Lebanon, Syria and Egypt are Arab and they form the core of the Arab countries. We live and we die for Arabism.

Gébran Tuéni[1]

Opposition to the concept that the Lebanese were descendants of the ancient Phoenicians crystallized only when the Christian Lebanese national movement became identified with the Phoenician idea. This occurred only around World War I and it is, therefore, difficult to find expressions against Phoenicianism before 1914. Naturally, the most vociferous opposition came from the Muslim population, which thoroughly opposed the formation of Greater Lebanon as an independent entity, let alone as a Christian non-Arab state. It can be said without doubt that the overwhelming majority of the Sunnis, Shi'is and Druze abhorred the view that their newly-founded state was a mere political and cultural continuum of the ancient Phoenician city-states and that they were actually the children of a civilization utterly foreign to them. Only following the "arabization" of the Phoenicians were intellectual Muslims willing to incorporate the idea into the Lebanese national narrative. This process was supported by the thesis that all ancient civilizations of the Near East originated from the Arabian Peninsula and all of them were of Semitic-Arabic descent.

Among the Christian communities, opinions varied. The Maronites, Greek Catholics, and other smaller Uniate communities generally supported the formation of Greater Lebanon and endorsed the historical narrative of the Lebanese nation beginning with the ancient Phoenicians. There were, nevertheless, Maronites who publicly denounced the Phoenician idea. We have already encountered the Maronite journalist Ibrahim Salim al-Najjar who rejected the Phoenician claims made by the Lebanese delegation to the Versailles Peace Conference in 1919, and we shall discuss below the views of another Maronite, Amin al-Rihani, who called for the inclusion of Lebanon into a larger Arab political unit.

The Greek Orthodox community was divided, too, over the Phoenician idea. On the one hand, the vast majority of Greek Orthodox throughout the Middle East supported and even led the pan-Arab movement, and in Lebanon many Greek Orthodox supported Antun Sa'adeh and his *Parti populaire syrien* (PPS). On the other hand, there were Greek Orthodox families in Beirut who were part and parcel of the Lebanese upper middle class, and for them Greater Lebanon represented a financial blessing. They supported the Lebanist idea, intermarried with other Christian haut-bourgeois families, and formed a cohesive social class that was the spine of the Lebanese state. The Sursuks, the Trads and the Dabbas' were part of this class, and they endorsed Greater Lebanon with the Phoenician historical narrative.[2] Hector Klat was a Greek Orthodox and we have already seen his Phoenician enthusiasm. Charles Malik was also Greek Orthodox and a devout supporter of Western-oriented Lebanon-Phoenicia. In general, Lebanese society and politics are characterized by intra-communal cleavages just as much as by inter-communal dynamics and it would, therefore, be erroneous to label all of the Christian communities in Lebanon as supporters of this or that camp; we have already seen that even among the Muslims in Lebanon, there were some cracks in the opposition to the Phoenician idea.

Nor were the French unanimous in their opinions about the Phoenician-Lebanese historical narrative. The French *Mission laïque* aspired to provide an alternative to the Jesuit domination in Syria and Lebanon and to the pro-Christian policy of France. As part of this stand they rejected the Phoenician narrative, seeing it as another negative factor contributing to the political and cultural cleavages in the mandatory territories. In April 1919, the head of the *Mission laïque* attacked the Phoenician tendencies of the Maronites and the Greek Catholics in Beirut and protested against the pro-Christian policy of France in Syria.[3] The *Mission laïque* continued to hold similar ideas after the formation of Greater Lebanon. At a gathering of *L'association syrienne arabe*, the Syrian club in Paris, Gabriel Besnard, the General Secretary of the *Mission laïque*, called for a more balanced French policy in Syria and vehemently attacked the Jesuit domination in the mandatory territories.[4] These opinions of the *Mission laïque* were, of course, in a minority among the French and, to a large extent, directed more towards the Jesuits than towards the Lebanese themselves. The animosity between the two missions and their polarized worldviews continued to exist throughout the mandate period, often erupting in exchanges of verbal insults.[5]

In the sections to follow I shall elaborate on several opponents of the Phoenician myth of origin in Lebanon. I examine these adversaries through the ideological writing of a spectrum of authors: the pan-Arab Muslims Rashid Rida and (the Druze) Shekib Arslan; the pan-Arab Christians Edmond Rabbath and Qonstantine Zurayk; the Maronite Lebanese author Amin al-Rihani; the

Muslim Lebanese writer and politician Muhammad Jamil Bayhum; and the leader of the Syrian Social Nationalist Party Antun Sa'adeh. These personalities provide a wide range of views and opinions, which not only disclose their own beliefs, but also tell us more about the weight and content Phoenicianism possessed in its formative years from the turn of the 20th century to the 1950s.

Arab-Muslims: Rashid Rida and Shekib Arslan

The *Mission laïque* was not the first to recognize the connection between Phoenicianism and Christian Lebanese national aspirations. Rashid Rida was perhaps the first to be aware of the association between separatist Lebanese notions and the Phoenician narrative.[6] A Muslim from Qalamun, a village next to Tripoli, living in Egypt since 1897, Rida was well acquainted with the political activity of the Syrians and the Lebanese in the Nile Valley. In 1914, before Phoenicianism became solely identified with the Lebanese national movement, he wrote in his journal *al-Manar* against notions of non-Arab identity in Syria and Lebanon. Attacking the aspirations of the *Alliance libanaise* branches in Egypt and America to form a separate political entity in Lebanon, Rida denounced their claims for a non-Arab identity. Using the platforms of the Lebanese Revival of Na'um Mukarzal in New York and the *Renaissance libanaise* of Faris Najm in São Paulo as the basis of his assault, he attacked their pretension of having Phoenician descent, affirming that

> ... It is a clear mistake, for many of the inhabitants of the Mountain [Mount Lebanon, A.K.] know that they are of Arab descent, among them its princes [*umara*] like the Bani Ma'n, the Bani Shihab, the Amir Fakhr al-Din, the Amir Bashir, Bani Arslan and other Druzes. The rest descend from the Arab and the Phoenician lineage, but they have all turned Arabs through the unity of language.[7]

National identity, according to Rida, was directly related to language. Many of the Spaniards, for example, were of Arab descent, but they stopped speaking Arabic and, therefore, were no longer considered Arabs. The Lebanese, he concluded, dream about something that is beyond their capacity. They want to depart from their "grandmother," the Arab *umma* and their "mother," Syria itself.

Rashid Rida played a significant role in the political struggle over the fate of Syria, from the Young Turk revolution in 1908 until his death in 1935. He participated in the activities of various associations — the Party of Decentralization before 1914, the Syrian Congress of 1920, and the Syro-Palestinian delegation in Geneva in 1921, to mention a few. He always advocated the establishment of an Islamic state, granting the Arabs the prime and leading role in this enterprise. Islamic religion and Arab ethnicity were intertwined in his ideology. He often claimed to be a brother of the non-Muslim Arabs, but he just as often spoke in derogatory terms against Arab Christians.[8] Therefore, in his struggle for the establishment of Greater Syria as an Arab-Islamic state, Lebanon was definitely a disturbing hindrance to Rida. As a Christian entity, claiming to have a non-Arab identity in the heart of the Arab Islamic *umma*, which he aspired to establish, Lebanon was not easy to swallow.

The battle Rida conducted against separatist tendencies in the Arab world did not begin with the Lebanese and their Phoenician inclinations. Although he was a marginal figure in the Egyptian political arena, this did not prevent him from expressing his opinions about internal Egyptian issues. He vehemently rejected the attempts made by the Copts to prove their "Egyptianness" through ties with ancient Pharaonic Egypt. By 1920, the majority of the Egyptian national movements claimed to be "Pharaonic," but in 1908, the Copts were among the first to claim to be the descendants of the ancient Egyptians. They were the real Egyptians, they asserted, unlike the Muslims who only arrived in the Nile Valley in the 7th century.[9] Rida, fighting for the Arab-Islamic cause on all possible fronts, denounced these attempts of the Copts to stress a Pharaonic, pre-Islamic, identity in Egypt.[10]

With time Rashid Rida honed his criticism against the Lebanese and the Syrian national movements. He utterly opposed the idea of the establishment of a Christian state in Lebanon and a secular Syrian state.[11] He also sharply criticized the French policy of divide and rule, blaming France for promoting a pro-minority policy by encouraging the Christian denominations in the Levant to possess a separate and falsified national identity with a distinct historical narrative.[12] This idea, that the centrifugal forces against Arab unity were a result of colonial schemes, was shared by most of the adversaries of the separatist national movements in the Middle East, as we shall see below.

In his attacks against the non-Arab separatist movements in the Middle East, Rida constructed a historical narrative for the Arabs that preceded the Phoenician or the Pharaonic narratives. Like many national thinkers, he created a comprehensive romantic myth of origin with all the required elements: descent, unity, occupation, golden age, dark age and rebirth. The Arabs, according to him, were a more ancient nation than the Phoenicians and the Egyptians. In fact, they inhabited these lands even before the ancient civilizations of Phoenicia and Egypt, from the point at which the entire region of what is known today as the Middle East was ethnically Arab. Islamic faith, as delivered to them by the Prophet Muhammad, was the glue that united them and provided the strength to sweep over the Middle East, North Africa and Spain. But then came separation and disunity, bringing upon them an era of stagnation. It was now time, said Rida, for the Arabs, through their faith, to recuperate and regain the strength emanating from their lofty and ancient history that had even preceded the days of Muhammad.[13]

Rida was not the only opponent of the Lebanese national movement who tried to expropriate the Phoenicians from the Lebanese historical narrative by asserting that the Phoenicians were actually Arabs. Rida's ally and friend to the Arab-Islamic cause, Shekib Arslan, did the same. Arslan, a member of the distinguished Druze family from Mount Lebanon, joined the Arab-Islamic camp, and with Rida and others relentlessly worked to create the envisioned Arab-Islamic state. He spent most of his time working on the European front for the realization of his political aspirations. In one of his appeals to the League of Nations against the mandate system, he spoke on the question of Palestine, stating that smaller and more backward countries had received complete independence and become members of the League of Nations:

> We think that also Palestine deserves to become part of the League of Nations; Palestine, the land of Christ, of the Phoenicians who invented the alphabet and who were the best seafarers of their time; Palestine, the cradle of the Arabs that had long ago occupied the world [...] this population is considered inferior to the Blacks. It is unthinkable.[14]

Shekib Arslan did not, of course, consider himself a Phoenician. He only used whatever historical ingredients he thought would advance his political inclinations. Expressions about the ancient past of one's nation/country prevailed in every national movement, especially in front of a Western audience. National speakers from the Middle East felt the need to demonstrate to the West that their nation and culture contributed the most to Western civilization. The Lebanese did so through the Phoenicians and Arslan did so as well, using, in fact, the same claims made by the Lebanese national movement of being a bridge between East and West, from antiquity to modernity:

> The awakening of the oppressed and, above all, of the Arabs, will be a beneficial event and the civilized world needs to welcome its arrival with sympathy, because a people, who bestowed throughout their history glorious services to humanity can be but an element of peace and of social undertaking at the present and in the future. This people's intermediary character between East and West makes its independence the primordial reason for the equilibrium of the nations that covet today the possession of the ways of the world. The Arabs need to retake their historic role and all the nations should be interested in helping them in this sacred work, in the best interest of civilization.[15]

It is no surprise that from a very early point the Arab-Islamic camp opposed the Lebanist idea and its historical Phoenician narrative. Rashid Rida's life in Egypt allowed him to observe up close the two most powerful centrifugal forces in the Arab world, the Egyptian and the Lebanese national movements. Phoenicianism, as advocated by the *Alliance libanaise* in Egypt and elsewhere, challenged Rida's two-fold ideology of Islam and Arabism. Not only was Phoenicianism advocated by Christians, but these Christians rejected their "Arab-ness" and adopted a new identity, tied to the West. In Rida's utopian Arab-Islamic state, Islamic law would prevail, granting the "People of the Book" rights according to the *Shari'a* [Islamic law], and this was exactly what his Christian adversaries feared and wished to prevent.

Christian Arab Nationalists: Qonstantine Zurayk, Edmond Rabbath and Amin al-Rihani

Interestingly, despite, or perhaps because of, the unequivocal opposition of the Muslims to the Lebanese state and its non-Arab symbols, it was actually Christian Syrians and Lebanese who predominantly wrote and deliberated against the Phoenician myth of origin. Their arguments are engaging, because, though belonging to minority groups, they challenged the *raison d'être* of Lebanon as an asylum for minorities. Two of the most vocal Christian Arab nationalists who opposed the Lebanese national movement and its historical narrative were Qonstantine Zurayk and Edmond Rabbath. They represent the views shared by many Arab nationalists in Syria in the 1930s, when the Syrian national movement was gearing up its struggle against the French mandate, and the debate in Lebanon over its cultural and political orientation was reaching a crucial point.

Qonstantine K. Zurayk

Qonstantine K. Zurayk (Qustantin Zurayq) (1909-2001) was born into a Greek Orthodox family in Damascus. He attended the primary and high schools of the Greek Orthodox Church in the city. In 1926, just as Greater Lebanon became a constitutional republic, he began studying at the American University in Beirut. After graduation in 1928, he pursued his higher education at the University of Chicago and at Princeton University, receiving his Ph.D. from the latter in 1930. He returned to AUB and began teaching medieval history of the Middle East. Soon, he evolved into a respected professor with strong secular Arab convictions, which befitted the general atmosphere of the university. The AUB campus had been the center of anti-French and pro-Syrian activity since the inception of the French mandate and Zurayk became a political philosopher for many Arab students attending the university.[16]

In 1939, Zurayk published in Beirut one of his most famous works, *al-Wa'i al-Qawmi* [National Consciousness]. He noted in the introduction that the book had been drafted with the purpose of clarifying and spreading the national idea, so that it would become a basis for collective action by the Arabs. Soon after its publication, the book was adopted by the Arab national movement, providing an ideological platform that described Arab nationalism and its tenets. *Al-Wa'i al-Qawmi* was published two years after Antun Sa'adeh's work, *Nushu' al-Umam* [The Evolution of Nations], which caused a stir in Syria by framing the idea of nationalism in a way opposed to the Arab national movement. Sa'adeh claimed that nationality was a combination of geographical factors and human will. People and territory were the required ingredients of nationalism, not religion or language. Zurayk answered Sa'adeh and other opponents of Arab nationalism in his book, claiming that it was language, religion and history that were indispensable for the creation of a nation. Therefore, equipped with all three, the Arabs were a full-fledged nation.

According to Zurayk, since the end of the 19th century a socio-political and cultural storm had been sweeping the Arab world, awaking it from its state of dormancy. In order to complete the change the Arabs were in need of a national philosophy (*falsafa qawmiyya*), which would form the spirit of their national movement, define its direction and assign missions to its adherents. The objective of *National Consciousness* was to provide this philosophy. Zurayk gave critical roles to Islam and the Arabic language as the most important components in the formation of the Arab national consciousness. He saw no contradiction between his Christian faith and his acknowledgement of the role of Islam in the formation of Arab nationalism. Unlike Rashid Rida, Islam did not mean the establishment of an Islamic state for Zurayk. Rather, he perceived Islam as an agent through which all Arabs live a rich cultural life. Islam provides the Arabs a cultural solidarity that can be shared by all Arabs, Muslims and non-Muslims. Christian Arabs, therefore, share this civilization with their Muslim brothers, and are an inseparable part of the Arab nation.[17]

After a lengthy preoccupation with nationalism in general and Arab nationalism in particular, Zurayk moved on to deal with the opponents of the Arab national movement. Lebanon, his new home, was the focus of his criticism. A full chapter in the book is dedicated to confronting the Lebanese-Phoenician national movement. There is a struggle in Lebanon, Zurayk wrote, between different national doctrines "creating a disturbed atmosphere and dividing the people of our country [sic.]." Lebanon needs to clear up this murky atmosphere and establish an appropriate national dogma, which would unite all the people of Lebanon.[18]

> Today in Lebanon there is a group that says: we are Phoenicians, we are descended from this people that has inhabited Lebanon since time immemorial, from where they departed to near and remote coasts, trading and colonizing. Yes! they say, indeed other peoples entered Lebanon: Aramaeans, Arabs, Franks and others, but they all, including the Arabs, consisted of a minority, which did not leave a memorable mark. The Phoenician race remained firm, and it still is.[19]

Among the adherents of Arabism (*'uruba*) there are those who say: the prevailing blood in Lebanon is Arab. The Arabs penetrated this country in ancient times, thereafter they occupied it in the seventh century and spread throughout the land until racially they controlled the country. The Arab race (*jins*) absorbed the other races that had dominated the country before. Thus Lebanon was painted with a new human color.[20]

These two groups, continued Zurayk, claim to have distinct and different blood, Arab or Phoenician. In order to discover who the Lebanese really are and what the color of their blood is, one needs to look at the different peoples that have inhabited Lebanon since the beginning of time. Just before the beginning of history, Zurayk wrote, Semitic peoples began entering the Fertile Crescent. They inhabited the entire region from the Syrian coast to the Arab Peninsula. The oldest known Semitic wave brought the Phoenicians to Lebanon. After them came the Egyptians, the Babylonians and the Assyrians. Their domination, however, was only political and they did not leave their ethnic imprint on the land. The Persians, the Greeks and the Romans, all belonging to the Aryan race, also occupied the land and did leave some ethnic mark on the people of the region. Of all the peoples that inhabited the land, the Aramaeans, also Semitic, came in the largest numbers and soon constituted the majority.[21] Then, in the 7th century, came the Arab invasion. But even before that, Arabs began penetrating Lebanon and all the Syrian lands through different avenues: commerce, warfare and peaceful settlement. It is no wonder that Arabs settled in the Fertile Crescent. The borders between the desert and the fertile lands have never been sealed. Arab settlement had an effect on the entire region, not only on Lebanon. The occupation of the 7th century carried with it a flood of people of the Arab race (*'unsur*) who utterly changed the human geography of the region.[22] Three main facts, Zurayk concluded, emerge from this quick survey. First, the inhabitants of this country do not belong to one single people, but rather to various peoples and races. Second, the majority of the peoples who inhabited the land were Semites: the Phoenicians, the Aramaeans and the Arabs. In lesser numbers came the Aryan race: Persians, Greeks, Romans, Franks, Turks and Mongols. Lastly, it is a historical misjudgment to claim that the Arabs were an insignificant minority in the formation of the human face of Lebanon.

In order to prove the point that the peoples who had resided in Lebanon since time immemorial were ethnically similar to the Arabs, Zurayk turned to racial theories that had dominated the fields of sociology and anthropology since the late-19th century.[23] Scholars, Zurayk explained, divide the human race into three main groups: Caucasian, Mongoloid and Negroid. The majority of the peoples that inhabited Lebanon throughout time have been members of the Mediterranean sub-group of the Caucasian race. They shared the same size of head, color of eyes and hair and blood composition.[24] Given the fact that race (*jins*) relies on biological, and not on geographic and cultural factors, there is no difference between Arab blood and Phoenician blood. They both belong to the same race, the Caucasian Semitic Mediterranean race. Therefore, he continued, the question of identity in Lebanon should be discussed in political, social and cultural realms and not in the racial realm.[25] Besides, even if the Arabs and the Phoenicians belonged to two different branches of the same race, or to two different races, does this prevent them from integrating into one joint nation (*qawmiyya*), Zurayk asks rhetorically. Nationality is not based on physical features, but rather on social, intellectual and spiritual foundations. France is a model of national cohesiveness and unity, although it is composed of three different branches of the Caucasian race — Northern in the north, Alpine in the center and Mediterranean in the south. In the case of Lebanon, the Phoenicians and the Arabs are from one branch and one race, so why cannot they unite like the French did?[26]

Zurayk concluded his arguments with high-flown words:

> Let us tear apart the veil of 'race;' and the ghost of 'blood' that block the light from our thoughts and discussions. Let us look at the language, the culture, the customs and the historical memories. Let us start looking towards the future so that we form the kind of life we desire [...]. It is not enough that a Lebanese should ask himself, 'What is the language which I inherited from my forefathers: Phoenician or Arabic?' But rather he should ask, 'What is the language that I want and that I am interested in speaking, and that I would embrace as an instrument for my culture now and in the future?' The Lebanese should not torment his soul with the question, 'What is my culture — Phoenician or Arab?' He should take a different path and ask a different question, 'What direction do I want to take in my culture: the Phoenician or the Arab one?' And last, and here lies the essential question, 'Where would I find my best interest, and implement my ultimate goal — with the creation of an independent Lebanon separate from the other Arab countries, or with the connection of Lebanon and the Arab world working towards a shared national life?'[27]

Several interesting points surface from Zurayk's disapproval of the Phoenician myth of origin in Lebanon. To begin with, he did not dismiss Phoenicianism as a figment of the Lebanese imagination. He acknowledged the historical validity of the existence of descendants of the ancient Phoenicians in modern times. He simply believed that racially they were not different from the Arabs because they belonged to the same racial family. Second, Zurayk perceived national consciousness as a cultural phenomenon, shaped by language and human history. Lebanon for him was, therefore, an integral part of the Arab world. The argument made by some modern Phoenician-Lebanese of belonging to a different ethnicity was invalid for him, because it was not biology or geography that carved a nation, but rather historical experience. These differences in perception of national consciousness lay at the center of the ideological debate among Arab and Lebanese nationalists (Antun Sa'adeh included). The former referred to language (Arabic) and history (Islamic civilization) as the two most important pillars of the Arab collective identity; while the latter considered biology (a distinct Lebanese or Syrian ethnicity) and geographical determinism (Lebanese are molded by the distinct topography of their land) as the most important pillars. In his lengthy preoccupation with races and ethnicities, Zurayk actually made an attempt to answer some of his Lebanese opponents with their own ethnic arguments that claimed they possessed a different ethnic and racial identity than the Arabs.

Zurayk never mentioned, not even in a footnote, the fact that Phoenicianism was identified with Christianity in Lebanon. Possibly because he gave a crucial role to Islam as the most important pillar in shaping Arab national consciousness, Lebanon as a Christian entity posed a problem for his argument. How could Christian Lebanese join an Arab national movement so closely identified with Islam? The whole *raison d'être* for the formation of Greater Lebanon had been the establishment of a Christian entity where religion and nationality were intertwined, just as Zurayk himself claimed, but for the Arab national movement in which Islam played the adhesive role.

Last, but certainly not least, in using the French example of nationalism as a model of emulation, Zurayk broke away from the conventional Arab national thought that looked to Germany as a model.[28] Zurayk was addressing the Lebanese national movement that saw French nationalism as its *beau idéal*. Many Maronites, especially in the 1920s before the days of disillusionment, looked at France as the pinnacle of perfection, and Zurayk, although a student of the Anglo-Saxon school, referred to France and its national cohesiveness to demonstrate that even the guardian angel of Lebanon overcame ethnic differences and formed a tenacious nation.

The fact that Qonstantine Zurayk dedicated a full chapter in a book about Arab national consciousness to challenge the Phoenician myth in Lebanon indicates, again, the importance of this myth in the Lebanese political and cultural arenas in the 1930s. It reflects the fact that Phoenicianism was not a marginal intellectual effort supported by a select group of people; it was a symbol of the entire Lebanese national movement. It was the historical justification and foundation for the separate existence of a Lebanese *ethnie*.

When dealing with opposition to the Lebanist idea and its historical narrative, the American University in Beirut automatically surfaces as a center of Arab political activity. It became conventional wisdom that AUB always hosted and nurtured pro-Arab activities and that within its walls, future leaders and thinkers of the Arab world acquired their education. AUB, Zurayk's academic home, has been portrayed as the antithesis of USJ — the former, anglophone, the latter francophone; one pro-Arab, the other anti-Arab.[29] The French certainly contributed to this image of AUB. From the very beginning of their mandate in Syria and Lebanon they looked on AUB with extreme suspicion, considering it a center for anti-French activity.[30] The Jesuits of USJ, who basically managed Lebanon for its first twenty years, regarded the American University as nothing less than a foe. AUB was not only anglophone, it was also sacrilegiously Protestant. In French reports on political activity at AUB, one can read about Arab student associations being active in Arab cultural and political activity, to the immense displeasure of the French.[31] Qonstantine Zurayk, therefore, fit well in AUB with his Arab convictions.

AUB had another facet, which often tends to be overlooked. Philip Hitti, whom we met previously, was a graduate of AUB. Despite the fact that his educational background more closely resembled that of many Arab nationalists, Hitti evolved to be one of the most important scholarly voices for the distinct separatist identity in Lebanon. Similarly, Asad Rustum graduated from AUB and, after receiving his Ph.D. from the University of Chicago, returned to teach history of the Middle East; we have already seen his role, too, in the dissemination of the Phoenician idea in the educational system in Lebanon. Charles Malik, a Greek Orthodox graduate and teacher at AUB, advocated, wrote and extensively proclaimed his support of the Western orientation of Lebanon-Phoenicia. Rushdi Ma'luf was also a product of anglophone education, notably AUB, and yet he joined the group of poets who congregated around Sa'id 'Aql, composing verse about the ancient Phoenician past of Lebanon. Furthermore, AUB, like USJ, not only provided higher education, but also managed an entire schooling system from kindergarten on up. In its schools, the history of Lebanon was taught in a manner similar to that used in the rest of the schools in Lebanon, regarding the history of Lebanon as one unit, beginning in antiquity with the Phoenicians and proceeding to other eras, through to modernity and the formation of Greater Lebanon.[32]

It is apparent that AUB, although a clear pro-Arab center, also produced "neo- Phoenicians;" at the same time, USJ, clearly a pro-Western, Christian, non-Arab center, produced its own pro-Arab students, as the following example of Edmond Rabbath illustrates.

Edmond Rabbath

Unlike Zurayk, Edmond Rabbath (1906-1991), a Syrian Catholic from Aleppo, acquired his education in French establishments: USJ and the Sorbonne in Paris, where he received his doctorate in law and political science.[33] It is, therefore, interesting to observe his political convictions, considering the fact that both his origin as a Uniate and his French-Jesuit educational background resembled the Lebanese whose political views he rejected.

Rabbath actually began his scholarly and political career supporting the Syrian national idea, separate from Arab nationalism. When aged only nineteen he wrote the book *Les Etats-Unis de la Syrie*, endorsing the idea of a Syrian nation, as professed by Henri Lammens. For the young Edmond

Rabbath, the Syrians were a full-fledged nation.[34] Muslim Syrians are not Arabs; they had lived in Syria before the Arab occupation in the 7th century and they simply adopted the religion of the occupier who brought to Syria a faith and not a race. Therefore, Christians and Muslims shared the same Syrian origin. Rabbath's francophone Jesuit education surfaced when he used his Jesuit teachers, Lammens and René Dussaud, to strengthen his arguments with scholarly bases.[35] These views corresponded well with Rabbath's confessional belonging as a Uniate from Aleppo. In Greater Lebanon most of the Uniate communities were in full support of the Lebanist idea. In Syria before 1920, they supported the formation of a non-Arab Syria,[36] as advocated by Georges Samné, another Uniate (Greek Catholic) from Damascus, and Chékri Ganem.

Twelve years later, Rabbath, older and more experienced not only in academia but also in politics, expressed entirely different views. By 1937, the Syrian national movement was far more developed and sophisticated than it was in the mid-1920s. The Franco-Syrian agreement had recently been ratified by the Syrian parliament. Rabbath, by then a deputy in the Syrian parliament and an activist in the Syrian National Bloc, was one of the architects of this agreement, making him an important protagonist in this national movement.[37] Syrian nationalism perceived the Syrians as part of a larger Arab world and Rabbath expressed his political views accordingly. In his *Unité Syrienne et Devenir Arabe*, published in 1937, he stated clearly in the first chapter, "La Syrie arabe:"

> Il n'y a pas de nation syrienne. Il y a une nation arabe, produit de cet agglomérat de peuples qui, jadis, forma l'Empire arabe [...] La nation arabe prend conscience d'elle-même. Elle existe, en ce vingtième siècle, sous des formes plus ou moins nettes, là ou l'arabe est parlé et l'Islam professé.[38]

Language and religion, he claimed, form the Arab nation. The first Arab to seed the "national sentiment," as defined by Renan's *Qu'est-ce qu'une nation?* was the Prophet Muhammad.[39] Syrian nationalism, as part of the larger Arab nation is, therefore, psychologically and politically manifested only through the Arab framework.[40] These views of Rabbath were very similar to the ideas of Qonstantine Zurayk who published his aforementioned book two years after Rabbath's *Unité Syrienne*. In the sub-chapter "Origin of Identity," Rabbath elaborated on the ethnic composition of the inhabitants of Syria. Like Zurayk, he claimed that all the ancient peoples that had inhabited Syria were Semites. More importantly, all Semites came from Arabia through waves of migration and invasion. The Arab-Islamic invasion was simply the last wave of Semitic migration to the region of Syria. Semites and Arabs are, therefore, synonymous appellations. In reality all the ancient peoples, whether Babylonians, Assyrians or Phoenicians, were "arabes par l'esprit qui les concevait, arabes par les bras qui les élevaient."[41]

Language, Rabbath maintained, had always been the national factor par excellence.[42] Since the Roman era, Arabic language had been dominant in the Syrian countryside. There had been a continuous struggle between Arabo-Semitic and Latin Roman races until the last years of the Byzantine Empire. With the Arab conquest, the Roman-Latin culture was eliminated from every single Syrian mountain and valley.[43] This argument was a direct response by Rabbath to the claims professed by some Lebanese concerning their cultural Latin orientation. The poem by Michel Chiha, quoted in Chapter II, plainly elaborates on this Latin culture of which Lebanon was part, as a result of its Christian nature and its location in the Mediterranean basin. The fact that Rabbath himself belonged to a community that had been latinized through its "Unia" with Rome did not prevent him from stating these views that challenged the religious orientation of his own community.[44]

Knowing the French up close and challenging them as a Syrian nationalist, Rabbath blamed the French mandate for generating the idea that the Christians were descendants of the ancient Phoenicians. He asked rhetorically whether the Christians in Syria were Arabs or simply Arabic speakers, and then answered:

Le Mandat a donné le jour à une théorie qui voit en eux, dans un but politique, les descendants des hardis navigateurs de Sidon et de Tyr. Et cependant, la tradition et les faits rejettent un phénicisme aussi intéressé.[45]

This "Phoenicianism," continued Rabbath, cannot vanquish traditions and facts that attest to an unequivocal Arabism in Syria and Lebanon. The Maronites in Mount Lebanon, although they have a distinct local identity, are as Arab as the entire Syrian population. They came to Lebanon from Hamma, an Arab region, and all attempts to link them to the Phoenicians or the *Marada* are futile.

After completing the discussion on race and ethnicity in Syria, proving that all Syrians were Arabs, Rabbath moved to confront the Lebanese national movement. A quarter of the book is occupied with his attempt to prove the historical injustice in the formation of Greater Lebanon.[46] As in the case of Qonstantine Zurayk, the weight and volume Rabbath devoted to Lebanon's Phoenician proclivities demonstrate the significance of the Phoenician myth in Lebanon. The chapter begins with a quote from *La Montagne Inspirée*, indicting Charles Corm as Rabbath's main adversary in this context:

Ah! dites-nous surtout les siècles magnifiques
Où nous eûmes, sans cesse, un cœur religieux;

Comment nos paysans, près de deux mille anées,
ont maintenu la Croix, au milieu des turbans,

Depuis les mers de Chine aux Méditerranées,
Dans notre seul Liban.

Mon frère musulman, comprenez ma franchise:
Je suis le vrai Liban, sincère et pratiquant.[47]

Interestingly, although a devout Arab nationalist, Rabbath recognized the distinct nature of the Lebanese case in the context of the Arab world. This duality, claiming, on the one hand, that Lebanon is an inseparable part of the Arab world and, on the other, recognizing its distinct features, is reflected throughout this section of the book. Rabbath supported the idea of the existence of an autonomous region in Mount Lebanon — a *foyer chrétien* — as had existed before 1914 and acknowledged its particular culture, different from the rest of the Arab world. Historical and social facts, he averred, enabled the existence of Lebanese patriotism, an existence that cannot be denied. Nevertheless, this particularism had always lived side by side with Arab sentiments. Rabbath not only acknowledged that Lebanon had evolved to become a distinct entity within the Arab world, but even more, he wrote, Lebanon was culturally influenced by the Mediterranean and the ancient peoples that inhabited this basin:

> Liban s'imprègne de l'esprit occidental, pour produire en définitive ce merveilleux mélange culturel, composé de substance arabe rajeunie par l'Occident [...]. La mentalité et les mœurs ne tardent pas à subir l'influence de ce renouveau. Plongeant d'ailleurs ses racines dans une atmosphère méditerranéenne, puisant une partie de son inspiration dans les antiques réminiscences phéniciennes, l'esprit de cette population intelligente s'ouvrait aisément aux idées de l'Europe.[48]

Turning the Phoenician myth upside down, Rabbath claimed that an Arab civilization with Western penchant had been formed in Lebanon. Lebanon, for him, was an "advanced lighthouse of Arab culture in the Latin Mediterranean."[49] It was an *Oriental* beacon of the Arab culture and not vice versa, as Christian Lebanese believed. They viewed Lebanon as a *Western* lighthouse in the East, the farthest extension of the West in an ignorant East.

The criticism of Rabbath's and Zurayk's of Lebanese independence and the Phoenician narrative was similar in essence. Both dreamt of an Arab nation founded on unity of language, history and religion (Islam). Rabbath, however, gave more space to the existence of an autonomous Lebanese entity in Mount Lebanon and recognized, unlike Zurayk, its particular culture, influenced by ancient civilizations and the Mediterranean basin. The reason for this recognition derives, possibly, from his Syrian Catholic origin and his Jesuit French education.[50] Rabbath was a francophile at heart and his views on nationalism were very close to French national thought.[51] Looking at the footnotes in the chapter on Lebanese independence, one can easily see that, although an Arab nationalist, Rabbath's francophone educational background led him to draw on the exact same studies that the Lebanese-Phoenicians used to prove their non-Arabness.[52]

In their own views, Rabbath and Zurayq represented mainstream Arab nationalism of the 1920s and 1930s, as professed by many Arab Christians. The question of who an Arab was had been dominant in the Middle East since the end of the 19th century, and the political ramifications of the answer to this complex question were critical in the 1920s-1930s. Christians had to come to grips with the fact that Islam and Arab-ness were intertwined to a point of almost complete congruity. It was clear to all that before the 7th century, the ancient Near East was inhabited by mostly Christians, and that these Christians, in one genealogical way or another, were descendents of the ancient peoples who inhabited the region. The question that remained to be answered was how these peoples were related to the Arabs from the Arabian Peninsula. In answering this question, Rabbath and Zurayq followed the thesis supported by many Arabs. They saw the Arabian Peninsula as a human well, from which human waves of Semites poured out around the Middle East, the Arab-Islamic conquest being the most distinguished and notable flow.[53] The Phoenicians, according to this narrative, were Arabs through and through, by their Semitic race and their origin from the shores of the Arab (Persian) Gulf. It was a powerful thesis that later enabled Muslim Lebanese to accept the Phoenicians as their Arab ancestors.[54]

Amin al-Rihani

Among the adversaries of the Phoenician myth of origin in Lebanon, Amin al-Rihani was one of the most intriguing and interesting. Al-Rihani long ago gained a reputation of being a devout Arab secularist, who fought for Arab culture and Arab political unity in most of his literary and political activity. His religious and social background seemingly should have made him a strong supporter of the Lebanist idea, a staunch Maronite and a Phoenician at heart. After all, this is exactly what happened to Na'um Mukarzal, who was born and raised in the same village where al-Rihani was born, where he spent the first twelve years of his life, and to which he later returned after long years in New York. Al-Rihani, nevertheless, developed an entirely different worldview from Mukarzal about Maronitism, Lebanon and the Arab world, for reasons that may require a psychologist rather than a historian to analyze.

Amin Faris al-Rihani was born in 1876 to a Maronite family in Freiké (Furayka), a village in the Metn district, twenty kilometers north-east of Beirut. In 1888, Amin accompanied his uncle to New York and began attending regular American public schools. In 1897, he returned to Lebanon, the first of many trips between Freiké and New York. Al-Rihani began writing short stories and articles in Arabic and English for various journals published by Syro-Lebanese in America and in Beirut. Na'um Mukarzal was the first to publish his works in *al-Hoda*.[55] When Mukarzal established the Lebanese League of Revival in 1910, al-Rihani wrote a passionate article in *Mir'at al-Gharb*, calling for all Lebanese in America to leave behind past disagreements and join forces in the struggle for the homeland, Lebanon. Al-Rihani demanded that the Lebanese community look at other communities in Egypt and South America as examples of political action and emulate their devotion for Lebanon.[56]

In May 1917, al-Rihani began collaborating with Ayyub Tabet[57] to set up the Syrian-Lebanese League of Liberation along with two other Lebanese authors, Gebran Khalil Gebran and Mikha'il Nu'aima. Tabet himself was an atheist, who, like al-Rihani, strongly believed in the message of the French Revolution.[58] In 1908, inspired by the liberal winds drifting in from Istanbul as a result of the Young Turk revolution, Tabet wrote an essay about the French Revolution.[59] Yet, unlike al-Rihani, he remained a devout francophile throughout the mandate period. The civil principles of the French Revolution may have been the bonding factor between the two, but it did not hold them together for long. Tabet was a strong believer in the non-Arab identity in Syria and Lebanon and a pro-French politician.[60] Al-Rihani held the exact opposite convictions, and was ultimately labeled by the French as a firm francophobe.[61]

By 1922 a famous author and nicknamed "the Philosopher of Freiké," al-Rihani traveled through the Arab world for a year and a half. He published articles and books concerning this trip, all calling for Arab political and cultural unity. At the end of this long and famous journey, he permanently moved to Freiké and left his village only to give lectures and defend the Arab cause. Throughout his literary life, al-Rihani was considered an eminent author in Arabic and English who defended Arabism in a very distinctive way. He was a dedicated secular Arab who disliked all forms of organized religion. He thus differed from Rabbath and Zurayk who acknowledged the role and importance of Islam in the Arab collective identity. For the same reason, al-Rihani disapproved of the Christian nature of Lebanon and regarded its religious leaders as a devastating factor for Lebanon.

Al-Rihani's relations with Lebanon were ambivalent. His love and affection towards Lebanon and the scenery of his village, Freiké, can be easily seen in his writings.[62] He, nevertheless, did not confuse this empathy with his strong Arab convictions and his belief that Lebanon belonged, culturally and politically, to a larger Arab world. His ideas about the history of Syria and Lebanon were very unique. In an environment where every nationalist looked at the past in order to cling to some lofty pedigree, al-Rihani judged the entire history of the region as a chain of calamities. In *Al-Nakabat* [The Calamities][63] he elaborated this view in detail, criticizing the entire history of Syria. He felt that the multitude of conquerors and migration waves were negative factors in the history of the land. They all contributed to the numerous rites and nationalities, which had torn the country apart. The Phoenicians, the Assyrians, the Hittites, the Cannanites, the Nabateans, the Greeks, the Romans and the Arameans had, and still have, a degrading influence on the social and national life of the Syrians, he claimed. It was time to admit that even the Umayyads were not the perfect rulers, as we tend to refer to them today. The Crusaders also received their share of his criticism. They were oppressors who raped the land and its women.[64] Al-Rihani concluded one of the chapters saying: "Syria, you are my country, you are the Babel of the nations, you are the Babel of religions." Elsewhere he asked, "Is there any wonder that there is no country like mine?" and answered, "My country — the residence of tribalism (*'asabiyyat*) and the cemetery of nationalism (*wataniyya*)."[65]

An example of the ambivalent relations between al-Rihani and Lebanon and the Phoenician narrative arises from his relationship with Charles Corm. As noted in Chapter IV, following Corm's publication of *La Montagne Inspirée* in 1934, al-Rihani wrote a critique of the epic in al-Ma'rid, the literary journal of Michel Zakkur.[66] It is a review mixed with positive and negative remarks and references to his friendship with Corm. His major criticism of the work was Corm's unconditional love of France. This love was expressed particularly in the first part of the book, a long stanza praising the French arrival in Lebanon at the end of WWI. Al-Rihani also disapproved of Corm's attempt to "phoenicianize" different emigrant Lebanese authors, including al-Rihani himself, by attributing their talent and the drive to emigrate as inherited characteristics from their ancestors, the ancient Phoenicians.[67] Corm's Phoenician inclinations won some cynical commentary from al-Rihani. Good for us, Lebanese, al-Rihani wrote sarcastically, that Corm found remnants of our country in the distant corners of the Mediterranean basin.

Corm, according to al-Rihani, was "the living example of the misfortune of poetry and nationality." Writing in a foreign language made Corm a lonely (*farid*) poet instead of a happy (*sa'id*) poet, because he did not use Arabic, the language of Lebanon. Referring to the ancient Phoenicians, al-Rihani wrote that Corm's *diwan* was "*the* Phoenician hymn of hymns," although al-Rihani was not sure if they deserved it. He was sure, however, that Lebanon deserved all the love that had flowed from the pages of Charles Corm.[68]

Despite such criticism, al-Rihani did not judge *La Montagne Inspirée* entirely negatively. He praised Corm for his exquisite descriptions of Lebanon's countryside and applauded his passion for Lebanon. This duality between the love of Lebanon and the strong conviction that Lebanon is part of a larger national collective, as manifested in al-Rihani's review of Corm's epic, surfaces also in al-Rihani's book *Qalb Lubnan*, a travelogue he wrote following a trip to Mount Lebanon in 1936. The travelogue again refers to the friendship between al-Rihani and Corm. Al-Rihani dedicated the book to "my friend Charles Corm," and Corm joined him for a section of the trip. The book not only includes descriptions of al-Rihani's experiences in Mount Lebanon, but also contains a very interesting essay he wrote as an integral part of the travelogue on the history of the ancient Phoenicians, indicating again the importance of this past to the modern history of Lebanon.

The essay is a long and educated attempt by al-Rihani to put the history of the Phoenician city-states in a new perspective. He called the Western historians who had been writing the history of Phoenicians the extremists (or exaggerators) of Phoenicia (*ghulat al-finiqiyya*), stating that they overestimated this people by attributing to them lofty characteristics and achievements. Al-Rihani also criticized the indiscriminate use of two of the most important texts of that period, those of Herodotus and Sanchuniathon. He claimed they could not be taken at face value, because their descriptions had been found to be erroneous. Herodotus and Sanchuniathon, along with the Bible, the writings of Josephus Flavius and the Assyrian annals, provided the most detailed contemporary account of the Phoenician civilization. Herodotus described a trip to the Phoenician coast in the 5th century BC and wrote about the origin of the Phoenicians from the Persian Gulf. Sanchuniathon, the Beirut historian (segments of whose book, *History of the Phoenicians,* survived thanks to the translation of Philo of Byblos in the 1st century AD) described the Phoenician civilization as it existed around the 10th century BC.[69] Sanchuniathon and Herodotus should not be the basis of the study of Phoenicia, al-Rihani asserted, because of the chain of translations and interpretations that prevent us today from regarding these texts as genuine descriptions of Phoenicia.[70]

Unlike other opponents of the Phoenician idea, al-Rihani did not discredit the Phoenicians, nor did he insist that they were Arabs whose achievements should be credited to the Arab civilization. He wrote about their accomplishments with a sober eye, and when needed he challenged many of the "truths" concerning their civilization. There is no shame in the fact that the Phoenicians imitated other civilizations, he wrote, for it does not diminish the importance of theirs. They did not invent the use of glass, nor were they the first to use silk and cotton, as is often claimed. Al-Rihani dedicated a full chapter to demonstrating that the Phoenicians did not even invent the alphabet. It was a joint effort of the civilizations in the Fertile Crescent, an effort that lasted from the beginning of the second millennium until 1400 BC. Archeologists found signs of alphabet use in the Sinai desert and in Ras Shamra that preceded the Phoenicians. As admirable merchants, the ancient Phoenicians needed the alphabet as a means of communication and they did perfect it. They deserve all the credit for this deed, but they did not invent the alphabet *ex nihilo*.[71]

Discussing the relationship between the Greeks and the Phoenicians, al-Rihani challenged the Frenchman Victor Bérard, one of the most important scholars to lay the foundation for the theory that it was the Phoenicians and not the Greeks who civilized the Mediterranean basin from East to West. As noted in the Introduction, Bérard used the Odyssey of Homer to prove his argument that the Phoenicians not only brought their merchandise to Greece on their boats, but that they also carried with them their civilization to introduce to the Greeks, a theory that was embraced with excitement by Charles Corm and the new Phoenicians. Through his criticism of Bérard, al-Rihani challenged the crux of the Phoenician image of the past. He claimed that there was no trace of Phoenician presence in Greece in the writings of other Greek authors, such as Sophocles, Herodotus, Pericles and others. The Greeks did borrow, but they did so from many Eastern civilizations — from the Egyptians, the Babylonians, the Assyrians and the Phoenicians. They borrowed from a civilization 2,500 years old, of which the Phoenicians were only one small part.

Al-Rihani's essay continues in the same vein and addresses many other issues concerned with the civilization of the ancient Phoenicians. Reading his work, the realization arises that it is not a rejection of the Phoenicians and their civilization, but rather a more critical view thereof. Thus, in several parts of the essay, al-Rihani has no difficulty in referring to Phoenicians as "our forefathers" (*'Ajdaduna*). Sometimes even the writer himself fell into the trap of Phoenician romanticism, for example when he wrote that the Phoenicians had emigrated in the same manner as modern Lebanese emigrate today.[72]

What made al-Rihani develop his worldview? He studied at the village school in Freiké until he emigrated to New York, and there he was cut off from the Maronite educational track. By the time he began his literary life in 1898, he had already spent 10 years in America. There he developed a strong belief in secularism, separation between religion and state, and in the civil values of the French Revolution. When Syro-Lebanese associations were formed in the second decade of the 20th century, he supported them because he believed they called for the establishment of a civil, non-confessional society. However, when the end result was the establishment of Lebanon, defined as a Christian state, al-Rihani could no longer support its existence as such.

Al-Rihani appreciated freedom of speech and religious liberty in America, but the cultural life and American materialism did not appeal to him. His first return visit to Freiké in 1897, and his numerous trips back and forth, were a lengthy root-searching journey, seeking out his own cultural identity. The culture al-Rihani favored upon his return to Lebanon was strongly Arab, the antithesis of American Western culture, towards which he had mixed feelings. Upon returning to Lebanon he had to re-learn Arabic, because as a child in Freiké, he had learned primarily French and some colloquial Arabic. He testified that his mother commonly used the terms Bedouin and *A'arabi* (Arab from the desert) to frighten him when he misbehaved.[73] He immigrated to America afraid of speaking Arabic and hating Arabs, lest a drop of their blood flow in his veins. His attraction towards the Arabs and Arabic surfaced as a result of several English books he read in New York about their civilization.[74]

The contrast between American culture and the new culture he rediscovered through these books was not easy for him to ignore.

Al-Rihani was a literary person and his preoccupation with Lebanon and its past was manifested through literary essays. In a way, he spoke in the same language of those who expressed the Phoenician idea in Lebanon: literary pieces exalting Lebanon, its people and its scenery. By doing so he did not see any dissonance between writing about the Phoenicians, albeit with a critical eye, and viewing Lebanon as an Arab country. This complexity is expressed in his self-perception. "My personality," al-Rihani testified, "consists of several opposed and harmonious personalities. Religiously, this personality is of Ba'al, Adonis, monotheistic, Christian, Muslim and Sufi [...]."[75] His self-identity was similar to the identity he prescribed for Lebanon:

> I am a born Lebanese, my language and nationality (*qawmiyya*) are Arab, and in my veins flows Phoenician, Canaanite, Aramaic and Chaldean blood. My heart is in Lebanon but my soul is in every Arab country. Even if I were a Christian Maronite, I would still be part of the rest of the sects and religions, which dissect this [Arab] nation. I believe there is no life for the Lebanese without the proximity to the Syrian, and there is no life for the Syrian without the proximity to the Arab. There is no life for the Arab without detesting the restraints of religions and tribal fanaticism [...].[76]

The lengthy preoccupation with the Phoenician narrative of Lebanon by Zurayk, Rabbath and al-Rihani reflects the fact that it was mainly Christian Arabs who made the effort to write against the Lebanist idea. Lebanon as a Christian entity was, ideologically, more problematic for them than for their Arab Muslim counterparts in the Arab movement. Sati' al-Husri, for example, gave little attention to the Phoenician narrative in Lebanon, although there was no question that he unconditionally rejected these claims. Al-Husri, the Arab national educator par excellence, had other, more important adversaries to challenge than the Lebanese national movement and its presumed Phoenician ancestors. Egypt, which al-Husri considered the *Piedmont* of the Arab nation, was his major concern; the Pharaonic tendencies in Egypt tormented him far more than the neo-Phoenicians in Lebanon.[77] He only referred to the Phoenician claims several times in passing, seeing it as a foreign idea imported by the French.[78]

For Christian Arab thinkers who believed in the formation of an Arab state where all citizens of all sects were equal, Lebanon (just like the Zionist movement) was a disturbing factor. The way to challenge it was, at first, to defy the historical and ethnic reasons for its separate existence. Rabbath, the Uniate, was the most moderate of the above three adversaries. He actually recognized the existence of a separate Christian entity in the restricted area of Mount Lebanon. Hence, his mild criticism of the Phoenician narrative. Zurayk, the

Greek Orthodox and Arab national thinker, was more critical of the existence of Lebanon and did not accept its historical narrative. Al-Rihani, the Maronite and the devout secularist, was more complex in his criticism. Although he shared with Rabbath and Zurayk the idea of a large Arab country united by language and shared culture, he also recognized Lebanon's Phoenician past, albeit not in the way Corm did. The Phoenicians belonged to the ancient history of the land, constituting one facet of its character. Rabbath and Zurayk represented, more than al-Rihani, the mainstream opposition to Lebanon and its Phoenician narrative. It was views such as those of al-Rihani, though, that finally mitigated the opposition to the Phoenician idea in Lebanon. Phoenicianism as a non-Arab identity did not become part of mainstream Lebanon in the 1940s-1950s, but by normalizing the idea that Lebanon did hold Phoenician features, albeit with Arab lineaments, it was possible for many Lebanese, who at first utterly opposed the formation of Greater Lebanon, to reconcile to some extent with a national historical narrative beginning with the Phoenicians.

Antun Sa'adeh and the Syrian Social Nationalist Party

Of all the adversaries discussed in this chapter, only one, Antun Sa'adeh, led an organized movement with a clear political agenda and a distinct historical theory that challenged the Lebanese-Phoenician view of the past. His party, the Syrian Social Nationalist Party (better known as the *Parti populaire syrien*, or PPS), posed a major threat to the existence of Greater Lebanon from its inception in 1932 until Sa'adeh's execution by the Lebanese government in 1949 and even after, during the 1950s-1960s. Not only did Sa'adeh defy the right of Lebanon to exist as an independent state, separate from Syria, but, as we shall see, he often used arguments similar to those raised by Lebanese nationalists to accommodate their own reasoning for the existence of Lebanon as a viable national community.

When Sa'adeh established the PPS, the idea of a greater Syrian, non-Arab nation had been in existence for at least three decades. Already in 1904, Henri Lammens wrote about the importance of the geographical composition of Syria, highlighting the uniqueness of a Syrian nation circumscribed within the limits of greater Syria, and utterly different from the Arab ethnicity.[79] In fact, well until April 1919, the Syrianism that Lammens professed was dominant among intellectuals in geographical Syria, particularly in Beirut, more than Arabism or Lebanism. As we have already noted in the first two chapters, Chékri Ganem, Bulus Nujaym, Jacques Tabet, Georges Samné, Charles Corm, and many others publicly expressed their desire to establish *"la plus grande Syrie,"* as a secular non-Arab nation, granting Lebanon a leading role in its formation. They based these aspirations on the scholarly works of Elisée Reclus, Henri Lammens and other French scholars,[80] who scientifically "proved" the existence of a Syrian nation since time immemorial. For reasons already explained, by the end of 1919 most of the Lebanese who supported the formation of a greater Syrian state had modified their views and begun advocating the formation of an independent Greater Lebanon. They nevertheless continued to base their political beliefs on the same learned works of Lammens and his peers. Thus, Syrian ideology as expressed by Sa'adeh can be best understood against the backdrop of this stream that existed in greater Syria long before the establishment of the PPS and which was the foundation of Sa'adeh's Syrian convictions. This is also the reason why Sa'adeh's ideology was appealing to more than a few Lebanese at its inception. Simply put, Syrianism was not a far-fetched ideology in the 1930s. Greater Lebanon had been in existence for little more than a decade when Sa'adeh established his party with enough supporters for his doctrines in Lebanon. Sa'id 'Aql, for example, began his literary career as a supporter and member of Sa'adeh's party.[81] The flirtation 'Aql conducted with the PPS did not last long, and by the mid-1930s he left the party and departed on an individual path of literary and political activity. Another Lebanese who was infatuated with the Syrianism of Sa'adeh was Salah Labaki. For a few years, Labaki was vice president of the PPS and in charge of its propaganda. He ceaselessly called for the inclusion of Lebanon into greater Syria and the formation of a Syrian, non-Arab, state.[82] On March 1936, Labaki even participated in the Conference of the Coast as a representative of the PPS and together with prominent Muslim Lebanese leaders called for the annexation of Lebanon to Syria.[83] Like 'Aql, by the end of 1936, Labaki left the party to become a leading literary figure in Lebanon and, as we have already seen, he wrote extensively about Lebanon using Phoenician symbols to glorify the country. Seemingly, one might notice a contradiction between Sa'adeh's ideology and the Lebanese idea, but in fact Lebanism was conceived along with Syrianism and not in contradiction to it. Bulus Nujaym comes to mind as the perfect example for this illusive incongruity. In 1908, when he wrote *La Question du Liban*, solving the problem of *Lebanon* was in his mind, but he thought this problem would be best resolved in the wider context of a secular non-sectarian federated Greater Syria. Although Nujaym of 1908 spoke about a Greater Lebanon in a Syrian federation, he was no less a Lebanese nationalist. In 1919, once the Ottomans were out of the picture and the Syrian national movement had been taken over by the Arab government of Faysal, he no longer supported the formation of a greater Syrian federation. With this in mind, it is easier to understand how persons like 'Aql, the Lebanese nationalist par excellence, and Salah Labaki, both began their literary careers as members of the PPS.[84] It is exactly for this reason that Sa'adeh's opposition to Lebanon's integrity was so threatening. More than al-Rihani, Zurayk and Rabbath, Sa'adeh was very clear and adamant about his disapproval of the narrative of Lebanese nationalism, i.e., the Phoenician myth of origin. In *A'da' al-'Arab A'da' Lubnan* [The Enemies of the Arabs, the Enemies of Lebanon] he clearly stated:

There are those who claim, misleading the people, that the Lebanese question is not a religious one, but rather a racial, social and historical question. They justify this by affiliating the Lebanese with the Phoenicians, distinguishing them from the rest of the Syrians, asserting that the Lebanese have always been an independent country, and other similar groundless arguments. The descent between the Lebanese and the Phoenicians is baseless. Its falsity is proved by anthropological and genealogical scientific facts. [...] It is not Lebanon that derives its origin from the Phoenicians, but rather Syria![85]

Clearly, Sa'adeh's disapproval of Phoenicianism emanated from its association with Lebanese Christian nationalism, which he rebuked. Lebanon's existence was based on a religious rationale and Phoenicianism was invalid for him not so much because he thought it was fictitious, but more because he believed these Phoenicians were actually Syrians and Syrianism was not a religious identification. As we shall see below, this theme of utter rejection of Phoenicianism in the Lebanese context and its embrace in the Syrian context was a recurrent motif in his writings about the national identity of the two.

In 1947, two years before his swift overnight trial and execution by the Lebanese government, Antun Sa'adeh published the principles of the PPS in a book entitled *Kitab al-Ta'alim al-Suriyya al-Qawmiyya al-Ijtima'iyya* [The Syrian Social Nationalist Book of Teachings].[86] The book is divided into two parts: the first contains eight "fundamental principles" for the existence of a Syrian nation and the second carries five additional "reform principles." The fourth principle in part one deals with the historical unity of the Syrian nation and is summarized by Sa'adeh as follows: "The Syrian *umma* is the unity of the Syrian people, born out of a lengthy history going back to prehistoric times."[87] A careful reading of this section of the book reveals that it was, in fact, a direct response by Sa'adeh to the political and cultural division in Lebanon. Sa'adeh referred to the two major political groups that divided Lebanese society, naming them the "Arab-Muslim" and "Phoenician-Christian" camps. He began this fourth principle by demonstrating that he did not view the Syrian nation as one pure racial stock but rather as an amalgam of races, ethnicities and peoples that had lived in the Syrian land throughout history, left their ethnic imprint, and added another component to the Syrian identity. Thus he stated that the Syrian nation

> constitutes the final outcome of a long history comprised of all nations that have settled in these countries and mingled therein, from the Late Stone Age, prior to the Chaldeans and Canaanites, down to the Amorites, Aramaeans, Assyrians, Hittites, and Akkadians, all of whom eventually became one nation. Thus, we see that the principle of Syrian nationality is not based upon common descent but upon the social and natural unity of a mixture of stock.[88]

The Phoenicians, for Saʻadeh, were one more group of people that inhabited Syria and assisted in the composition of the Syrian nation. Syria, he believed, was no more Phoenician than it was Chaldean or Aramaean, although, as we shall see below, in other writings he did attribute to the ancient Phoenicians much credit for their contribution to humanity. Interestingly, referring to the Arabs in Syria, Saʻadeh clearly stated that:

> This [fourth] principle does not absolutely rule out that the Syrian nation is one of the nations of the Arab world, or one of the Arab nations. Similarly, the existence of the Syrian nation as an Arab nation does not rule out that Syria is a full-fledged nation with rights to absolute self-rule for itself and its *watan*, and, consequently, has a self-existing national cause, independent of any other cause.[89]

Neglecting this fundamental principle, explained Saʻadeh, was the reason for the religious rivalries that had divided Syria between Arab-Muslim inclinations and Christian-Phoenician propensities, that had torn apart the unity of the nation and diminished its strength. Implementing this principle would save Syria from the racial arrogance that characterized Syrian communal life today. The Syrians who felt they were Aramaeans, Phoenicians, Arabs or Crusaders could hold on to their beliefs as long as they followed this principle of national, social and egalitarian unity of rights and duties indistinguishable from blood or genealogical differences. This principle, Saʻadeh concluded, offers a synthesis between the thesis of Phoenician chauvinism and the antithesis of Arab chauvinism, or vice versa. It allows us to think about one Syrian nation, united in its history and geography.[90]

Similarly to Zurayk and Rabbath, Saʻadeh divided Lebanon into two camps, Phoenician and Arab. He knew well that Phoenicianism was directly related to the Christian, Western-oriented camp in Lebanon and, therefore, he could not agree with the arguments supporting the existence of a modern Phoenician nation in the image of Greater Lebanon. His ardent secular worldview, on the one hand, and the firm identification of Phoenicianism in the 1930s with the francophones of Beirut, on the other, alienated Saʻadeh from the social group that advocated the francophone Phoenician idea. He strongly disliked the Maronite hegemony in Lebanon for social and ideological reasons. Ideologically, he could not agree with the correlation the Maronites made between religion and national sentiments. Socio-politically, the Maronite's francophone tendencies and their hegemony in Lebanon in general and in Beirut in particular was disturbing for Saʻadeh. As a returning immigrant he was an outsider in Beirut without concrete contacts to any local power-base. He was not part of the francophone circles, nor was he a member of the wealthy Greek Orthodox families that dominated the financial life in the city. He found part-time work in AUB as a German teacher — a marginal position that enabled him to meet students and teach his ideology — but it did not introduce him to any socio-political power in the city.

As part of Sa'adeh's attempt to appropriate the Phoenicians into his ideology, he often referred to the ancient Phoenician-Syrians in his nationalistic writing, almost always using parentheses for the word "Phoenician" next to the synonymous term "Canaanite." As noted in the Introduction, the ancient Phoenicians did call themselves Canaanites, but the latter term was more inclusive than the term Phoenician, for it included the entire land of Canaan, which roughly corresponded with Sa'adeh's definition of geographical Syria. In his most famous nationalistic pamphlet, *Nushu'al-Umam* [The Evolution of Nations], Sa'adeh granted the Canaanites with no less than the discovery of nationalist sentiments.[91] They were the first people who practiced patriotism (*mahabbat al-watan*) and social cohesion in accordance with national sentiment. Moreover, the Canaanite-Phoenicians, he claimed, brought into being the civil state that later served as a model for the Greeks and the Romans. The Phoenicians, wrote Sa'adeh, also founded other forms of government such as the electoral monarchy and the democratic state. Thus, while the neo-Phoenicians in Lebanon bestowed on their ancestors, the ancient Phoenicians, the civilizing role of the ancient world; Sa'adeh granted the Syrians, as a whole, the same attributes. "It was they [the Syrians]," he wrote, "who civilized the Greeks and laid the foundations of Mediterranean civilization which the Greeks later joined."[92]

The ancient Phoenicians, it seems, then, were a desired commodity not only for the Lebanese national movement. Syrianism *à la* Sa'adeh was just as eager to incorporate them into its own national narrative. Yet, for Lebanese nationalists such as Corm, 'Aql and al-Saouda, Phoenicianism was *the* national identity of Lebanon, whereas for Sa'adeh, the Phoenician past was one facet, albeit glorious, of a lengthy historical experience of the entire Syrian terrain. In a way, it was another variant of Phoenicianism, out of several, that existed in Lebanon in the 1930s and 1940s. It clarifies why 'Aql and Labaki found the ideology of the PPS so appealing at first, and why the poet Adonis was also attracted to the party. It also helps explain why Sa'adeh's ideology posed such a threat to the Lebanese national movement. It was the major secular ideological alternative to Lebanese nationalism that provided a whole worldview, from its perception of history to its understanding of contemporary national conduct. Moreover, it came from within Lebanese society and was based on existing political currents among many intellectuals who believed that the objectives for which Greater Lebanon was established could actually best be met through the formation of a large secular Syrian nation. If we strip Sa'adeh's ideology from its vociferous nature and fascist tendencies, we would find, at the core, that it was not too far from the Lebanist idea, as conceived in the first decade of the 20th century by liberal lay Lebanese such as Bulus Nujaym and Philip and Farid al-Khazin, who sought to solve the problem of Lebanon by expanding its borders, but in a context of a Syrian federation.

Muhammad Jamil Bayhum and Sunni Lebanese

It is impossible to conclude a discussion about the adversaries to the Phoenician idea in Lebanon without referring to the largest opposition group. This was, of course, the Sunni community, for years the second largest sect, which the national pact of 1943 named a partner of the Maronites in the division of political power in Lebanon. Muhammad Jamil Bayhum, the Beiruti Sunni politician and writer, who lived through much of the era discussed in this study, is a good representative of the Sunni bourgeoisie in Beirut. In his arguments against the non-Arab identity of Lebanon Bayhum set the ground for most of the arguments of the Muslim Lebanese and, therefore, he is an appropriate person to round out the discussion of the Phoenician adversaries. Bayhum (1887-1978)[93] was born into one of the wealthiest Sunni families in Beirut. He acquired his education at the Ottoman Islamic College in the city[94] and at the *Mission Laïque* School. As a member of this fortunate class, he assumed leadership positions from an early stage of his political career. In 1916 he was a member of the municipal council of Beirut and in 1919-1920, he participated in the short-lived government of Faysal in Damascus as a delegate from Beirut — to mention two of his posts. Throughout the mandate years he stood out as a staunch supporter of Arab unity, a devoted adversary of the French mandate and a dedicated activist in various Islamic associations and clubs. With such a résumé there is no doubt that Bayhum opposed the Phoenician idea on all levels: as an Arab, as a Muslim, and as a Lebanese, once Lebanon became a *fait accompli* even for the Muslims.

In 1957, Bayhum published a book called *Al-'Uruba wa al-Shu'ubiyyat al-Haditha* [Arabism and the New Shu'ubiyyat].[95] It contained discussions with four distinguished personalities about Ibn Khaldun, Arab unity and its contemporary adversaries. Bayhum opened the book with an introduction containing a survey of the various modern *Shu'ubiyyat* in the contemporary Arab world. The educated and erudite writer did not choose this term accidentally. The *Shu'ubiyya* was a political and literary movement of non-Arabs formed in the days of the 'Abbasi *Khalifa* al-Mansur (754-775). It rejected Arab superiority in the Caliphate and demanded equal rights for all Muslims, regardless of their race. The movement aspired to gain recognition for the rights and achievements of the non-Arab ethnicities and extolled the ancient eastern civilizations of the Pharaohs, the Persians, the Indians, the Greeks and the Romans. With time, the term *Shu'ubi* evolved to denote a non-Arab who objected to Arab pride and who supported separatist groups within the Arab-Muslim world. In the 20th century another interpretation was added to the term. Many non-conformist Arabs were now labeled as *Shu'ubis*, from leftist thinkers such as Sadik Jalal al-'Azm to avant-garde Arab literary authors such as the poet Adonis.[96] For Bayhum, all modern separatist movements in the Arab world were novel forms of *Shu'ubiyyat*, especially in Egypt and Lebanon where these movements had large groups of followers. The use of this term by Bayhum was directly related to his Arab-Islamic world-view. By using this familiar designation, he placed all separatist groups in a specific historical context. The Arabs, the originators of Islamic religion and culture, fought in the past against anti-Arab tendencies and are still doing so today. These patterns of history do not change.

According to Bayhum, the prime reason for the modern existence of the *Shu'ubiyyat* was Western imperialism that sought to facilitate the colonial process through a policy of division and confusion in the Arab world. Bayhum surveyed the various separatist movements, beginning with Pharaonicism in Egypt, proceeding to Phoenicianism in Lebanon, to Syria, Iraq and other movements in the Arab countries. France, for Bayhum, initiated the *Shu'ubiyya* in Lebanon with the help of the Jesuit missionaries. Books written by the missionaries totally ignored the fact that Muslims, in addition to Christians, had inhabited Lebanon.[97] Bayhum condemned the French for using the Ministry of Education in the mandatory years in order to create a new curriculum bare of the elements of Arab civilization. In 1926, he protested, the French planned to designate the colloquial Arabic of Lebanon as a formal language in the *baccalauréat* (General Certificate of Education), in order to cut Lebanon off from its Arab neighbors.[98] Some Lebanese, influenced by the French, began writing Phoenician poetry and fiction, published Phoenician magazines and established Phoenician literary and economic associations.[99] These new Phoenicians, he wrote, soon learned that the ancient Phoenicians were actually Arabs who came to Lebanon from the Arab Gulf (definitely not the Persian Gulf, Arab nationalists would argue). When they realized this fact they no longer wished to be identified as Phoenicians. Thus, they created a new *Shu'ubiyya*, which they called Mediterreanianism. But it made no difference for Lebanon, because it was the same old *Shu'ubiyya* simply with a new disguise.[100]

Bayhum's critique of the Phoenician narrative reflected the convictions shared by Muslim opponents of Lebanese Christian nationalism. To begin with, they all saw it as a product of French colonial misconduct rather than a genuine desire of Lebanese Christian self-determination. Second, Muslim opponents of the non-Arab orientation of Lebanon arabized the Phoenicians through the theory that argued that all ancient peoples of the Near East originated from the Arabian Peninsula and, therefore, they were all Arabs.[101] This enabled them, on the one hand, to ridicule the "non-Arab" neo-Phoenicians and, on the other, to accept the Phoenicians as a legitimate page in the history of Lebanon without abandoning their Arab-ness. Thus, even Bayhum himself could bluntly write: "the truth is that our first forefathers the Phoenicians who were praised in poetry and prose and who were a source of pride for the

Arabian Peninsula are worthy of all admiration and we cannot exaggerate eulogizing them."[102] Third, Muslims held the view that the Mediterranean began to be appealing to the *Shu'ubis* in Lebanon once they realized that the Phoenicians were actually Arabs. Not desiring to be associated with the Arabs, these *Shu'ubis* fabricated Mediterraneanism as their new identity. As I have already elaborated in the previous chapters, Phoenicianism had walked hand in hand with Mediterraneanism in Lebanon since its inception. One facet of becoming a Phoenician in modern Lebanon was being part of the Mediterranean basin rather than the Arab East. Charles Corm, *the* neo-Phoenician par excellence, regarded the Mediterranean basin as an integral part of Lebanese culture at least since the early 1930s and Michel Chiha wrote already in 1919 that Lebanon is an inseparable part of the Latin Mediterranean civilization. In the 1940s, the Mediterranean Sea began to be more commonly used to describe the special culture of Lebanon, not because of the reason Bayhum provided, but more as a result of a process of normalization of the Phoenician past and its symbols. One of these symbols was the Mediterranean, a term easier to digest than the Phoenicians.

Muhammad Jamil Bayhum was part of a generation of Muslim Sunnis that had lived in Beirut through the last two decades of the Ottoman Empire, witnessed the fall of the Ottoman system, supported the formation of an Arab-Syrian state and fought against the separatist tendencies of Lebanon. Phoenicianism for Bayhum was an utterly foreign concept, which he by no means could accept. If we saw among Christian adversaries of the Lebanist idea a sort of willingness to recognize, even to a minor extent, the Phoenicians as a legitimate page in Lebanon's history, then, in the case of Bayhum, there was a total rejection of the idea. Phoenicianism, Pharaonicism, Syrianism *à la* PPS, were all labeled by him as *Shu'ubiyyat*, a phrase that touched a historical chord and put the struggle over the identity of Lebanon into an Arab-Islamic historical context.

From Rida to Bayhum to Rabbath to Zurayq to al-Rihani and to Sa'adeh, opposition to the Phoenician idea in Lebanon shared some common denominators. Had the six sat together in 1934 to discuss Charles Corm's *La Montagne Inspirée*, Bayhum, who socio-economically was closer to Corm than all six, and Rida would presumably reject Corm's epic from beginning to end. They would defy Corm's Christian, non-Arab Lebanon and ridicule the Phoenicians as portrayed by the author. Sa'adeh would join them in rejecting the Christian foundation of Corm's worldview but at the same time would disapprove any religion as the base of any nation, Islam included. Zurayq and Rabbath would probably call on Corm to think about the future, rather than the past, and to consider Lebanon's best interest today. They would understand Corm's view, but would, nevertheless, claim that Lebanon, even if it is culturally unique, is still Arab with a local Mediterranean flavor. Al-Rihani would unduly praise Lebanon's countryside and people as portrayed in Corm's epic, but would disagree with Corm's attempt to Phoenicianize every rock and tree in Lebanon. Sa'adeh would praise the sections of *La Montagne Inspirée* that extol the Phoenicians, but would simply say that they were Syrians and not Lebanese. He would share with al-Rihani his disapproval of Corm's use of French, the language of the colonizer, rather than Arabic, the local language. All six would converse in elevated Arabic and agree, with the exception of Sa'adeh, that al-Qurm (the accurate transliteration from Arabic) was clearly an Arab who, had it not been for the French, would have recognized his Arab roots and written about them, in Arabic, with the same poetic talent that he used to praise the Phoenicians, his imaginary forefathers.

References

1 AD Nante, carton 1365, Rapport sur les partis politiques au Liban, p. 57, December 17, 1942.
2 Just three examples out of many: Aurore Trad was the owner and editor of the Francophile journal *Phénicia* (1938-1939); Emile Eddé was married to Lody Sursuk; Charles Dabbas had a French wife, both were part of the francophile milieu to which the Corms, the 'Amouns, the Eddés and so forth belonged. In Beirut of July 1919, a delegation to the American King Crane Commission of the city's Greek Orthodox community supported the formation of independent Greater Lebanon under the aegis of France. See *Lisan al-Hal*, July 9, 1919; *Al-Hoda*, August 18, 1919.
3 MAE Paris, Vol. 103, p. 151. Rapport présenté au conseil d'administration de la Mission laïque française par P. Deschamps, directeur-fondateur du Collège de Beyrouth. February-April 1919.
4 MAE Paris, Vol. 398, p. 13. Réunion organisée par l'association syrienne arabe de Paris, February 11, 1927. At the same gathering, Georges Samné gave a lecture about Syria in history demonstrating the continuous significant role of Syria through history. He used Elisée Reclus to demonstrate the geographical and national unity of Greater Syria, stating that the division of Syria into small petty states (including Lebanon) is not viable.
5 Jesuit Archives, Vanves. Fond Louis Jalabert, Paquet VII, Chemise GP. A report of M. Besnard (General Secretary of the Mission Laïque), *La Culture Française en Orient*, June 1934.
6 On Rashid Rida's Arab-Islamic ideas, see Hourani, *Arabic Thought*, pp. 222-244; C. Ernest Dawn, *From Ottomanism to Arabism* (Urbana: University of Illinois Press 1973), pp. 137-138.
7 Rashid Rida, "al-Jinsiyya al-Lubnaniyya wa Ghulu Talabiha," [Lebanese Nationality and its Exceeding Demands], *al-Manar*, Vol. 17 (1914), pp. 617-627. Rida's article provides another indication that Phoenicianism as an alternative identity for the Lebanese was first expressed in the Americas.
8 Rashid Rida, *al-Wahy al-Muhammady* [The Revelation of Muhammad] (Beirut, 1987), pp. 22-25. See also Hourani, *Arabic Thought*, p. 236.
9 Long before Egyptian territorial nationalism became identified with Pharaonicism, Copts were nicknamed by their Muslim neighbors *Jins Fara'auni* (Pharaonic race or *genus Pharaonicus*). See in S. H. Leeder, *Modern Sons of the Pharaohs*

(London: Hodder and Stoughton, 1918), p. 312. See also Samir Seikaly, "Coptic Communal Reform 1860-1914," *Middle East Studies,* 6(1970), p. 269; and the preface to Kyriakos Mikhail, *Copts and Moslems* (London: Smith & Elder, 1911), p. viii, written by A. H. Sayce, a professor at Oxford University: "The genuine Egyptians are the Christian Copts. They alone trace an unadulterated descent from the race to whom the civilization and culture of the ancient world were so largely due. Thanks to their religion, they have kept their blood pure from admixture with semi-barbarous Arabs and savage Kurds [...]."

10 "Al-Muslimun wa al-Qubt" [The Muslims and the Copts], *al-Manar*, Vol. 11 (1908), pp. 338-347.

11 "Al-Mas'ala al-Suriyya wa al-Ahzab" [The Syrian Question and the Parties], *al-Manar*, Vol. 21 (1919). "Al-Rahla al-Suriyya al-Thaniyya" [The Second Syrian Journey], Vol. 26 (1921).

12 "Al-Thawra al-Suriyya wa al-Hukuma al-Faransiyya wa al-Tanazu' bayna al-Sharq wa al-Gharb" [The Syrian Revolution, the French Government and the Struggle between East and West], *al-Manar*, Vol. 26 (1925), pp. 699-712.

13 "Al-Shiqaq bayna al-'Arab wa al-Muslimun" [The Disunity between the Arabs and the Muslims] *al-Manar*, Vol. 34 (1935), pp. 782-786.

14 MAE Paris, Vol. 209, p. 85-86. Extract of an article in *La Suisse*, entitled: "La Syrie et la Palestine devant la Société des Nations," September 14, 1924.

15 "La Renaissance arabe," *La Nation Arabe* (Geneva, 1930). The first issue of the journal (edited by Shekib Arslan and Ihsan Bey al-Jabiri) of the Syro-Palestinian delegation to the League of Nations in Geneva.

16 Information on Zurayk: George N. Atiyeh & Ibrahim M. Oweiss (eds.), *Arab Civilization; Studies in Honor of Qonstantine K. Zurayk* (Albany, N.Y.: State University of New York Press), pp. 1-38. See also Hourani, *Arabic Thought*, pp. 309-310.

17 Qostantin Zurayq, *al-Wa'i al-Qawmi* [National Consciousness] (Beirut: Dar al-Makshuf, 1939), p. 112.

18 *Ibid*, p. 97.
19 *Ibid*, p. 98.
20 *Ibid*, p. 98-99.
21 *Ibid*, pp. 100-101.
22 *Ibid*, p. 102.

23 See, for example, Carlos C. Closson, 'The Hierarchy of European Races,' *American Journal of Sociology*, 3, November 1897, pp. 314-327. On page 315 of this research there is a lengthy bibliographical list of scientific studies on racial hierarchy that dominated the field of sociology from the late-19th century. Zurayk does not refer to specific studies, but it is evident that he draws on the same body of works as appeared in Closson's study.

24 The preoccupation with the racial physical features and their impact on human behavior was very common in ethnological studies of the time. Compare with Closson, *Ibid*, p. 316. See Antun Sa'adeh's engagement with the same subject, *Nushu' al-Umam*, pp. 34-35.

25 *Al-Wa'i al-Qawmi*, p. 106.
26 *Ibid*, p. 107.
27 *Ibid*, p. 108-109.

28 Bassam Tibi, *Arab Nationalism*, 2nd Edition (New York: Macmillan, 1990), pp. 127-138.
29 Munir Bashshur, *The Role of Two Western Universities in the National Life of Lebanon and the Middle East. A Comparative Study of the American University in Beirut and the University of Saint Joseph* (Ph.D. Dissertation, University of Chicago, 1964). A more recent portrayal of the atmosphere in AUB can be found in Fouad Ajami, *The Dream Palace of the Arabs* (New York: Pantheon Books, 1998), pp. 100-110.
30 AD Nantes, carton 390, Instruction publique, Service des renseignements, March 25, 1923.
31 See, for example, MAE Paris, Vol. 191, p. 116. Weigand to MAE, June 19, 1923, a report on anti-French activity at AUB. According to the report, an Arab association, *Zahrat al-Adab* [The Splendor of Literature], was formed at the university. Its purpose was to fight French language and mores. The report stated that association meetings took place at the university and students as well as professors attended them.
32 AD Nantes, carton 137, Curriculum of the Elementary, Middle and High Schools of the American Mission in Syria, Beirut, 1928. In 1927, the American Junior College for Women was established by the American Presbyterian Mission, adopting a Phoenician vessel as its logo. The Lebanese American University is the latest incarnation of this college, still carrying the same Phoenician vessel as its formal logo. See the web site http://www.lebanonlinks.com/le/uni.html.
33 Biographical information on Edmond Rabbath is taken from *Who's Who in Lebanon* (Beirut, 1963-1991); see also Hourani, *Arabic Thought in Liberal Age*, pp. 310-311.
34 Rabbath, *Les États Unis de la Syrie* (Aleppo: October 1925), p. 4.
35 *Ibid*, p. 7.
36 See, for example, MAE Paris, Vol. 13, p. 221-224. The Greek Catholic Patriarch Rahmani to MAE, June 10, 1919. Similar opinions were expressed by the Armenian Catholics in Aleppo, in MAE Paris, Vol. 43, pp. 174-175. See also the memorandum to the American Commission of the Greek Orthodox Archbishop Cyrille Moghabghab, *Le Grand Liban à la Conférence de la Paix* (Oct. 1919, Paris), in MAE Paris, Vol. 125.
37 Philip S. Khoury, *Syria and the French Mandate* (Princeton: Princeton University Press, 1987), p. 464.
38 Rabbath, *Unité Syrienne*, p. 33
39 *Ibid*, p. 35. See the vehement Jesuit attack on Rabbath's arguments in *al-Bashir*, May 13, 1937.
40 Rabbath, *Unité Syrienne*, p. 40.
41 *Ibid*, p. 48.
42 *Ibid*, p. 79.
43 *Ibid*, p. 80. The idea that the Arab occupation put an end to the Latin-Semitic rivalry, by injecting Semitic features to the Syrian population, was already expressed by Bulus Nujaym in 1908 in *La Question du Liban*, pp. 7-10.
44 The formation of an eastern Catholic Church in the 17th century created a new hybrid of a church that was disconnected from its historical eastern Orthodox roots and found a new affiliation within the European Catholic Churches. The

end result was that, lacking the historical bonds with Eastern Christianity, the eastern Catholics were the most facile at adapting to the new winds from the West and latinized, as indeed Michel Chiha wrote in Alexandria in the poem quoted in Chapter II. About this process see Robert Haddad, *Syrian Christians in Muslim Society,* pp. 49-58. There is no surprise in the fact that Chiha, the Chaldean Catholic, ferociously challenged the pro-Arab beliefs of Rabbath the Syrian Catholic. Parts of Chiha's arguments against Rabbath were expounded upon in *Liban d'Aujourd'hui,* discussed in Chapter III.

45 Rabbath, *Unité Syrienne*, p. 92
46 *Ibid*, pp. 110-199.
47 The quotation is taken from *La Montagne Inspirée*, p. 57, 61.
48 Rabbath, *Unité Syrienne,* p. 150
49 *Ibid,* p. 153.
50 Rabbath used Lammens to demonstrate the geographical and ethnic unity of greater Syria. He ignored the fact that Lammens totally rejected the idea that the Syrians were Arabs; see, for example, *Ibid,* pp. 198-199. Rabbath may have also forgotten that twelve years earlier he used Lammens to demonstrate that Syria was Syrian and not Arab.
51 Rabbath's francophilism is expressed, for example, when he praises the ideas of the French Revolution and the French national idea. He uses the term of Edgard Quinet, the French thinker, and calls France *"Christ des Nations." Ibid,* pp. 406-407.
52 The bibliographical list includes the works of Bulus Nujaym, Farid al-Khazin, Lamartine, Ernest Renan, René Ristelhuber, the Maronite Patriarch Monsignor Arida, Henri Lammens, *La Revue Phénicienne* and more. See, *Ibid,* pp. 109-110.
53 Kenneth Cragg, *The Arab Christian* (Louisville: Westminster/John Knox Press, 1991), pp. 13-14; Hitti, *History of the Arabs*, pp. 3-13.
54 See, for example, Hassan Hallaq, *Lubnan: Min al-'Finiqiyya ila al-'Uruba* (Beirut: al-Dar al-Jami'iyya, 1993).
55 Al-Rihani's first article in *al-Hoda*, "Tawhid al-Lugha al-'Arabiyya fi al-Dawla al-'Uthmaniyya" [The Unity of the Arabic Language in the Ottoman Empire], appeared on April 5, 1898, two months after the first issue of *al-Hoda* was published.
56 "Ila al-Lubnaniyyin fi al-Mahjar" [To the Lebanese in the New World], *Mir'at al-Gharb*, March 11, 1910, as quoted in Henri Melki, *al-Sahafa al-'Arabiyya*, pp. 191-195. The Maronite and Greek Orthodox communities in New York were in disagreement over the leadership of the Syro-Lebanese community in the city. This dispute was reflected in the two papers: the Maronites' *al-Hoda* and the Greek Orthodox *Mir'at al-Gharb*. It is, therefore, significant that al-Rihani used Mukarzal's rival paper to call for the unity of all Lebanese and support the political activity of Mukarzal.
57 See a pamphlet written by Ayyub Tabet: *Syria before the Peace Conference*, in MAE Paris, Vol. 46. The pamphlet explains that the Syrians, ethnically and culturally, are not Arabs, but rather of Aramaic descent. There is no mention of the Phoenicians. On the cooperation between al-Rihani and Tabet, see Tauber, *The Arab Movements in World War I,* p. 226.
58 Al-Rihani's famous essay on the French Revolution appeared in *al-Hoda* in 1902. See Henri Melki, *al-Sahafa al-'Arabiyya*, p. 58.

59 Tabet's article about the French Revolution can be found in Ra'if Khury, *Modern Arab Thought* (Princeton: Princeton University Press, 1983), pp. 295-208, translated by Ihsan 'Abbas from *al-Fikr al-'Arabi al-Hadith* (Beirut: Dar al-Makshuf, 1943).
60 The journal *Correspondance d'Orient*, No. 209 (March 15, 1919), quoted an article by Tabet that first appeared in *The Evening Sun*, January 8, 1919, stating that "despite the fact that the Syrians speak Arabic, they are almost exclusively from Aramaic, Phoenician, Greek or Roman descent. Part of the population is even from Frankish origins." Tabet expressed the same views about the *Lebanese* after the establishment of Greater Lebanon. See CZA S25 4549, Tuvia Arazi to Political Department April 8, 1945, a report of a meeting with Ayyub Tabet in which the latter elaborated about the Phoenician descent of the Lebanese and explained to Arazi why he did not need to know Arabic.
61 MAE Paris, Vol. 627, p. 4. Haut Commissaire to MAE January 12, 1934. Renseignement au sujet de Amin Rihani. The French authorities were about to deport al-Rihani from Lebanon, had it not been for his American citizenship and the intervention of the American consul in Beirut. This incident occurred following a lecture al-Rihani gave at the *Association de la solidarité littéraire* on December 23, 1933 where he vehemently attacked all the enemies of the Arab cause: the French mandate and its collaborators, the separatist movements in the Middle East and the religious establishments in Lebanon. The speech begins with the following sentence: "We have moved from the regime of Abdülhamid to the regime of the admirers of Ba'al [...]." The admirers of the Phoenician god were, of course, the Lebanese government.
62 Especially in *Qalb Lubnan* [The Heart of Lebanon], written around 1936, following a long trip al-Rihani took in Lebanon's countryside, but published for the first time in 1949, nine years after the author passed away.
63 *Al-Nakabat, aw khulasat Tarikh Suriyya Mundhu al-'Ahd al-Awwal ba'd al-Tufan ila 'Ahd al-Jumhuriyya bi Lubnan* [The Calamities, or a Summary of the History of Syria Since the Days of the Flood to the Era of the Republic of Lebanon] (Beirut: al-Matba'a al-'Ilmiya, 1928).
64 *Ibid*, pp. 58-59.
65 *Ibid*, pp. 6-7.
66 "Jabal al-Tajalli," in *al-Ma'rid*, July, 2, 1934. This article was reproduced in Amin al-Rihani, *Adab wa Fann* [Literature and Art] (Beirut: Dar Rihani lil-Tiba'a wa al-Nashr, 1957), pp. 94-99.
67 See in *La Montagne Inspirée*, p. 67-68.
68 Al-Rihani, *al-Ma'rid*, (July, 2, 1934), pp. 9-10.
69 Maria Eugenia Aubet, *The Phoenicians and the West*, p. 22-24.
70 *Qalb Lubnan*, p. 548.
71 *Ibid*, pp. 568-577.
72 *Qalb Lubnan*, p. 591.
73 See the interesting introduction to his travelogue, *Muluk al-'Arab* (Beirut, 1924), especially pp. 4-6, where he describes the process through which he re-discovered his Arab roots.
74 Al-Rihani mentions Thomas Carlyle, *Heroes and Hero-Worship*; and Washington Irving, *The Alhambra*.

75 Amin al-Rihani, *al-Rihaniyyat,* as quoted in, *Amin al-Rihani* (Beirut: Itihad al-Kutab al-Lubnaniyyin, 1988), p. 98.
76 *Ibid,* p. 92.
77 See, for example, al-Husri's response to a lecture Taha Hussein gave in Iraq in which he claimed that Egypt was culturally Pharaonic and not Arab. Hussein's lecture and Husri's reaction can be found in AD Nantes, carton 407, Lescuyer to MAE, December 9, 1938. Note de presse, December 12, 1938.
78 Sati' al-Husri, *Nushu' al-Fikra al-Qawmiyya* [The Evolution of National Thought] (Beirut: Matba'at al-risala, 1951), p. 268; see also Sati' al-Husri, *al-'Uruba, Bayna Du'atiha wa Mu'aradiha,* [Arabism between Its Advocates and its Opponents] (Beirut: Dar al-'Ilm lil-Malayin, 1951). This was an answer of al-Husri to a series of articles in *al-'Amal,* the Phalange journal: *Al-Wahda al-'Arabiyya Baynana wa Bayna Faylasufiha al-'Alama al-Husri* [Arab Unity between Us and Its Philosopher, the Savant al-Husri] July 23, to August 2, 1951.
79 Lammens, *La Syrie et son Importance Géographique* (Lourain, 1904).
80 Nujaym, in his book *La Question du Liban,* p. xi, p. 1, provides long lists of primarily French scholars who established this theory. Lammens was, of course, Belgian, but for all matters of convenience and in practice he was part of this group of French scholars.
81 According to Jamil Sawaya, one of the founders of the PPS and a friend of Sa'adeh, Sa'id 'Aql wrote the party's anthem set to the tune of *Deutschland Deutschland, über alles*; see Kemal H. Karpat (ed.), *Political and Social Thought in the Contemporary Middle East* (New York: Praeger, 1968), p. 100. Sa'adeh himself referred to 'Aql once in *al-Sira' al-Fikri fi al-Adab al-Suri* [The Intellectual Crisis in Syrian Literature], 2nd edition (Beirut, 1947), pp. 60-63. He criticized *Bint Yaftah,* the first long tragedy 'Aql wrote, as not Syrian enough. It seems that 'Aql himself tried to erase this part of his biography. He did not republish *Bint Yaftah,* which he wrote while a member of the PPS. See Yusuf al-Sumaily, *al-Shi'r al-Lubnani, Itijahat wa madhahib* [Lebanese Poetry, Directions and Schools] (Beirut, 1980), p. 124.
82 AD Nantes, carton 457, Meyrier to MAE, au sujet de PPS, July 10, 1936. Labaki is mentioned as the *ministre de la propagande* of the PPS; carton 943, Salah Labaki to the Haut Commissaire, March 2, 1936. In this letter Labaki calls on the High Commissioner to include Lebanon in a larger Syrian framework, because the Lebanese are tired of religious divisions. The majority of Lebanese would like to be back to "*la mère patrie*" — Syria.
83 See the minutes of the Conference and the closing statement in Hassan Hallaq, *Mu'tamar al-Sahil wa al-Aqdiya al-Arba'a,* especially pp. 46, 54, 68-70.
84 It should be recalled that both 'Aql and Labaki were non-Beiruti arabophones, two factors that made their cooperation with Sa'adeh easier. Although Sa'adeh did not consider language an essential ingredient in national consciousness, Arabic for him was the language the Syrians should speak. He hated the French and disliked the Lebanese francophiles, viewing them as collaborators with the colonizing power. See in Sa'adeh, *A'da' al-'Arab A'da' Lubnan* [The Enemies of the Arabs, the Enemies of Lebanon] (Beirut, 1954), p. 120, p. 171, p. 173.
85 *Ibid,* pp. 55-56.
86 Sa'adeh, *Kitab al-Ta'alim al-Suriyya al-Qawmiyya al-Ijtima'iyya* (Beirut, 1947).
87 *Ibid,* p. 17.

88 *Kitab al-Ta'alim*, p. 18. Translated by Karpat, *Political and Social Thought*, p. 60.
89 *Kitab al-Ta'alim*, p. 23. Scholars who wrote about Sa'adeh's ideology exaggerated their analysis of his dislike of the Arabs. It is true that he rejected the pan-Arab movement, but it is just as true that he recognized the role and importance of Arab culture in the composition of the Syrian nation.
90 *Kitab al-Ta'alim*, pp. 23-24.
91 *Ibid.*
92 Karpat, *Political and Social Thought*, p. 61.
93 Information on Bayhum is taken from Hassan Hallaq, *al-Mu'arikh al-'Alama Muhammad Jamil Bayhum* [The Historian and the Savant Muhammad Jamil Bayhum] (Beirut, 1980), and *Who's Who in Lebanon* (Beirut, 1963-1976).
94 The Ottoman College was a greenhouse for Beirut Arabists, as indeed was Bayhum. See Cleveland, *Islam against the West*, pp. 8-10.
95 *Al-'Uruba wa al-Shu'ubiyyat al-Haditha* (Beirut, 1957).
96 See Anwar al-Jundi, *al-Shu'ubiyya fi al-Adab al-'Arabi al-Hadith* [The-Shu'ubiyya in the Modern Arabic Literature] (Tripoli, Lebanon, 1987), p. 16, p. 68. Special place is given to Sa'id 'Aql as an Arch-*Shu'ubi*, pp. 204-209. For general information about the historical movement, see "Shu'ubiyya," *Encyclopaedia of Islam,* First Edition, p. 345.
97 Bayhum uses as an example the Syrian Jesuit teacher Louis Cheikho and his book, *Udaba al-Qarn al-Tasi' 'Ashar* [The Authors of the Nineteenth Century], in which no Muslim author is mentioned.
98 *Lubnan bayna Musharriq wa Mugharrib* [Lebanon between Eastern and Western Orientations] (Beirut, 1969), pp. 118-123.
99 Bayhum did not mention specific names but I assume he referred to the Phoenician literary group of Charles Corm and to the economic club of Michel Chiha and Gabriel Menassa, *"Les Nouveaux phéniciens."*
100 See *Lubnan bayna Musharriq wa Mugharrib*, especially pp. 17-18, where Bayhum refers to a debate about the Phoenicians he conducted with "my friend Charles Corm." See also on p. 42, about a disagreement he had with Na'um Mukarzal over the Zionist movement in Palestine.
101 See a recent use of this view in Hassan Hallaq, *Lubnan min al-Finiqiyya ila al-'Uruba* (Beirut: Dar al-Jami'iyya, 1993).
102 Bayhum, *Lubnan bayna Musharriq wa Mugharrib*, p. 19.

6

Chronicle of a Dream and Disillusionment

The ancient era is, undeniably, a source of legitimate pride. How could the Lebanese be indifferent to the fact that their predecessors on this land played a definitive role in the invention of the alphabet, for example, or in the founding of dozens of cities around the Mediterranean and the Atlantic? […] How could they forget, when they arrived in Europe, that this continent bears, according to the beliefs of the ancient Greeks, the name of a princess from Phoenicia?
But history, of course, does not stop in this glorious chapter. There was Alexander, Rome, then Byzance […] then came the Muslim conquest, that squarely brought the country into the sphere of Arab civilization. […] Lebanese from all faiths have been long considered the bearers of Arab culture.

Amin Maalouf[1]

The three decades between Lebanon's attainment of independence and the eruption of the civil war tell a chronicle of a dream and its disillusionment. The dream was the great promise of a pluralistic society, delicately balanced between its multifaceted members. It foretold a prosperous country distinctively different from others in the region that were plagued by social and political upheavals. But the disillusionment became evident as Lebanese society and state first frayed and then totally disintegrated. The "inter-sectarian balance" proved to be unstable and the "bridge between East and West" could not hold the internal and external socio-political tensions exerted on the newly independent society. For a while, though, the Lebanese dream did seem to be coming true, particularly in the 1950s-1960s. The Phoenician narrative was part of that dream, and for some time it also seemed to be coming into its own. Phoenicianism in the mid-20th century continued to develop along two different trajectories. One saw Christian ultra-nationalists continuing to express their vision of Lebanon as modern Phoenicia. Some, but by no means all, also couched their views in non-Arab terms. The other trajectory took Phoenician symbols and "language" into the national discourse of mainstream Lebanese elites. Simultaneously, opposition to the Phoenician ideal continued to exist mainly among Arab nationalists who opposed all forms of separatist tendencies within the Arab world, Lebanese nationalism included.

Beirut continued to be the center of Phoenician writing both in French and in Arabic. *Les cahiers de l'Est*, for example, first published in Beirut in 1945, followed the pattern of literary francophone journals such as *Phénicia* and *La Revue du Liban*. Its owner and editor, Camille Aboussouan, came from similar social and cultural circles to Michel Chiha and Charles Corm.[2] He opened his journal to a range of voices, from Phoenician Lebanists such as Chiha, Corm and Hector Klat to Arab nationalists such as Edmond Rabbath. Yet, as in other francophone journals, readers did not need to extrapolate much about the political and cultural orientation of *Les cahiers de l'Est*, which was unequivocally Western-oriented, adorned with Phoenician poems and essays.[3] Kamal Junblatt, who after 1958 would become one of the most outspoken Arab nationalists in Lebanon, was among the frequent contributors.[4] Even he elaborated freely in those pages about the 5,000 years of Lebanese history starting with the first Mediterranean navigators who invented the alphabet and carried it across the seas.[5] In 1949, the same year this article was written, Junblatt also founded the Progressive Socialist Party, which championed the idea of a secularized Lebanese state closely aligned with the Arab world. A scion of a feudal Druze family, Junblatt was associated with Beirut's haute-bourgeoisie, possibly as a result of his francophone education.[6] He therefore participated in their cultural enterprises, such as *Les cahiers*, and more importantly he took part in the activities of the *Cénacle libanais*, an intellectual and cultural Lebanese club, to be discussed below.[7]

Beirut also continued to produce Arabic writers who were fascinated by the Phoenician past of Lebanon and incorporated it into their essays, prose and poetry, although by no means were they labeled "Phoenicians." Roused by Corm's book of poetry, *La montagne inspireé*, a group of largely Muslim writers established in 1951 a literary association named *Usrat al-Jabal al-Mulham* [The Society of the Inspired Mountain]. Reflecting the mainstream path that Phoenician expressions began to acquire, this literary group believed that, on the one hand, Lebanese thought was tied to a Lebanese reality of multiple cultures reverting back to Greek, Roman and Latin civilizations and, on the other, Lebanon was also tied to the Arab reality and was an inseparable part of the Arab-Islamic civilization.[8]

Arguably, the two most notable examples of this school are Yusuf al-Khal and 'Ali Ahmad Sa'id, better known by his pen name, Adonis. Already in the 1940s, al-Khal stood out among the Arabic writers of Lebanon and in 1945, he published poems about the country's ancient Phoenician history.[9] The newspaper *l'Orient* stated that this young Lebanese poet should be praised for his poetry about the ancient glorious days of Lebanon, especially in face of the tendency to reject the preoccupation with Lebanon's most distinguished eras.[10] Similarly, 'Ali Ahmad Sa'id, by choosing the pen name Adonis, made an explicit statement that his sources of inspiration reached as far back as ancient Lebanon. Both al-Khal and Adonis viewed themselves as Arab poets, but at the same time they also regarded the entire history of Lebanon and the Middle East as their world of reference. It was an inevitable process that began with the writings of Sa'id 'Aql, Salah Labaki, Rushdi Ma'luf and others and extended to wider circles of Arabic writers. Many years later Adonis wrote in his semi-autobiography that as a young poet 'Aql was his major source of inspiration.[11] But unlike 'Aql, Adonis did not reject his Arab identity; he composed verses about the ancient Phoenicians, Greeks, Romans, and yes, also Arabs, and pointed to the contribution of these civilizations to the crystallization of a remarkable and unique Lebanese identity. As the founders and editors of the renowned literary journal *Shi'r*, the importance of Adonis and al-Khal in the literary circles of the Arab world was considerable. Their views about the region's history, as a source of their literary creation, were widely discussed by Arab social and political circles that had previously paid little heed to the ancient civilizations of the Middle East, including the Canaanite-Phoenicians. In his semi-autobiography, Adonis referred to three different poetic schools that prevailed in Beirut in the 1940s and 1950s. The first school focused on Arab nationalism and was marked by rigidity of the theme and the poetic structure. The second was Marxist Communist poetry. The third school was also preoccupied with nationalistic inclinations, but it read the Arab heritage differently, including therein the cultural inheritance of the Sumerian, Babylonian and Canaanite civilizations that preceded the Arabs. Thus, claimed Adonis, Arabism was interpreted differently by this school, unrelated to ethnicity or race but rather connected to language and culture; it fused into Arabism the ancient, non-Arab, civilizations of the Near East. This school did not view Arab civilization as a separate whole, existing unto itself, but rather as a continuation of a cultural heritage 5,000 years old, which needed to be acknowledged and eulogized.[12]

Biographically, Adonis was distant from the Phoenician circles of Corm, Chiha, Klat and Naccache. He was a Syrian 'Alawi who first arrived in Beirut in 1956. Unlike the others, he began studying French at a relatively old age. He was attracted to the PPS for its secular platform and its comprehensive interpretation of the region's history. He became an active member of the party and, for that reason, was arrested and jailed. Upon arriving in Beirut, he found a city that was engaged in numerous streams of politics and beliefs, one of which was devoted to the Phoenician past of Lebanon. The arabophone literary circles in the city embraced him and enabled his literary talent to flourish. Despite the fact that he chose the Phoenician god, Adonis, as his literary name, he was not a "Phoenician" like Corm and 'Aql, although he was often treated by Arab nationalists as if he were. The "republic of merchants" was not his main preoccupation as it was for Chiha and for the haute-bourgeoisie of Beirut for whom Phoenicianism was often tied to their commercial interests. Neither was Adonis part of the Maronite nationalism of the Mountain and its Phoenician manifestations as expressed by al-Saouda and 'Aql. Referencing the Canaanite-Phoenician past of Lebanon had deep cultural implications for him, emanating from his belief that today's civilization could only be understood in the light of five millennia of human experience. Beirut, accustomed to similar beliefs voiced by Antun Sa'adeh and his supporters or by Christian Lebanese nationalists, also had space for a cultural interpretation of the Phoenician past that did not negate the Arab component of the national identity of Lebanon.

With the exception of a "brief" civil war in 1958, which the Lebanese discounted as a "mishap," the 1950s-1960s appeared to be joyous times for Lebanon. Its reputation as the Switzerland of the Middle East and Beirut's as a Levantine version of the City of Lights seemed well justified. Indeed, the vision of Michel Chiha appeared to be fulfilled. In Beirut, one of the most important intellectual clubs, the *Cénacle libanais,* was advocating Chiha's "Idea of Lebanon"[13] as an open, liberal, Mediterranean society, with 6,000 years of history starting with its ancient inhabitants. Michel Asmar founded the Cénacle libanais to provide an intellectual forum that could "bring together every authentic Lebanese value, to make these values work together to rediscover the essence of our country that reaches back six millennia but whose identity has been hidden by long Ottoman rule and 25 years of Mandate."[14] A leading and honorary participant in the Cénacle, Michel Chiha and other Lebanese intellectuals, businessmen and economists, such as Gabriel Menassa, Henri Pharaon and Alfred Kettaneh, utilized this forum to promote a *laissez faire* economy and justified the country's recent economic success using Phoenician terminology. Dubbing themselves "The New Phoenicians," they claimed that Lebanese inherited their commercial talents from their ancient forefathers who were no less than the first entrepreneurs in human history.[15] This Beirut-based elite, of which Chiha was no doubt the most outstanding model, helped to establish both the "merchant republic of Lebanon" and, what concerns us, its image — inward as well as out. A cursory look at tourist books and photo albums of Lebanon in the 1950s-1960s, compiled by Lebanese and non-Lebanese alike, exposes unambiguously the image of Lebanon which this group communicated to the world.[16] Likewise, at the 1964-65 New York World's Fair Lebanon displayed itself in a manner suspiciously similar to its exhibition 25 years earlier at the 1939 Fair.[17] Charles Corm, who died a year earlier, would have been proud to see New-Phoenicia being displayed again in New York.

Perhaps there is no better event than the International Festival of Baalbeck that represents this image. From 1955 until the eruption of the civil war in 1975 the Baalbeck annual festival was the country's most important and celebrated cultural undertaking, depicting Lebanon as a beautiful postcard, steeped in wealth, benevolence and cosmopolitanism. Yet, an astute observer would also notice in the festival the "Lebanese paradox" of the era.[18] Whereas most of those patronizing the event traveled from Beirut in their luxurious cars, dressed in their best robes and embellished with their most expensive adornments, the residents of the town of Baalbeck, mostly Shi'is and overwhelmingly poor, were left out of the festivities. In order to facilitate the arrival of the bourgeoisie to the festival the Beirut-Baalbeck road was improved and paved. Thus, the festival, just like the wealth of Lebanon itself, was an exclusive event enjoyed mainly by the Beirut elite. The event was held in the temples of Jupiter and Bacchus at the archeological site of the ancient Roman city Heliopolis. There was nothing formally Phoenician in this festival. In fact, Arab singing, theater and dancing were an integral part of the festival's programs. Nevertheless, the cultural orientation which the organizers were trying to depict for Lebanon was transparent. The event was always divided into two sections, an international repertoire and a local, Lebanese one. And each year, the festival committee produced a magnificent program that was an event in and of itself.[19] The programs generally followed Michel Chiha's vision of Lebanon: pieces by Charles Corm, Sa'id 'Aql, Hector Klat, Elie Tyan, Georges Naccache, Adonis, the Mediterraneanist philosopher René Habachi, Umar Fakhuri, Fouad Abi Zayd and numerous others embellished these booklets, all unequivocally emphasizing the country's 5,000-year-old cultural mission, starting with the Phoenician endowment to humanity. Thus, Phoenician and Arab symbols coexisted side by side in the Baalbeck festivals, demonstrating the multifaceted nature of Lebanese society.

For those fortunate, affluent Lebanese who made the annual pilgrimage to the Baalbeck Festival, the Phoenician ideal became the symbol of the Lebanese success story. For Sélim Abou, then a young professor at USJ, Phoenicianism was a symbol of Lebanon's pluralism, of its liberal propensity and its triumph. In his 1962 book, *Le bilinguisme arabe-français au Liban*, Abou dedicated large segments of his work to explain the cultural meaning of the Phoenician ideal. Phoenicianism, he stated, was born as an affirmation of the spirit of the Lebanese people who, liberated from long years of servitude and reacquiring their self-consciousness, passionately collected the privileged moments of history where the traits of their personality lay. "Le Liban phénicien," for Abou:

> c'est d'abord la continuité selon laquelle le cadre géographique et historique a informé l'âme libanaise; c'est la multiplicité culturelle libanaise, reculée dans le temps jusqu'au point où elle trouve le principe de son unité dans l'image de cette race d'aventuriers, dont la vocation était l'échange et la rencontre, le don et l'accueil, la médiation sous toutes ses formes. Le paysage naturel développe des images de type explicatif, des métaphores: la montagne-creuset, la mer carrefour, la ville- phare, le village-foyer, etc. Le 'Liban phénicien,' c'est ensuite

l'appropriation subjective spontanée de la multiplicité originelle; c'est le sujet libanais, tel que la continuité à travers les siècles des mêmes gestes et des mêmes traditions l'a façonné, réceptacle de la dualité, toujours déchiré entre deux mondes qui sont deux manières d'être, et tirant de ce déchirement le contenu d'une affirmation de soi propre. Ici, le paysage naturel devient le lieu de transfert de la dualité, il entre lui-même dans une dialectique de l'opposition et de la synthèse: ce sont les couples — devenus classiques dans la littérature libanaise — de la montagne et de la mer, de la ville et du village, du couchant et de l'orient, de l'ombre et de la lumière, en tant qu'ils sont chargés d'une signification morale et spirituelle. Le 'Liban phénicien,' c'est enfin la dualité elle-même, comme structure de base de l'âme libanaise, de ses tendances et de ses appétits; c'est un dosage particulier de la sensorialité et de l'intelligence, du cœur et de la raison, dont l'antinomie subsistante tente sans cesse de se délivrer dans le mythe des métamorphoses, et en tous cas s'y exprime. Ici le paysage naturel, presque toujours présent, tend à la plasticité absolue. Il n'a plus de forme propre, mais celle qu'y insuffle l'idée ou la vision. C'est aussi à cette limite que la correspondance des écrivains libanais à leur paysage élémentaire délivre sa signification globale.[20]

Abou did not refer to the Phoenician past as a reflection of the ethnic, non-Arab origin of Lebanon, but rather as a demonstration of the country's cultural uniqueness and its multifaceted people. Writing from within the bastion of Christian Lebanon — USJ — Abou's writing reflected the view shared by many Christian intellectuals in the 1960s about the nature of Lebanon and its national identity. They believed that, give and take a few problems, their Lebanon was realizing itself, and the Phoenician heritage was an integral part of this realization. Christian writers produced a plethora of books about the land's history and identity, all focusing on Lebanon as a unique and pluralistic society whose characteristics, even as an Arab country, were partly a result of its Phoenician heritage.[21] This vision was not restricted to those at the Jesuit University but reached also the country's first (and last) public institute for higher education, the Lebanese University. Fouad Afram al-Bustani, a leading Christian intellectual who supported the separatist Christian vision of Lebanon, was the first president of the Lebanese University from its inception in 1951until 1970, and set its political and cultural orientation. The head of the Department of Philosophy, Kamal Yusuf al-Hajj, was another Christian intellectual who adamantly supported the vision of a Lebanese identity based on its Phoenician heritage.[22] Nor is there coincidence in the fact that, in 1966, when the university's Department of Geography began publishing a journal of Lebanese geography, it entitled it *Hannon*, a common name in ancient Carthage in general and, in particular, the name of the son the great Phoenician military commander Hannibal. If this was not blatant enough demonstration of the journal's political orientation, May Murr, a professor at the university and one of the most avid neo-Phoenicians from the 1960s to this day, wrote an introductory essay eulogizing the geographical determinism that molded the Lebanese identity from the Phoenician era to the formation of Greater Lebanon in 1920.[23]

As during the mandate years, fascination with the Phoenician past was not only expressed through literature and in academia. The Lebanese lira coin, for example, was decorated with a cedar tree and a Phoenician vessel. Lebanese journals and newspapers often dedicated articles to archeological discoveries of the country's ancient eras. In some cases even esoteric subjects related to the Phoenicians were published — a hairdresser who styled a Phoenician haircut[24] or a designer who produced Phoenician clothes.[25] More importantly, Lebanese artists, from sculptors to architects, used Phoenician symbols liberally in their work. The great basilica of Our Lady of Lebanon in Harissa is a case in point. Located just above the bay of Junieh, in the heartland of Maronite Lebanon, the statue of Mary and its shrine have served as a symbol of Christian presence and dominance in Lebanon since their construction in 1908. As a result of the popularity of the shrine it was decided in the 1960s to build a larger place of worship at the same location. In 1970, Pierre el-Khoury, one of Lebanon's most distinguished architects, designed a new basilica. He claimed his work was inspired by images of Phoenician triremes and the Lebanese cedar tree, the two primary emblems of Lebanese separatism.[26] In addition, sculptors and painters such as Halim al-Hajj, Aref Rayes, Omar Onsi and César Gemayel frequently drew on Phoenician symbols to create their art.[27]

By the 1960s, the generation of neo-Phoenicians who were first to express their vision of Lebanese nationalism in Phoenician terms had either reached old age or passed away. Michel Chiha died in 1954, Charles Corm in 1963. Hector Klat continued to publish poetry in *French*, eulogizing Lebanon until his death in 1973. Yusuf al-Saouda, meanwhile, kept publishing books in *Arabic* displaying his radical vision of Lebanon as neo-Phoenicia, utterly unrelated culturally and ethnically to its Arab neighbors; he died in 1971.[28] As recalled from Chapter II, from the time of the French mandate al-Saouda was persistent in his radical interpretation of Phoenicianism. It is no wonder, therefore, that during the civil war some Christian Lebanese who sought to totally disassociate themselves from their Arab-Muslim neighbors used his writings to base their claim for a non-Arab, if not anti-Arab, Lebanon.

Sai'd Aql reached the apex of his literary career in the 1960s. 'Aql pursued his linguistic enterprise, which he started in the 1940s, to turn colloquial Lebanese into the national language. He created his own 36 "'Aqlien letters," based on Latin characters with diacritic marks which he invented, and used this script to write and publish literary pieces in "Lebanese," beginning with the 1961 book of poetry, *Yara*.[29] Writing poetry in colloquial Lebanese was not novel, but 'Aql's venture had a clear political message. At the height of

Arab nationalism in general and Nasserism in particular, 'Aql dared to defy the most important pillar of Arab identity — Arabic language. "Arab linguistic unity, a concept made by political consideration, is an illusion,"[30] he stated. Literary Arabic, for him, was a dead language, whereas the Lebanese dialect was a living language, very different in grammar and syntax from Arabic. Not surprisingly, 'Aql's "language" caused a stir. Arab nationalists saw it as nothing less than an imperialist plot against Arab language and nations, whereas some Christian Lebanese, such as the Maronite historian Jawad Bulus, applauded it.[31] 'Aql continued this project through the 1960s. He translated Lebanese and foreign literary pieces to this language and founded a special publishing house for their printing and dissemination. On the eve of the civil war, 'Aql intended to launch a journal, entitled *Melkart* after the Carthaginian king, totally dedicated to his Lebanese language. However, because of the outbreak of the war, this journal did not materialize and 'Aql, along with so many compatriots, was plunged into the murky waters of war. Still, his linguistic venture reflected, and attempted to resolve, the long-time conflict between the idea of Lebanese separatist nationalism, on the one hand, and its linguistic manifestation, on the other. 'Aql, the "theoretician of Lebanism" tried to achieve this by presenting a Lebanese national language with its own sets of rules and historical, non-Arabic, roots. This enterprise remained marginal within Lebanese literary circles and it ultimately failed. In some manner, 'Aql's language and its demise represented in general the status of Lebanese exclusive nationalism, its intellectual manifestations and its limited circulation before 1975. In the 1960s, Lebanon as a society seemed to be turning away, politically and culturally, from separatist streams of thought. The regimes of President Fouad Chéhab and his successor Charles Helou seemed to find the golden path between Lebanon's belonging and attachment to its Arab neighbors and its inherent separatist tendencies. In such a political atmosphere, an exclusive historical narrative beginning with the ancient Phoenicians could subside or at least be used without its negative political weight, ready to be used again if and when the national identity and political orientation of Lebanon were to be challenged.

Clear signs of internal unrest in Lebanon began surfacing after the 1967 War. Palestinian military activities and Israeli retaliation exacerbated the delicate socio-political balance within Lebanese society. Not coincidentally, the reaction of some Christians to this challenge was to revive the discussion of the old, almost worn-out, debate over Lebanon's identity. In July 1969, amidst heavy clashes between Palestinian militias and the Lebanese army, a group of Christian intellectuals gathered in a restaurant on the outskirts of Bikfaya, the Phalange stronghold, to establish an "Association for the Revival of the Phoenician Heritage in Lebanon." They drafted a platform and an agenda aimed at revitalizing interest in the ancient Phoenicians in order to remind the Lebanese who they were and what their national and cultural legacy was.[32] I suspect that none of their "revival" projects was accomplished. But more importantly, this association reflects the role Phoenicianism played in the political struggle that began storming Lebanon in the late 1960s. As had happened before, once the character of Lebanon was threatened, Phoenicianism was taken "out of the attic" and reused to put Lebanon back on the right track, at least in the eyes of the beholder.

If pluralism and cosmopolitanism dominated the Christian national discourse in the 1950s and 1960s, then by the early 1970s separatism and seclusion prevailed. By then, Université Saint Esprit de Kaslik (USEK), founded in 1950 by the Lebanese Maronite Order, evolved to be a prime center of Christian Lebanese national thinking and writing. Etienne Saqre, the Rector from 1968-1974, was one of the key advocates of the political and cultural orientation of the university. As of the late 1960s until the Civil War broke out, USEK initiated the publication of several works focusing on Lebanon's national identity and the meaning of Lebanism.[33]

The Civil War radicalized all aspects of local life. Consequently, it also exacerbated the process of reconstruction of communal boundaries within Lebanese society. This process, which is ceaseless and an inseparable part of human experience in general, is often intensified in cases of internal and external violent struggles. Thus, to a large extent the Lebanese civil war evolved to be a war over the redefinitions of the Lebanese collective identities. Previously, Lebanese intellectuals could speak about their country as a culturally pluralistic society, recognizing therein its multiple members. However, after the outbreak of the war, this language was replaced by terminology of absolutism of identities and communal boundaries. Thus, teachers at USEK and other Christian intellectuals, such as Bulus, Malik, al-Bustani, Honein and 'Aql who, before the war, regarded the Phoenician past as the foundation of pluralistic Lebanon and wished to use it as the historical common denominator for all Lebanese, drastically changed their views. Some of them became aligned with the Lebanese Forces. They became their leading ideologues and took on the belligerent tone of the Christian camp with historical deterministic justifications.[34] Kaslik became a hothouse for their views, which rendered the Phoenician claims as one of their prime arguments for the existence of Christian Lebanese nationalism, thoroughly different from the Arab-Muslim population of Lebanon, let alone the Palestinian refugees. Not coincidentally, Maronite clergymen led this move. Etienne Saqre established the Guardians of the Cedars in 1976, and very aggressively advocated the Phoenician historical narrative as a solely Christian ideology.[35] One of the prime works that made similar claims was written by another Maronite priest, Butrus Daw. From 1977-1981 Daw published his weighty work, *Tarikh al-Mawarina*, emphasizing the uninterrupted history of the Maronites in Lebanon.[36] He dedicated sections of his work to demonstrate the autochthonous nature of the ancient inhabitants of Lebanon — the Phoenicians — who, according to him, had converted to Christianity by the 4th century and a century later joined the Maronite Church. His writing reflected Christian nationalism during the civil war at its peak. Lebanon, for him, was an outright Christian, non-Arab entity. The history of the Maronites was portrayed as a constant struggle against foreign occupiers, defending their national rights. Other Maronite clergymen wrote in a similar tone about the Maronite identity and the meaning of Lebanism.[37] More than anything else, these views demonstrated that Phoenicianism found its place anew within the valleys and summits of Mount Lebanon. The vision of Lebanon, as advocated by Daw and other Christian intellectuals who congregated around Kaslik, differed from that of Chiha and the haute-bourgeoisie in Beirut. In a way, Phoenicianism made its way up to the Mountain after long years of residence in Beirut. The Mountain and its image of a closed, conservative and obstinate society dominated the Christian discourse during the long fifteen years of civil war. As is well known, there was no one Christian discourse during the war. Christian sects, like other sects in Lebanon, were often internally divided on political, familial, geographical and even ideological lines. Intra-communal divisions have always been a prime factor in Lebanese society, as have inter-communal rivalries. However, the idea of a unique Christian experience in Lebanon was shared by the majority of the Maronite and other Catholics sects. USEK, the Maronite Patriarchate and especially the Maronite Order, and the Lebanese Forces supported to a large extent the Christian vision of Lebanon as a separate entity with a historical narrative starting with the ancient Phoenicians.

The Civil War terminated with the ultimate collapse of Christian Lebanese nationalism. In fact, in hindsight, one could say that this Christian nationalism sealed its fate already in 1920 with the formation of Greater Lebanon and the annexation of non-Christian areas to the fledgling political entity. It took, however, seventy more years before it weakened to the point of insignificance. The Ta'if Accord (1989) not only brought the conclusion of the war but also marginalized the socio-political forces within Lebanese society that advocated for a distinct, non-Arab identity. Moreover, the text of the accord begins and ends with assertions of the Arab-ness of Lebanon, implicitly declaring that after lengthy years of civil war, Arabism triumphed and non-Arab tendencies were defeated. The dominance of Syria in Lebanon and the rise of Hizballah as a powerful political and social force only add to this sense of victory. Hizballah, as an Islamist movement, defies in principle non-Islamic historical narratives and could by no means accept any sort of discussion over a Phoenician heritage. There is no doubt that the dominance of both Hizballah and Syria in Lebanon since the early 1990s created an atmosphere which encourages alignment with Arab-Islamic stances and suppresses other narratives.

In defiance of Syria's dominance and its Lebanese allies, supporters of Michel 'Aoun, the symbol of Lebanese Christian ultra-nationalists since 1990, have used the Phoenician narrative to support their political demands for the evacuation of Syrian forces from Lebanon and for an annulment of the Ta'if

Accord.³⁸ Similarly, when Pope John Paul II visited Lebanon in May 1997, his hosts, led by the highest echelons of the Maronite clergy, used the most visual Phoenician symbol to assert Christian presence in Lebanon. The Pope gave a mass in front of hundreds of thousands Christian believers at Our Lady of Lebanon Basilica at Harissa. On stage, behind the seat of the Pope, the producers of the event constructed a large Phoenician vessel made out of red and yellow flowers. Yellow represented the colors of the Vatican, whereas red was the color that endowed the Phoenicians with their Greek appellation. In front of the highest Lebanese dignitaries and in the presence of the Maronite patriarch, Nasrallah Butrus Sfeir, the event sent a message of Maronite defiance in the face of the post-civil war political reality.³⁹

The marginalization of the separatist Christian political forces meant their radical interpretation of the history of Lebanon was sidelined too. Yet, the preoccupation with the ancient past of the land is far from ebbing. In Beirut "classic" Phoenician texts continue to be published: Ernest Renan's *Mission de Phénicie* was reprinted by Editions terre du Liban in 1998; in 1996 Dar al-Nahar reissued *La revue phénicienne* and *Phénicia*; and a biography of Charles Corm was published in 1995 by the still active *Éditions de la revue phénicienne*.⁴⁰ In addition, in Lebanese immigrant communities across the world Phoenicianism continues to flourish even more than in the homeland.⁴¹ It is much easier today to express unpopular views, such as adherence to Phoenicianism, outside of Lebanon than inside. As in the early 20th century, Christian Lebanese diasporas that wish to hold on to their Lebanese identity tend cling to Phoenicianism. There are far more Christian Lebanese residing outside of Lebanon today than there are at home. The Lebanon they left no longer exists, at least not as they imagine it. What is left for them is to romanticize over the imagined identity of Lebanon and its equally-imagined desired future. The Phoenician narrative offers a romantic and nostalgic past, a tool to challenge the present and a wishful vision for the future.

The ancient Phoenicians remain in the Lebanese national psyche simply because they constitute an inseparable — and celebrated — chapter of the chronicles of the land. To understand this, one need go only as far as the post-war-renovated National Museum in Beirut, which focuses mainly on the Phoenician, Greek and Roman eras and leaves a very small portion to Arab and Islamic art. In addition, since 1993, following the major reconstruction of Beirut, the central district has become the largest excavation site in the world, unearthing the city's multiple archeological layers including its Canaanite-Phoenician precursor, Be'erot.⁴² Lebanese can now view, up close, the first civilizations that built and settled their capital. Lebanese Prime Minister Rafiq al-Hariri's firm, Solidere, in charge of the reconstruction work, has financed large parts of the excavations. He decided to name the part of the project underway in the impoverished Shi'i neighborhoods of south Beirut Elisar, after the Phoenician queen who, legend has it, fled Tyre to establish Carthage.⁴³

As the slogan accompanying the gentrification project — "Beirut, the Ancient City of the Future" — indicates, its vision is future-oriented, of course, but it is rooted in the past, recovering the rich patrimony which the land's ancient inhabitants bequeathed to the modern Lebanese. Arabs by culture, Arabs by language, but Lebanese through the unique history of the land on which they reside as a less than cohesive national community.

References

1 *Liban: l'Autre Rive* (Paris: Institut du Monde Arabe, 1999), pp. 14-15.
2 Born in Beirut in 1919, Camille Aboussouan acquired his education in the Lazarist college in 'Aintoura and at USJ, becoming a devout francophone and a strong advocate of the Phoenician identity in post-mandatory Lebanon. See, for example, his *ex-libris*, a drawing of Europa carried by Zeus, in *The Library of Camille Aboussouan* (London: Sotheby's, 1993), p. 12.
3 See, for example, Bishara Tabbah, "Rôle de Béryte dans le fixation du 'Corpus Juris' romain," 1 (1945); Elie Tyane, "Poème du Liban," 2 (1945); Yusuf al-Saouda, "Colonies libanaises, émigration et immigration," 3 (1945); Charles Corm, "La symphonie de la lumière," 4 (1945), pp. 57-77; Said 'Aql, "Les fondements historiques d'un humanisme libanais, le Liban et l'homme," 4 (1945); Nagib Dahdah, "Évolution de la nation libanaise," 5 (1945).
4 See, for example, Kamal Jimblatt [sic.], *Démocratie nouvelle* no. 3, 1 series (1945), p. 7; *La démocratie mondiale et la paix*, no. 1, 2 series (1947), p. 7; *Visage moral des druzes*, n. 4-5, 2 series (1949), p. 158.
5 Kamal Jimblatt, *Le Liban et le monde arabe*," no. 6, 2 series (1949), p. 86.
6 Junblatt completed his secondary education at the Lazarist College in 'Aintoura in 1937. He then traveled to the Sorbonne in Paris to study law. When World War II broke out he returned to Lebanon and obtained his law degree from USJ. See in Farid al-Khazen, Kamal Jumblatt, "The Uncrowned Druze Prince of the Left," *Middle Eastern Studies,* Vol. 24, No. 2 (April 1988), p. 179, especially note 4.
7 Kamal Junblatt, *La Démocratie Économique* (Beirut: Cénacle libanais, 1950); *La Démocratie Sociale* (Beirut: Cénacle libanais, 1953).
8 Riad Fakhuri, " Lubnan: al-Jam'iyyat al-Adabiyya min al-In'izaliyya ila al-Taqaddumiyya," [Lebanon: The Cultural Associations from Isolationsim to Progressivism,, *Al-Sayad,* April 25-May 2 (1974), p. 66.
9 Yusuf al-Khal, *Al-A'amal al-Shi'iriyya al-Kamila, 1938-1968* [The Complete Works of Poetry] (Beirut: 1973), pp. 71-116, especially the poems "Lubnan" [Lebanon], "Biladi" [My Country], and "Shu'a' al-Gharb" .The Ray of the West]. These were originally published in al-Khal's first book of poetry, *al-Hurriya* [Freedom] (Beirut: Dar al-Kitab, 1944).
10 *L'Orient,* May 20, 1945.
11 Adonis, *Ha Anta Ayyuha al-Waqt* [You there, O Time], (Beirut: Dar al-Adab, 1993), pp. 25-26.
12 *Ibid*, pp. 99-102; see also Shemuel Moreh, "Ha-Zeramim ha-Ra'ayoniyyim ba-Shirah ha-'Aravit ha-Modernit," [Ideological Trends in Modern Arab Poetry], *Hamizrah Hehadash,* 19(1969), pp. 31-49.

13 Nadim Shehadi, *The Idea of Lebanon: Economy and State in the Cénacle libanais, 1946-1954* (Oxford: Centre for Lebanese Studies, 1987).
14 *Ibid*, p. 14.
15 Carolyn L. Gates, *The Merchant Republic of Lebanon* (London: Centre for Lebanese Studies and I. B. Tauris, 1998), p. 82.
16 See, for example, Colin, Thubron, *The Hills of Adonis* (London: Heinemann, 1968); Robert Boulanger, *Lebanon* (Paris: Hachette, 1955).
17 http://peace.expoarchive.com/6465/international/intpav25.shtml
18 Annie Tohme, "Le Festival de Baalbek au carrefour des paradoxes libanais d'avant guerre," in Hélène Sader et al. (eds.), *Baalbek: Image and Monument; 1898-1998* (Stuttgart: Steiner, 1998), p. 221.
19 See the different programs of the Baalbeck Festival. See also *Les Riches Heures du Festival* (Beirut: Dar al-Nahar, 1998).
20 Sélim Abou, *Le Bilinguisme Arabe-Français au Liban*, pp. 421-422.
21 See, for example, the works of Jawad Bulus, *Tarikh Lubnan* [The History of Lebanon] (Beirut: Dar al-Nahar, 1972); *Les Peuples et les Civilisations du Proche-Orient,* especially Vol. 1-2 (Paris: Mouton & Cie, 1961-1968); Jean Salem, *Le peuple libanais* (Beirut: Librairie Smir, 1968). See also the Sunni historian 'Adil Isma'il, *Le Liban; histoire d'un people* (Beirut: Dar al-Makchouf, 1965).
22 Kamal Yusuf al-Hajj, *Mujaz al-Falsafa al-Lubnaniyya* [The Concise Philosophy of Lebanon] (Juniyah: Matabi' al-Karim al-Hadithah, 1974), especially pp. 129-166; al-Hajj, *al-Falsafa al-Lubnaniyya al-Haditha: Muhadara* [The Modern Philosophy of Lebanon: A Lecture] (Beirut: Manshurat Dar al-Intilaq, 1964).
23 May Murr, "Réflexions sur le géographie du Liban," *Hannon*, Vol. 1(1966).
24 *Al-Hawadith*, October 26, 1979.
25 *Al-Sayyad*, July 27-August 3, 1972.
26 See the brochure, Our Lady of Lebanon Shrine, year 2000. See also Pierre el-Khoury, *Pierre el-Khoury architecture, 1959-1999* (Beirut, Paris: Dar el-Nahar and Moniteur, 2000), pp. 52-65.
27 See photos of their work and others in Edouard Lahoud, *L'Art Contemporain au Liban*.
28 See, for example, his *Tarikh Lubnan al-Hadari* (Beirut: Dar al-Nahar, 1972).
29 *Yara* (Beirut: Maktabat Antoine, 1961).
30 *Al-Jarida*, March 5, 1961. Quoted in Simon Jargy, "Vers une révolution dans les lettres arabesø" *Orient,* Vol. V, no. 17 (1961), p. 311.
31 *Ibid*, p. 94.
32 *Al-Hayyat*, July 9, 1969; August 6, 1969.
33 *Ab'ad al-Qawmiyya al-Lubnaniyya* [Lebanese National Dimensions] (Kaslik: Jami'at al-Ruh al-Qadis, 1970); *Al-Baramij al-Lubnaniyya wa al-Tanshi'a al-Wataniyya* [Lebanese Programs and National Development] (Kaslik: Jami'at al-Ruh al-Qadis, 1971); Joseph Mouwanès, *Les Éléments Structuraux de la Personnalité Libanaise* (Kaslik: Bibilothèque de l'Université Saint-Esprit, 1973).
34 Walid Phares, *The Rise and Fall of Christian Lebanese Nationalism*, p. 110. See also Edward Hunein, 'Ala Durub Lubnan [About the Paths of Lebanon] (Kaslik, 1979); Fouad Afram al-Bustani, *Mawaqif Lubnaniyya* [Lebanese Positions] (Beirut: Manshurat al-Da'ira, 1982); "Al-Muqawama al-Lubnaniyya fi Shi'r Sa'id 'Aql," [Lebanese Resistance in the Poetry of Sa'id 'Aql], *Al-Masira,* 27 (April 25, 1983), pp. 42-43.

35 *Al-Masira* (April 13, 1984), pp. 16-19.
36 Butrus Daw, *Tarikh al-Mawarina* [History of the Maronites] (Beirut: Dar al-Nahar, 1977-1981).
37 See, for example, Michel 'Uwayyet, Al-Mawarina: Min Hum wa-Madha Yuridun? [The Maronites: Who are they and what do they want?] (Juniyeh 1987);
38 See the website of the Free Patriotic Movement of the supporters of General Michel 'Aoun, http://www.lebanon-world.org. See also the websites of the banned Lebanese Forces and note their obsessive preoccupation with the Phoenician past: http://www.lebaneseforces.org; http://www.lebanese-forces.org.
39 *La Revue du Liban,* 1945 (May 17-24, 1997), on-line edition. See also pictures of the Phoenician vessel in the same article.
40 Jamil Jabar, *Sharl al-Qurm, Sha'ir al-Jabal al-Mulham* [Charles Corm, the Poet of the Inspired Mountain] (Beirut: Éditions de la Revue Phénicienne, 1995).
41 See some examples of Lebanese immigrants' fascination with the Phoenicians: John G. Moses, *How the Lebanese Advanced Civilization* (New York: Published by the author, 1998). Peter Wadih Tayah, *The Maronites: Roots and Identity* (Miami: Bet Moroon Publishers, 1987). Jim McKay, *Phoenicia Farewell: Three Generations of Lebanese Christians in Australia* (Melbourne: Ashwood House Academic, 1989).
42 Nasser Rabbat, "The Interplay of History and Archeology in Beirut," in Peter Rowe and Hashim Sarkis (eds.), *Projecting Beirut* (Munich: Prestel, 1998), p. 20.
43 Mona Harb el-Kak, "Transforming the Site of Dereliction into the Urban Culture of Modernity: Beirut's Southern Suburb and Elisar Project," in *Ibid*, p. 176.

Conclusion

"Of all cults," wrote Ernest Renan in his classic text *Qu'est-ce qu'une nation?*, "that of the ancestors is the most legitimate, for the ancestors have made us what we are. A heroic past, great men, glory, this is the social capital upon which one bases a national idea."

For Renan, shared language, religion, customs and geography may be important ingredients for the formation of a nation, but they are, by far, exceeded by the ultimate and most important element of national consciousness which is "the fact of sharing, in the past, a glorious heritage and regrets, and of having, in the future, [a shared] program to put into effect, or the fact of having suffered, enjoyed and hoped together."[1] Yet, for Renan, by no means does this past require an absolute or impeccable historical veracity. Forgetting the actual past and reconstructing anew a historical narrative, drawing even on historical errors, is an inseparable part of the process of the creation of a nation. Only someone like Renan could have the courage — and the audacity — to proclaim in the Sorbonne, one of France's most sacred intellectual shrines, such words of heresy against the eternal existence and perennial genuineness of the nation.

Following Renan, it would not be an exaggeration to say that all national communities have deliberately forgotten parts of their history and have overstated or even fabricated other parts in the process of their national creation. "The cult of the ancestors," as Renan vividly put it, is that which facilitates the formation and maintenance of any nation, and grants its members a sense of belonging, allowing them to imagine themselves as part of a historical collective rooted in a common and imposing past, and headed towards a shared and auspicious future. The Middle East in general, and Lebanon in particular, are no exception to this worldwide universal phenomenon.

Phoenicianism was born as an attempt of a few intellectual Syro-Lebanese to provide the wares of the "cult of the ancestors" in Syria and Lebanon at least two decades before Arab nationalism became a challenging force in the Middle East. World War I was the time when Phoenician expressions began to be associated solely with Christians in Syria and Lebanon, and by its end the entire movement for the formation of Greater Lebanon had been labeled Phoenician. In 1920, there may have been a Lebanese state but a Lebanese nation had not yet emerged. Lebanon may have had a body but, using Renan's metaphor, it still lacked a unifying soul for its inhabitants. At first, Phoenicianism served as the "cult of the ancestors" for the majority of the Christian population in Mount Lebanon and in Beirut, and it only provoked the Muslim population which was coerced into this newly founded political entity. Yet within two decades, independent Greater Lebanon became a reality even for the Muslim population which, led by Beirut's Sunni upper class, acquiesced to its existence. The "cult of the ancestors" did not cease; it only changed course. Phoenicianism as *the* national, non-Arab, identity of Lebanon continued to be articulated by a select group of Christians in Beirut and in the Mountain. But at the same time, Phoenicianism for many non-Christians evolved to denote the history of the *land* no less than the history of its people. Some Muslim Lebanese who agreed with Lebanon's independent existence, justified by its distinct national — yet Arab — features, were willing to incorporate the Phoenician past into their national narrative because, after all, the ancient Phoenicians did dwell in the *land* and the history of Lebanon, as the history of any other nation with self-pride, does begin in antiquity. And if one wanted to scrutinize the people and not only the land, than it could be easily proved that the Phoenicians, who, according to Arab nationalists, undoubtedly came from Arabia, were actually of Arab descent. Thus, by the 1950s and 1960s two kinds of Phoenicianism existed and were thriving side by side. One was the "cult of the ancestors," as articulated by intellectuals from Beirut who regarded the ancient Phoenicians as the forefathers of cosmopolitan, liberal, open-minded Lebanon. The second was embedded in the ideology of Christian Lebanese nationalism that continued to view Lebanon as a Christian non-Arab bastion — a neo-Phoenicia — in a predominantly Arab-Muslim region. In 1975, this kind of Phoenicianism became the dominant ideology. The civil war radicalized all streams of thought and as a result liberal Lebanon subsided, clearing the arena for radicals of all sorts.

There is no doubt that the French assisted in all possible means to disseminate Phoenicianism in Lebanon; many Lebanese critics of the Phoenician identity have bitterly noted this fact. Yet, it should be asked if, in an era of national imagining, the Lebanese national movement actually needed the French to come up with their own "cult of the ancestors" or was it an inevitable process that would have occurred with or without French guidance? As we have seen, the first local signs of interest in the ancient Phoenicians began before France dominated education in Lebanon and before the Jesuits took control of the country. The ancient Phoenicians were there for the Lebanese (and the Syrian) national movement to be reclaimed from the abyss of historical oblivion and to be used, just as were the Gauls for the French, the Saxons for the English, the Pharaohs for the Egyptians, the Babylonians for the Iraqis, and the Assyrians for the Syrians. As Renan, followed by numerous scholars of nationalism, explained, the spirit of nationalism is constituted by the past and the present, the past being "the common possession of a rich legacy of memories." Looking at the past, any national movement would have taken the ancient Phoenicians, who created one of the most impressive civilizations in the Near East, and incorporated them into its rich legacy of memories; and it is entirely irrelevant whether these memories were fabricated, as long as they were well-imagined.

More than a movement, a party or an ideology, Phoenicianism developed as a state of mind in the Lebanese national idea. It had leading thinkers and scores of followers, but it did not develop as a systematic worldview with a clear agenda. It was often exploited politically to mobilize certain groups into political action. Yet culturally Phoenicianism had very little impact on Lebanese society. Charles Corm named his second son Hiram, after the famous Tyrian king, and truly believed that he, Charles, slept, ate, laughed, wrote, did business and made love in the same spirit as his Phoenician ancestors. Yet there were very few Lebanese, even passionate Phoenicians, who took this identity as seriously as did Corm. There were a few "Phoenician" street names in Beirut, and when Corm died a street in the Achrafiyyeh neighborhood was named after him.[2] Phoenician poetry, prose, painting and sculpture have been produced since 1920 to this day, but, with the exception of the 1930s and the 1960s, it remained marginal within the general artistic production of the country. Phoenicianism, then, remained a cult of the *past* but it had little impact on modern Lebanon's cultural *present*.

* * *

In 1988, when the cannons were still roaring and Lebanese were killing each other in horrendous numbers, Kamal Salibi published his soul-searching book *A House of Many Mansions*. In his conclusion, he wrote a statement antithetical to Renan's view regarding the role of fabricated history in national formation. "For any people to develop and maintain a sense of political community," Salibi wrote, "it is necessary that they share a common vision of their past."[3] For communities with natural solidarity, Salibi continued, fictionalized history can suffice for this purpose. However, such self-deception can only work in communities confident of their unity and solidarity. Divided societies cannot afford this imaginary luxury. To achieve solidarity these societies must "know and understand the full truth of the past." Lebanon, Salibi concludes, is a case in point. As a politically divided society, Lebanon is condemned to know and understand its past, if it seeks to survive. No political settlement could last unless Lebanon came to terms with its history and adjusted to its veracities. The Lebanese had to know exactly who they were, why and how they came to be Lebanese. Otherwise they would continue to be so many tribes and fail to overcome the cleavages that tear their society apart.

If the positivist vision of history "as it actually was," is left aside, what radiates from Salibi's words is an engaging statement that argues succinctly that Lebanon needs to reevaluate its history in order to survive as a national community. And so, in *A House of Many Mansions*, Salibi, who, prior to 1975, was one of the prime historians to provide the Lebanese with their [false?] national history, deconstructs this historiography, which he himself helped to construct, and offers a new evaluation of the most important foundation myths of Lebanon. He disputes the myth of the Emirate as the precursor of modern Lebanon; he challenges the view of the Maronite community as a (Christian) rose among (Muslim) thorns; he contests the theories of the Mountain as a refuge for minorities and as a distinct autonomous region within the Ottoman Empire; and, finally, he also critically analyzes the phenomenon of Phoenicianism in Lebanon, charging it as one of the most faulty and historically groundless ideas conceived in Lebanon.

Can Lebanese today follow Salibi's appeal and agree on a common history that would reflect their desire to live in a cohesive national community? After all, as Salibi himself remarked at the beginning of his book, paradoxically, Lebanese of all sects came out of the war with "a strong sense of common identity, albeit with some different nuances."[4] According to Salibi, the construction of a common history is possible if, on the one hand, Christian Lebanese reconcile with the Arab identity of Lebanon and, on the other, Muslim Lebanese explain this identity in terms that do not alienate their Christian compatriots, i.e., clearly separating between Arab and Muslim histories. What Salibi fails to say is that one of the major reasons for the fighting during the war was Lebanon's identity. Thus, before reaching the point of drafting an "accurate" common history for Lebanon, one first has to reconcile with the war and its reasons, one of which was the disagreement over the "identity" of Lebanon and its place within the Arab regional system. Unfortunately, discussion of the war in today's Lebanon is regarded as beyond the limits of politesse. Even language itself has been manipulated to avoid a direct reckoning with the past. When Lebanese mention the civil war at all, many refer to it as "the events," or "the war of the others." Thus, the tenth anniversary of the end of the war — an opportunity for evaluation of this horrendous war and its consequences — passed almost unmentioned in Lebanon.

Since Kamal Salibi published his book in 1988, Lebanese historians have worked tirelessly to reconstruct the history of Lebanon "as it actually was," at least in their eyes.[5] Old habits die hard and indeed narratives are being removed from history books only to be replaced by new ones, truth-telling according to their writers and fictitious according to others. There is no better arena that reflects the complexity of the issue than the Lebanese state education system. In an attempt to construct an accepted unified historical narrative, the 1989 Ta'if Accord itself stipulated that "the curricula shall be reviewed and developed in a manner that strengthens national belonging, fusion, spiritual and cultural openness, and that unifies textbooks on the subjects of history and national education." In accordance with this clause, the Educational Center for Research and Development initiated the composition of a new unified history textbook. The plans for the publication of the book have caused a stir. Lebanese educators have objected to the process of compiling the unified history book, which they said would ignore much of the country's history out of fear of offending sectarian sensitivities. The same Educational Center is also in charge of supervising textbooks used in state schools. In October 2001, it decided to remove a page from an academic history book, *A Window to the Past*, taught to public school students in the third grade. The president of the Center, Nimr Freiha, also froze the teaching of the lesson until the book was amended the following year. This act followed a series of allegations from politicians who accused the authors of comparing the Arab conquest to invasion and occupation. Beirut Member of Parliament, Bassem Yammout, stated that the authors disregarded Lebanon's Arab identity. He complained of a sentence that reads: "They all went, and Lebanon stayed," in reference to Arabs being an occupying power that passed through Lebanon. "It is true that Lebanon stayed," Yammout added, "but it remained an Arab country ... a feature that is prevalent today and stressed in the Taif Accord."[6] These examples demonstrate that, unfortunately, not much has changed in this sphere in Lebanon. Back in the 1930s the Ministry of Education made a similar attempt by initiating the writing of a unified historical textbook. The book, written by Asad Rustum and Fouad Afram al-Bustani, analyzed in Chapter III, evoked a public stir and ultimately failed to provide Lebanon with a historical narrative accepted by all.

The attempt to compose a unified narrative that would satisfy all parties in Lebanon is probably doomed to fail, but more importantly, this initiative and the reactions it drew reflect the complexity of reconciliation in post-war Lebanon and the role that is attributed to the history of Lebanon in this process. This was already understood by the drafters of the Ta'if accord. They were aware of the fact that to a large extent the civil war was a battle over Lebanon's identity and its place within the Arab sphere. The accord, therefore, starts and concludes with the following statements: "Lebanon is Arab in belonging and identity," and "Lebanon, with its Arab identity is tied to all the Arab countries by true fraternal relations." The accord is indeed the first official document that bluntly states the national identity of Lebanon. But the preoccupation with the Arabism of Lebanon in the Ta'if Accord is so intense that a reader of the document may wonder if, by insisting on its Arab-ness, the drafters of the accord actually emphasized the fact that for not a small number of Lebanese the identity of their country is not crystal clear. There is no doubt that the accord merits high praise for ending violence in Lebanon, but there is also no doubt that it did not establish any mechanism for reconciliation. Its treatment of the history and of the identity of Lebanon has not yet unearthed the reasons for the long fifteen years of Lebanese internal destruction.

Lebanese have been preoccupied with their national identity since the formation of Greater Lebanon in 1920. From Muhammad Jamil Bayhum's *'Urubat Lubnan* to Hassan Hallaq, *Min al-Finiqiyya ila al-'Uruba* and from Yusuf al-Saouda's *Istiqlal Lubnan fi al-Tarikh* to Sa'id 'Aql's recent *Sagesse de Phénicie*, the subject does not leave the forefront of the public sphere. An example of this preoccupation is a recent exhibition entitled *Liban l'Autre Rive* presented at the Institut du Monde Arabe in Paris from October 1998 to May 1999. The exhibition recounted the story of Lebanon from pre-history to modernity, drawing on its very rich annals. Conceived and realized by the Institut du Monde Arabe and the Lebanese General Office of Antiquities, the exhibition manifested the assertion (mixed with hope) that Lebanon has been resurrected from the ashes of the civil war that tore its society apart. Notions of assurance and optimism are interlaced in the texts of the exhibition catalogue, recognizing the multifarious nature of the history and society of Lebanon. Thus, the Minister of Culture and Higher Education, Faouzi Hobeiche, opened the catalogue asserting Lebanon's attachment to its Arab-ness and at the same time acknowledging its rich historical patrimony as manifested in the archeological richness of the country. From the invention of the first linear alphabet to the Arab cultural renaissance, the patrimony of Lebanon, Hobeiche wrote, is presented in this exhibition. The celebrated francophone author Amin Maalouf also wrote an introductory essay for the catalogue. From the first sentence he acknowledged the fact that the exhibition is in fact a manifestation of Lebanon's national identity, as reflected from its rich history. Countries, like people, Maalouf wrote, are often troubled by their identity, especially when they experience dire crises that put into question their very existence. How did they come to be, one day, a separate entity, they ask? What distinguishes them from close as well as distant countries? Some people, Maalouf continued, look for the most simplistic answer: it is this or that religion, this or that language, or it is the ethnic appearance that provides them their *raison d'être*. People, he wrote, manipulate history, lie and deceive in order to find support for their political beliefs. The merit of this exhibition is to demonstrate that Lebanon's history, Maalouf added, cannot be reduced to one epoch. Thus, the Phoenician era is a source of pride for all Lebanese. But the history of Lebanon does not halt there. Rather it continues to other pages of different eras, such as the Muslim conquest in the 7th century which irreversibly connected Lebanon to the Arab civilization. An Arab past, Greek-Roman past, Ottoman past, and Phoenician past — certainly, people in Lebanon and elsewhere made them bones of contention, Maalouf wrote, as if the names of these civilizations are only instruments or codes for contemporary political quarrels. Indeed, every community finds certain eras more appealing then others but the history of Lebanon as a whole does not belong to anyone. It is characterized by diversity and not by clinging to this or that epoch. This diversity is not a fable, because it is exactly within this subtle mélange that the distinctiveness of Lebanon and its history reside. Thus, Maalouf actually argues that, indeed, Lebanon is attached to the Arab world, but its history and identity are comprised of thousands of years of long human experience. The ancient history of the country and its people, therefore, is an inseparable component of its identity, which, by its diversity is, in fact, the first model of the Global Village. Interestingly enough, these views are not that different from those expressed in the 1950s in Beirut by Muslim authors such as Adonis or members of *Usrat al-Jabal al-Mulham*. These writers believed in the Phoenician heritage of modern Lebanon, though, at the same time, they did not abandon their Arab-ness for even a moment.

Very few Lebanese question the Arab-ness of Lebanon today. Yet, as the Parisian exhibition demonstrated, the ancient Phoenicians still hold an important place in the historical annals of modern Lebanon. One need only look at the front cover of the exhibition catalogue: pictures of Phoenician figurines, unearthed in Byblos, decorate this page (rather than pictures of an ancient mosque, an Ottoman palace, or conversely a Crusader castle), leaving no room for doubt that the ancient Phoenician patrimony to modern Lebanon, although recuperating from long years of civil strife, is still very much alive. Similarly, Marcel Khalife, one of the most important musicians in the Arab world and a passionate advocate of Lebanon's attachment to its Arab-ness, saw no difficulty in composing music for a ballet named "Alisar Queen of Carthage," which told the escape story of the princess of Tyre to the most important Phoenician colony.[7] On the other — popular — side of the cultural spectrum, the Phoenicians even entered the realm of Lebanese jokes. In a "Top 16 list of why it's great to be Lebanese," circulating on the Internet, we learn that "We are everything: Lebanese, Arab, Phoenician, Martian ..."

Indeed, viewing Phoenicianism as an alternative identity to Arabism is restricted to a small group in post-civil war Lebanon. Nevertheless, it is apparent that the interest in the phenomenon of Phoenicianism is far from subsiding. As discussed earlier, in Lebanese immigrant communities the Phoenician identity still flourishes and Beirut itself continues to issue old and new Phoenician works. Lebanon, rehabilitated after the civil war, is still attempting to define its collective identity and the place of its distant and near history therein. Although the "neo-Phoenicians" and most of their Christian supporters, often ridiculed by their rivals, have been nudged off the central stage of Lebanese society, the ancient Phoenicians are still there to be used as a legitimate backdrop in the history of Lebanon and its people, demonstrating that the long years of preoccupation with the ancient inhabitants of Lebanon planted those Phoenicians deep in the heart of the much disputed Lebanese national consciousness.

References

1 *Qu'est-ce qu'une nation?* Translated and annotated by Martin Thom in Homi Bhabha (ed.), *Nation and Narration* (London, 1990), pp. 8-22.

7 "Al-Asma' al-Jadida li-Shawari' Bayrut" [New Names to the Streets of Beirut], *Al-Hayyat*, April 5, 1966.

3 Kamal Salibi, *A House of Many Mansions* (London: I.B. Tauris, 1988), pp. 216-217.

4 *Ibid*, p. 2.

5 Elizabeth Picard, *Lebanon: A Shattered Country*, p. 1.

6 *The Daily Star*, 23.10.2001.

7 The ballet was performed in 1998 by the Lebanese Caracalla Dance Troupe. See/listen to Khalifeh's album *Bisat al-Rih* [Magic Carpet], Nagam Records, Inc. 1998.

Bibliography

Archival Sources

A. France

Ministère des Affaires Etrangères (MAE), Paris, Série E-Levant 1918-1940.
  Private papers of Robert de Caix.
Ministère des Affaires Etrangères, Les Archives Diplomatiques de Nantes
  (AD), Mandat Syrie-Liban, 1918-1948
Protectorat Maroc, 1907-1956
Jesuit Archives, Vanves.
Private papers, Louis Jalabert.

B. Britain

The Private Papers Collection. St Antony's College, Oxford, Middle East
  Centre. Yale Papers Microfilm and Photostats.
Centre for Lebanese Studies, Copies of the regional files of the American
  Consulate in Beirut.

C. Israel

Central Zionist Archives (CZA), Jerusalem. The Political Department of the
  Jewish Agency, record group S25.

D. The Unites States

U.S. Congress. House. Reports of the Immigration Commission, *Immigration Legislation*, 61st Congress, 3rd session.
U.S. Congress, House. Reports of the Immigration Commission, *Abstracts of Reports of the Immigration Commission.* Washington D.C., 1911.
U.S. Congress. House. Reports of the Immigration Commission, presented by Mr. Dillingham, *Dictionary of Races or Peoples.* Washington, D.C., 1911.

Reference Works and Bibliographies

AbuKhalil As'ad. *Historical Dictionary of Lebanon.* London, 1998.
Berchet, Jean-Claude. *Le Voyage en Orient.* Fourth edition. Turin, Italy, 1997.
The British Lebanese Association. *Lebanon - the Artists View.* London, 1989.
Al-Bustani, Buturs, Salim al-Bustani, Suleyman al-Bustani, Najib al-Bustani. *Da'irat al- Ma'arif.* Beirut, 1876-1900.
Dagher, Joseph. *L'Orient dans la Littérature Française de l'Après Guerre 1919-1933.* Beirut 1937.
Daghir Yusuf As'ad. *Qamus al-Sahafa al-Lubnaniyya, 1858-1974* [Dictionary of Lebanese Press]. Beirut, 1978.
Fani, Michel. *Dictionnaire de la Peinture au Liban.* Paris, 1998.
Furayha, Anis. *Mu'jam Asma' al-Mudun wa al-Qura al-Lubnaniyya* [A Dictionary of Names of Cities and Villages in Lebanon]. Beirut, 1972.
Lahoud, Edouard. *L'Art Contemporain au Liban.* New York-Beirut, 1974.
Maouad, Ibrahim. *Bibliographie des Auteurs Libanais de Langue Française.* Beirut, 1948.
Masson, Paul. *Éléments d'une Bibliographie Française de la Syrie.* Marseille, 1919.
Sacre, Maurice. *Anthologie des Auteurs Libanais de Langue Française.* Beirut, 1948.
Zein, Ramy. *Dictionnaire de la Littérature Libanaise de Langue Française.* Paris, 1998

Newspapers, Journals and Periodicals

Al-Bashir (Beirut).
Davar (Jerusalem).
AL-Hilal (Cairo).
Al-Hoda (Philadelphia, New York).
Al-Manar (Cairo).
Al-Ma'rid (Beirut).
Al-Mashriq (Beirut).
Al-Muqtataf (Beirut, Cairo).
L'Asie Arabe (Paris).
L'Asie Française (Paris).
Association Amicale des Anciens Élèves de l'USJ (Beirut).
Association amicale des Anciens Élèves des Pères Jésuites en Orient; Alexandrie, Beyrouth, le Caire (Cairo).
Bulletin Annuel de l'Association Amicale des Anciens Élèves de l'USJ (Beirut).
Bulletin de l'Association des Anciens Élèves de l'USJ (Beirut).
Bulletin de l'Union Économique de Syrie (Beirut).
Bulletin du Musée de Beyrouth (Beirut).

Les Cahiers de l'Est (Beirut).
Correspondance d'Orient (Paris).
Études (Paris).
Le Jour (Beirut).
Le Journal du Caire (Cairo).
Mélanges de l'Université Saint Joseph (Beirut).
La Nation Arabe (Geneva).
L'Orient (Beirut).
La Revue de Deux Mondes (Paris).
La Revue du Liban et l'Orient Méditerranéen. (Paris, 1928-1939).
La Revue du Liban et l'Orient Arabe. (Beirut, 1939-1945).
La Revue Phénicienne (Beirut).
La Voix du Liban (Paris).
The Palestine Post (Jerusalem).
Phénicia (Beirut).
Proche Orient, Revue Économique et Financière (Beirut).
SYRIA, Revue d'Art Oriental et d'Archéologie (Paris).
La Syrie (Beirut).

Dissertations and Theses

Bashshur, Munir. 'The Role of Two Western Universities in the National Life of Lebanon and the Middle East. A Comparative Study of the American University in Beirut and the University of Saint Joseph.' Ph.D. dissertation, University of Chicago, 1964.

Bulus, Samawil. 'Ha-Patriarch ha-Maroni Elias Butrus al-Howayyek ve-Hakamat Medinat Levanon ha-Gadol' [The Maronite Patriarch Elias Butrus al-Howayyek and the Formation of Greater Lebanon]. MA. Thesis, Haifa University, 1987.

Campbell, Robert Bell. 'The Arabic Journal, Al-Mashriq: Its Beginning and First Twenty-Five Years under the Editorship of Père Louis Cheikho, S.J.' Ph.D. dissertation, The University of Michigan, 1972.

Dugast, Olivier. 'Automobiles, chauffeurs et transports routiers en Syrie et au Liban pendant la période mandataire.' MA Thesis, Université de Rennes II, No date.

Hakim-Dowek, Carol. 'The Origins of the Lebanese National Idea, 1840-1914.' Ph.D. dissertation, St. Antony's College, 1997.

Kearny, Helen McCready. 'American Images of the Middle East, 1824-1924: A Century of Antipathy.' Ph.D. dissertation, University of Rochester, 1976.

Kerr, David, A. 'The Temporal Authority of the Maronite Patriarch, 1918-1958: A Study in the Relationship of Religious and Secular Power.' Ph.D. dissertation, Oxford University, 1977.

Melki, Henri. 'Al-Sahafa al-'Arabiyya fi al-Mahjar wa 'Alaqatuha bi-al-Adab al-Mahjari' [Arab Journalism in the New World and its Relations with

Arab American Literature], Ph.D. dissertation. Georgetown University, 1972.
Naff, Alixa. 'A Social History of Zahle, The Principal Market Town in Nineteenth Century Lebanon.' Ph.D. dissertation, UCLA, 1972.
Sayegh, Joseph. 'Le phénomène poético-social dans le vallée de Zahleh.' Ph.D. dissertation, University of Paris, 1964.
Schreier-Zachs, Fruma. 'From Communal to Territorial Identity: the Emergence of the 'Syrian Concept' 1831-1881' (Hebrew), Ph.D. dissertation, Haifa University, 1997.
Traboulsi, Fawaz. 'Identités et solidarités croisées dans les conflits du Liban contemporain.' Ph.D. dissertation, University of Paris, 1993.

Primary Sources: Books, Articles and Pamphlets

Ab'ad al-Qawmiyya al-Lubnaniyya [Lebanese National Dimensions]. Kaslik, 1970.
Abou, Sélim. *Le Bilinguisme Arabe-Français au Liban*. Paris, 1962.
Abu Khalil, Shawqi. *Mawdu'iyyat Filib Hitti* [The Objectivity of Philip Hitti]. Damascus, 1985.
Abu Zayd, Sarkis. *Tahjir al-Mawarina ila al-Jazai'r* [The Emigration of the Maronites to Algeria]. Beirut, 1994.
—. *'Urubat Yusuf Karam* [The Arabism of Yusuf Karam]. Beirut, 1997.
Adib, Auguste, Pasha. *Le Liban après la Guerre*. Paris, 1918.
Adonis, *Ha Anta Ayyuha al-Waqt* [You there, O Time]. Beirut, 1993.
'Ammoun, Blanche. *Histoire du Liban*. Beirut, 1940.
Antonius, George. *The Arab Awakening*. London, 1938.
'Aql, Sa'id. 'Al-Shi'r al-Lubnani bi-al-Lugha al-Faransawiyya' [Lebanese Poetry in French Language]. A*l-Mashriq* (July-September, 1935): 381-393.
—. *Lubnan, in Haka* [Lebanon, If It Could Speak]. Beirut, 1960.
—. *Bint Yaftah* [Japhteh's Daughter]. Beirut, 1935.
—. *Al-Majdaliyya* [The Magdalene]. Beirut, 1937.
—. *Mushkilat al-Nukhba fi al-Sharq* [The Problem of the Elite in the East]. Beirut, 1954.
—. *Qadmus*. Beirut, 1944.
—. *L'Or est Poèmes*. Beirut, 1987.
—. 'Les fondements historiques d'un humanisme libanais, le Liban et l'homme.' *Les Cahiers de l'Est*. 4 (1945).
—. *Sagèsse de Phénicie*. Beirut, 1999.
Association amicale des anciens élèves de l'USJ, *Livre d'Or*. Beirut, 1949.
Azar, Abbé. *Les Marounites d'après le Manuscrit Arabe du R.P. Azar*. Cambari, 1852.
Babikian, J. A. *Civilization and Education in Syria and Lebanon*. Beirut, 1936.

Al-Baramij al-Lubnaniyya wa al-Tanshi'a al-Wataniyya [Lebanese Programs and National Development]. Kaslik, 1971.
Barrès, Maurice. *Une Enquête aux Pays du Levant* (Paris: 1923).
—. *La Colline Inspirée*. Paris, 1913.
de Baudicour, M. *La Colonisation de l'Algérie* (Paris, 1847).
Bayhum, Muhammad, Jamil. *Lubnan bayna Musharriq wa Mugharrib* [Lebanon between Eastern and Western Orientations]. Beirut, 1969.
—. *Al-'Uruba wa al-Shu'ubiyyat al-Haditha* [Arabism and the new Shu'ubiyyat]. Beirut, 1957.
—. *'Urubat Lubnan* [The Arabism of Lebanon]. Beirut, 1969.
Bérard, Victor. *Les Phéniciens et l'Odyssée*. Paris, 1902.
—. *De l'origine des Cultes Arcadiens; Essai de Méthode en Mythologie Grecque*. Paris, 1894.
Blanchard, Désiré, and Jules Toutain. *Histoire Ancienne des Peuples d'Orient*. Paris, 1901.
Bordeaux, Henry. *Voyageurs d'Orient*. Paris: 1926.
Bulus, Jawad. *Tarikh Lubnan* [The History of Lebanon]. Beirut, 1972.
—. *Les Peuples et les Civilisations du Proche-Orient*. Paris, 1961-1968.
Bustros, Eveline. *Evocations*. Beirut, 1956.
Bustani, Fouad Afram. *'Ala 'Ahd al-Amir* [During the Time of the Prince]. Beirut, 1926.
—. *Limadha?* [Why?]. Beirut, 1930.
—. *Mawaqif Lubnaniyya* [Lebanese Positions]. Beirut, 1982.
Cedar of Lebanon. *Syria Reborn*. Alexandria, 1919.
Cham'un, Camille. *Marahil al-Istiqlal* [Stages of Independence]. Beirut 1949.
Chamberlain, W. S. *The Foundations of the Nineteenth Century*. London, 1910.
Chambre de Commerce de Marseille. *Congrès Français de la Syrie*. (January, 3-5 1919).
Cheikho, Louis. *Souvenir des Noces d'Or de l'USJ de Beyrouth*. Beirut, 1925.
—. *USJ; Catalogue des Ouvrages, 1875-1925*. Beirut, 1925.
Chiha, Michel. *Liban d'Aujourd'hui*. Beirut, 1944.
—. *Palestine*. Beirut, 1956.
—. *Variations sur la Mode Méditerranéenne*. Beirut, 1994.
—. *La Maison de Champs*. Beirut, 1935.
Closson, Carlos, C. 'The Hierarchy of European Races.' *American Journal of Sociology* 3(November 1897): 314-327.
Comité Central Syrien. *L'Opinion Syrienne à l'Étranger pendant la Guerre*. Paris, 1918.
—. *La Syrie devant la Conférence*. Paris, 1919.
Comité de l'Orient. *Les Oeuvres Françaises en Syrie*. Paris, 1919.
Comité Libanais de Paris. *Mémoire sur la question du Liban*. Paris, 1912.
Conklin, Nancy, Faires, and McCallum, Brenda. 'Final Report: Greek School, Holy Trinity-Holy Cross Orthodox Cathedral, and Lebanese Arabic School,

St. Elias Maronite Catholic Church, Birmingham, Alabama.' In *Project on Ethnic Heritage and Language Schools in America*. Washington D.C., 1982.

Corm, Charles. *6000 Ans de Génie Pacifique au Service de l'Humanité*. Beirut, 1988.

—. 'Au congrès de la Méditerranée, témoignage d'un poète libanais.' *Études* (January 1936): 74-83.

—. *L'Art Phénicien*. Beirut, 1940.

—. *La Symphonie de la Lumière*. Beirut, 1973.

—. *Les Miracles de la Madone aux Sept Douleurs*. Beirut, 1948.

—. *La Montagne Inspirée*. Beirut, 1934.

Coze, Edouard. 'La Syrie et le Liban,' conférence faite le 8 Mars 1922 aux officiers de la 10eme division d'infanterie sous le présidence de M. le Général Lebouc.

Cromer, Earl of. *Modern Egypt*. London, 1908.

D'ancre, Alfred. Silhouettes Orientales. Paris, 1869.

Dahdah, Najib. 'Lubnan al-Kabir fi al-Tarikh.' *al-Mashriq*. 34 (1936).

—. 'Evolution de la nation libanaise.' *Les Cahiers de l'Est*. 5(1945).

Darian, Yusuf. *Nubdha Tarikhiyya fi Asl al-Ta'ifa al-Maruniyya wa Istiqlaliha bi Jabal Lubnan* [A Historical Note on the Origin of the Maronite Church and its independence in Mount Lebanon]. Alexandria, 1918.

Daw, Butrus. *Tarikh al-Mawarina* [History of the Maronites]. Beirut, 1977-1981.

Debs, Yussuf. *Lettre de Mgr Debs touchant le Patriarche des Maronites, 30 December1893*. Amiens, 1894.

Al-Dibs, Yusuf. *Kitab Tarikh Suriyya* [The Book of Syrian History]. Beirut, 1893.

Duruy, V. *Histoire de l'Orient*. Paris, 1896.

Eddé, Jacques. *Géographie de la Syrie et du Liban*. Beirut, 1924.

Fakhuri, 'Umar. *Al-Haqiqa al-Lubnaniyya* [The Lebanese Truth]. Beirut, 1945.

Flaubert, Gustave. *Salammbô*. Paris, 1862.

Furayha, Anis. *Tabsit Qawa'id al-'Arabiyya* [Simplification of the Rules in Arabic]. Beirut, 1952.

Ganem, Chékri. *Écrits Politiques: Oeuvres Complètes*. Beirut, 1994.

Gagnol, M. l'Abbé. *Histoire Ancienne des Peuples de l'Orient*. Paris, 1891.

Gédéon, E. & G. *L'Indicateur Libano-Syrien*. 5th edition. Beirut, 1928-1929.

Ghanem, Robert, Abu. *Les Éléments de la Formation d'un État Juif en Palestine*. Beirut, 1946.

al-Ghaziri, Bernard, Ghobaira. *Rome et l'Eglise Syrienne Maronite d'Antioche, 517-1531*. Beyrouth, 1906.

Gobineau. *Essai sur l'Inégalité des Races Humaines*. Paris, 1853-1855.

de Gontaut-Biron, Comte R. *Comment la France S'est Installée en Syrie. 1918-1919* Paris, 1922.

Haddad, Farid. *Sirat Hanib'al Shi'iran* [The Epic of Hannibal in Poetry]. Alexandria, 1925.

Haddad, Marie. *Les Heures Libanais.* Beirut, 1937.
Al-Hajj, Kamal, Yusuf. *Mujaz al-Falsafa al-Lubnaniyya* [The Concise Philosophy of Lebanon]. Juniyah, 1974.
—. *Al-Falsafa al-Lubnaniyya al-Haditha: Muhadara* [The Modern Philosophy of Lebanon: A Lecture]. Beirut, 1964.
Hallaq, Hassan 'Ali. *Mu'tamar al-Sahil wa al-aqdiya al-Arba'a* [The Conference of the Coast and the Four Districts]. Beirut 1983.
—.*Lubnan: Min al-Finiqiyya ila al-'Uruba.*[Lebanon: From Phoenicianism to Arabism]. Beirut 1993.
Haqqi Isma'il. *Lubnan; Mabahith 'Ilmiyya wa Ijtima'iyya* [Lebanon: Scientific and Social Studies]. 1918. Reprint. Beirut, 1968.
Hanotaux, Gabriel, and Alfred Martineau, eds. *Histoire des Colonies Françaises et de l'Expansion de la France dans le Monde.* Paris,1931.
Harun, Jurj. *A'lam al-Qawmiyya al-Lubnaniyya, Yusuf al-Sawda* (The Eminent Persons of Lebanese Nationalism, Yusuf al-Saouda]. Kaslik, 1979.
Haut Commissariat de la République française en Syrie et au Liban. *La Syrie et le Liban en 1921.* Paris, 1922.
Himadeh, Said. *Economic Organization of Syria.* Beirut, 1936.
Hitti, Philip. *Amrika fi Nadhar Sharqi* [America in the eyes of an Oriental]. New York, 1919.
—. *Muhajarat al-Suriyyin wa Isti'imaruhum bayna al-'Ahd al-Finiqi wa al-'Ahd al-Hadir* [The Emigration and Colonization of the Syrians between the Phoenician and the New eras]. New York, 1917.
—. 'Ist'imar al-Surriyyin bayna al-'Ahdayn' [The Colonization of the Syrians between Two Eras]. *al-Muqtataf* (July 1917): 9-18.
—. *The Syrians in America.* New York, 1924.
—.*Testimony before the Anglo-American Committee on Palestine.* Washington, D.C., 1946.
—. *History of the Arabs.* London, 1937.
—. *A Short History of Lebanon.* New York, 1965.
—. *Educational Guide for Syrian Students in the United States.* New York, 1921.
—. *History of Syria, Including Lebanon and Palestine.* New York, 1951.
—. *Lebanon in History.* London, 1957.
—. *The Arabs: A Short History.* Princeton, 1943.
—. *The Near East in History, a 5000 Year Story.* Princeton, 1961.
Hobeika, Pierre. *Emile Eddé.* Beirut, 1939.
Hunein, Edward. *'Ala Durub Lubnan* [On the Paths of Lebanon]. Kaslik, 1979.
Al-Husri, Sati'. *Al-'Uruba, bayna Du'atiha wa Mu'aradiha* [Arabism Between Its Advocates and its Opponents]. Beirut, 1951.
—. *Nushu' al-Fikra al-Qawmiyya* [The Evolution of National Thought]. Beirut, 1951.
Isma'il, 'Adil. *Le Liban; Histoire d'un Peuple.* Beirut, 1965.

Itihad al-Kutab al-Lubnaniyyin. *Amin al-Rihani.* Beirut, 1988.

Jabar, Jamil. *Lubnan fi Rawa'i Aqlamihi* [Lebanon According to Its Distinguished Pens]. Beirut, 1964.

—. *Sharl al-Qurm, Sha'ir al-Jabal al-Mulham* [Charles Corm, the Poet of the Inspired Mountain]. Beirut, 1995.

Jabotinsky, Ze'ev. *Shimshon* [Samson]. In *Ketavim* [Works]. Jerusalem, 1964.

Jalabert, Louis. 'Au pays de l'amitié française, à travers le Liban.' *Études* (1933): 416-435.

—. 'La France abandonnera-t-elle la Syrie?' *Études* (1927): 161-182.

—. 'L'amitié française au Liban.' *Études* (1919): 235.

—. *Syrie et Liban – Réussite Française?* Paris, 1934.

Jenks, Jeremiah, and Lauck, Jett. *The Immigration Problem.* New York, 1911.

Jimblatt [sic.], Kamal. 'Le Liban et le Monde Arabe,' *Les Cahiers de l'Est*, no. 6, 2 series (1949).

Jouplain, M. [Bulus Nujayam]. *La Question du Liban; Étude d'Histoire Diplomatique et de Droit International.* 1908. Reprint. Jounieh, 1961.

Jullien, M. *La Nouvelle Mission de la Compagnie de Jésus en Syrie.* Paris, 1899.

Al-Jundi, Anwar. *Al-Shu'ubiyya fi al-Adab al-'Arabi al-Hadith* [The-Shu'ubiyya in Modern Arabic Literature]. Tripoli, Lebanon, 1987.

Khairallah, K. T. *Les Régions Arabes Libérées.* Paris, 1919.

—. *La Syrie.* Paris, 1912.

—. *La Question du Liban.* Paris, 1915.

Khalidi, Mustafa, and Farukh, 'Umar. *Al-Tabshir wa al-Isti'mar fi al-Bilad al-'Arabiyya* [Missionary Activity and Colonialism in the Arab Countries]. Beirut, 1957.

Al-Khal, Yusuf, *al-A'amal al-Shi'iriyya al-Kamila, 1938-1968* [The Complete Work of Poetry]. Beirut, 1973.

Khatir, Lahd, Sa'b. *Mukhtasar Tarikh Lubnan* [The Short History of Lebanon]. Beirut, 1914.

Al-Khoury, Béchara, *Majmu'at Khutab* [A Selection of Speeches]. Beirut, 1951.

—. *Haqa'iq Lubnaniyya* [Lebanese Facts]. Beirut, 1961.

Khury, Ra'if. *Modern Arab Thought.* Princeton, 1983. Translated by Ihsan 'Abbas from *al-Fikr al-'Arabi al-Hadith.* Beirut, 1943.

Klat Hector. *Les Miettes du Festin.* Beirut, 1939.

—. *Feuilles Mortes.* Beirut, 1969.

—. *Le Cèdre et le Lys.* Beirut, 1935.

—. *Ma Seule Joie.* Beirut, 1966.

Labaki, Salah. *Arjuhat al-Qamar* [The Moon's Cradle]. Beirut, 1938.

—. *Min A'amaq al-Jabal* [From the Depth of the Mountain]. Beirut, 1945.

—. *Al-Tayyarat al-Adabiyya al-Haditha fi Lubnan, Lubnan al-Sha'ir* [Modern Literary Currents in Lebanon]. Beirut 1954.

Lammens, Henri. *Al-Mudhakarat al-Jughrafiyya fi al-Aqtar al-Suriyya* [Geographical Studies in the Syrian Lands]. Beirut, 1911.

—. *La Syrie et Son Importance Géographique.* Lourain, 1904.

—. *La Syrie; Précis Historique.* Beirut, 1921.

—. *Tasrih al-Absar fi ma Yahtawi Lubnan min al-Athar* [Panorama of Lebanese Antiquities]. Beirut, 1906.

—. Ferdinand Taoutel, and René Moutèrde. *Petite Histoire de Syrie et du Liban.* Beirut, 1924.

Levantine H. (pseudonym of Lammens). 'Le Liban et son role géographique en Syrie.' *Études* (1908) 116: 487-505.

Lapouge, G.V. *Les Sélections Sociales.* Paris, 1888-1889.

Lavigerie, Mgr. *Souscription Recueillie en Faveur des Chrétiens.* Paris, 1861.

Ledrain, E. *Notice Sommaire des Monuments Phéniciens du Musée du Louvre.* Paris, 1900.

Levenq, Gabriel. *Géographie Élémentaire de la Syrie.* Beirut, 1920.

Lortet, Pierre. *La Syrie d'aujourd'hui; Voyage dans la Phénicie, le Liban et le Judée, 1875-1880.* Paris, 1884.

Ma'luf, Michel. *Histoire de Ba'albek.* Zahle, 1890.

—. *Tarikh al-Amir Fakhr al-Din al-Ma'ni al-Thani* [The History of the Prince Fakhr al-Din II]. Junieh, 1934.

Ma'luf, Rushdi. *Awwal al-Rabi'* [The Beginning of Spring]. Beirut, 1944.

Masson, Paul. *Eléments d'une Bibliographie Française de la Syrie.* Marseille, 1919.

Mathews, Roderic, D, and Metta Akrawi. *Education in the Arab Countries of the Near East.* Washington D.C., 1946.

McKay, Jim. *Phoenicia Farewell: Three Generations of Lebanese Christians in Australia.* Melbourne, 1989.

Mélia, J. *Chez les Chrétiens d'Orient.* Paris, 1929.

Mikhail, Kyriakos. *Copts and Moslems.* London, 1911.

Mill, Hugh, R. ed. *The International Geography.* London, 1909.

Moses, John G. *How the Lebanese Advanced Civilization.* New York, 1998.

Moutèrde, René. 'Le congrès archéologique en Syrie, April 8-7, 1926.' *Études* (April- June, 1927): 564-570.

—. *Précis d'Histoire de la Syrie et du Liban.* Second edition. Beirut, 1931.

Moutran, Nadra. *La Syrie de Demain.* Paris, 1916.

Mouwanès, Joseph. *Les Éléments Structuraux de la Personnalité Libanaise.* Kaslik, 1973.

Mukarzal, Naum. *Qissat Yusuf bek Karam* [The Story of Yusuf Bey Karam]. NewYork, 1909.

—. *Tarikh Hanib'al* [The History of Hannibal]. New York, 1924.

Murad, Nicolas. *Notice Historique sur l'Origine de la Nation Maronite et sur Ses Rapports avec la France.* Paris, 1844.

Mutran, Khalil. *Diwan al-Khalil.* Cairo, 1947.

Nammur, César. *Al-Naht fi Lubnan* [Sculpting in Lebanon]. Beirut, 1990.

Nasr, Anis. *Al-Nubugh al-Lubnani fi al-Qarn al-'Ishrin* [Lebanese Genie in the Twentieth Century]. Aleppo, 1938.
Nasr, Naji Salim. *Sa'id 'Aql, Faylasufan* [Said 'Aql, a Philosopher]. Beirut, 1980.
Official Guide Book, New York World's Fair 1939. New York, 1939.
Pharès, Emmanuel, Mgr. *Les Maronites du Liban.* Lille, 1908.
Al-Qatar, Ilyas, et al. *Asad Rustum, al-Insan wa al-Mu'arikh* [Asad Rustum, the Person and the Historian]. Beirut, 1984.
Raphaël, Pierre. *Le Cèdre du Liban.* Beirut, 1924.
Rabbath, Edmond. *Les États Unis de la Syrie.* Aleppo, October 1925.
—. *Unité Syrienne et Devenir Arabe.* Beirut, 1937.
Rapport sur la Situation de la Syrie et du Liban. Paris, 1928.
Reclus, Elisée. 'La Phénicie et Les Phéniciens.' *Bulletin de la Société Neuchâteloise de Géographie.* XII(1900).
—. *Nouvelle Géographie Universelle.* Vol. XI. *L'Asie Antérieure*, Paris, 1884.
Renan, Ernest. 'Qu'est-ce qu'une nation?' Translated and annotated by Martin Thom in Homi Bhabha. (ed.). *Nation and Narration*. London, 1990: 8-22.
—. *Mission de Phénicie.* Paris, 1864.
—. *Caliban: Suite de la Tempête.* Paris, 1878.
Rida, Rashid. 'Al-Jinsiyya al-Lubnaniyya wa Ghulu Talabiha' [Lebanese Nationality and its exceeding demands]. *Al-Manar*. 17 (1914): 617-627.
—. 'Al-Shiqaq bayna al-'Arab wa al-Muslimun' [The Disunity between the Arabs and the Muslims]. *al-Manar*. 34 (1935): 782-786.
—. 'Al-Thawra al-Suriyya wa al-Hukuma al-Faransiyya wa al-Tanazu' bayna al-Sharq wa al-Gharb' [The Syrian Revolution, the French Government and the Struggle between East and West]. *Al-Manar*. 26(1925): 699-712.
—. 'Al-Mas'ala al-Suriyya wa al-Ahzab' [The Syrian Question and the Parties]. *al-Manar*. 21(1919).
—. 'Al-Muslimun wa al-Qubt' [The Muslims and the Copts]. *al-Manar*. 11 (1908): 338-347.
—. 'Al-Rahla al-Suriyya al-Thaniyya' [The Second Syrian Journey]. *al-Manar*. (1921): 26.
—. *Al-Wahy al-Muhammadi* [The Revelation of Muhammad]. Beirut, 1987.
Al-Rihani, Albert. *Al-Rihani wa Mu'asiruhu* [Al-Rihani and his Contemporaries]. Beirut, 1966.
—. *Rasa'il al-Rihani* [Al-Rihani's Letters]. Beirut, 1959.
Al-Rihani, Amin. *Adab wa Fann* [Literature and Art]. Beirut, 1957.
—. *Al-Nakabat, aw khulasat Tarikh Suriyya Mundhu al-'Ahad al-Awwal ba'd al-Tufan ila 'Ahad al-Jumhuriyya bi-Lubnan* [The Calamities, or a Summary of the History of Syria Since the Days of the Flood to the Era of the Republic of Lebanon]. Beirut, 1928.
—. *Muluk al-'Arab* [The Arab Kings]. Beirut, 1924.
—. *Qalb Lubnan* [The Heart of Lebanon]. Beirut, 1978.

—. *Nubdha fi al-Thawra al-Faransiyya* [A Note about the French Revolution]. New York, 1902.

Al-Riyashi, Iskandar. *Ru'asa Lubnan kama 'Araftuhum* [Lebanese Presidents as I Knew Them]. Beirut, 1961.

Ripley, William. 'Races in the United States,' *Atlantic Monthly* (1907).

Ristelhueber René. 'Les Maronites.' *La Revue de Deux Mondes* (January 1, 1915): 198-212.

—. *Les Traditions Françaises au Liban.* Paris, 1925.

Rustum, Asad, and Fuad Afram al-Bustani. *Hurub Ibrahim Basha al-Misri fi Suriya wa al-'Anadul* [The Wars of Ibrahim Pasha in Syrian and Anatolia]. Beirut, 1927.

—. *Tarikh Lubnan* [The History of Lebanon]. Beirut, 1938.

Rustum, Asad. *Lubnan fi 'Ahd al-Amir Fakhr al-Din al-Ma'ni al-Thani* [Lebanon in the Time of the Prince Fakhr al-Din al-Ma'ni II]. Beirut, 1936.

—. *Lubnan fi 'Ahd al-Umara' al-Shihabiyyin* [Lebanon in the Time of the Shihabi Princes]. Beirut, 1933.

Sa'adeh, Antun. *al-Sira' al-Fikri fi al-Adab al-Suri* [The Intellectual Crisis in Syrian Literature]. 2nd edition. Beirut, 1947.

—. *A'da' al-'Arab A'da' Lubnan* [The Enemies of Lebanon, the Enemies of the Arabs]. Beirut, 1954.

—. *Kitab al-Ta'alim al-Suriyya al-Qawmiyya al-Ijtima'iyya*, Beirut, 1947.

—. *Marahil al-Mas'ala al-Filastiniyya* [Stages of the Lebanese Problem]. Beirut, 1953.

Sa'adeh, Jurj 'Arij. *Al-Sahafa fi Lubnan* [Journalism in Lebanon]. Beirut, 1965.

Salem, Jean. *Le Peuple Libanais.* Beirut, 1968.

Samné, George. *La Syrie.* Paris, 1920.

—. *Les Oeuvres Françaises en Syrie.* Paris 1919.

—. *Vers le Petit Liban.* Paris, 1926.

Sarkis, Khalil, Ramiz. *Sawt al-Gha'ib* [The Voice of the Absent]. Beirut, 1956.

Al-Samrani, Filib. *Al-Dhakha'ir al-Saniyya.* [The Splendid Treasures]. Junieh, 1931.

Al-Saouda, Yusuf. *Istiqlal Lubnan wa al-Itihad al-Lubnani fi Iskandariyya* [Lebanese Independence and the Alliance Libanaise in Alexandria]. Alexandria, 1920.

—. *Étude Juridique sur la Protocole d'Alexandrie.* Beirut, November, 1944.

—. *Tarikh Lubnan al-Hadari* [The Cultural History of Lebanon]. Beirut, 1972.

—. *Fi Sabil al-Istiqlal* [For the Sake of Independence]. Beirut, 1967.

—. *Fi Sabil Lubnan* [For the Sake of Lebanon]. Alexandria, 1919.

Segond, Emile. *Histoire Ancienne de l'Orient.* Paris, 1920.

Sfeir, 'Abdallah, Pasha. *Le Mandat Français et les Traditions Françaises en Syrie et au Liban.* Paris, 1922.

Sotheby's. *The Library of Camille Aboussouan.* London, 1993.

Stanford's Compendium of Geography and Travel. London, 1893-1899.

Syrie et Liban, Rapport Mensuel d'Ensemble. Beirut, June 1921.
Tabet, Jacques. *La Syrie.* Paris, 1920.
—. *Helissa.* Paris, 1924.
—. 'À la Syrie.' *Correspondance d'Orient.* 209 (March, 15 1919).
Taoutel, Ferdinand. *Mukhtasar Tarikh Suriya wa Lubnan* [The Short History of Syria and Lebanon]. Beirut, 1924.
di Tarazi, Filib. *Asdaq ma Kana 'an Tarikh Lubnan* [The Reliable History of Lebanon]. Beirut, 1948.
Tawil, Edgard. *La Syrie.* Alexandria, 1919.
Tayah, Peter, Wadih. *The Maronites: Roots and Identity.* Miami, 1987.
de Thoron, Le Vicomte Ontroy. *Les Phéniciens à l'île d'Haïti et sur le Continent Américain.* Paris, 1889.
Tarikh Jaridat al-Hoda wa al- Jawali al-Lubnaniyya fi Amrika, 1898-1968 [The History of the journal al-Hoda and the Lebanese communities in America]. New York, 1968.
Tyan, Elie. *Le Château Merveilleux.* Beirut, 1935.
—. *Lumière sur la Montagne.* Beirut, 1935.
Tyan, Ferdinand. *Sous les Cèdres du Liban, la Nationalité Maronite.* Montligeon, 1905.
—. *France et Liban: Défense des Intérêts Français en Syrie.* Paris, 1917.
Université Saint Jospeh. 'In memoriam, Le père Henri Lammens,' *Mélanges de la faculté orientale* (1937-1938): 335.
—. *Les Jésuites en Syrie, 1831-1931.* Beirut, 1931.
Usbu' al-Taqafa fi Lubnan. Beirut, 1942.
'Uwayyet, Michel. *Al-Mawarina: Man Hum wa Madha Yuridun?* [The Maronites: Who are they and what do they want?]. Juniyeh 1987.
Vayssettes, E. *Sauvons les Maronites par l'Algérie et pour l'Algérie.* Algeria 1860.
Vellay, Charles. *Le Culte et les Fêtes d'Adônis-Thammouz dans l'Orient Antique.* Paris, 1904.
Wallace, O. M. *Egypt and the Egyptian Question.* London, 1883.
Woodruff, C. *The Expansion of Races.* New York, 1909.
Al-Zein, Ahmad 'Arif. *Tarikh Sayda* [The History of Sidon]. Sidon, 1913.
Zurayq, Qostantin. *Al-Wa'i al-Qawmi* [National Consciousness]. Beirut, 1939.

Secondary Sources, Books and Articles

Abu Zayd, Sarkis. *Tahjir al-Mawarina ila al-Jazai'r* [The Emigration of the Maronites to Algeria]. Beirut, 1994.
Abrams, L, and D. J. Miller. 'Who were the French Colonialists? A reassessment of the Parti Colonial, 1890-1914.' *The Historical Journal.* 19 (1976): 685-725.
Abu-Manneh, Butrus. 'The Christians Between Ottomanism and Syrian

Nationalism: The Ideas of Butrus al-Bustani,' *International Journal of Middle Eastern Studies.* 11 (1980): 287-304.
Addi, Lahouari. 'Colonial Mythologies: Algeria in the French Imagination,' in L. Carl Brown and Matthew S. Gordon, eds. *Franco-Arab Encounters.* Beirut, 1996.
Adra, Hoda. *Flaubert et le Liban.* Beirut, 1985.
Ageron, Charles-Robert. *L'Algérie Algérienne de Napoléon III à de Gaule.* Paris, 1980.
Ajami, Fouad. *The Dream Palace of the Arabs.* New York, 1998.
Akarli, Engin Deniz. *The Long Peace: Ottoman Lebanon 1861-1920.* Berkeley, 1993.
Anderson, Benedict. *Imagined Communities.* 1983. Revised Edition. London, 1991.
Andrew, C. M. and A. S. Kanya-Forstner. 'The French 'Colonial party:' its Composition, Aims and Influences, 1885-1914.' *Historical Journal,* 14 (1971).
—. *The Climax of French Colonial Expansion.* Stanford, 1981.
—. 'The French Colonialist Movement during the Third Republic: the Unofficial Mind of Imperialism.' *Transactions of the Royal Historical Society,* 5th series, 26 (1976).
Anhoury, Najwa, Aoun. *Panorama de la Poésie Libanaise d'Expression Française.* Beirut, 1987.
Armstrong, John, A. *Nations before Nationalism.* Chapel Hill, North Carolina, 1982.
Assali, Jean, Charles. 'Napoléon et l'antiquité.' in Michel Ganzin, ed. *L'Influence de l'Antiquité sur la Pensée Politique Européenne XVI-XX siècles.* Aix-en-Provence, 1996: 423-431.
Atiyeh, George N. & Ibrahim M. Oweiss, eds. *Arab Civilization; Studies in Honor of Qonstantine K. Zurayk.* New York, 1988.
Aubert, Maria, Eugenia. *The Phoenicians and the West.* Trans. Mary Turton. Cambridge, 1993.
'Awad, Walid. *Ashab al-Fakhama: Ru'asa' Lubnan* [Their Excellencies, the Presidents of Lebanon]. Beirut, 1977.
Ayalon, Ami. *The Press in the Arab Middle East.* Oxford, 1995.
Baron, Beth. 'Nationalist Iconography: Egypt as a Woman,' in Jankowski and Gershoni, eds. *Rethinking Nationalism in the Arab Middle East.* New York, 1997.
Berlinerblau, Jacques. *Heresy in the University.* New Brunswick, 1999.
Bernal, Martin. *Black Athena: The Afroasiatic Roots of Classical Civilization.* 2 volumes. New Jersey, 1987, 1991.
Betts, Reimond. *Assimilation and Association in French Colonial Theory.* London, 1973.
Betts, Robert, Brenton. *Christians in the Arab East: A Political Study.* Atlanta, 1978.

Beydoun, Ahamd. *Identité Confessionnelle et Temps Social chez les Historiens Libanais Contemporains.* Beirut, 1984.

Bidwell, Robin. *Morocco under Colonial Rule.* London, 1973.

Boulanger, Robert. *Lebanon.* Paris, 1955.

Bregeon, Jean-Joel. *L'Egypte de Bonaparte.* Paris, 1998.

Brown, L. Carl. 'France and the Arabs: An Overview.' in L. Carl Brown and Mathew S. Gordon, eds. *Franco-Arab Encounters* (Beirut, 1996): 1-31.

Brunschwig, Henri. *Mythes et Réalités de l'Impérialisme Colonial Français.* Paris, 1960.

Buheiry, Marwan, ed. *Intellectual Life in the Arab East.* Beirut, 1981.

Burke, Edmond. 'A Comparative View of French Native Policy in Morocco and Syria, 1912-1925.' *Middle Eastern Studies* (May 1973): 175-186.

—. 'The Image of the Moroccan State in French Ethnological Literature: A New Look at the Origin of Lyautey's Berber Policy,' in Ernest Gellner and C. Micaud, eds. *Arabs and Berbers.* London, 1973.

Carter, B. L. *The Copts in Egyptian Politics.* London, 1986.

Charmot, François. *La Pédagogie des Jésuites.* Paris, 1951.

Chatterjee, Partha. *Nationalist Thought and the Colonial World.* London, 1986.

Chéhab, Maurice. *Tyre; History, Topography, Excavations.* Beirut, 1960.

—. *Monuments of Baalbeck and Arjan.* Beirut, 1970.

—, and André Porrot and Sabastian Moscati. *Les Phéniciens.* Paris, 1975.

Chevallier, Dominique. 'Lyon et la Syrie en 1919: Les bases d'une intervention.' *Revue Historique* (October-December, 1960).

Cioeta, Donald J. 'Ottoman Censorship in Lebanon and Syria, 1876-1908.' *International Journal of Middle Eastern Studies.* 10(May 1979): 167-181.

Cleveland, William L. 'The Arab Nationalism of George Antonius Reconsidered' in Jankowski and Gershoni, eds. *Rethinking Nationalism in the Arab Middle East.* New York, 1997: 65-86.

Cleveland, William, L. *Islam against the West.* Austin, Texas, 1985.

—. *The Making of an Arab Nationalist; Ottomanism and Arabism in the Life and Thought of Sati' al-Husri.* Princeton, 1971.

Conrad, L. ed. *The Formation and Perception of the Modern Arab World: Studies by Marwan R. Buheiry.* Princeton, 1990.

Cragg, Kenneth. *The Arab Christians.* Louisville, 1991.

Dawn, Ernest. 'The Origins of Arab Nationalism,' in Rashid Khalidi, et al, eds. *The Origins of Arab Nationalism.* New York, 1991: 3-30.

—. *From Ottomanism to Arabism.* Chicago, 1973.

Dib, Pierre. *Histoire de l'Église Maronite.* Beirut, 1962.

Donhue, John, W. *Jesuit Education.* New York, 1963.

Dubar, Claude and Salim, Nasr. *Les Classes Sociales au Liban.* Paris, 1976.

Duclos, Louis-Jean. 'The Berbers and the Rise of Moroccan Nationalism,' in Ernest Gellner and C. Micaud, eds. *Arabs and Berbers.* London, 1973: 217-229.

Durtal, Jean. *Saïd Akl, Un Grand Poète Libanais.* Paris, 1970.

Elath, Eliahu. 'Ha-Tziyonut ha-Finikit be-Levanon.' [Phoenician Zionism in Lebanon] *Cathedra* (1985) 35: 109-124.
—. *Shivat Tziyon ve-'Arav* [Zionism and the Arabs], Tel Aviv, 1974.
—. *Mi-Ba'ad le-'Arafel ha-Yamim* [Through the Mist of Time]. Jerusalem, 1989.
Eley, Geoff, and Ronald Grigor, Suny. eds. *Becoming National.* New York, 1996.
Entelis, John P. *Pluralism and Party Transformation in Lebanon; al-Kata'ib.* Leiden, 1974.
Esman, Milton, J. and Itamar Rabinovitch. *Ethnicity, Pluralism and the State in the Middle East.* Cornell, 1988.
Faris, Nabih, Amin. 'Lebanon, 'Land of Light.'' in James Kritzek and Bayly Winder. *The World of Islam.* London, 1959: 336-350.
Fawaz, Leila. *Merchants and Migrants in Nineteenth Century Beirut.* Cambridge, Mass, 1983.
Fieldhouse, D.K. *Colonialism 1870-1945.* London, 1981.
Fontaine, Jean. *La Crise Religieuse des Écrivains Syro-Libanais Chrétiens de 1825 à 1940.* Tunis, 1996.
Gates, Carolyn L. *The Merchant Republic of Lebanon.* London, 1998.
Gellner, Ernest. *Nations and Nationalism.* London, 1983.
—. *Thought and Change.* London, 1964.
Gelvin, James. *Divided Loyalties.* California, 1997.
Gemayel, Nasser. *Les Echanges Culturelles entre les Maronites et l'Europe 1584-1789.* Beirut, 1984.
Gershoni, Israel. 'Rethinking the Formation of Arab Nationalism in the Middle East, 1920-1945.' in James Jankowski and Israel Gershoni, eds. *Rethinking Nationalism in the Arab Middle East.* New York, 1997: 3-11.
Ghalib, Ghanim. *Shi'r al-Lubnaniyyin bi al-Lugha al-Faransiyya 1903-1968* [Poetry of Lebanese in French Language]. Beirut. 1981.
Gilseman, Michael. *Lords of the Lebanese Marches; Violence and Narrative in an Arab Society.* London, 1996.
Girardet, Raoul. *L'Idée Coloniale en France.* Paris, 1972.
Gordon, Cyrus. H. *Before Columbus.* New York, 1971.
—. *The Ancient Near East.* New York, 1965.
Gordon, David C. *Self-Determination and History in the Third World.* Princeton, 1971.
—. *The French Language and National Identity.* London, 1973.
Gras, M, R. Rouillard, and J. Teixidor. *L'Univers Phénicien.* Paris, 1989.
Guha, Ranajit. *An Indian Historiography of India: A Nineteenth Century Agenda an its Implications.* Calcutta, 1988.
Haddad, Robert. *Syrian Christians in Muslim Societies.* Princeton, 1970.
Haddad, William, W. 'The Christian Arab Press and the Palestine Question: A Case Study of Michel Chiha of Bayrut's *Le Jour.*' *Muslim World.* 65, no. 2 (April 1975): 119-130.

Hajjar, Joseph. *Les Chrétiens Uniates du Proche-Orient.* Paris, 1962.
Hallaq, Hassan. *Al-Mu'arikh al-'Alamah Muhammad Jamil Bayhum* [The Historian the Savant Muhammad Jamil Bayhum]. Beirut, 1980.
Hamdan, Umaya. *Al-Ramziyya wa al-Rumantiqiyya fi al-Shi'r al-Lubnani* [Symbolism and Romanticism in Lebanon]. Baghdad, 1981.
Harik, Iliya. *Politics and Change in a Traditional Society Lebanon, 1711-1845.* Princeton, 1968.
Harrison, Helen, A. *Dawn of a New Day; The New York World's Fair, 1939-40.* New York, 1980.
Hobsbawm, Eric. *Nations and Nationalism since 1788.* Cambridge, England, 1990.
Hoogland, Eric, J. ed. *Crossing the Waters.* Washington D.C., 1987.
Hournai, Albert, and Nadim Shehadi, eds. *The Lebanese in the World.* London, 1992.
—. *Syria and Lebanon; a Political Essay.* Oxford, 1946.
—. *Arabic Thought in the Liberal Age 1798-1939.* Oxford, 1962.
Hudson, Michael, C. *The Precarious Republic.* New York, 1968.
Hutchinson, John and Smith, Anthony. *Nationalism.* Oxford, 1994.
Institut du Monde Arabe, *Liban, l'Autre Rive.* Paris, 1999.
Jabar, Jamil. *Sharl al-Qurm, Sha'ir al-Jabal al-Mulham* [Charles Corm, the Poet of the Inspired Mountain]. Beirut, 1995.
Karam, Georges, Adib. *L'Opinion Publique Libanaise et la Question du Liban.* Beirut, 1981.
Karpat, Kemal, H. ed. *Political and Social Thought in the Contemporary Middle East.* New York, 1968.
Katzenstein, H. Jacob. *The History of Tyre.* Beer Sheva, 1997.
Kayal, Philip, M, and Joseph, M. Kayal. *The Syrian-Lebanese in America.* Boston, 1975.
Kayali, Hasan. *Arabs and Young Turks.* California, 1997.
Khalaf, Saher. *Litterature Libanaise de Langue Française.* Sherbrook, 1974.
Khalidi, Rashid, L. Anderson, M. Muslih, and R. S. Simon. eds. *The Origins of Arab Nationalism.* New York, 1991.
Khalifah, Bassem. *The Rise and Fall of Christian Lebanon.* Toronto, 1997.
al-Khazen, Farid. 'Kamal Jumblatt, The Uncrowned Druze Prince of the Left,' *Middle Eastern Studies,* Vol. 24, No. 2(April 1988).
Khoury, Gérard, D. *La France et l'Orient Arabe.* Paris, 1993.
Khoury, Philip S. *Syria and the French Mandate.* Princeton, 1987.
Kritzek, James, and Bayly Winder, eds. *The World of Islam.* London, 1959.
La Fascination de l'Egypte: du Rêve au Projet. Paris, 1998.
Lahoud, Rachid. *La Littérature Libanaise de Langue Française.* Beirut, 1945.
Lewis, Bernard. *History - Remembered, Recovered, Invented.* Princeton, 1975.
—, and P. M. Holt, eds. *Historians of the Middle East.* London, 1962.
Lohéac-Amoun, Lynne. *Daoud Amoun et la Création de l'État Libanaise.* Paris, 1972.

Momsen, Wolfgang. *Theories of Imperialism*. New York, 1980.
Moosa, Matti. *The Maronites in History*. New York, 1986.
Moreh, Shemuel. 'Ha-Zeramim ha-Ra'ayoniyyim ba-Shirah ha-'Arvit ha-Modernit' [Ideological Trends in Modern Arab Poetry]. *Hamizrah Hehadash*, 19 (1969): 31-49.
Moscati, Sabatino. *The Phoenicians*. Milan, 1987.
Moubarac, Youakim. *Recherches sur la Pensée Chrétienne et l'Islam dans les Temps Modernes et à l'Époque Contemporaine* (Beirut, 1977).
—. *Le Dialogue Islamo-Chrétien au Liban*. Beirut, 1965.
—. *Les Chrétiens et le Monde Arabe*. Beirut, 1972-73.
Mukarzel, Mary. *Al-Hoda, 1898-1968*. New York, 1968.
Myers, David, N. *Re-Inventing the Jewish Past*. Oxford, 1995.
Naff, Alixa. *Becoming American: The Early Arab Immigrant Experience*. Illinois, 1985.
Owen, Roger and Bob Sutcliffe, eds. *Studies in the Theory of Imperialism*. London, 1972.
Owen, Roger, ed. *Essays on the Crisis in Lebanon*. London, 1976.
Phares, Walid. *Lebanese Christian Nationalism*. Boulder, 1995.
Philipp, Thomas. *The Syrians in Egypt*. Stuttgart, 1985.
—, ed. *The Syrian Land in the 18th and 19th Century*. Stuttgart, 1992.
—. *Gurgi Zaydan: His Life and His Thought*. Beirut, 1979.
Pohl, Frederick, J. *Atlantic Crossings before Columbus*. New York, 1961.
Polk, William, R. *The Opening of South Lebanon, 1788-1840*. Cambridge, Mass, 1963.
Pritchard, James B. *Archeology and the Old Testament*. Princeton, 1958.
Rabinovich, Itamar. 'Syria and the Syrian Land: The 19th Century Roots of 20th Century Developments,' in Thomas Philipp, ed. *The Syrian Land in the 18th and 19th century* Stuttgart, 1992: 43-54.
Reimer, Michael, J. *Colonial Bridgehead; Government and Society in Alexandria, 1807- 1882*. Boulder, 1997.
Les Riches Heures du Festival. Beirut, 1998.
Robinson, R. 'Non-European Foundations of European Imperialism: Sketch for a Theory of Collaboration.' in Owen and Sutcliff, eds. *Studies in the Theory of Imperialism*. London, 1972: 117-142.
Rondot, Pierre. *Les Chrétiens d'Orient*. Paris, 1955.
Rosenblum, Mort. *Mission to Civilize, the French Way*. Florida, 1986.
Rowe, Peter, and Hashim Sarkis, eds. *Projecting Beirut*. Munich, 1998.
Russell, Malcolm. B. *Syria Under Faysal, 1918-1920*. Minneapolis, 1985.
Sader, Hélène, et al., eds. *Baalbek: Image and Monument; 1898-1998*. Stuttgart, 1998.
Salem, Jean. *Introduction à la Pensée Politique de Michel Chiha*. Beirut, 1970.
Salhab, Nasri. *La France et les Maronites*. Beirut, 1997.

Saliba, Najib. 'Emigration from Syria.' *Arab Studies Quarterly* (1981) 3, No. 1: p. 61.

Salibi, Kamal. 'Islam and Syria in the Writings of Henri Lammens.' In Bernard Lewis and Peter Malcolm Holt, eds. *Historians of the Middle East*. London, 1962: 330-342.

—. *A House of Many Mansions*. London, 1988.

—. *Maronite Historians of Medieval Lebanon*. Beirut, 1959.

—. *The Modern History of Lebanon*. London, 1964.

Seikaly, Samir. 'Coptic Communal Reform 1860-1914,' *Middle East Studies* 6(1970).

Shehadai, Nadim. 'The Idea of Lebanon: Economy and State in the Cénacle Libanais 1946-1954,' in *Papers on Lebanon*. No. 5. Centre for Lebanese Studies. Oxford, 1988.

Silberman, Neil Asher. *Between Past and Present*. New York, 1989.

Sivan, Emanuel. *Mitosim Politiyyim 'Arviyyim* [Arab Political Myths]. Tel-Aviv, 1985.

Smith, Anthony. 'The Myth of the 'Modern Nation' and the Myths of Nations' *Ethnic and Racial Studies* II (January, 1988).

—. *The Ethnic Origins of Nations*. Oxford, 1986.

Sokhn, Joseph. *Les Auteurs Libanais Contemporains*. Beirut, 1972.

Spagnolo, John. P. *France and Ottoman Lebanon; 1861-1914*. Oxford, 1977.

Al-Sumaily, Yusuf. *al-Shi'r al-Lubnani, itijahat wa madhahib* [Lebanese Poetry, Directions and Schools]. Beirut, 1980.

Tauber, Eliezer. *The Arab Movements in World War I*. London, 1993.

—. *The Emergence of the Arab Movements*. London, 1993.

Thubron, Colin. *The Hills of Adonis: A Quest in Lebanon*. Boston, 1968.

Tibawi, A. L. 'History of the Syrian Protestant College,' *Middle East Journal*, 21 (1967): 199-212.

Tibi, Bassam. *Arab Nationalism*. 2nd edition. New York, 1990.

Traboulsi, Fawaz. *Silat bila Wasl: Mishal Shiha wa al-aydiyulujiya al-Lubnaniya* [Michel Chiha and the Lebanese ideology]. Beirut, 1999.

Younis, Adele L. *The Coming of the Arabic-Speaking People to the United States*. New York, 1995.

Zamir, Meir. *Lebanon's Quest*. London, 1998.

—. *The Formation of Modern Lebanon*. London, 1985.

Zim, Larry, Mel, Lerner and Herbert, Rolfes. *The World of Tomorrow; The 1939 New York World's Fair*. New York, 1988.

Zittrein-Eizenberg, Laura. *My Enemy's Enemy*. Detroit, 1994.

Zuwiyya-Yamak, Labib. *The Syrian Social Nationalist Party*. Cambridge, Mass., 1969.

Index

Abbasids, 81, 220
Abbé, Azar, 36-37
'Abdo, Jabbour Ibrahim, 156
'Abduh, Muhammad, 7
Abdülhamid (Ottoman Sultan), 6, 40
Abi Zayd, Fouad, 234
Abou Sélim, 191n, 234-235
Aboussouan, Camille, 231
AbuKhalil, As'ad, 1
Achou, Emile, 84
l'Action française, 121, 137n
Addada, Abdel-Wahab, 156
al-Adib, 130
Adib, Auguste Pasha, 62-63, 75, 84, 85, 90, 94, 97n
Adonis (god), 131, 156, 186n, 214
Adonis (Ibrahim) River, 25, 146, 147, 186n
Adonis ('Ali Ahmad Sa'id), 221, 231-232, 234
Afghani, Jamal al-Din, 7
Ahdab, Khair al-Din, 129
'Alawites, 111, 133-134n, 232
'Alayli, 'Abdallah, 131-132
Aleppo, 111, 112, 124, 205
Alexandria, 40-41, 55, 57-70, 120, 159, 170
Algeria,
  Maronite immigration to, 29; French colonial policy in, 13-15, 23
Alliance libanaise (Egypt), 34, 61-63, 70, 75, 83, 84, 170, 197, 199
Altounian, Mardiros, 156

America,
  Syrian immigration to, 70-71, 100n; U.S. Policy towards immigration, 71-75; Attitudes towards Arabs and Turks, 72-73, 101n; Lebanese clubs in, 75, 197; Arrival of ancient Phoenicians to, 78
American Council on Education, 118-119
American Protestant mission (See also AUB and Syrian Protestant College), 30, 39, 42, 75, 117, 225n
American University of Beirut, 75, 76, 78, 112, 117, 171, 218;
  as center of Arab Nationalism, 200, 205
'Amoun, Blanche, 156, 188n
'Amoun, Charles, 156
'Amoun, Iskandar, 7, 87
'Amoun, Daoud, 61, 75, 86, 105n, 156
Anderson, Benedict, 10, 11, 52n, 123, 182
Antioch, 175
'Aoun, Michel, 239
'Aql, Sai'd, 124, 129, 141, 151, 158, 162, 163, 169-183, 192n, 205, 216, 228n, 232, 233, 234, 248; and language, 172-173, 181, 236-237; and Israel, 181
Arab, Emile, 90, 91
Arab League, 132, 174
Arabia, 81, 83, 131, 195, 202, 206, 209, 222, 245

Arab government in Damascus (1918-1920), 7, 36, 83-84, 86, 89, 93, 139n, 197, 216, 220
Arab identity in Lebanon, 81-82, 129-133, 152, 156, 197-215, 220-223, 232, 239
Arab nationalism (also pan-Arabism), 6-8, 116, 131, 167, 195, 196, 200-215, 231, 232, 237
Arab-Syrian Congress (Paris 1913), 75, 80-81
Aramaeans, 3, 83, 84, 201, 202, 211, 217, 218
Arcache, Chécri, 84, 107n
Archeology,
  French policy towards, 21-23, 58, 123-124; Influence on Lebanese nationalism, 124-125; Excavations in Phoenicia, 21-23, 122
'Arida Antoine, Monsignor, 139n, 170
Arslan, Shekib, 7
l'Asie arabe, 86
Asmar, Michel, 233
l'Association nationale de la jeunesse syriene, 88-89, 91-92
l'Association syrienne arabe, 196
Assyria, 23, 24, 82, 165, 206, 211, 217
Astarte, 147
'Awad, Tawfiq, 139n, 154, 155
al-Azhar university, 131
'Azm, Sadik, Jalal, 221

Ba'al, 36-37, 122, 157, 185n, 214, 227n
Babylon, 23, 206, 232
Bacchus, 149
al-Bachir, 128
Balbeck, 146, 147-149
Balbeck international festival, 233-234
Baroudy, Samia, 142
Barrès, Maurice, 49n
  visit to the Levant, 24-25, 64, 147; influence on *La Montagne Inspirée*, 144, 185n
Bashir II, 118, 155
Baudelaire, Charles, 171

Bayhum, Muhammad Jamil, 135n, 186n, 197, 220-223, 248
al-Bayrut, 118, 128
Beirut, 31, 45, 56, 57, 64, 67, 68, 75, 77, 79, 84, 85, 87-96, 111, 113, 120, 122, 123, 124, 127, 130, 132, 155, 156, 157, 168, 173, 175, 180, 231
  bourgeoisie class in, 57, 59, 60, 61, 69, 76, 81, 88, 109, 158-159, 159, 163, 166, 171, 196, 218, 220, 232-233, 245; ancient city of (Béryte), 66, 67, 90
Bérard, Victor, 4, 144, 163, 212
Berbers, 13-14, 19n, 27, 29
Besnard Gabriel, 120, 196
Bhamdoun, 80
Bikfaya, 61, 170, 171, 181, 237
The Biqa', 33, 45, 56, 73, 81-82, 144, 171, 180
Birmingham, Alabama, 73-74
Black Athena, 4
Bonaparte, Napoleon, 22, 58, 96n
de Bonneville, Christophe, 156, 188n
Bounoure, Gabriel, 115
Britain, 8, 84, 111, 127, 167
Bulus, Jawad, 237, 238
al-Bustani, Butrus, 7, 40, 44
al-Bustani, Fouad Afram, 117-118, 170, 235, 248
al-Bustani Najib, 41-42
Byblos, 22, 124, 131, 147, 157
Byzantine, 114, 165, 175, 207

Cadmus (god), 157, 177
Cadmus: Epic by Sa'id 'Aql, 173-180
Caetani, Leon, 17n,
Les Cahiers de l'Est, 231
Cairo, 40-41, 55, 57- 61, 63, 68, 69, 75
de Caix Robert, 27-28, 89, 112
Canaan-Canaanites, 1, 2, 23, 35, 42, 211, 217, 219, 232
Capitualtions Agreement, 22, 26
Cardahi, Choucri, 60
Carthage, 22, 23, 118, 155, 165, 240
le Cénacle libanais, 233

Cercle de la jeunesse catholique de Beyrouth, 142, 164
Chatterjee, Partha, 12
Chéhab, Maurice, 124, 163
Chéhab, Fouad, 237
Cheikho, Louis, 31, 34, 35, 54n, 63
Chiha, Michel, 84, 93, 94, 96n, 98n, 129, 236, 239, 141, 151, 153, 158, 171, 172, 182, 234, 236; sojourn in Alexandria, 60, 64-67, 159; contribution to *la Revue Phénicienne*, 90, 93-94, 107n; place in Lebanese society, 94, 159-160, 233; and Lebanese Nationalism, 159-169, 180
la Colline Inspirée, See Barrès Maurice
Comité central syrien, 69, 80, 82-84, 87, 89
Comité libano-syrien, 69
Congress of the Coast and the Four Districts, 128-129, 139n, 216
Copts, 198, 223n
Corm, Charles, 63, 236, 64, 87-96, 108n, 122, 123, 124, 129, 160, 163, 166, 167, 170, 171, 180, 182, 183, 215, 232, 234, 236, 246
  family background, 87-88; education, 88, 95; Syrian inclinations, 88-89; noms de plumes, 89-93; as a businessman, 96, 141, 183n; friendship with Amin al-Rihani, 142-143, 211-212; and Mediterraneanism, 152-153; and language, 143, 144-145, 151-152, 182; *La Montagne Inspirée*, 87, 93, 122, 141-153, 155, 158, 172, 173, 179, 207-208, 211-212, 222-223, 231; *La Revue Phénicienne*, 83, 85, 87-96, 158, 160, 240, 161, 163
Corm, Daoud, 87, 90, 123
Corm, Georges, 90
Corm, Jean, 90
Correspondance d'Orient, 83
Coury, Georges, 156
Coussa, Emile, 90
Cromer, Earl of, 59-60
Crusades, 26, 86, 114-116, 118, 119, 123, 125, 145, 154, 156, 201, 211

Da'irat al-Ma'arif, 40, 41, 44
Dahdah, Najib, 128
Damascus, 36, 42, 83, 84, 86, 87, 111, 123, 124, 126, 134n, 175, 180, 200, 206
Darian, Monsignor, 69-70, 99n
Daw, Butrus, 238-239
Debbas, Charles, 80, 223n
Decentralization party, 197
Deir al-Qamar, 62
Delahalle, Romain, 156
al-Dibs, Yusuf, 32, 75
Dodelle, Jean, 156, 188n
Douaihi, Saliba, 156
Druzes, 34, 57, 75, 111, 143, 155, 195, 199, 231
Dugas, Charles, 125
Dunand, Maurice, 157
Dussaud René, 123, 206

École de la Sagesse (Madrasat al-Hikma), 61, 75, 76, 170
Eddé, Emile, 80, 95, 152, 153, 158, 181
  sojourn in Alexandria, 60, 67; rivalry with Béchara al-Khoury, 67, 94, 115, 127, 160; friendship with Charles Corm, 142; and the 1929 Public School Crisis, 115; presidency of, 122, 126-129; attitude towards Phoenicianism, 142, 184n
Egypt, 22, 118, 125, 127, 159, 166, 195, 199, 221
  Syrian and Lebanese immigration to, 40, 57-61, 165; Syro-Lebanese journals in, 41-45; Syro-Lebanese communities in, 57-70, 210; Egyptian nationalism, 60-61, 214; Lebanese nationalism in, 6, 170; Rashid Rida in, 197-198
Elections 1936 (presidential), 126-127
Elections 1937 (parliamentary and municipal), 127, 129
Epstein (Elath) Eliahu, 106n, 158, 187n, 189n

Études, 112
Europa, 157, 163, 177-180, 183

Fakhr al-Din al-Ma'ni, 5, 10, 57, 96n, 117, 118, 132, 155, 176
Fakhuri, 'Umar, 109, 130, 132, 139n, 234
Farroukh, Mustapha, 156
Faysal Ibn Hussayn, See: Arab government in Damascus
Flaubert Gustave, Salammbô, 22, 49n,
France, 166, 203, 204, 208, 210, 245
  Syro-Lebanese in, 79-87; attitude towards Maronites, 26-29; rivalry with Britain, 89; and taking control over Syria, 79, 83; Franco-Lebanese treaty, 127; Franco-Syrian treaty, 127, 206
Franjiyyeh, Hamid, 154
Freiké, 75, 209, 210, 213
French colonialism, 13-15, 111, 123, 131, 198;
  in North Africa, 13-15, 111; in Egypt, 58-59; in Lebanon, 27-28, 31, 123-124, 176, 221, 245; and Christianity, 28-29
French Mandate, 109-129, 157, 160, 196, 199, 170, 200, 204, 207, 210, 220; transfer from Ottoman to French rule, 110-112; High Commission, 110-112, 120-121, 123, 127, 160; policy towards education, 110-119; policy towards museums and archeology, 123-126; and Lebanese Francophiles, 91-92, 142-143, 144, 157, 160, 211
French Revolution, 210, 213
Frères Maristes, 171
Front national libanais (of Yusuf al-Saouda), 128, 139n
de Freige, Jean Marquise, 107
Freiha, Anis, 182
Freiha, Nimr, 247

Gabriel, Chucri, 156
Ganem, Chékri, 7, 69, 79, 80, 84-85, 87, 89, 90, 91, 95, 102n, 206, 215
Gebran, Khalil Gebran, 210

Gellner, Ernest, 10
Gemayel, César, 156, 183, 236
Gemayel, Joseph, 90, 95
Gemayel, Pierre, 128, 193n
Germany, 22, 24, 204
Ghasan, 82
Ghazir, 30, 31, 62, 97
Ghousta, 87, 157
de Gontaut-Biron, R. Comte, 88, 105n
Gouraud, Henri, 27-28, 30, 55, 99n, 108n, 111-113, 134n
Greece (ancient), 2-4, 5, 47, 113, 116, 118, 148, 152, 153, 154, 163, 166, 177-180, 202, 213, 219, 231, 232
Greek Catholics, 28, 61, 73, 74, 81, 82, 83, 84, 195, 196, 206
Greek Orthodox, 41, 42, 61, 63, 82, 84, 117, 129, 155, 163, 181, 195, 196, 200, 205, 215, 218, 223n
La Guardia, Fiorello, 153
Guardians of the Cedars, 238

Habachi, René, 234
Haddad, Marie, 156, 163, 188n
al-Hajj, Halim, 142, 156, 184n, 236
al-Hajj, Kamal Yusuf, 235
Hakim-Dowek, Carol, 5
Halabi, Chafic, 151
Hallaq, Hassan, 248
Hannibal, 102n, 155, 176, 235
Hanotaux, Gabriel, 28-29
Haqqi, Isma'il Bey, 33, 35, 169
al-Hariri, Rafiq, 1, 240,
Harissa (Basilica of Our Lady of Lebanon), 236
Helou, Charles, 237
Herodotus, 3, 213
Hijaz, 84, 88
al-Hilal, 41-44, 169
Hitti, Philip, 75-79, 103n, 131, 132, 165, 205
Hittites, 211, 217
Hizballah, 239
al-Hoda, 75-76, 210
Hobeiche, Faouzi, 249

Homer, 163, 212
Honein, Edward, 238
al-Hoyeck, Youssef, 142, 156, 163, 184n
Hoyek, Elias, 38, 85-86, 95, 144
Hugo, Victor, 171
al-Husri, Sati', 133n, 214, 228n
Hussein, Taha, 228n
Huvelin, Paul, 30, 107n

Ibn Khaldun, 220
Iraq, 127, 159, 166, 221
Islam and Muslims, 45, 55, 168, 180, 214
as pillar of Arab nationalism, 6, 7, 43, 77, 165, 201, 206; in French colonial policy, 14, 29, 112, 123; and Henri Lammens, 32; arrival in Lebanon and Syria, 35, 42, 47, 78, 82, 230; attitude of Lebanese nationalists towards, 89, 145, 146, 152, 153, 160, 161, 182, 236, 238, 239, 240; and Lebanese nationalism, 115, 183, 195, 196, 197-200, 209, 216, 220-222, 231, 244, 245, 247; in school textbooks, 117, 173; at the New York World's fair, 154-156; in Antun Sa'adeh's thought, 217, 218
Isma'il, Khedive of Egypt, 58
Israel, State of, 181, 237
Istanbul, 56, 123
Italy, 3, 48, 166

Jahiliyya, 113
Jalabert, Louis, 31, 63, 105n, 134n
Jalkh, Jean, 90, 107n, 172
Jam'iyyat Shams al-Birr, 41
Jerusalem, 126, 158, 175
Jesuit Order (See also USJ), 123
establishment of, 26; domination in Lebanon, 29-36, 110, 113, 142, 196; education, 29-30, 158, 159, 170, 208
Jesus, 2, 126, 146, 157, 166, 199
le Jour, 160
Junblatt, Kamal, 231
Jupiter, 149

Kadicha valley, 146-147
Karam Yusuf, 155, 177, 187n
Karameh, Anna, 69
Kata'ib – Phalanges, 127, 128, 180-181, 237
Kettaneh, Alfred, 233
Khabbaz, Gabriel, 160
Khairallah, Khairallah, 79
al-Khal, Yusuf, 231-232
Khalid Tawfiq (Grand Mufti of Lebanon), 115
Khalife, Marcel, 250
al-Khazin, Philippe and Farid, 9, 56-57, 96n, 219
Kheir, Abdallah, 90
al-Khoury, Béchara, 132, 142, 152, 154, 155, 164
sojourn in Alexandria, 60, 64-65, 98n, 159; relations with Michel Chiha, 159, 162, 167; rivalry with Emile Eddé, 127, 155
al-Khoury, Fouad, 90
al-Khoury, Pierre, 236
King-Crane Commission, 84-85, 89, 90, 97n, 223n
Klat, Hector, 90, 163, 172, 196, 231, 234, 236; in Alexandria, 63-65, 98n, 159
Kseib, Khalil, 118

Labaki, Salah, 139n, 172, 182-183, 216, 232
Laissez-faire economy, 167
Lammartine, 147
Lammens, Henri, 31, 51n, 169,
and Syrian nationalism 32-33, 215; influence on Lebanese nationalists 48, 61, 63, 68, 69, 90, 91, 97n, 98n, 119, 124, 164, history textbooks of, 116, 134n; influence on Edmond Rabbath, 205, 226n
Language and Lebanese nationalism, Jacques Tabet, 68; Na'um Mukarzal, 76; importance of Arabic 129; Amin al-Rihani, 143, 211; Charles Corm, 144-145, 150-151; Michel Chiha,

165, 167-168, Sa'id 'Aql, 169-173, 237; comparison between thinkers, 182; Rashid Rida, 197; Constantine Zurayk, 201; Edmond Rabbath, 207; Muhammad Bayhum, 221; Antun Sa'adeh, 228n; Sélim Abou, 234
Latinism, 67, 166, 207, 208, 226n
Lavigerie Monsignor, 23
Lazarist Order, 30, 46
League of Nations, 123, 199
Lebanese Forces, 181, 238, 239
Lebanese League of Revival (Na'um Mukarzal), 75
Lebanese National Museum, 69, 123-124, 240
Lebanese University, 117, 170, 235-236
Lebanist idea, 76, 78, 87, 94, 174, 180-181, 196, 199, 214, 216, 219, 222
Levenq, Gabriel, 61, 116, 119
Lortet, Louis, 23
Louvre Museum, 23, 124
Lyautey, Louis-Hubert, 13

Maalouf, Amin, 230, 249
al-Ma'luf, 'Isa Inskandar, 34, 171
Ma'luf, Rushdi, 173, 182-183, 205, 232
Makhluf, Ibrahim and Emile, 131, 231
Malik, Charles, 132, 196, 205, 238
Mamluks, 114, 116, 119
Ma'ni dynasty, 117, 119
al-Manar, 197-198
al-Marada, 82, 109, 207
Maronite, 61, 74, 142, 150, 155, 158, 161, 163, 195, 213
  church, 36-38, 132, 153, 180; patriarch, 128, 154; relations with France, 26-29; college in Rome, 26, 29, 30; historiography, 36-38, 109; internal political rivalries, 127, 209; nationalism, 166, 168, 169-183, 207, 218, 236-237, 245
Marseille, 21, 31 166
Martin, Pierre, 32, 37
Marun, Saint, 9
al-Mashriq (journal), 128, 172

Maurras, Charles, 94
Mediterranean Sea and culture, 2-3, 47, 83, 88, 94, 125, 130, 174, 203, 207, 208, 219, 231, 233
Mediterraneanism, 152-153, 157, 159-169, 221
Menassa, Gabriel, 233
Mir'at al-Gharb, 210
Mission laïque, 106n, 120, 135n, 196, 197, 220
al-Malat Shibly, 171
La Montagne Inspirée: see Corm Charles
Morocco, 111, 134n
Moubarac, Ignace, Monsignor, 132
Moubarak, Youakim, 33
Mouchahwar, Amin, 90, 94
Mount Lebanon, 55, 56, 57, 75, 81, 82, 88, 155, 197, 199, 207, 239, 244
  and the 'long peace,' 44; as refuge of minorities, 47, 164, 214; immigration from, 70, 72; as a symbol of Lebanese nationalism, 92, 107n, 147, 150, 157, 159, 164, 166, 167, 168, 181, 208, Amin Rihani's trip in 211
Mouterde, René, 116, 119, 125
Moutran, Nadra, 7, 81-82
Muhammad (Prophet), 112, 113, 116, 198, 206
Muhammad 'Ali, 57, 58
Mukarzal, Na'um, 75-76, 80, 102n, 169-170, 209-210
al–Muqtataf, 41-42, 77, 169
Murad, Nicholas, 36-37
Murr, May, 236
Musa, Salama, 182
Mutasarrifiyya, 5-6, 34, 35, 46, 95, 169
Mutran, Khalil, 171

Nabateans, 211
Naccache, Albert, 34, 51n, 90, 142, 156, 158, 167, 181
Naccache, Alfred, 90, 121-122, 138n, 142, 163
Naccache, Georges, 120-121, 136n, 160, 234

INDEX

al-*Nahar*, 128, 129
al-Nahda (literary movement), 7, 39-40, 44, 118
al-Najjar, Ibrahim Salim, 7, 86, 105n, 195
Najm, Faris, 197
Nakhla, Rashid, 171
National Pact, 13, 94, 115, 132, 164
New Testament, 35
New York, 70, 75, 76, 88, 209-210, 213
New York World's Fair 1939-1940, 153-157, 233
New York World's Fair 1964-1965, 233
Nimr, Faris, 41, 103n,
Nu'aima, Mikha'il, 210
Nujaym, Bulus, 34, 45-48, 68, 90, 94, 215, 216, 219
Nushu' al-Umam, 201, 219

The Odyssey, 94, 212
Onsi Omar, 236
l'Orient, 120-121, 128, 231
Ottoman Islamic College (Beirut), 220
Ottomanism, 6-8, 56
Ottoman Empire, 26, 36, 38, 55, 72, 76, 79, 81, 111, 118, 222, 233
Oughourlian, Joseph, 163
Ougour, Aurore, 129, 163, 190n, 223n

Palestine, Palestinians, 127, 132, 158, 181, 199, 237, 238
Pan-Arabism: see Arab nationalism
Paris, 46, 55, 56, 57, 69, 79-87, 112, 123, 167, 175, 180
Pharanonicism, 70, 182, 195, 198, 214, 221, 223-224n
Pharaon, Habib, 107n
Pharaon, Henri, 233
Phoenicians,
  history of, 2-5, 212-213, 235; study of, 22; mythology of, 144-151, 177-180; discovery of America, 78, 103n; origins of, 131-132, 152, 202; in school textbooks, 49n 110-119; arabization of, 195, 197, 206, 209, 221, 245

Phénicia (journal), 129, 156, 163, 167, 231, 240
Philistines, 2, 42
Piepape, Colonel, 111
Pope, John Paul II, 240
Progressive Socialist Party, 231
Protestants, 39, 41, 45, 61, 80, 117

Qa'imaqamiyya, 5, 181
Qalb Lubnan, 142, 211-212
Quai d'Orsay, 70, 79, 112, 120

Rabbath, Edmond, 129, 196, 205-209, 214, 226n, 231
Race,
  theories on, 71-74, 100n, 202, 224n; in Lebanon, 35, 63, 68, 116, 165-166, 202-203; in Syria, 33, 42-43, 47, 72, 74, 76, 77, 83, 217; Arab race, 42-43, 47, 72-73, 68, 77, 83, 202, 206
Radio Levant, 129-130
Rayes, Aref, 236
Reclus, Elisée, 8, 18n, 46, 101n, 104n, 215, 223n
Règlement organique (organic law), 56, 61, 62
Renaissance libanaise (São Paulo), 197
Renan, Ernest, 21-22, 39, 240, 50n, 90, 92-93, 122, 162, 206, 244, 246
la Revue du Liban et l'Orient Méditerraneen, 131, 231
la Revue Phénicienne, See Corm Charles
Rida, Rashid, 7, 104n, 196-200, 201
al-Rihani, Amin, 142-143, 152, 173, 185n, 195, 196, 209-215, 226n
Roman Empire, 4, 5, 77, 90, 148-149, 152, 154, 202, 207, 219, 231, 232
Romanticism (literary school), 171
Rome, 88, 118
Ronzavelle, Sébastian and Louis, 31
Rostand, Edmond, 67, 98n, 171
Rustum, Asad, 117-118, 205, 248

Sa'adeh, Antun, 107n, 171, 172, 183, 192n, 196, 204, 215-220, 222, 232-233,
al-Sa'ad, Habib Pasha, 95, 107n, 170
Saad, Edmond, 163
de Saint Quentin, René, 153
Salammbô, see Flaubert Gustave
Salhani, Antun, 34, 61
Salibi, Kamal, 103n, 168-169, 246-247
Salonika, 59
Samné, Georges, 7, 69, 79, 102n, 103n, 104n, 206, 215, 223n
Sanchuniathon, 89
al-Saouda, Yusuf, 75, 76, 84, 85, 97n, 102n, 128, 132, 162, 166, 181, 236
  in Alexandria, 61-63, 159, 169-170
Saqre, Etienne, 238
Sarkis, Ramiz, 129
Sarrail, Maurice, 121
Sarruf, Ya'aqub, 41
Sfeir, Maroun, 156
Sfeir, Nasrallah, Butrus, 240
al-Shahbandar, 'Abd al-Rahman, 85
Shakespeare, 90, 92-93
Shekib, Arslan, 196, 199
al-Shartunui, Rashid al-Khuri, 32
Sidon, 67, 86, 124, 157, 178
Shi'is, 115, 127, 143, 195, 240
al-Shidyaq, Tannus, 39
Shihabi Dynasty, 117, 119
Shimlan, 75
Shu'ubiyya, 220-221
Slouschz, Nahum, 189n
Smith, Anthony, 9-10, 147, 176
Smyrna, 59, 166
Spain, 3, 166, 198
al-Sulh, Riad, 132, 135n, 164
al-Sulh, Taki al-Din, 143, 173, 186n
Sunnis, 61, 110, 115, 127, 130, 132, 143, 154, 155, 161, 181, 195, 220
Suq al-Gharb, 75
Sursock Alfred Mussa, 84, 99n
Symbolism (literary school), 171
Syria, 23, 29, 38, 45, 46, 47, 55, 56, 79, 80, 85, 109, 111, 167, 169, 239, 169, 170, 195, 221; and the *Nahda*, 39-44; opposition to Lebanese separate existence, 34, 86, 115, 118, 127, 160, 162, 197- 215, 220-223; Syrian secular nationalism, 6-8, 68-69, 77-78, 81-84, 88-89, 172, 205-206, 215-220, 226n; Syrian Arab nationalism, 7-8, 200-209; Christians in, 25; France in, 26-28, 30-31, 111-115, 122-123; Syrian immigration to Egypt, 57-59, immigration to America, 70-73; historiography of, 32-33, 37; dominance in Lebanon, 239

Syria, 124
Syrian identity, 7-8, 42-43, 215-220
Syrian National Bloc, 206
Syrian Protestant College (see also AUB), 30, 35, 41, 45, 111, 123
Syrian Social Nationalist Party (Parti Populaire Syrien), See Sa'adeh Antun,
Syrian-Lebanese League of Liberation, 210
la Syrie, 156, 188n, 190n

Tabbah, Béchara, 60
Tabet, Ayyub, 80, 154, 210, 226n
Tabet, Georges, 106n
Tabet, Ibrahim J., 90
Tabet, Jacques, 83, 85, 90, 91, 95, 99n, 108n, 215
  sojourn in Alexandria, 60, 67-69; establishment of national museum, 69, 124; Lammens' influence on, 98-99n
Ta'if Accord, 239, 247-248
Talhamé, Michel, 90
Tanzimat, 38
Taoutel, Ferdinand, 116
Taqi al-Din, Khalil, 143, 186n
de-Tarrazi, Philippe, 84, 90, 91, 124, 138n
Trad, Gabriel, 60
Trad, Michel Namé, 84
Trad, Pierre, 84
Tresca, Louis, 125

Tripoli, 34, 63, 64, 67, 127, 197
Tuéni, Gébran, 129, 154, 155
Tuéni, Michel, 84, 95, 108n
Tunisia, 3, 134n
Tyane, Elie, 90, 91, 107n, 163, 172, 234
Tyre, 22, 35, 67, 86, 124, 157, 163, 168, 177, 240

Ugarit, 5, 124
Umayyad Dynasty, 81, 211
Uniate Churches, 26, 46, 49n, 98n, 195, 205, 206, 215, 225n
Université de Lyon, 23, 30, 125
Université Saint Ésprit de Kaslik, 238
Université Saint Joseph, 23, 30-36, 37, 88, 111, 164, 169, 205, 235
  alumni association of, 121-122, 124; influence on Lebanese society, 112-113, 137n, 119-122, 129, 205; books by teachers of, 116-117; Oriental Faculty, 31, 117, 121, 125
Usrat al-Jabal al-Mulham, 231

Valéry, Paul, 171, 180
Vatican, 26, 30
Venus, 147, 149, 156
Versailles Peace Conference, 11, 61, 75, 80, 84-87, 88, 89, 195
Virgin Mary, 179, 236
Virolleaud, Charles, 124

al-Wa'i al-Qawmi, 201-204
Weygand, Maxime, 112
World War I, 6, 7, 33, 36, 45, 48, 57, 60, 64, 79, 80, 82, 88, 92, 111, 125, 159, 169, 195, 211
World War II, 154, 163, 164, 174

al-Yaffi Abdallah, 135n, 155
Yammout, Bassem, 248
Yared, Gabriel, 60
Yazbek, Adele, 171
Yazbek, Yusuf, 139n, 172
Young Turk revolution, 55, 56, 60, 79, 197, 210
Yunis, As'ad, 143, 152

Zahle, 73, 81, 82, 171, 180
Zakkur, Michel, 152, 211
Zamir, Meir, 36
Zaydan, Jurji, 41-44
al-Zein Ahmad 'Arif (*al-'Irfan*), 44, 99n
Zeus, 157, 163, 177-180, 187n, 241n
Zionist movement, 78, 132, 158, 167, 181, 214
Zubaida Sami, 10
Zurayk Qonstantine, 196, 200-205, 206, 208, 214

www.ingramcontent.com/pod-product-compliance
Lightning Source LLC
Chambersburg PA
CBHW071239230426
43668CB00011B/1500